DISABILITY RIGHTS IN EUROPE

This book is based on a conference organised jointly by the editors to mark the European Year of Disabled People. It explores the range of legal strategies which have been adopted, both nationally and internationally, to achieve equality for disabled people and facilitate their inclusion into mainstream society. It examines current developments in anti-discrimination law, both within Member States and at EU level. It also assesses the effectiveness and potential of the human rights framework for disabled Europeans. In addition, a number of approaches to the enforcement and promotion of disability rights are considered.

Contributors to this book, drawn from across Europe, represent a variety of different backgrounds. They include leading academics in the field, as well as campaigners and others working to improve or enforce disability-related legislation. The book is a unique and timely contribution to an important and rapidly expanding field of study. It will be of relevance to all those, whether lawyers or not, with an interest in disability and equality issues.

D1080889

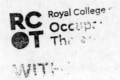

Disability Rights in Europe

From Theory to Practice

Edited by

Anna Lawson

University of Leeds

Caroline Gooding

Special Adviser to the Disability Rights Commission

·HART·
PUBLISHING

OXFORD AND PORTLAND, OREGON
2005

Hart Publishing
Oxford and Portland, Oregon

Published in North America (US and Canada) by
Hart Publishing
c/o International Specialized Book Services
5804 NE Hassalo Street
Portland, Oregon
97213–3644
USA

Hart Publishing is a specialist legal publisher based in Oxford, England. To order further copies
of this book or to request a list of other publications please write to:

Hart Publishing, Salter's Boatyard, Folly Bridge,
Abingdon Road, Oxford OX1 4LB
Telephone: +44 (0)1865 245533 or Fax: +44 (0)1865 794882
e-mail: mail@hartpub.co.uk
WEBSITE: http://www.hartpub.co.uk

British Library Cataloguing in Publication Data
Data Available
ISBN 1–84113–486–4 (paperback)

Typeset by Compuscript Ltd, Shannon
Printed and bound in Great Britain by
MPG Books Ltd, Bodmin, Cornwall

Foreword

BERT MASSIE*

THIS BOOK, AND the conference from which it emerges, marks the growing maturity of disability rights. In Britain this is signalled by the unfolding of the Disability Discrimination Act 1995 and the Human Rights Act 1998; in Europe, by the implementation of the Employment Framework Directive and proposals for a disability-specific directive; and globally, by long overdue progress towards a UN Convention.

Disability rights are, of course, not new to me or to many of you. I certainly grew up with an awareness of the need for legal rights for disabled people.

Nevertheless, disability rights and the disability dimension of broader equality and human rights are just beginning to gain recognition on statute books and in court judgments.

Whilst disability rights are young, both as legal and academic concepts, the need to strengthen and deepen our understanding of the disability agenda is urgent. We need to mature rapidly if we are to promote disabled people's distinctive needs and experiences within the broader equality debate. The chapters in this book aim to develop our thinking—to hold our deep-seated assumptions up to scrutiny. Is disability discrimination distinctive? If so, in what way? What similarities are there with the struggle of other groups for equality and human rights? What have we to learn from each other?

My own view is that human rights have a particular importance for disabled people. I think we might win the battle for civil rights (for protection against disability discrimination) in the next ten years but the battle for human rights more generally will be a long, hard slog. The proposed Commission for Equality and Human Rights will be able to promote human rights but not enforce them.[1] The more cynical amongst you might think that what this means is that the new body will be able to talk about human rights but not enforce them. I suspect you are right.

---

* Chair of the Disability Rights Commission.
[1] *Fairness for All: A New Commission for Equality and Human Rights* (London, Women and Equality Unit, Department of Trade and Industry, 2004).

We must not think of this as an abstract issue. As Richard Light's chapter makes clear, it is a life or death struggle for many, many people. Nor should we fall into the tempting trap of believing that human rights abuses somehow only occur in other countries. Here much of the struggle for basic human rights revolves around the claim for 'independent living'. The term refers to all disabled people having the same choice, control and freedom as any other citizen—at home, at work, and as members of the community. This does not necessarily mean disabled people 'doing everything for themselves,' but it does mean that any practical assistance people need should be based on their own choices and aspirations.

Access to appropriate social support is a fundamental pre-condition to the full participation of many disabled people in social and economic life. Any restrictions on such support impede disabled people's freedom to exercise their human and civil rights.

At present access to independent living options is still essentially granted on a discretionary, rather than mandatory, basis. There are considerable restrictions on both the levels of resources people can receive, and on the ways in which they are allowed to use these resources to organise their support systems. So, for example, disabled people might be eligible to receive services to enable them to access personal assistance at home, but not at work. Similarly, assistance with travel might be available for certain activities (such as going to school), but not for participation in social or leisure activities.

In practice this often means that, instead of being able to participate freely in the full range of community life, disabled people have to organise their lives around whatever kinds of practical support are available. These might tackle some of the practical barriers they face, but rarely deal with all of them. And, in a lot of cases, the minimum support people can expect to receive does not guarantee much more than simply being able to stay alive. Independence, in the words of Ann McFarlane, means more than 'being able to make yourself a cup of tea and feed the cat.'[2]

We need to question why, in the 21st century, it is still seen as acceptable for disabled people to be living in institutions against their wishes, to be denied access to basic support to enable them to enjoy a family or social life, and to be guaranteed no more than the bare minimum services necessary for day-to-day survival.

Disabled people do not have any effective guarantees of support, as budgets come under pressure. Some local administrations are raising the threshold for eligibility for services with the result that, in some cases, disabled people are denied help even with very basic activities like washing and eating. In one case, which the Disability Rights Commission (DRC) has dealt with in the past few months, disabled people were told that they could only be guaranteed a bath or shower once a fortnight and, even then, only if there was a substantial risk to their health.

[2] Personal conversation.

The DRC is aware of children being out of school because no-one is prepared to administer medication to them during the day or because best practice in supporting teachers in managing behaviour is not in place.

A right to independent living must mean, as a minimum, a right to protection against enforced admissions into institutional care. It is outrageous that in this day and age individuals should be forced to live in institutions purely because it is deemed too expensive to support them in the community. The DRC is aware of a recent increase in reports of disabled people being threatened with enforced admission into institutional care as a result of cuts in social services budgets.

A 2003 John Grooms Inquiry found that nearly 80 per cent of local authorities limit the cost of community care packages, and 75 per cent of them use the cost of alternative residential care as the ceiling.[3] As a result disabled people are forced against their will into institutions simply in order to receive the basic support they require to survive. For some disabled people the 'workhouse' of 19th century infamy still looms large in its 20th century incarnation. More than 8,000 pre-retirement age adults are living in care homes designed primarily for a different client group, usually elderly people.

The idea that enforced admission into institutional care could be outlawed does not seem quite so ambitious if we consider recent decisions of the US Supreme Court and Federal Government. In the recent *Olmstead* case, the US Supreme Court ruled that

> unjustified isolation or segregation of individuals with disabilities through institutionalisation is a form of disability-based discrimination prohibited by the Americans With Disabilities Act 1990.[4]

This does not establish unconditional protection against enforced institutionalisation as, importantly, it is permissible for States to take availability of resources into account when making placement decisions. However, the Court also ruled that the objective of ensuring that all disabled people are enabled to live independently should be pro-actively supported by the provision of Federal Government funding.

Consequently, the Federal Government has recently announced a $2.1 billion funding programme under the 'New Freedom Initiative' to assist disabled people who currently live in institutions to return to the community. There will also be a comprehensive review of federal policies and regulations that impede community living.

We need to develop and articulate the equality and human rights arguments for a right to independent living; and then we need to work out

---

[3] J Ackroyd, *Where do you think you're going? Report of the John Grooms Inquiry into the needs of young disabled people* (London, John Grooms Association, 2003).

[4] *Olmstead, Commissioner, Georgia Department of Human Resources v L C* (98–536) 527 US 581 (1999) 138 F3d 893.

how to make such a right a living reality, not just an academic nicety. If we are to influence public policy so that it serves rather than oppresses disabled people, however, those of us involved in that process need the support of academia. We need you to supply the bullets for us to use as ammunition. It seems to me that the manner in which public bodies calculate the cost of supporting disabled people is at best crude, and possibly misleading. Is the cost of residential care just the weekly invoice? What is the cost of a person's dignity? Can we put a price on it, and, if so, how? How do we calculate the cost of the fear in which many disabled people live, knowing that without committing a crime, and without the trial given to even the most menial felon, they could face a lifetime of incarceration from which there is no escape and no parole. I recently had lunch with one severely disabled woman who has an expensive care package and is in just this position. She is afraid in case the package is withdrawn. And, of course, she can never move to another part of the country because a different local authority might refuse to pay anything. Her freedom is limited to her postcode.

Who are the 'experts' anyway? Richard Light speaks powerfully of the urgency of the task of making human rights a reality for disabled people, and our need for humility in the face of it:

> The real 'experts' on disability and human rights are the disabled people who have endured denial of their fundamental human rights, but will never have the opportunity of addressing a conference or contributing to a publication (save in the role of anonymous victim). No matter how vital we may consider our place in this process, we are all drawn from the substitute's bench; we presume to right the wrongs inflicted on others and, in this, I fear that none of us is equal to the task.

In the UK, this challenge is given a particular significance at present by plans to replace the DRC with a unified Commission for Equality and Human Rights, charged with addressing issues in relation to gender, race, religion, sexuality, age and disability. Whilst I recognised the attractions of such a body, my worry (shared by my Commissioners, and by many in the 'disability movement') is that this might lead to the further marginalisation of disabled people and of our concerns. Above all, my concern was that there would be no room for disabled people to determine disability policy within the new body. At the DRC, 11 of my 15 Commissioners are disabled. So are almost 40 per cent of my staff. They are a massive strength and resource. I believe in the mantra of the disability movement—'nothing about us without us', but am aware that some think it should be 'everything about us without us'. We are working to retain the distinctive voice of disabled people within a unified Commission. Time will tell whether we have succeeded in this vital task.

The same point, of course, applies equally to academia itself. If, as I have said, we need academia, we must not forget that academia needs us too! If research in whatever field, from law to economics to social policy, is to accurately reflect life, it needs to capture the experience of disability which is an intrinsic part of the human experience and it will not be possible to do this without the presence of disabled people working on equal terms as students, lecturers, professors, commissioners of research, and as active participants within an 'emancipatory research' framework.[5]

This is not to say that non-disabled academics should not contribute to these debates. On the contrary, I warmly welcome their contributions to this book and elsewhere. Disabled people and their insights and concerns must not be shut into a self-contained box; 'disability studies' must not be made into an academic 'ghetto' but must, rather, participate in and challenge every aspect of every discipline. In Richard Light's words, we need 'a dialogue of equals', in which disabled people inform, and are informed by, broader debates.

I hope that in the future disability studies will grow in our universities and that it will promote a free and open debate in which disagreement is welcomed as a way of honing ideas. I also hope that, even more than in the past, academia and those working on public policy can work closely together and together achieve the results which we all desire and which some of us so desperately need.

---

[5] See eg E Stone and M Priestly, 'Parasites, pawns and partners: disability research and the role of non-disabled researchers' (1996) 47 *British Journal of Sociology* 699–716.

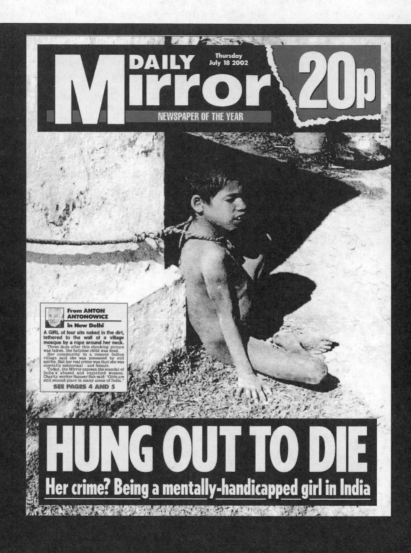

Contents

Table of Cases

Table of Legislation

National Legislation

AUSTRALIA

AUSTRIA

BELGIUM

BOLIVIA

BRAZIL

CANADA

CHILE

CHINA

COSTA RICA

CZECH REPUBLIC

HUNGARY

INDIA

IRELAND

PANAMA

PHILIPPINES

PORTUGAL

SOUTH AFRICA

SPAIN

SRI LANKA

SWEDEN

SWITZERLAND

UGANDA

UNITED KINGDOM

Statutes

Statutory Instruments

Part I
Preliminary

1

Introduction

ANNA LAWSON and CAROLINE GOODING*

UNTIL RECENTLY, DISABLED people were largely invisible in the context of anti-discrimination and human rights law. Legal recognition, for them, was generally confined to the spheres of welfare and charity law. This, however, was only a partial recognition which failed to see disabled people as citizens whose lives were just as valuable as those of their non-disabled counterparts and who had rights to be included and to participate fully in the world around them. The advent of the Americans With Disabilities Act in 1990 marked the beginning of a much fuller legal recognition of the claims of disabled people to equality and inclusion, both in the US and elsewhere; though subsequent developments have in many ways been rapid, that recognition is still far from complete.

Within Europe the debate about disability rights intensified last year. This was due, in part, to the fact that 2003 was the year in which Member States were required by the Framework Employment Directive[1] to consider the implementation of anti-discrimination legislation protecting disabled people in employment. For many countries this provided the first occasion on which legislators considered disability rights legislation. For others it provided renewed impetus for change.

2003 was also the European Year of Disabled People. The European Disability Forum, representing organisations of disabled people across Europe, highlighted the need for a disability-specific Directive[2] (comparable to the Race Directive) which would apply to all aspects of social life within EU competence, not merely employment. This proposal has gained support from the relevant European Commissioner,[3] though the Commission

---

* Anna Lawson is a Lecturer in Law and member of the Centre of Disability Studies and the Human Rights Research Unit, University of Leeds. Caroline Gooding is Special Adviser to the Disability Rights Commission.
[1] Council Directive 2000/78/EC of 27 November 2000 establishing a general framework for equal treatment in employment and occupation, [2000] OJ L303/16.
[2] See Appendix III below.
[3] Statement by Employment and Social Affairs Commissioner, Anna Diamantopoulou, in Rome at the closing ceremony of the European Year of People with Disabilities on Sunday 7 December 2003.

itself has not yet indicated that it has any plans to introduce such a directive.

Outside Europe, within the United Nations Framework, the global disability movement entered into detailed discussions relating to the establishment of the first ever convention specifically recognising the rights of disabled people.

The conference from which this book emerges was designed to provide a forum for debate on these exciting developments, and to allow space to review the basic principles that underpin them. It brought together a stimulating mix of politicians, lawyers, academics and campaigners from a wide range of countries to compare experiences, exchange ideas and consider strategies for achieving legal change to bring about meaningful equality and to facilitate the full inclusion of disabled people in the lives of their communities.[4] The strategies considered related to law at national, European and also the wider international level. Speakers, like delegates, were drawn from a wide variety of countries and backgrounds. Regrettably, however, space, time and other constraints make it impossible to include all the papers delivered at the conference in this volume.[5]

The chapters in this book have been divided into four sections: Part 1 is preliminary only and needs no further explanation. Part 2 deals with issues relating to the human rights of disabled people, whereas the focus of Part 3 is on anti-discrimination law. It must be stressed, however, that there is in reality no bright-line distinction between these two areas. Such a division has been used, with unfortunate effect, to limit the power of the UK Disability Rights Commission to support disabled litigants in human rights cases which do not concern the Disability Discrimination Act 1995 (DDA). Nevertheless, the practical impact of both forms of violation will be to disempower and disable the individual concerned. Not surprisingly, then, the chapters in Part 2 contain some discussion of anti-discrimination concepts; that of Olivier De Schutter, for instance, contains a thought-provoking analysis of the relationship between the duty to make reasonable adjustments or accommodations and the concept of indirect discrimination. Similarly, many of the chapters in Part 3 (particularly those by Theresia Degener, and Jacqueline Schoonheim and David Ruebain) draw heavily upon, and closely examine, human rights laws and principles. Finally, Part 4 contains a wide-ranging discussion of what the notion of 'equality' for disabled people actually means and of strategies that might be used to achieve and enforce it in practice.

Part 2 opens with Richard Light's discussion of the on-going process of achieving a UN convention providing protection specifically to disabled

---

[4] Held at the University of Leeds on 25–26 September 2003 and organised by the editors with generous sponsorship from the UK Disability Rights Commission.

[5] We are particularly sorry that the book does not include chapters from two speakers (Gerard Quinn and Richard Whittle) who, along with Theresia Degener, Aart Hendriks and Lisa Waddington, made up our Conference Advisory Panel.

people. He offers a disturbing account of the abuses to which disabled people around the world are routinely subjected and a powerful reminder of the importance of remaining passionate in the campaign for change. Academic objectivity must not be allowed to sterilise or neutralise the loneliness, horror and fear which continue to pervade the lives of millions of disabled people. Nor must it be allowed to suffocate or sideline the voices of those people; effective change will occur only if it is led by disabled people themselves.

Luke Clements and Janet Read then examine the disturbing silence of disabled people in the context of the European Convention on Human Rights. Given that they are routinely subject to human rights abuses, and denied the protection that the Convention would appear to offer them, why have so few cases been brought? Olivier De Schutter also examines the relevance of the ECHR to disabled people, focusing on its potential as a means of requiring states to take positive steps to accommodate the needs of disabled people in all areas of life. The final chapter in Part 2, by Ian Cram, analyses the problem of hate speech directed at disabled people. It examines possible sources of protection for the victims of such hateful expression and draws upon analogous debates in the US. Again, it draws attention to the silence of disabled people; people who have been victimised in this way and not reported the problem to police or other authorities.

Part 3 begins with a comparative analysis of the laws of 45 countries, from all regions of the world, which provide explicit protection from discrimination to disabled people. Despite the fact that many of these laws were inspired by the same sources (the Americans With Disabilities Act 1990 and the UN Standard Rules on the Equalisation of Opportunities for People with Disabilities 1993), Theresia Degener identifies key differences between them in their approach and consequent levels of protection. In Chapter 7 Lisa Waddington examines the Framework Employment Directive which requires Member States to implement anti-discrimination legislation for disabled people in the area of employment. As well as analysing the requirements of the Directive itself, she compares the ways in which a number of countries have chosen to implement it.

Caroline Gooding and Catherine Casserley then provide an account of the legislative protection from discrimination by providers of goods and services offered to disabled people in four EU countries. Again, they contrast approaches, identifying strengths and weaknesses. They also outline the proposals put forward by the European Disability Forum for a new directive requiring all Member States to implement comprehensive legislative protection for disabled people in this field.

In Chapter 9, Jacqueline Schoonheim and David Ruebain consider legislative strategies (at the international, European and national levels) to promote the inclusion of disabled children in mainstream education. Part 3 concludes with a more general overview of the current battle for disability rights in Europe by Aart Hendriks. He draws attention to obstacles encountered by campaigners for disability equality in the US and suggests some practical steps that may enable Europeans to avoid experiencing the same difficulties.

In Part 4, Sandra Fredman draws attention to parallels between claims for, and legal responses to, disability rights and those which have arisen in the contexts of sex and race. She examines the meaning of equality, linking different conceptions of it to different campaigning strategies for disability rights. Colm O'Cinneide's chapter builds on this discussion by examining how, in practice, a positive legal duty to promote equality of opportunity for disabled people might operate. The potential power of such a duty to effect meaningful change is also explored.

In Chapter 13 Nick O'Brien provides an account of the experiences of the Disability Rights Commission in law enforcement. He draws attention to the limits of litigation as a strategy for achieving societal change and outlines other, potentially more effective, approaches. In the final chapter Anna Lawson explores the way in which law itself can operate as a disabling force. If negative stereotypical conceptions of people with impairments are embedded within it, they are likely to manifest themselves in a legal system which in a variety of ways, and despite anti-discrimination or human rights statutes, devalues disabled people and undermines their claims to equality and inclusion. It is important, then, that disabled people are conceived of as human beings to be valued in the same way as others and as citizens with useful contributions to make.

As might already be apparent, the present time is an exciting one for Europeans striving for improved legal protection for the rights of disabled people. The Framework Employment Directive will require anti-discrimination legislation covering employment to appear on the statute books of all Member States by 2006. There is now a serious possibility that this Directive will, in the next few years, be accompanied by another requiring such legislation to extend to goods and services (including education and transport). Article 15 of the Revised European Social Charter also offers new possibilities for requiring signatory countries to enact legislation protecting disabled people from discrimination in the context of economic and social rights.[6] Further protection, in Europe and beyond, may also be conferred by the emerging UN Convention on disabled people.

The introduction of positive duties to promote equality for disabled people, as proposed in the current UK Disability Discrimination Bill, is also highly significant. Many of the chapters in this book (in particular, those by Olivier De Schutter, Caroline Gooding and Catherine Casserley, Sandra Fredman, Colm O'Cinneide and Nick O'Brien) emphasise the limitations of a legal system which merely requires employers, service providers and others to respond reactively to the needs of a particular disabled person.

[6] See the discussion of this in O De Schutter, ch 4 below.

Equality and social inclusion will be achieved only by requiring such people to remove potentially disabling barriers as an anticipatory measure or, better still, to design their policies, practices and premises in such a way as to avoid creating those barriers at the outset.

There is an interesting conceptual link between these emerging positive duties to promote equality for disabled people and the social model of disability. The latter focuses on the disabling barriers created by the structures and organisation of society which prevent people with impairments from participating fully in the life around them. It is these very barriers which positive duties are designed to tackle. They impose obligations on those who design and operate structures and organisations to do so in a manner that keeps such barriers to a minimum. It is fitting that, despite the fact that it was in the US that anti-disability-discrimination legislation first appeared, these positive duties to promote disability equality should emerge from Europe, which is the home of the social model.

Exciting though these developments are, there is no room for complacency. Many of the legal changes anticipated above have not yet materialised in concrete form. Even when they do, much thought and effort will be required to ensure that they are implemented effectively so as to have a genuine impact on the lives of disabled Europeans. The enactment of well designed legislation is as preliminary a step as is the first move in a game of chess. However, as Richard Light stresses in the next chapter, this is no game: it is, for many, a battle for meaningful existence and indeed for life itself.

Part II
Human Rights

2

Disability and Human Rights: The Persistent Oxymoron

RICHARD LIGHT*

1 INTRODUCTION

O N 18 JULY 2002, the front page of the *Daily Mirror* carried a disturbing photograph of a four-year old girl tethered to a building by a rope tied around her neck. The girl was sat, naked, in the dirt and in the full glare of the sun. In the stark words of the report: 'three days later, the helpless child was dead ... her crime was being mentally subnormal [*sic*] and female'.[1] The death of this unnamed girl, although it was reported some years after I first began reviewing and reporting cases recorded in the Disability Awareness in Action (DAA) Human Rights Database,[2] has become a persistent companion (as has Marta Russell's powerful description of the death of Baby Knauer, the first officially recorded death under the Nazi Government's 'Law for the Prevention of Genetically Diseased Offspring').[3] It is not the most horrific or graphic case that I have reviewed, but somehow that grainy photograph exemplifies the betrayal of trust and denial of common decency that lies at the root of this book. It also serves to remind us that protecting disabled people's human rights concerns a great deal more than access to rehabilitation, transport or education, important though such issues are. If it is to be meaningful, such protection

---

*Richard Light is an independent researcher and consultant, specialising in law and public policy.

[1] A A Antonowicz, 'Hung out to die' *Daily Mirror*, 18 July 2002 p 1. See Frontispiece.

[2] The DAA Human Rights Database was the first international project to systematically record human rights abuses against disabled people. Supplemented by tailored support to grassroots disability organisations, the Database is a significant element in DAA's prolonged efforts to increase the profile of disability as a human rights issue. See, for a review of recent cases, R Light, *Review of Evidence Contained on the DAA Human Rights Database* (London, Disability Awareness in Action, 2003).

[3] M Russell, *Beyond Ramps: Disability at the End of the Social Contract* (Maine, Common Courage Press, 1998). I encourage those with an interest in human rights or bioethics to read her chilling account of the eugenics programmes and reflect on their resonance with current debates, including New Labour's 'Contract for Health'.

must extend to the most fundamental rights: to life and freedom from degrading and inhuman treatment.

As may already be clear, I write, not as an academic or policy maker, but as an activist: a role that adopted me over a decade ago. I hope that what I have to say will not simply be dismissed as subjective or emotional. On the first charge, and as will shortly become clear, my views have been shaped by managing the first international database of human rights abuse inflicted on disabled people. Far from being subjective, my presentation will be influenced by an exceptional empirical resource. On the second charge, *mea culpa*; the systemic and obscene abuse of disabled people's human rights is something about which I get *very* emotional, and for that I am unrepentant. We are not, after all, dealing with some arcane matter of international jurisprudence or public policy, but the endemic and appalling abuse of the community to which I choose to belong: the international community of disabled people.

I have been asked to discuss, in this chapter, proceedings at the UN Ad Hoc Committee on a Comprehensive and Integral International Convention to Promote and Protect the Rights and Dignity of Persons with Disabilities and, specifically, to address three substantive issues: First, why we need an international convention to protect and promote the human rights of disabled people. Second, the impact such a convention might have. Third, an assessment of the chances of winning a convention adequate to the task. To these questions I have made two additions: First, I provide an extremely brief introduction to human rights activity at the UN, particularly in relation to disability. Second, I have tried to posit current discussion within what I know to have been the active efforts of disabled people, and our representative organisations, to raise the profile of disability as a human rights issue.

Inevitably, my responses to the questions posed will be personal; colleagues who have been at various meetings associated with the convention may disagree with some, or even all, of what I have to say. That there are differing views and interpretations is both inevitable and essential. Even where we share similar aspirations for the convention, each of us is a victim of biography, geography and organisational bias, such that we interpret the process differently. To add to an already tangled plot, we have spent a maximum of six weeks together at the UN over the past two years; during the intervening period we have attended separate meetings and briefings and, as significantly, been fed different pieces of 'insider information' from various sources, some more reliable than others. In short, we have been engaged in a political process and, therefore, subjected (and party) to games of Chinese whispers; with genuine respect for my colleagues, I fear none of us can provide *the* definitive assessment of where we are, how we got here and where we will be next week.

No matter how committed to, and involved in, the process we are, none of us are more than bit-players. Promoting and protecting disabled people's human rights is part of a wider process of challenging negative attitudes toward disabled people. It is a process that has continued for decades in a multitude of venues and, as is so often the case, those who have the honour of participating in this potentially historic event do so as a result of others' labour.

The real 'experts' on disability and human rights are the disabled people who have endured denial of their fundamental human rights, but will never have the opportunity of addressing a conference or contributing to a publication (save in the role of anonymous victim). No matter how vital we may consider our place in this process, we are all drawn from the substitutes bench; we presume to right the wrongs inflicted on others and, in this, I fear that none of us is equal to the task.

2 THE UN, DISABLED PEOPLE AND HUMAN RIGHTS

I do not intend to spend a great deal of time describing the background to current efforts to elaborate a thematic convention; the 2002 UN report by Gerard Quinn, Theresia Degener and others[4] offers a thoughtful and precise description that requires no reiteration here.

What I should like to emphasise is that efforts to win political support for such a convention have been sustained since at least 1987, when the Global Meeting of Experts to Review the Implementation of the World Programme of Action concerning Disabled Persons recommended the drafting of a thematic convention. The Italian government wasted no time and broached the subject later the same year at the 42nd Session of the General Assembly. The Assembly responded equally promptly, by declining to pursue the matter. In 1989 Sweden sought to promote discussion of disability and human rights at the 44th Session and, once again, there was insufficient support from the international community to proceed.

For our purposes, attention must shift from the General Assembly to the Commission on Human Rights in Geneva where, in 1994, a resolution[5] on disability and human rights was adopted. So began a bi-annual tradition of adopting a disability resolution at the Commission, guided (until recently) by the skilled and committed efforts of Ireland. In company with colleagues from the disability movement, I spent some time at the Human Rights Commission and with the High Commissioner's Office in Geneva, believing that Geneva would take the lead on disability and human rights. I was wrong. On 19 December 2001, the General Assembly adopted Resolution 56/168, on a 'Comprehensive and integral international

---

[4] G Quinn, T Degener, A Bruce, C Burke, J Castellino, P Kenna, U Kilkelly and S Quinlivan, *Human Rights and Disability: The current use and future potential of United Nations human rights instruments in the context of disability* (New York, United Nations, 2002).
[5] Resolution 1994/27, adopted at the Commission's 50th Session.

convention to promote and protect the rights and dignity of persons with disabilities' proposed, initially, by Mexico.

Vitally, this Resolution confirmed the Assembly's commitment to:

> ... establish an Ad Hoc Committee, open to the participation of all Member States and observers of the United Nations, to consider proposals for a comprehensive and integral international convention to promote and protect the rights and dignity of persons with disabilities, based on the holistic approach in the work done in the fields of social development, human rights and non-discrimination ...

The Ad Hoc Committee has, thus far, met twice at UN Headquarters in New York: from 29 July to 9 August 2002, and from 16 to 27 June 2003. At the time of writing, preparations are well in hand for the third meeting of the Committee, beginning on 24 May 2004.

3 WHY DO WE NEED AN INTERNATIONAL CONVENTION?

The simplest questions are invariably the hardest to answer; to do this question justice would require a book all of its own. The succinct response is that disabled people's human rights are, demonstrably, ineffectually protected.

The last report on the DAA Human Rights Database summarises material entered at 14 March 2003 and measured against the 1948 Universal Declaration of Human Rights.[6] At that time, the Database contained a total of 1,890 cases committed since 1990 and affecting at least 2,093,114 disabled people. In 11.5 per cent of these cases, the abuse directly caused or materially contributed to the death of the victim. I should emphasise that these figures *significantly under-represent* the scale of the problem, not least because systemic abuse is habitually enumerated in broad percentage terms rather than precise figures[7] and also because of the substantial difficulties associated with evidence gathering.[8]

Article 5 of the Universal Declaration of Human Rights 1948 (UDHR)—prohibiting torture, cruel, inhuman and degrading treatment or punishment—remains the article concerning which DAA receives most reports.[9]

---

[6] The Universal Declaration, rather than the substantive instruments, was chosen as the appropriate yardstick in an effort to emphasise DAA's inability to found action or complaints and to emphasise the aspirational aspects of the Declaration.

[7] For example, there is evidence to support the contention that the vast majority of disabled children in developing countries are denied access to even the most basic education; however, percentage estimates of participation rates vary and there are few dependable datasets from which the number of children affected could be reliably calculated. In such cases, DAA records one entry on the Database, although there are a great many more than one victim.

[8] The difficulties associated with such evidence gathering are summarised in R Light, *A Real Horror Story: The Abuse of Disabled People's Human Rights* (London, Disability Awareness in Action, 2002).

[9] 487 of the 1,890 reports.

Breaches of Article 5 have affected at least 416,290 disabled people whose cases have been recorded in the database.

As can be seen from even this cursory review of the data, the widely held perception that human rights and disability amounts to little more than access to rehabilitation services, transport or welfare is significantly wide of the mark. Whatever the reasons for this extensive disparity between perception and data, it is abundantly clear that it presents a significant impediment to the promotion of disabled people's human rights. A second, and equally pernicious, impediment is the apparent inability of some agencies to cast aside a fixation on prevention and rehabilitation, so as to more effectively include disabled people within the wider panoply of human rights and fundamental freedoms. This is not to claim that these matters are extraneous or that the concerns of disabled people in the majority world should be ignored; rather, I am seeking to emphasise that disablement is multi-faceted and that the need to provide adequate healthcare and treatment, themselves established human rights,[10] should be pursued in parallel with efforts to promote the full range of human rights.

Finally, the failure to mainstream disability within the human rights agenda ensures that our needs are marginalised and treated as a 'special' case. At some point, human rights practitioners and agencies must acknowledge and address the 'disability dimension' in their work. Development, the rights of women, children, displaced persons and civilians in areas of armed conflict, for example, all have a disability dimension. Wherever there is a humanitarian crisis, it is safe to assume that, even if it goes unrecognised and unreported, disabled people will bear an additional burden due to a failure to construct programmes that account for their needs or, perhaps more accurately, a failure even to acknowledge their existence.

It is, then, palpably the case that current human rights instruments and mechanisms inadequately protect disabled people's human rights but, to be frank, a thematic convention, in and of itself, is incapable of rectifying the problem. Nonetheless, I believe that the elaboration of a convention is necessary for four main reasons: First, we require and merit tangible acknowledgement of our humanity; something that is routinely denied and suppressed. Second, it would be iniquitous to allow abuse to continue unchecked; meaningful and concerted action is already long overdue. Third, we should move beyond the ubiquitous rhetoric, reports and resolutions; there is a compelling case for the international community to implement measures of substance. Finally, whatever political horse-trading is necessary to achieve a convention, the *process* of elaborating such a convention has intrinsic value.

Having attended both sessions of the Ad Hoc Committee on a Comprehensive and Integral International Convention to Promote and

---

[10] Art 25 UDHR; Art 12 International Covenant on Economic, Social and Cultural Rights 1966.

Protect the Rights and Dignity of Persons with Disabilities, I can assure you that there *has* been a dramatic improvement in the quality of the debate. We *are* increasing understanding of the social process of disablement, the necessity to formally acknowledge our humanity and the concomitant obligation to ensure that our human rights are better protected. Some states that have not, to my knowledge, previously had much to say about disability were, by the last meeting, eloquent and passionate advocates for change. Such opportunities are priceless and it behoves us to seize them as they arise.

Nevertheless, there are arguments against the formulation of a thematic convention. Perhaps the most compelling of these is that disabled people are included within the existing human rights instruments[11] and that it is preferable to mainstream disability within that framework. To be frank, I have no objections to such an argument put in such terms. However, I believe that it begs further questions: First, why have existing instruments had so little impact on the protection of disabled people? Second, how will the existing regime be changed so as to protect disabled people more adequately in future? Third, what will provide the catalyst for effective and sustained reform? No matter how sincere the question, the UN's own reports have repeatedly shown that existing instruments have failed adequately to protect disabled people, *period.*[12]

A second, and perhaps more world-weary, objection to a thematic convention simply questions its value. It should be acknowledged that this objection has often been expressed by disabled people. There is some scepticism and concern as to whether a thematic convention will be capable of initiating the required change and, in view of the current status of the monitoring and investigation machinery, the point is a fair one. My only

---

[11] That human rights apply to all human beings—that they are universal—is specifically acknowledged by the UN Charter: 'the promotion and encouragement of respect for human rights and fundamental freedoms is an undertaking to be carried out for all.' The Vienna Declaration makes it abundantly clear that disabled people are included within the protection afforded by the International Bill of Rights; Art 63 UDHR states:

> The World Conference on Human Rights reaffirms that all human rights and fundamental freedoms are universal and thus unreservedly include persons with disabilities. Every person is born equal and has the same rights to life and welfare, education and work, living independently and active participation in all aspects of society. Any direct discrimination or other negative discriminatory treatment of a disabled person is therefore a violation of his or her rights.

[12] See eg E–IA Daes, *Principles, Guidelines and Guarantees for the Protection of Persons Detained on Grounds of Mental Ill-Health or Suffering from Mental Disorder* (United Nations publication, Sales No E85 XIV.9, 1986); L Despouy, *Human Rights and Disabled Persons* (United Nations publication, Sales No E92.XIV.4, 1993); B Lindqvist, *Monitoring the Implementation of the Standard Rules on the Equalisation of Opportunities for Persons with Disabilities* (New York, United Nations, document A/52/56, 1997); B Lindqvist, *Monitoring the Implementation of the Standard Rules on the Equalisation of Opportunities for Persons with Disabilities* (New York, United Nations, document E/CN.5/2000/3, 2000); and D Michaelakis, *Government Action on Disability Policy: A Global Survey* (Stockholm, Office of the United Nations Special Rapporteur on Disability, 1997).

response to this objection is that we should not, and cannot, abandon efforts to promote respect for human rights or ensure their universal applicability.

4 THE POTENTIAL IMPACT OF SUCH A CONVENTION

As I have already made clear, I am persuaded that the process of elaborating a convention is every bit as important as the convention itself. What I am unable to decide is whether that view is influenced by concerns about the *form* that the eventual instrument may take. The reality is, however, that it is still too early to predict what form and, therefore, what effect, a convention might have.

Without wishing to appear cynical, it is not the convention, but the resolve of states to give effect to our human rights, that will be decisive; it is not the letter of the law, but the determination to realise its aims that is crucial. The short answer is that the convention will achieve as much, or as little, as states are prepared to permit.

A convention founded on a genuine desire to protect and promote disabled people's human rights, encapsulated within a painstakingly constructed text and policed by a rigorous monitoring regime, has the capacity to effect radical and rapid change.

Such a convention could ensure that disabled people's human rights—including our right to life—are no longer rendered meaningless by prejudice and ignorance; prevent the kind of nauseating abuse and neglect that has repeatedly been revealed by, for example, Mental Disability Rights International; and promote our dignity. It is sincerity of intent that will decide whether 'could' becomes 'did'.

Precedent, perhaps especially recent precedent, discourages me from speaking to the question in greater depth. I imagine that the impact of a convention will depend on politics rather than law, and on economics rather than ethics. Despite such equivocation, however, I think we can take heart from the fact that there are a great many individuals and organisations that are wholeheartedly committed to the elaboration of an effective convention. The disability movement has high expectations of the international community and is committing substantial resources (despite diminishing funds and an uncertain future) to this process. We are combining expert advice, skilled negotiation and steadfast activism to ensure that an effective convention is not only ratified, but also honoured.

5 ASSESSMENT OF THE CHANCES OF WINNING A CONVENTION ADEQUATE TO THE TASK

In my estimation, there are still competing themes and aspirations: some UN agencies and Member States appear keen to give emphasis to social development; other states (including Britain) would prefer an instrument that adheres to existing instruments and adopts what might be described as a 'strong' human rights approach. There has been mention of a convention that gives legal effect to the Standard Rules[13] and, regrettably, it appears that there are still states that remain resolutely opposed to *any* convention. I fear that there may be only one issue about which the international community is undivided: the convention should *not* create significant financial burden.

Having established the mechanisms for a Working Group, comprising representatives from 27 Member States, 12 NGOs and one representative from national human rights institutions, the Group met for two weeks at the beginning of 2004. The resulting report is a testament to the efforts of the members of the Group and the diplomatic skills of its chairman and, in accordance with the Ad Hoc Committee Decision of 27 June 2003, will 'be the basis for negotiation by Member States and Observers at the Ad Hoc Committee'.

Despite the excellent Working Group Report, it is feasible that the Ad Hoc Committee will be unable to adopt its proposals, thereby ensuring that the text will have to be discussed, word-by-word and comma-by-comma, in Committee. If so, the progress of the convention will be measured in decades and the content will be an uneasy compromise between the very different positions held by the various Member States. My fear is that the further states move from a 'strong' human rights approach, the less significant the resulting convention will be; adopting a text that merely expresses the aspiration that states will do more to 'promote and protect the rights and dignity of disabled people' will, I am afraid, merely add to the already extensive, but empty, rhetoric that has been expended in the name of disability, to the discredit of all involved.

6 THE IMPORTANCE OF THE DISABLED PEOPLE'S MOVEMENT

Having attended to the questions posed by the editors, albeit inadequately, I would like to spend a few moments addressing some additional issues that I believe should be acknowledged.

First and foremost, efforts to promote disabled people's human rights did not begin with Mexico's Resolution or, indeed, the previous efforts of Italy, Sweden or Ireland. Many within our movement have been active in promoting disability as a human rights issue for decades and their contribution should be acknowledged: Javid Abidi, Bill Albert, Schuaib Choklein, Justin Dart, Theresia Degener, James Donald, Rachel Hurst, Rodrigo Jimenez, Klaus Lachwitz, Joshua Malinga, Moses Masamene, Friday Mavuso, Frank Mulcahy, John O'Gorman, Gerard Quinn, Enrique Sarfati, Victor

---

[13] *Standard Rules on the Equalization of Opportunities for Persons with Disabilitie*s, adopted by the UN, Resolution 48/96, annex, 20 Dec 1993.

Wahlstrom and Richard Wood; all have worked vigorously and spoken eloquently in support of disabled people's human rights. As always, having singled some out for mention, I have inadvertently caused offence to others. There are also countless individuals who, whilst they may never have spoken publicly about human rights, have put their own safety, and that of their loved ones, at risk to undertake grassroots endeavours aimed at promoting and protecting human rights in their own community. They are the epitome of what the UN describes as 'human rights defenders'.

Disabled people and our supporters have not sat back, passively, waiting for others to protect us. We have demanded that our rights be respected, unambiguously and consistently; but, until recently, no-one was listening.

As will already be clear, no matter how much I *might* wish to approach this subject with academic detachment and objectivity, it is an unrealistic aspiration. Neither do I accept that it is a subject about which any of us should be dispassionate. The systemic and endemic abuse of disabled people's human rights is a travesty that has gone unchallenged for too long.

Prior to Resolution 56/168, introduced by Mexico without fanfare or advance warning, during the 2001 UN General Assembly, there were few outside of the disability movement who were prepared to use the words 'disability' and 'human rights' in the same sentence; disability may have had something to do with health or welfare but, or so the popular orthodoxy went, it had absolutely nothing to do with human rights. Not only was such rejection perverse on the evidence available, it too often evidenced more than mere ignorance: few who have spent time in the intellectual company of the 'new' eugenicists could doubt that it was not merely our human rights, but our very humanity that was being given short shrift. In the dispassionate world of the academy, there is little space for such observations but, in my opinion, unless and until such issues are acknowledged, practitioners, theorists and advocates will remain ignorant of the pressing need to promote debate about disability and human rights. To seek to divorce the sordid reality of 'disablement' from human rights analysis is akin to treating pulmonary oedema with throat lozenges.

Such concerns ensured that I was initially ambivalent about contributing to the conference from which this publication flows, all the more so because my own academic endeavours had emphasised the extent to which history has been written with scant regard for disabled people, even recent history. The point that I am seeking to make here is vital, both for what follows in this book and for a proper understanding of the process of *disabling* people. I am not seeking to score cheap points against those working within the academy or, indeed, those who are temporarily non-disabled, but I am trying to illustrate the extent to which subjugation, disparagement and rejection are too often synonymous with the experience of disablement.

I do not believe that the evidence supports the thesis that disabled people's absence from history is accidental or free from bias: we appear principally as a testament to the good works and sacrifice of others. The history of disability has been written from the perspective of the non-disabled, not as a dispassionate record, but as marketing puff for the reputation of the biographer. So one-sided a result can only occur when there is a chronic disparity in power, a hackneyed acknowledgement that history is written by the victor, wherever the 'field of battle'.

If the emerging field of disability and human rights conforms to the usual pattern, the decades-long struggle of disabled people to promote and protect our human rights will also vanish from the historical record, to be replaced by a crusade by benevolent experts, who seek to pull us from our slough of despair. If this chapter, or indeed the book in which it appears, achieves little else, my hope is that it will serve to acknowledge that we have reached this point through the consistent effort of the disabled people's movement and some dedicated individuals within it.

I am delighted that such effort is beginning to elicit change and warmly welcome any and all who are committed to protecting and promoting the human rights and fundamental freedoms of disabled people but, if commitment to such rights is to survive its novelty status, it will be essential to ensure a dialogue between equals. Overpowering benevolence has already inflicted too much harm.

There are also particular challenges facing disabled people's organisations, too many of which have been forced to cease operating in a climate where not-for-profit organisations are being encouraged to adopt for-profit approaches. There is little doubt in my mind that, if such 'marketisation' continues, efforts to promote disabled people's human rights will be irretrievably damaged. Precisely those who most need the support and advocacy of our organisations are the least likely to have the resources—financial, professional or emotional—to combat abuse unaided.

7 CONCLUSION

I am yet to be convinced that our demands will produce the outcome that we so desperately need. Few activists and campaigners can have been spared the unedifying experience of witnessing trivial power struggles, petty vendettas, blatant self-promotion, organisational intransigence, manipulation by those with vested interests, arrogance, asininity and political horse-trading that have bedevilled efforts to improve the situation of disabled people.

I wish that I could tell you that, having seen the work of the Ad Hoc Committee, UN agencies and Member States, I am confident that such failings will be absent from the elaboration of a thematic convention. I regret that I am unable to do so. I pray for innovation but fear 'business as usual'.

There are no states that can afford to be complacent about disabled people's human rights; some of the most liberal and progressive democracies host quite appalling abuse with barely a murmur of dissent. This can occur precisely because disabled people's very humanity is denied: hastening the death of a disabled person is, after all, a 'blessed relief', to the extent that the modern lexicon now includes the nauseating phrase: 'altruistic filicide'. There can be no more robust authority for my contention that our humanity is denied than this discursive conflation of charity with murder.

As I complete this chapter, the European Union will expand from fifteen to twenty-five member states in a matter of days and the BBC is reporting the British Prime Minister's opposition to the free movement of European citizens 'unable to work', a significant proportion of whom are likely to be disabled. Disabled people's status as right bearers and citizens remains contested, particularly where the social process of disablement restricts, or entirely removes, opportunities to be economically active.

Despite ongoing work at the UN, disability and human rights has failed to win adequate attention from *any* sector of civil or political society; indeed, there is evidence that a great many relevant agencies—including grant-making bodies—continue to deny the relevance of disability to human rights. It would be reassuring to attribute such tendency to ignorance but, as the range and severity of abuse contained in the DAA Database confirms, the reality may be far less comforting. Before a rights discourse can be adequately developed, there is a pressing need to counter equivocal attitudes toward disabled people's very humanity. I hope that this publication will encourage wide debate and more detailed analysis by, and in collaboration with, disabled people and their representative organisations. I bid those who join the effort a fond welcome.

3

The Dog that Didn't Bark: The Issue of Access to Rights under the European Convention on Human Rights by Disabled People

LUKE CLEMENTS and JANET READ*

1 INTRODUCTION

T HE INFLUENCE OF the European Convention on Human Rights (ECHR) has grown steadily since its adoption in 1950. Today its jurisdiction runs to 45 European states. The workload of its Strasbourg Court is no less impressive, with over 30,000 pending cases in 2002.[1] Its judgments span the entire spectrum of civil and political rights, dealing with issues such as murder, torture and disappearances as well as newspaper restrictions, sexual rights, unfair court hearings and property rights. These judgments have been highly influential in shaping the legislative codes of many countries.[2]

Although there is no current survey of the Court's activities (by reference to the subject matter of complaints), certain facts are readily apparent from the case list of past judgments. It is clear, for example, that the Article 6 right to a fair hearing attracts the highest number of complaints, followed by the Article 5 right not to be unlawfully detained. It is also clear that certain countries, including Italy, Turkey and increasingly Russia, appear

---

* Luke Clements is a solicitor and senior Research Fellow at Cardiff Law School; Janet Read is a Senior Lecturer at the School of Health and Social Studies, Warwick University. The title is inspired by the following literary extract:

'Is there any point to which you would wish to draw my attention?'—'To the curious incident of the dog in the night-time.'—'The dog did nothing in the night-time.'—'That was the curious incident,' remarked Sherlock Holmes. [*Silver Blaze*, Sir Arthur Conan Doyle.]

[1] Council of Europe (2003) *Survey of Activities 2002* available at www.echr. coe.int/Eng/EDocs/2002SURVEY.pdf
[2] See for UK examples, the Mental Health Act 1983 and the Children Act 1989.

with great frequency. These patterns are generally explicable. The high number of Article 5 and 6 complaints is probably due to the fact that they arise from situations already likely to involve lawyers who would generally be aware of the Strasbourg process. The high number of complaints made against Italy is due to particular problems relating to delay in Italian court proceedings; Turkey's frequent appearance is attributable to the activities of its security forces in the south-east of its country; and many of the complaints against Russia concern either unfair interferences with property rights or the problems in Chechnya.

What such a review suggests is that the number of complaints generated bears no direct relationship to the severity of the human rights violation involved and that certain complainants (for instance prisoners and litigants in the civil justice process) make a disproportionate number of the applications. Such a review also suggests that certain groups, like the sound of Sherlock Holmes' infamous dog, are notable by omission. Only a handful of judgments, for instance, concern the rights of disabled people. Few text books give space to an analysis of disabled people's rights under the Convention and few monographs have addressed this question.[3] Whilst the dearth of learned papers may be partially explained by the dearth of reported cases, the absence of significant numbers of complaints by disabled people is curious, particularly given that there is substantial evidence of the violation of their human rights.[4] It has been established, for instance, that the deaths of many disabled babies have been deliberately caused or hastened, even since the Convention, by 'selective non-treatment' or by the withholding of food and essential medical treatment.[5] There has also been long-standing concern over discriminatory assumptions underpinning the withholding of medical treatment from some disabled adults.[6] There has been growing recognition of the fact that both disabled children and disabled adults have been vulnerable to abuse and to unwarranted restriction of their liberty.[7] Many have been routinely separated from family, friends and community.[8] Unlike those living without impairments, they have been unable to take for granted their home or their social and personal life.[9]

[3] See eg L Clements and J Read, *Disabled People and European Human Rights* (Bristol, Policy Press, 2003).

[4] See generally L Clements and J Read, *ibid*.

[5] See generally R Weir, *The Selective Non-treatment of Handicapped Newborns* (New York, Oxford University Press, 1984); and I Kennedy, *Treat Me Right. Essays in Medical Ethics* (Oxford, Clarendon Press, 1988).

[6] See eg A Asch, 'Disability, bioethics and human rights' in G Albrecht, K Seelman and M Bury (eds), *Handbook of Disability Studies* (London and Thousand Oaks, Sage Publications, 2001).

[7] H Westcott, *Abuse of Children and Adults with Disabilities* (London, NSPCC, 1993); Department of Health and the Home Office, *No Secrets: Guidance on Developing and Implementing Multi-agency Policies and Procedures to Protect Vulnerable Adults from Abuse* (London, Department of Health, 2000).

[8] J Read and C Harrison, 'Disabled children living away from home in the UK: recognising hazards and promoting good practice' [2002] 2 *Journal of Social Work* 211–31.

[9] M Hirst and S Baldwin, *Unequal Opportunities* (London, HMSO, 1994).

Many are left without any means (whether formal or informal) of communicating their preferences or their dissent.[10]

The Convention, then, would appear to have immense relevance to disabled people. It would provide them with a means of enforcing rights such as the right to life and to protection from abuse; the right to access to justice; the right to privacy and to a family life; the right to freedom to receive and impart information; and the right to associate and assemble. Why, then, has such potentially fertile ground not been cultivated by disabled people? In this chapter we argue that the low profile of disabled people in the Convention case law is not because Convention rights have no relevance to disabled people. The problem lies, rather, in the difficulty they experience in accessing them.

2 THE ISSUE OF ACCESS

Responsibility for the dearth of cases can, in large measure, be placed at the door of the usual culprits; the physical, social and economic barriers that prevent disabled people from exercising their rights. Some of these barriers to access are embedded in the circumstances in which many disabled people live their lives. Some are related to the unresponsiveness of the law, the judiciary and the practicalities of enforcement mechanisms to the needs and rights of disabled people.

Taking action to gain redress for a grievance always requires knowledge, support, confidence, energy and staying-power. Due process is complex and frequently time-consuming. Worthwhile outcomes cannot be guaranteed. These issues, problematic enough in any circumstances, are likely to be magnified for many people with impairments. Disabled people often live in circumstances which are poorer, and more constraining and limiting than those of their non-disabled peers.[11] It is not uncommon for many to have faced years of stress, exhaustion and poor health without adequate support. In such circumstances it may well be difficult to exercise even a limited degree of autonomy and choice or to carry out activities regarded by the general population as ordinary. Embarking on the complex, taxing procedures attendant on bringing a challenge under the Convention would be regarded by many such disabled people as impossible. Research suggests that some disabled people feel ill-equipped to make complaints in the standard way and that they are often fearful of the possible negative consequences of voicing dissatisfaction. One important study of social welfare complaints procedures and people with learning difficulties[12] found that

[10] P Russell, *Having a Say! Disabled Children and Effective Partnership in Decision-Making* (London, Council for Disabled Children, 1998).

[11] See eg C Barnes, *Disabled People in Britain and Discrimination* (London, Hurst and Company in association with the British Council of Organisations of Disabled People 1991).

[12] K Simons, *I'm Not Complaining, but* ...(York, Joseph Rowntree Foundation, 1995).

'fear of the consequences' was 'by far the most commonly cited reason for not making formal complaints'. In short, the barriers disabled people face in their daily lives are complex and multi-layered.

Further, some disabled people will lack the intellectual capacity to make decisions about issues which fundamentally impact on their human rights. Such people are among those who are most at risk of human rights violations. They will often require another to act on their behalf. The fact that no appropriate person may be available to take on this role, and the very ambiguity of the law on representative action, undoubtedly constitutes an additional barrier in the way of their access to rights.

Whilst these particular types of barrier may help to explain the dearth of complaints brought by disabled people, they do not explain the reluctance of the Court and Commission to entertain sympathetically the few such complaints that do reach them. Other barriers reside within the judicial process itself.

Problems of access are of course not unique to disabled people, and the Strasbourg Court has long accepted that human rights are of little value if inaccessible. Implicit within the Convention process is the existence of the 'right of access' to the courts and other bodies able to provide redress. Whilst the Court has, in general, robustly challenged inappropriate barriers to the judicial process,[13] it has not done so where the barriers in question have affected disabled people specifically. *Skjoldager v Sweden*[14] is a good illustration of this point. The applicant, a psychologist, visited a care home for people with learning disabilities where he found a number of residents unlawfully locked in their rooms. Following his report, action was taken which eventually resulted in the removal of the locks. He was, however, denied further access to the residents. Where unlawful detention of this nature has occurred, Article 5(5) requires that compensation be paid. Because none was offered to the residents, the applicant complained to the European Commission. He did so in a representative capacity, but in his own name because the municipality had refused to provide him with the names of the residents (who were incapable of lodging the complaint themselves). The case was rejected on the ground that the applicant had no specific authority to make the complaint. The residents were, therefore, effectively outside the protection of the Convention.

Malone v UK[15] raises similar issues. Mandy Malone, a wheelchair-user, was the defendant in possession proceedings relating to her council house. Her request that these be heard in a court near to her home was refused. Consequently, in order to reach the court, she had to leave home at 4.30 am and undertake a 950 kilometre round trip. As a result, she was confined

---

[13] See eg in relation to prisoners rights, *Golder v UK* (1975) 1 EHRR 524.
[14] (1995) 22504/93.
[15] (1996) 25290/94.

to her bed for four days and required medical assistance. Her complaint related to the unfairness of the process and the inaccessibility of the court building (she had to be carried up the steps of the court and experienced 'excruciating discomfort' due to the lack of suitable toilet facilities). The Strasbourg complaint was rejected on the grounds that she had 'failed to appropriately bring to the attention of the court her difficulties'.

3 JUDICIAL INDIFFERENCE

Why is it, then, that the courts are prepared to be robust in their defence of the rights of prisoners but not of institutionalised people with learning disabilities? Why is it that the courts view disability as something that administrators need address only if forewarned; if, in effect, 'booked in advance'? Given that there are in the region of 8,600,000 disabled people in the UK, and given the extent of concern about the possible abuse and human rights violations to which they may be exposed, the lack of sympathy typified by the *Skjoldager* and *Malone* decisions is deeply troubling. It is simply inconceivable that the court would have responded to a complaint concerning a prisoner held *incommunicado* in the way that it responded in *Skjoldager*. It is simply unacceptable that the court should respond, as it did in *Malone*, by requiring disabled defendants to submit, in effect, to trial by battle; to litigate the able-bodied way, without becoming drained, without requiring rest and without requiring a toilet.

There are various possible explanations for these leaden judicial responses. One might suggest that judges do not consider disabled people to be 'ripe for freedom'[16] in the same way that slaves, serfs, southern blacks and women were once thought not to be ripe for it. It would be pleasing if this suggestion could simply be dismissed out of hand, but the failure of the courts to conceptualise disability in any meaningful way, or to grasp any notion of what it feels like to live with the impairment and the social stigmatisation and exclusion that accompany it, does have throwbacks to such unfortunate times.

4 CONCEPTUAL BARRIERS

It may be, however, that the judicial misperceptions, or misconceptions, are altogether more jurisprudential in nature; that somehow human rights are not seen as relevant to disabled people. It is undoubtedly the case that disabled people have sometimes been considered by more powerful others as not entitled to full and automatic membership of the category of 'human'. They have sometimes been denied 'personhood' and been

---

[16] AW Wood and G Di Giovanni (eds), *Kant Religion Within the Boundaries of Mere Reason and Other Writings* (Cambridge, Cambridge University Press, 1998).

construed as having less value than those who are not disabled.[17] There have been times when the results of this approach have been catastrophic, both for individual disabled people and for disabled citizens as a group.[18] When (as a result of active intent, neglect, or ignorance) certain individuals or groups are denied the status of 'human' *on the same terms as their peers* the rights which accompany that status are also likely to be denied them. This tendency to regard disabled people as 'other', to place them in a separate category, may go some way towards explaining the failure of lawyers to articulate human rights in a language that renders justiciable[19] such concepts as a fundamental right to inclusion within society's mainstream institutions and processes, to independence and to a non-disabling personal and social environment. It might also help to explain the dearth of academic contributions in this field; the so-called 'silence of human rights scholars'.[20]

Disabled people are often viewed, even by some of those who do not dehumanise them in the sense just outlined, primarily as recipients of health and welfare services rather than as citizens with the same rights as others. Indeed, the conflation of disabled people's rights with socio-economic and collective rights may have done much to obscure the central relevance of the Convention to them. This is not, of course, to deny the importance of socio-economic rights to disabled people. They, in common with other socially marginalised and disempowered groups, have need of decent public housing, of income support, and of health and social care services. This means that the European Social Charter and many other socio-economic treaties have particular significance for disabled people. It does not mean, however, that the ECHR or any other civil and political rights treaty will have diminished significance for them. Many lawyers are in danger of perceiving (albeit subliminally) a trade-off in this domain; a trade-off between services and civil rights. In return for services, on this view, the recipient would either relinquish certain human rights, or at least cease to be in such immediate need of them. If this is indeed the case, then it constitutes a further, profoundly disabling, barrier in the way of people with impairments.

Whilst the problems of conceptualising disability in the language of the Convention should not be underestimated, the difficulty lies primarily in the lack of vision of those who doubt or deny its applicability. Magna Carta

[17] S Vehmas, 'Discriminative assumptions of utilitarian bioethics regarding individuals with intellectual disabilities' (1999) 14 *Disability and Society* 37–52.

[18] See eg A Shearer, *Everybody's Ethics* (London, Campaign for Mentally Handicapped People, 1984).

[19] See eg Arai-Takahashi's analysis of the non-justiciable nature of such rights, in Y Arai-Takahashi, 'The role of international health law and the WHO in the regulation of public health' in R Martin and L Johnson (eds), *Law and the Public Dimension of Health* (London, Cavendish, 2001).

[20] A Hendriks, 'Disabled persons and their right to equal treatment' in JM Mann, S Gruskin, MA Grodin and GJ Annas (eds), *Health and Human Rights* (London, Routledge, 1999).

was not undermined by the fall of feudalism nor the Bill of Rights by the abolition of slavery nor the US Constitution by the Supreme Court's ruling against racial segregation in education.[21] Nor has the Convention been devalued by its championing of the rights of women and racial minorities or those of gay and lesbian people. The recognition of civil and political rights in these new domains has required vision. It has challenged established modes of communication, requiring the language of 'justiciable rights' to be used in new ways to accommodate new paradigms and create new conceptual vehicles.

These challenges have fundamentally reconfigured the grammar of the law and resulted in many memorable judgements condemning contemporary injustices. From such endeavours we have seen, within the last 50 years, the courts conceptualising (in the language of the law) principles such as 'separate but equal', 'indirect discrimination', 'positive obligations' and 'legitimate expectation'. These concepts have emerged slowly, been highly contested and, as a result, undergone continual refinement. In relation to the rights of disabled people, there is clearly still a long way to go. In the last twenty years, in both the formal and the grey literature of disabled academics and activists and their supporters, emphasis has been increasingly placed on the discrimination faced by disabled people as well as on the social and political factors which inhibit their equal opportunities and full participation. With the development of the 'social model of disability', disability rights activists have increasingly identified themselves as citizens who are routinely prohibited from exercising their civil and human rights.[22] The identification of disability as a human rights issue has, nevertheless, been slow to find effective expression within the law. It is, however, not only in relation to the rights of disabled people that there continues to be a struggle to translate political concepts into legal language.

Wexler's[23] classic articulation of the failure of 'black letter law' to tackle the injustices experienced by poor people, for instance, remains valid today and has much resonance for other marginalised groups (including disabled people):

> Poor people are not just like rich people without money. Poor people do not have legal problems like those of the private plaintiffs and defendants in law school casebooks. ... Poverty creates an abrasive interface with society; poor people are always bumping into sharp legal things. The law school model of personal legal problems, of solving them and returning the client to the smooth and orderly world in television advertisements, doesn't apply to poor people.

---

[21] *Brown v Board of Education* 347 US 483 (1953).
[22] See eg M Oliver, *The Politics of Disablement* (London, Macmillan, 1990); and J Morris, *Accessing Human Rights: Disabled Children and the Children Act* (Barkingside, Barnardos, 1998).
[23] S Wexler, 'Practising law for poor people' (1970) 79 *Yale Law Journal* 1049.

The fact that Strasbourg continues to have profound difficulty in identifying and addressing state responsibility for discrimination against disabled people is, likewise, not an affirmation of the inappropriateness of the medium but, rather, a failure of imagination. It represents a failure of advocates and judges to find a new way of expressing the language of the Convention. The fact that Article 14 does not specifically include disability as an example of a ground of unlawful discrimination is a consequence of a lack of vision on the part of the drafters of the Treaty; it is not proof that discrimination on grounds of disability is intrinsically different from other forms of discrimination.[24] The Convention is similarly silent on the rights of children and gay and lesbian people, but this has not prevented the Court developing a jurisprudence which identifies, articulates and attempts to remedy the injustice they experience.

The very difficulty of articulating these disparate manifestations of injustice in the restrictive language of the Convention is what ultimately maintains its relevance as a 'living instrument'. Noam Chomsky in his essay on 'Language and Freedom'[25] argues that limitations within language and its principal structures reflect deeper 'restrictive attributes of the mind'. Far from regarding this as a negative characteristic, however, he argues that it is ultimately liberating:

> There is no inconsistency in the notion that the restrictive attributes of mind underlie a historically evolving human nature that develops within the limits that they set; or that these attributes of mind provide the possibility for self-perfection; or that, by providing the consciousness of freedom, these essential attributes of human nature give man the opportunity to create social conditions and social forms to maximize the possibilities for freedom, diversity, and individual self-realization.

5 ANALOGOUS STRUGGLES

For all its 'restrictive attributes', the Convention (like other civil and political rights instruments) has retained its relevance through its repeated application to new domains of injustice. It is, to use the jargon of the Strasbourg Court, a 'living instrument' which develops new principles and conceptualisations in order to address contemporary ills. Accordingly, the analogous struggles of other socially oppressed groups, such as Roma, gay and lesbian people, have produced a jurisprudence which may be adapted to serve the needs of disabled people. In applying such jurisprudence in a disability context, however, the Court should take care, on the one hand, to refrain from adopting a generic or formulaic approach which does not reflect the

---

[24] There has, however, still been no Court finding of a violation of Art 14 on grounds of disability and in *McIntyre v UK* (1995) [29046/95; 21 October 1998] the UK Government refused to accept that disability was a 'status' protected by Art 14.

[25] *TriQuarterly* nos 23–24 (7) 52 (Evanston, Northwestern University Press, 1972).

distinctiveness of the experiences of disabled people and, on the other, to recognise the many common themes running through the testimony of socially stigmatised people. J Sachs expressed this dilemma, in the context of the struggle of gay and lesbian people for equal status in South Africa, as follows:[26]

> Human rights are better approached and defended in an integrated rather than a disparate fashion. The rights must fit the people, not the people the rights. This requires looking at rights and their violations from a person-centred rather than a formula-based position, and analysing them contextually rather than abstractly.

It is not only from the injustices experienced by gay and lesbian people that disabled people may draw useful parallels. The struggle by Roma to persuade the Court to appreciate their 'untouchable' status has also resulted in the tentative development of a language of exclusion which can be 'read across'. In this discourse, Roma have focused on the incremental nature of the socio-legal restrictions confronting them. This has been described by Jean Pierre Liégeois[27] as 'an accumulation of handicaps'; the layer upon layer of social and administrative regulation, individually innocuous but cumulatively fatal. Judge Pettiti, in *Buckley v UK*,[28] expressed the oppressive nature of this socio-legal process in the following terms:

> The Strasbourg institutions' difficulty in identifying this type of problem is that the deliberate superimposition and accumulation of administrative rules (each of which would be acceptable taken singly) result, firstly, in its being totally impossible for a Gypsy family to make suitable arrangements for its accommodation, social life and the integration of its children at school, and secondly, in different government departments combining measures relating to town planning, nature conservation, the viability of access roads, planning permission requirements, road safety and public health that, in the instant case, mean the Buckley family are caught in a 'vicious circle'.

6 JUDICIAL RECOGNITION

It would be misleading to suggest that Human Rights Courts have not even begun to assemble the vocabulary and legal principles from which a jurisprudence of direct relevance to disabled people might eventually be constructed. In *Olmstead v LC*,[29] for instance, the US Supreme Court was prepared to conceptualise the disparate rates of institutionalisation of

---

[26] *National Coalition for Gay and Lesbian Equality v Minister of Justice* (1998) South African Constitutional Court–CCT11/98: 9 October 1998; 1999 (1) SA 6 (CC); 1998 (1) BCLR 1517 (CC) para 112.

[27] J-P Liégeois, *Gypsies and Travellers* (Council of Europe, 1987), p 111.

[28] (1996) 23 EHRR 101 at 137.

[29] 527 US 581 (1999); 119 S Ct 2176 (1999) at 2187.

disabled and non-disabled people in terms of unlawful discrimination. It held that:

> Institutional placement of persons who can handle and benefit from community settings perpetuates unwarranted assumptions that persons so isolated are incapable or unworthy of participating in community life

and that 'institutional confinement severely diminishes individuals' everyday life activities'.

Some very positive developments also emerge from a handful of Strasbourg judgments. The most important of these is *Botta v Italy*,[30] in which the applicant (who had physical impairments) complained that he was unable to use the beach at his holiday destination due to the lack of access ramps and specially equipped toilets. He alleged that this was a breach of Italian law and, when this claim failed, that it also violated his human rights. His argument involved transporting the language of the Convention (in that case, Article 8) into the territory of the social model of disability; a 'reading across' which the Court was able to understand and willing (but only in principle) to accept. It held that the Article 8 concept of private life 'includes a person's physical and psychological integrity';[31] and that this integrity is protected in order to 'ensure the development, without outside interference, of the personality of each individual in his relations with other human beings'.[32] Further, it ruled that:[33]

> While the essential object of Article 8 is to protect the individual against arbitrary interference by the public authorities, it does not merely compel the state to abstain from such interference: in addition to this negative undertaking, there may be positive obligations inherent in effective respect for private or family life. These obligations may involve the adoption of measures designed to secure respect for private life even in the sphere of the relations of individuals between themselves.

In *Price v UK*[34] (a case concerning the summary imprisonment of a thalidomide-impaired applicant), the Court was prepared to accept the uniqueness of a disabled person's experiences and, consequently, indicated that treating them in the same way as a non-disabled person might well amount to degrading treatment under Article 3. According to Judge Greve:[35]

> It is obvious that restraining any non-disabled person to the applicant's level of ability to move and assist herself, for even a limited period of time, would

[30] (1998) 26 EHRR 241.
[31] *Ibid* para 32.
[32] *Ibid*.
[33] *Ibid*.
[34] (2001) 34 EHRR 1285.
[35] *Ibid* at 1296.

amount to inhuman and degrading treatment—possibly torture. In a civilised country like the United Kingdom, society considers it not only appropriate but a basic humane concern to try to ameliorate and compensate for the disabilities faced by a person in the applicant's situation. In my opinion, these compensatory measures come to form part of the disabled person's bodily integrity.[36]

7 JUDICIAL CAUTION

Botta and *Price*, then, are cases in which the Court has been willing to listen and to recast its jurisprudence to accommodate the experiences of disabled people. As we noted at the beginning of this chapter, however, there are many cases in which Strasbourg has not been so amenable. Two recent cases which presented the Court with opportunities to develop its nascent jurisprudence in this field call for specific mention.

Zehnalová & Zehnal v Czech Republic[37] concerned the inability of the disabled (first) applicant to enter a large number of public buildings in her home town because of their inaccessibility to people with impaired mobility. The applicant sought to apply the *Botta* principles in the concrete environment of her home town. The Court, however, ruled the complaint inadmissible, observing that:[38]

Article 8 of the Convention cannot be taken to be generally applicable each time the first applicant's everyday life is disrupted; it applies only in exceptional cases where her lack of access to public buildings and buildings open to the public affects her life in such a way as to interfere with her right to personal development and her right to establish and develop relationships with other human beings and the outside world.

In the Court's opinion, then, although the State might have a positive obligation to ensure access to certain buildings, this particular complaint was 'too broad and indeterminate'. Had it wished to be imaginative, it could have developed the reasoning of Judge Pettiti in the *Buckley* complaint and acknowledged that Mrs Zehnalová had been confronted by an accumulation of barriers and been subjected to a form of discrimination which was many-layered. Such an approach would have allowed the Court to abandon its traditional search for a discrete and dramatic interference with a Convention right in favour of a new analysis that enabled it to respond to incremental injustices of the type in question. Indeed, the Court already has such a tool in the form of the principle of proportionality.

Sentges v Netherlands[39] is equally disappointing. The applicant (aged 7) was described as 'unable to stand, walk or lift his arms, and his manual and

---

[36] From the concurring opinion of Judge Greve.
[37] (2002) Application No 38621/97.
[38] *Ibid* at page 12.
[39] (2003) Application No 27677/02.

digital functions [were] virtually absent' so that, 'for every act he [needed] or [wished] to perform, including eating and drinking, he [was] completely dependent on assistance from third persons.' A request (endorsed by a rehabilitation specialist) for a robotic arm, that would enable him to perform many basic functions unassisted, was refused by the authorities on financial grounds. Although the cost of the arm was substantial (10,900 euros per annum), its purchase would have resulted in savings in other aspects of the care package.

Sentges presented the Court with an opportunity to develop the principles underlying the proportionality rule. On such extreme facts, the striking of a fair balance between the positive obligations inherent in Article 8(1) and the legitimate aims identified in Article 8(2) requires, if not a new dimension to the analysis, then at the very least a more sophisticated assessment of the competing claims. What is at stake is not mere discomfort or inconvenience but the very possibility of having meaningful relations with other human beings. In such cases, compensatory measures of this nature must form (to cite Judge Greve in *Price v UK*) part of the disabled person's bodily integrity. Instead of analysing the extent and character of this obligation, the court hid behind the discredited principle of the 'margin of appreciation'.[40] In its view, even if this was an exceptional case in which it could be argued that Article 8 might require positive state action:[41]

> regard must [also] be had to the fair balance that has to be struck between the competing interests of the individual and of the community as a whole,

especially when 'the issues involve an assessment of the priorities in the context of the allocation of limited State resources'.

No-one can sensibly disagree with this statement, but it does beg a number of questions: How is the balance to be struck? Is the process by which this balance is struck a legitimate concern of human rights law? Regrettably, the Court in *Sentges* had not the vocabulary, the vision or the humanity to conceptualise the applicant's predicament in terms of civil and political rights. As Lord Lester has observed, 'the court now appears to use the margin of appreciation as a substitute for coherent legal analysis'.[42]

8 CONCLUSION

In this paper we have endeavoured to identify the reasons why so few disabled people have sought the protection of the European Court of Human Rights; why so few disabled people have sought to articulate the injustices they experience in the language of civil and political rights. The

---

[40] See in particular, Lord Lester of Herne Hill, *Universality versus Subsidiarity: A Reply* [1998] 1 EHRLR 73–81.
[41] *Ibid* at page 7.
[42] *Ibid.*

multi-layered restrictions routinely experienced by disabled children and adults in many aspects of their lives are the focus of activity of disability rights organisations in Europe and elsewhere. Advocacy provision (including self-advocacy) and other similar services may prove useful in supporting and empowering disabled people to engage in the otherwise disabling process of litigation. The tangible restrictions which are embedded in the judicial system (physical barriers to courts, indifferent judges and unsympathetic institutions) also require attention from activists and those supportive of their endeavours. Over time, there is hope that a combination of awareness-raising and enforcement will foster more benign institutional environments that anticipate and respond to the concerns of disabled people. Initiatives of this nature may also address some judicial misconceptions and thoughtlessness.[43] Addressing the broader conceptual barriers, however, will present a greater challenge. Ultimately this will require the development of a new jurisprudence, a new vocabulary and grammar, which describes the particular discrimination and social exclusion experienced by disabled people. This will require the voice of disabled people to be heard by the legal system. It will require lawyers, including judges, to comprehend how, in this particular corner of the twenty-first century, the oppression experienced by disabled people manifests itself in a myriad of crude and subtle forms.

---

[43] The Judicial Studies Board of England and Wales has taken a very positive first step in this direction with the publication of *Equality before the Courts: A short practical guide for judges* (London, Judicial Studies Board, 2002).

4

Reasonable Accommodations and Positive Obligations in the European Convention on Human Rights

OLIVIER DE SCHUTTER*

1 INTRODUCTION

THIS CHAPTER SEEKS to identify whether the jurisprudence of the European Court of Human Rights (ECtHR) may lead it to require both the State and private actors to effectively accommodate the needs of disabled people and to ensure that they are not subject to discrimination because of the environment which they inhabit. The following section examines four cases in which disabled litigants asked the ECtHR, implicitly or explicitly, to impose an obligation on the defending State to provide reasonable accommodation. All these cases invoked the right to respect for private life, guaranteed by Article 8 of the European Convention on Human Rights (ECHR). The third section considers the ECtHR's imposition of positive obligations on States and seeks to identify the precise nature of such obligations as well as their future potential for disabled people. In fact, the lessons from the existing case-law are rather disappointing. The leading case in this area remains *Botta v Italy*, decided in 1998, where the Court held that Article 8 could not be invoked in the absence of a 'direct and immediate link' between the measures sought and the 'private life' of the applicant. This link has been construed narrowly and appears to relate exclusively to the applicant's immediate surroundings or everyday activities. The fourth section therefore examines the possible strategies which might be used to circumvent the restrictions of the *Botta* line of cases so as to result in the recognition of an ECHR obligation to provide reasonable accommodations for disabled people. It will consider, in particular, whether Articles 3 or 14 (which prohibit inhuman or

* Professor of Law, University of Louvain (Belgium); Co-ordinator of the EU Network of Independent Experts in Fundamental Rights; Visiting Professor at New York University. I am grateful to A Hendriks and G Quinn for their stimulating comments.

degrading treatment, and discrimination in the enjoyment of Convention rights) might be relied upon. Finally, in section 5, I will examine the impact of the Convention on the provision of reasonable accommodation in employment, which presents certain specific difficulties.

2 THE RIGHT TO RESPECT FOR PRIVATE LIFE AND THE REQUIREMENT OF ACCESSIBILITY

2.1 'Private Life'

The four ECHR cases, in which some form of accommodation for a disabled person was requested, all arose outside the context of employment. They invoked the right to respect for private life guaranteed by Article 8. Indeed, since the early 1990s, the notion of 'private life' which appears in Article 8 has been extended beyond the protection of information, and beyond the sphere of intimate relationships, to include a right to 'establish and develop relationships with other human beings and the outside world'.[1] This conception of private life is similar to the 'right to the free development of [one's] personality,' in Article 2 of the German Basic Law of 1949,[2] and also to the right to privacy, set out in the penumbra of the explicit clauses of the Bill of Rights appended to the US Federal Constitution and interpreted to include a right to make certain choices essential to one's existence.[3]

Indeed, it is such an extended notion of 'private life' that, in the case of *Pretty v UK*, Diane Pretty relied upon to claim the protection of an alleged right to make decisions about one's body and what happens to it. She argued that, because she was suffering from a neuro-degenerative disease leading to progressive muscle weakness affecting the voluntary muscles and would therefore be unable to commit suicide by herself, her right to private life conferred on her the right to be assisted in committing

[1] *Niemietz v Germany* (16 December 1992) Series A No 251–B, para 29.

[2] This provision states that:

> Everybody has the right to the free development of his personality, as long as he does not violate the rights of others and does not contravene the constitutional order or moral laws

(trans in S Michalowski and L Woods, *German Constitutional Law: The protection of civil liberties* (Dartmouth, Ashgate, 1999), p 108). The German Federal Constitutional Court (*Bundesverfassungsgericht*) has derived a 'general freedom to act' from this provision (*allgemeine Handlungsfreiheit*), protecting

> not only ... a limited area of personality development, but rather ... every form of human activity regardless of the importance of this behaviour for the development of personality (BverfGE 80, 153 (1989)).

[3] Such choices may relate, eg, to childrearing and education (*Pierce v Society of Sisters* 268 US 510, 535 (1925); *Meyer v Nebraska* 262 US 390, 399 (1923)), marriage (*Loving v Virginia* 388 US 1, 12 (1967)), procreation (*Skinner v Oklahoma* 316 US 535, 541 (1942); *Roe v Wade* 410 US 113 (1973); *Planned Parenthood of Southern Pennsylvania v Casey* 505 US 833 (1992)) or contraception (*Eisenstadt v Baird* 405 US 438, 453–4 (1972)).

suicide. It was held that, despite the absence of any case-law guaranteeing a right to self-determination under Article 8, 'the notion of personal autonomy is an important principle underlying the interpretation of its guarantees.'[4] *Pretty*, to which we shall return later, presented the Court with the new problem of determining whether the right to privacy could include a right to dispose of one's own body. Despite the high profile of that case, it constituted just one more development in the Article 8 case-law. Long before *Pretty*, Article 8 had been used to protect the physical and psychological integrity of the individual, as well as his/her social identity; thus guaranteeing 'autonomy' and the right to self-fulfilment, as opposed to a right to be simply 'let alone'. This approach to 'private life' has, for instance, led Judge Molinari to observe (in a case concerning the refusal of a disability allowance to the applicant on grounds of his nationality) that:[5]

> In my opinion, this case goes to the heart of Article 8 of the Convention. The Court's interpretation of that provision has evolved concerning rights affecting the private and family sphere of human beings, which is the most intimate of spheres, and one in respect of which the Court must ensure that their dignity and their private and family life are protected by the States signatory to the Convention. The Court has held that these States must in the first place respect the private and family life of anyone within their jurisdiction, but also remove the obstacles and restrictions which hinder the free development of the personality, and assume broader and broader positive obligations.

In her view, the granting of allowances to disabled adults fell within the ambit of Article 8, justifying the application of Article 14 where it operated in a discriminatory fashion. It is this notion of 'private life' that has been invoked in a number of recent applications in attempts to require States to adopt measures which would contribute to the social and professional integration of disabled people by removing the artificial barriers which currently prevent them from freely developing their personality.

2.2 The Disability Cases

In the first and best-known case, *Botta v Italy*,[6] the applicant complained that the bathing establishments at the seaside resort where he spent his vacations were not equipped with the facilities needed to enable disabled people to gain access to the beach and the sea. This was in breach of Italian law, which required a clause to be added to the relevant concession contracts obliging private beaches to facilitate access by disabled people, and made provision for compliance to be enforced by the competent local authorities. The Court, however, considered that Article 8 did not extend

---

[4] *Pretty v UK* (29 April 2002) Application No 2346/02, para 61.
[5] In her dissenting opinion in *Koua Poirrez v France* (30 September 2003) Application No 40892/98.
[6] *Botta v Italy* (24 February 1998) *Reports and Decisions of the ECtHR* 1998–I, No 66 412.

to the right to gain access to the beach and the sea at a place distant from the normal place of residence during holidays, as:

> there can be no conceivable direct link between the measures the State was urged to take in order to make good the omissions of the private bathing establishments and the applicant's private life.[7]

In the second case, also concerning Italy, the applicant, Mr Marzari, suffered from metabolic myopathy, leading to 'thermal disability.' Cold temperatures and changes in temperature caused him intense muscular pain, often forcing him to use a wheelchair. He complained that, in breach of Italian law, the local administrative authorities had failed to provide him with an apartment adequate to the needs arising from his impairment. However, the Court noted the willingness of the local authorities to carry out works on the apartment allocated to him and rejected the application as manifestly ill-founded. In its view, no positive obligation on local authorities to provide the applicant with a specific apartment could be inferred from Article 8. A suitable apartment had been offered to the applicant. He had refused it on the ground that it did not meet his needs, despite an assessment to the contrary by a Commission for the study of metabolic diseases.[8]

In a third case, *Zehnalová and Zehnal v the Czech Republic*, the applicants complained that in the town of Prerov where they were residing, a number of buildings providing services to the public (including the post office, the local tribunal, the police office, medical facilities and the local swimming pool) were not accessible to people with certain impairments because of inadequate enforcement of regulations which required the removal of architectural barriers.[9] Despite the fact that the inaccessible buildings in question were far more closely linked to the everyday lives of the applicants than the inaccessible beaches had been to the life of Mr Botta, the Court ruled that they had failed to establish the necessary special link between the buildings and their private life. Relying on the test laid down in *Botta*, it explained that:

> Considering the important number of buildings concerned, some doubt remains as to their everyday use by the applicant and as to the existence of a

---

[7] *Ibid* para 35. On this case, see the notes by RA Lawson and A Hendriks in *NJCM-Bulletin* 1998, p 597.

[8] *Marzari v Italy* (4 May 1999) Application No 36448/97.

[9] Because it concerned the provision of public services, the case of *Zehnalová and Zehnal* (14 May 2002) Application No 38621/97 is closest to the well-known case of *Eldridge v British Columbia* [1997] 3 RCS 624, where the Canadian Supreme Court recognised that deaf persons should be provided a sign interpreter to facilitate their communication with the personnel of a public hospital: the absence of such an accommodation of their disability would constitute discrimination under the Equality Clause of Art 15(1) of the Canadian Charter of Rights and Freedoms.

direct and immediate link between the measures required from the State and the private life of the applicants.

As in *Botta* therefore, Article 8 was considered as inapplicable.[10]

Finally, in the most recent case of *Nikky Sentges v the Netherlands*, the applicant had a disease characterised by progressive muscle degeneration. As a result, he had to rely on assistance from other people for every act he wished to perform, including eating and drinking. A robotic arm would have greatly reduced his dependence on the constant presence of carers and would have enabled him to continue living at home for a longer period of time. The health insurance fund rejected his request for such a device, however, as it was not covered by any social insurance scheme. After failing to have this decision annulled by the national courts, Mr Sentges turned to the ECtHR where he argued that he was not free to establish and develop relationships with other human beings of his choice. He contended that 'private life' encompassed notions pertaining to his quality of life, including personal autonomy, self-determination and the right to establish and develop relationships with others. However, it was held that even if Article 8 were applicable, the Court must consider the fair balance to be struck between the competing interests of the individual concerned and the community as a whole, and must also have regard to the wide margin of appreciation granted to States in determining how to ensure compliance with the Convention. In light of the fact that this margin is particularly wide where the issues involve the allocation of limited State resources, the Court ruled that the Netherlands were within this range of acceptable responses.[11]

2.3 An Interpretation

In all these cases the *Botta* test for determining the applicability of Article 8 was reaffirmed. According to this test the State will be under a positive obligation to ensure effective 'respect' for private life where two conditions are satisfied: First, there must be 'a direct and immediate link between the measures sought by an applicant and the latter's private and/or family life',[12] which renders Article 8 applicable. Second, the efforts required from the public authorities should not be disproportionate, so that a fair balance is achieved between the competing interests of the individual and of the community as a whole. In other words, the State will be obliged to take measures to remove obstacles encountered by a disabled person,

---

[10] *Zehnalová and Zehnal v the Czech Republic* (14 May 2002) Application No 38621/97. See the commentary by A Hendriks in *NJCM-Bulletin* 2003, p 321.

[11] *Sentges v the Netherlands* (8 July 2003) Application No 27677/02.

[12] *Botta v Italy* (24 February 1998), para 34.

where they relate to his/her immediate environment and constitute a permanent and important (rather than occasional or negligeable) barrier to the development of his/her personality, unless doing so would impose a disproportionate burden upon it.

No such 'direct and immediate link' to private life was found in *Botta*, where a disabled person sought access to the beach and the sea at a place distant from his normal place of residence during his holidays; or in *Zehnalová and Zehnal*, where such a person claimed a right to access public facilities.[13] On the other hand, such a 'direct and immediate link' was found to exist in *Marzari*, where access to housing was concerned, and in *Sentges*, where capacity to perform ordinary acts of daily life (such as switching a computer on, making telephone calls, eating or drinking) was concerned. In these two cases, Article 8 was held to be applicable, though not actually violated.

It has been rightly pointed out that what distinguishes the latter two situations from the former two is that, in *Marzari* and *Sentges*, the measures sought were personalised accommodation measures for the benefit of the particular individuals, as opposed to general measures for the benefit of an ill-defined community.[14] It should be noted, however, that a finding of violation in *Marzari* or *Sentges* would have had consequences reaching far beyond those individual cases, obliging the Italian authorities, for instance, to rethink the accessibility of social housing for disabled people and the Dutch legislator to broaden the scope of the relevant social insurance scheme. In fact, the main reason why Article 8 was found applicable in *Marzari* and *Sentges* but not in *Botta* or *Zehnalovà and Zehnal* lies in the 'direct and immediate link' to private life test set out in *Botta*. In *Marzari* and *Sentges*, the applicants were permanently affected in their everyday life by the alleged refusal to provide them with the accommodation they requested. According to the Court, this was precisely what the applicants in the other two cases failed to demonstrate.

3 THE JUDICIAL IMPOSITION OF POSITIVE OBLIGATIONS

3.1 Overview

These four leading ECHR cases illustrate the reluctance of the Court to impose far-reaching obligations on States to remove the architectural

[13] In those cases, since Art 8 was held to be inapplicable, the non-discrimination clause of Art 14 could not be engaged. On the non-discrimination clause of Art 14 ECHR, see below.
[14] See A Hendriks, on *Sentges v the Netherlands* (8 July 2003) (2004) 29 *NJCM-Bulletin* 57, at p 6: 'In de zaken *Botta* en *Zehnalovà en Zehnal* had de klacht betrekking op (de niet-naleving) van algemene toegankelijkheidseisen, dat wil zeggen regels die zijn geformuleerd ten behoeve van een grotere niet-gedefinieerde groep mensen. ... Niet kan worden gesteld dat de aanpassingen die Marzari en Sentges wensten voor hele groepen mensen gepast is.'

or other barriers which impede the full social and professional integration of disabled people. How are these results to be explained? Are the particular facts of these cases to blame, or are there more structural explanations? I will consider three factors which may be operating, before looking at possible ways to circumvent them.

In my view the explanation for the relatively 'hands-off' approach of the Court is to be found at the institutional rather than substantive level. Its apparent timidity is to be attributed to various constraints operating upon it, rather than to an understanding of Article 8 as having no bearing upon the adjustment of infrastructure to facilitate use by disabled people.

3.2 The Specificity of the Obligation to Progressively Realise

The Court faces a number of specific constraints when considering the imposition of an obligation of progressive realisation on States. This form of human rights obligation requires States to adopt measures which, although they move the State in the desired direction, cannot immediately ensure that the right is fully realised in all its dimensions. In *Zehnalová and Zehnal* the Court noted that, despite the fact that many public buildings were inaccessible to the applicants, the authorities had not remained inactive and the situation in the town of Prerov had improved in recent years.[15] In *Marzari*, the Court expressed the opinion that the authorities' refusal to provide relevant assistance to a disabled individual might raise an issue under Article 8 because of the impact of that refusal on the individual's private life. In that case it was the good faith of the authorities, their demonstrated willingness to find a solution to the applicant's housing problem, which led the Court to conclude that they had 'discharged their positive obligations in respect of the applicant's right to respect for his private life.'

Botta and *Zehnalová and Zehnal* exemplify the limits of the all-or-nothing approach, operating in the binary fashion which characterises the judicial function. This approach stands in contrast to that which might be expected, for instance, of a committee periodically reviewing the evolution of the situation in a particular State based on comparisons made over time. This latter mechanism (illustrated by the expert committees instituted by the UN human rights treaties) might appear better suited to the role of enforcing an obligation to adapt infrastructures for disabled people. Such

---

[15] Although the Court belittles the influence this may have exercised on the finding of non-violation it arrived at, the role of this element, which demonstrates the good faith of the authorities, cannot be ignored. In its words:

La Cour observe en outre, sans cependant y attacher une importance déterminante, que les autorités nationales n'ont pas été inactives et que, de l'aveu même des requérants, la situation dans la ville s'est améliorée depuis quelques années.

an obligation may have to be implemented progressively, over a number of years.

3.3 The Problem of Polycentricity

Two further explanations for the cautious approach adopted by the Court in these cases can be identified: First, there is the difficulty created by what Lon Fuller has described as the resolution of polycentric problems by adjudication.[16] Where an individual complaint presents the judge with a problem, the solution of which will have ripple effects elsewhere and perhaps worsen the situation of many others, how can the judge take this collective dimension into account? The alternatives would be either to deny the complaint or to adopt the role of social engineer, ordering and perhaps supervising large-scale changes to provide the necessary remedy.

O'Reilly and others v Ireland, which was ruled inadmissible by a Chamber of the ECtHR on 28 February 2002,[17] provides a good illustration of the difficulty. It concerned the failure of a County Council to discharge its statutory duty to repair a road which constituted the sole access to the applicants' homes. The road had not been repaired since 1974 and, as a result, the applicants experienced a number of problems including those arising from the fact that a bus to collect a disabled resident, and also a school bus, were unable to use it.

The Court did not deny the hardship caused to the applicants by the County Council's breach of its statutory duty to repair the road. However, it accepted that the Council did not have sufficient resources to fulfil this obligation and was, therefore, obliged to choose and prioritise the roads to be repaired according to certain criteria.[18] It was in response to this lack of funds that the Irish Supreme Court had refused to issue a mandamus order; the effective result of such an order would have been to 'ensure the repair of the roads in County Cavan in an arbitrary fashion by the elevation of certain roads to an unjustified priority in the road repair

---

[16] See L Fuller, 'The forms and limits of adjudication' (1972) 92 *Harvard Law Review* 353; and 'Adjudication and the rule of law' (1960) 54 *Proceedings of the American Society of International Law* 1. The notion of 'polycentricity', as a characteristic of problems which should not be solved by adjudication, is borrowed from M Polanyi, *The Logic of Liberty: Reflections and Rejoinders* (London, Routledge, 1951), pp 170 ff. See also, for a perspective similar to Fuller's, H Hart, 'The Supreme Court, 1958 term—foreword: the time chart of justices' (1959) 73 *Harvard Law Review* 84. For a discussion, see JWF Allison, 'Fuller's analysis of polycentric disputes and the limits of adjudication' (1999) 54 *Cambridge Law Journal* 367.

[17] *O'Reilly v Ireland* (28 February 2002) Application No 54725/00.

[18] These criteria are summarised in the description of facts by the Court. They are:

the degree of deterioration of the road, the number of families availing of the road, the needs of industry and employment, the types of traffic using the road, the volume of traffic, whether there exist particular cases of social or medical needs, the potential for tourism development and representations from local elected representatives and from private individuals.

programme.' Indeed, the Supreme Court had pointed out that the effect of any mandamus order would be the repair only of the particular road complained of, leaving other roads in the County in a state of disrepair. This illustrates the 'arbitrariness' of having priorities decided upon by the order in which suits are filed, rather than on the basis of other, more objective, criteria.

Confronted with the particular circumstances of an applicant, but largely uninformed about the more global context of that situation; ill-equipped to arbitrate in the face of delicate budgetary choices to be made by the State authorities and furthermore lacking any democratic legitimacy to make such choices in their place, the reluctance of the ECtHR to take the course requested by the applicants in *O'Reilly* is understandable.[19] It is confronted with the same dilemma whenever an individual alleges a violation but the State has insufficient resources to solve the problem for all those in similar circumstances. In *Sentges* the Court, mindful of this, observed that the margin of appreciation it will grant to the State

> is even wider when ... the issues involve an assessment of the priorities in the context of the allocation of limited State resources .... In view of their familiarity with the demands made on the health care system as well as with the funds available to meet those demands, the national authorities are in a better position to carry out this assessment than an international court.[20]

3.4 The 'Direct and Immediate Link' Test for the Identification of Positive Obligations

A third explanation for the outcomes of these cases may lie in the open-ended character of the notion of 'respect for private life,' and the scope of the positive obligations it could potentially impose on States. We know, perhaps, where the obligation begins; we hardly know where it ends. The introduction of the 'direct and immediate link' concept in *Botta* may be explained by the Court's desire to render the process by which it identifies the existence of positive obligations more objective. In earlier cases, in deciding whether such 'positive obligations' existed, the Court had regard to 'the fair balance that has to be struck between the general interest of the community and the interests of the individual.' In other words, the scope of the positive obligations imposed on States in the name of effective respect for private life was defined by a balancing of interests; the identification of the positive obligation being fused with the examination of

---

[19] Indeed, the Court cites its previous case-law to the effect that the States are granted a wide margin of appreciation 'when the issues involve an assessment of the priorities as to the allocation of limited State resources' (see *Osman v UK* (28 October 1998) *Reports and Decisions of the ECtHR* 1998–VIII, s 116).
[20] *Sentges v the Netherlands* (8 July 2003) Application No 27677/02.

whether the State could offer objective and reasonable justifications for refusing further protection to the individual.[21]

In the terminology of *Botta*, on the other hand, Article 8 will be applicable only where the failure by the State to adopt certain measures amounts to an interference with the right to respect for private life. This represents an attempt to define the scope of positive obligations imposed on the State as if they were simply a category of negative obligations. Under the *Botta* test, indeed, the Court will require that the State discharge a positive obligation to take measures ensuring effective respect for private life where the lack of such measures *infringes upon the individual's right to private life* by *directly interfering with* his/her capacity to exercise his/her right to self-determination. It is significant that, when announcing this test, the Court referred to earlier cases in which Article 8 had been violated by the passivity of the State: passivity which had resulted in a woman being unable to seek judicial protection from her violent and alcoholic husband;[22] a mentally disabled person being unable to invoke criminal proceedings against a sexual abuser;[23] a family being obliged to move from its residence to escape from the harmful effects of pollution caused by the activity of a waste-water treatment plant situated near the family home;[24] and the applicants being unable, in the absence of any information given by the authorities, to assess the risks they might be running by remaining in the vicinity of a factory producing toxic emissions.[25] In all these cases, the absence of appropriate measures by State authorities

---

[21] See eg *Abdulaziz, Cabales and Balkandali v UK* (28 May 1985) Series A No 94, para 67 (stating that the extent of the obligations inherent in an effective 'respect' for family life will be defined 'with due regard to the needs and resources of the community and of individuals'); *Rees v UK* (17 October 1986) Series A No 106, para 44 (in answering the question whether respect for the private life of transsexuals entails the obligation of UK authorities to alter the register of births or to deliver birth certificates which differ in their contents from the birth register), where the Court stated:

> [h]aving regard to the wide margin of appreciation to be afforded the State in this area and to the relevance of protecting the interests of others in striking the requisite balance, the positive obligations arising from Article 8 cannot be held to extend that far;

Gaskin v UK (7 July 1989) Series A no 160, para 42 stating that:

> the Court, in determining whether or not such a positive obligation exists, will have regard to the 'fair balance that has to be struck between the general interest of the community and the interests of the individual',

B v France (25 March 1992) Series A no 232–C, para 44. See, for a critique of this criterion, F Sudre, 'Les "obligations positives" dans la jurisprudence européenne des droits de l'homme', (1995) *Revue trimestrielle des droits de l'homme* 363.

[22] *Airey v Ireland* (9 October 1979) Series A no 32.

[23] *X and Y v the Netherlands* (26 March 1985) Series A no 91 at para 30.

[24] *López Ostra v Spain* (9 December 1994) Series A No 303–C at para 58.

[25] *Guerra and Others v Italy* (19 February 1998) *Reports of Judgments and Decisions of the ECtHR* 1998–I at paras 57–60.

directly impacted upon the physical or psychological integrity of the individual. As a result of this passivity, the individual was deprived of the enjoyment of his private or family life, just as much as if the State had directly committed such interference of its own initiative.

It is true that the methodology used by the Court to identify whether or not the State has 'positive obligations' in a particular situation is by no means uniform.[26] It is also true that in *Sentges*, when determining whether a positive obligation existed, the Court had regard not only to the *Botta* concept of a 'direct and immediate link' to the private life of the individual but also engaged in the exercise of balancing all the interests involved. Nevertheless, it is possible to identify a clear judicial approach running through these decisions.

In sum, the introduction of the concept of the 'direct and immediate link' in *Botta* is a domestication of the notion of 'positive obligations.' Pushed to its limits, the theory of positive obligations could have led to the imposition of a requirement to undertake wide-scale restructuring of the environment wherever such restructuring could contribute, at a reasonable cost, to facilitating the self-fulfilment of disabled individuals. But the *Botta* jurisprudence restricts this potential. Whilst it may be justifiable to impose obligations on States to take measures to protect the physical and psychological integrity of the individual, where there is a direct impact on his/her functioning in daily life, it is not viewed as justifiable for a judge to use the notion of 'respect for private life' as a lever to impose on the public authorities a requirement to bring about far-reaching transformations of the environment.

4 OVERCOMING *BOTTA*

4.1 Overview

Advocates of disability rights therefore need to find ways to circumvent the limits imposed on Article 8 by the *Botta* line of cases. The main problem, as we have seen, resides in the identification of the precise scope of the positive obligations which may be imposed on the State in the name of the 'effective respect for private life'. The fear is that, once a positive obligation to provide reasonable accommodations for disabled people is affirmed, this obligation may be stretched so far that it will be simply impossible for the State authorities to meet this obligation. Therefore, what we require are techniques which will facilitate the identification of clear parameters for

---

[26] For a more detailed discussion, see O De Schutter, 'The protection of social rights by the European Court of Human Rights' in P Van der Auweraert, T De Pelsmaeker, J Sarkin and J Vande Lanotte (eds), *Social, Economic and Cultural Rights: An Appraisal of Current European and International Developments* (Maklu, Antwerpen-Apeldoorn, 2002) at p 207, esp pp 225–32.

positive obligations to provide reasonable accommodations, which extend beyond the present concept of a 'direct and immediate link' with the private life of the individual, the restrictive effects of which have already been outlined. I will consider five potential routes to achieving this objective.

4.2 The Obligation to Ensure Compliance with Internal Law

A first possibility would be to require, as a minimum, that States act effectively against any violations of laws which they themselves have adopted, where this would ensure that the 'personal autonomy' of an individual is guaranteed. By enacting such laws the State has, in effect, chosen the extent to which it will seek to guarantee this capacity of the individual. In obliging the State to ensure that these laws are actively enforced, an international court would, therefore, neither be imposing its own particular views about what should be done in the local context, nor would it take the State by surprise or impose too heavy a burden upon it (since the State authorities could be expected to have made their own calculations before enacting the laws in question).[27] In *Hatton v UK* the ECtHR was asked to decide whether the implementation of a policy on night flights at Heathrow airport constituted a violation of the right to respect for the private lives of the local population disturbed by the noise. The Court insisted that:

> in previous cases in which environmental questions gave rise to violations of the Convention, the violation was predicated on a failure by the national authorities to comply with some aspect of the domestic regime.[28]

One of the reasons why the Court found that the night flights policy did not violate Article 8 was that it did not breach any provision of internal law.

To date, however, such arguments have failed in the context of disabled people's claims for accommodations. In *Botta*, as we have seen, the Court

[27] See eg the reasoning of the Irish High Court in *O'Reilly and others*, in which it agreed to make an order of mandamus against the competent County Council requiring it to repair the road leading to the domicile of the applicants as this was a statutory obligation imposed on the Council. According to the High Court:

> This is not a case of telling the Government how it must spend money. It is a case of the [Government] having imposed a statutory duty on local authorities, being required to provide the means of carrying out that duty

(cited by the ECtHR in *O'Reilly and others v Ireland* (28 February 2002) Application No 54725/00).

[28] *Hatton and others v UK* (8 July 2003) Application No 36022/97 at para 120. The Court cites the cases of *López Ostra v Spain* (9 December 1994) Series A No 303–C at para 58, and *Guerra v Italy* (19 February 1998) *Reports of Judgments and Decisions of the ECtHR* 1998–I as examples of cases where the measure complained of was in violation of the internal law: in *López Ostra* 'the waste-treatment plant at issue was illegal in that it operated without the necessary licence and, in *Guerra*, the refusal to provide the requested information to the inhabitants was in violation of a statutory obligation of the State'.

ruled Article 8 inapplicable despite the fact that the Italian authorities had failed to enforce their law requiring private beaches to install facilities for disabled people. In *Zehnalová and Zehnal*, the applicants placed strong reliance on the argument that positive obligations could, at the very least, be imposed on State authorities to ensure compliance with internal legislation. By amending the Law on buildings in 1994, they argued, the Czech Republic had accepted an obligation to guarantee people with certain impairments access to public buildings. The State had, on their view, imposed obligations on third parties (eg those constructing the buildings) and must ensure that they complied with the law. This responsibility should be treated as a positive obligation falling within the scope of Article 8.

This argument, however, failed to convince the Court. Thus, whilst any active interference with Article 8 rights must be in conformity with the law (because it may be justified only if it is 'in accordance with the law'), the same does not apply in the context of a State's positive obligations. It seems that a failure to ensure compliance with national legislation will not necessarily violate a positive obligation stemming from Article 8.

4.3 The Obligation to Comply with Other International Undertakings

A second possibility would be to assess the scope of the positive obligations arising from Article 8 in the light of undertakings made by the relevant State under other instruments of international human rights law. Admittedly the ECtHR is not entrusted with the supervision of the other international obligations of the States which are party to the European Convention on Human Rights. In *Zehnalová and Zehnal* (where the applicants invoked Articles 12 and 13 of the European Social Charter), not only did the Court reaffirm this position, but it also seemed to recreate a distinction between categories of rights, depending on whether they were protected under the ECHR or under the Charter. In its words:

> [t]he question is what are the limits of the applicability of Article 8 of the Convention and where the border lies which separates the rights guaranteed by the Convention on the one hand, and the social rights protected under the European Social Charter, on the other hand.

The impression this creates is misleading, however. As the decision in *Zehnalová and Zehnal* itself recognised, the European Social Charter may influence the interpretation of the ECHR, despite the fact that these instruments are endowed with different institutional enforcement machineries. The Court itself noted that:

> like other international instruments, the European Social Charter (... elaborated, like the European Convention on Human Rights itself, in the

framework of the Council of Europe), may be a source of inspiration for the Court.[29]

In *Botta*, the ECtHR was careful not to follow the argument of the European Commission on Human Rights that Article 8 was inapplicable because the rights claimed were 'social in character.' In the Commission's view:

the social nature of the right concerned required more flexible protection machinery, such as that set up under the European Social Charter.[30]

The position of the Commission, therefore, was that the rights guaranteed by the European Social Charter should not be read into the ECHR because each of these instruments had their specific sphere of engagement: the latter guarantees rights which are immediately justiciable; the former contains programmatic rights to be progressively realised. This position, however, would have re-installed a watertight division between these two categories of rights; a division which, since *Airey*,[31] the Court has systematically relaxed and in many cases overturned. It is worth emphasising that the ECtHR did not decide *Botta* on this basis. Its ruling does not rely on a division between civil and political rights and social and economic rights but is, rather, based on the Court's understanding of the term 'private life' and its requirements.

More significant still, where the Court has been asked to identify which positive obligations derive from Article 8 in other contexts, it has taken into account other relevant international obligations of the State concerned. It has used an estoppel-like argument: how could a State possibly argue that it would be unreasonable to expect it to adopt a particular measure, if the State has already undertaken to adopt that measure by agreeing to other international agreements? In general, the Court seeks to interpret the ECHR in the light of general public international law. It does so particularly where it needs to justify the meaning it attaches to notions which are, by definition, open and contextual, such as the positive obligations flowing from the duty to 'respect private life.' In *Ignaccolo-Zenide v Romania* and, more recently, in *Iglesias Gil v Spain*, the scope of the positive obligation of the State to adopt measures to ensure that children will be united with their parents in cases of parental kidnapping was defined with reference to the Hague Convention (to which the States concerned were parties).[32]

---

[29] (14 May 2002) Application No 38621/97.
[30] *Botta v Italy* (24 February 1998) *Reports of Judgments and Decisions of the ECtHR* 1998–I, No 66 412 at para 28.
[31] *Airey v Ireland* (9 October 1979) Series A no 32.
[32] *Ignaccolo-Zenide v Romania* Application No 31679/96, CEDH, 2000–I at para 94; *Iglesias Gil and AUI v Spain* (29 April 2003) Application No 56673/00 at para 51:

S'agissant ... des obligations positives que l'article 8 de la Convention fait peser sur les Etats contractants en matière de réunion d'un parent à ses enfants, celles-ci doivent s'interpréter à la lumière de la Convention de La Haye du 25 octobre 1980 sur les aspects civils de l'enlèvement international d'enfants.

In this respect, the doctrine which the European Committee on Social Rights (ECSR) has derived from Article 15(3) of the revised European Social Charter is of particular relevance to *Botta*-like cases. The ECSR has stated that the revised version of this Article:

> advances the change in disability policy that has occurred over the last decade away from welfare and segregation and towards inclusion and choice

and it has been interpreted by the Committee as requiring the adoption of positive measures to achieve the integration of disabled people in housing, transport, telecommunications, cultural and leisure facilities. Moreover, in the view of the Committee, Article 15(3):

> requires the existence of anti-discrimination (or similar) legislation covering both the public and the private sphere in the fields such as housing, transport, telecommunications, cultural and leisure activities, as well as effective remedies for those who have been unlawfully treated.[33]

4.4 The Obligation to Include Safeguards in the Decision-Making Process

A third line of development would be to focus on the issue of compliance with procedural norms, requiring States to weigh all relevant interests carefully when making decisions and, in particular, to analyse the impact of proposed measures on more vulnerable groups. In this regard it is no accident that, in *Marzari v Italy*, the Court was influenced by the fact that the State had set up a specific Commission for the study of metabolic diseases which had taken the view that the house offered to the applicant would have been adequate. This convinced the Court that the competent authorities had acted only after carefully weighing all the alternatives and collecting all relevant information regarding the possible impact on the fundamental rights at stake.

In cases relating to environmental issues, the Court's scrutiny has addressed two distinct issues: the first, material, involving an inquiry into the substantive merits of the measure; the second, procedural, focusing on the decision-making process. In *Buckley v UK* (which concerned the impact of land planning regulations on the nomadic lifestyle of the gypsy community) the Court said:

---

[33] Conclusion 2003–1 at p 170 (France—Art 15(3)); Conclusion 2003–1 at p 298 (Italy—Art 15(3)3); Conclusion 2003–2 at p 508 (Slovenia—Art 15(3)); Conclusion 2003–2 at p 614 (Sweden—Art 15(3)). In its last control cycle, the Committee defered its conclusion concerning the compliance of France with Art 15(3) of the Revised European Social Charter, pending receipt of the information requested on the existence of legislation protecting disabled people from discrimination in the domains cited (housing, telecommunications, transport, cultural and leisure activities). The conclusions of the Committee concerning compliance of Sweden with this provision of the Revised Charter were also deferred pending the receipt of further information. The Committee concluded that, as no such legislation exists in Italy or in Slovenia, the situation in these countries was not in conformity with Art 15(3).

Whenever discretion capable of interfering with the enjoyment of a Convention right such as the one in issue in the present case is conferred on national authorities, the procedural safeguards available to the individual will be especially material in determining whether the respondent State has, when fixing the regulatory framework, remained within its margin of appreciation. Indeed ... whilst Article 8 contains no explicit procedural requirements, the decision-making process leading to measures of interference must be fair and such as to afford due respect to the interests safeguarded to the individual by Article 8.[34]

Similarly, in *Hatton*, the Court observed that it had to consider:

all the procedural aspects, including the type of policy or decision involved, the extent to which the views of individuals (including the applicants) were taken into account throughout the decision-making procedure, and the procedural safeguards available.[35]

Such a procedural check could also be applied to the adoption of regulations or policies which adversely affect disabled people. This would require public authorities, before adopting such measures, to seek information about the extent of such an impact, the available alternatives, and the means by which the impact could be reduced and kept to a minimum. This approach would be in line with the requirement of the ECSR (in relation to Article 15(3) of the ESC) that:

persons with disabilities and their representative organisations should be consulted in the design, and ongoing review of such positive action measures [seeking to improve the integration of persons with disabilities in the life of the community] and that an appropriate forum should exist to enable this to happen.[36]

4.5 The Obligation Not to Discriminate

Fourth, we may seek to overcome the limits imposed by the *Botta* line of decisions by the combined effect of Article 8 and the non-discrimination requirement of Article 14 which, of course, may not be invoked independently. According to well-established case-law:

[34] See also eg *Beard v UK* (18 July 2001) Application No 24882/94 at para 103 (concerning the alleged violation of Art 8 ECHR resulting from the adoption of planning regulations ignoring the needs of the gypsy community):

the procedural safeguards available to the individual applicant will be especially material in determining whether the respondent State has, when fixing the regulatory framework, remained within its margin of appreciation. In particular, it must examine whether the decision-making process leading to measures of interference was fair and such as to afford due respect to the interests safeguarded to the individual by Article 8.

[35] *Hatton and others v UK* (8 July 2003) at para 104, see n 28.
[36] Conclusion 2003–1 at p 168 (France—Art 15(3)); Conclusion 2003–1 at p 507 (Slovenia—Art 15(3)).

Article 14 complements the other substantive provisions of the Convention and its Protocols. It has no independent existence, since it has effect solely in relation to 'the enjoyment of the rights and freedoms' safeguarded by those provisions. Although the application of Article 14 does not presuppose a breach of one or more of those provisions—and to this extent it is auto-nomous—there can be no room for its application unless the facts of the case fall within the ambit of one or more of the latter.[37]

Where Article 8 is not applicable, the Convention will therefore impose no requirement of non-discrimination. This was precisely the basis of the Court ruling in *Botta* as in *Zehnalová and Zehnal*.

However, the scope of Article 14 has sometimes been more broadly defined. Not only has it been held to be applicable where the alleged dis-crimination has its source in the exercise of a right protected by the Convention (eg in the exercise of the freedom to manifest one's religion[38] or to lead one's sexual life);[39] but it has also been held applicable where the relationship of the allegedly discriminatory measure, with the enjoyment of a right protected under the Convention, is comparatively indirect.

The case of *Petrovic* is perhaps most illustrative of this 'autonomisation' of Article 14.[40] The applicant, a father who was denied a parental leave allowance, alleged that the Austrian law which reserved such an allowance to mothers was discriminatory. The Court agreed that Article 14 was appli-cable, despite the fact that the refusal to grant the applicant a parental leave allowance did not amount to a failure to respect family life because Article 8 did not impose any positive obligation on States to provide the financial assistance in question. The Court reasoned that:

Nonetheless, this allowance paid by the State is intended to promote family life and necessarily affects the way in which the latter is organised as, in con-junction with parental leave, it enables one of the parents to stay at home to look after the children. The Court has said on many occasions that Article 14 comes into play whenever 'the subject-matter of the disadvantage ... con-stitutes one of the modalities of the exercise of a right guaranteed'[41] or the measures complained of are 'linked to the exercise of a right guaranteed'.[42] By granting parental leave allowance, States are able to demonstrate their

[37] See *Abdulaziz, Cabales and Balkandali v UK* (28 May 1985) Series A No 94 at p 35, para 71, and *Inze v Austria* (28 October 1987) Series A No 126 at p 17, para 36.
[38] *Thlimmenos v Greece* (6 April 2000) Application No 34369/97 at para 42.
[39] *Fretté v France* (26 February 2002) Application No 36515/97.
[40] *Petrovic v Austria* (27 March 1998) *Reports of Judgments and Decisions of the ECtHR* 1998–II. The validity of *Petrovic* has been recently reaffirmed by a chamber of the Court (1st section), unanimous on this point (see para 4 of the dissenting opinion of Mr Grabenwarter (*ad hoc* judge) joining with the majority on this issue), in *Karner v Austria* (24 July 2003) Application No 40016/98 at para 32.
[41] See the *National Union of Belgian Police v Belgium* (27 October 1975) Series A No 19 at p 20, s 45.
[42] See *Schmidt and Dahlström v Sweden* (6 February 1976) Series A No 21 at p 17, s 39.

respect for family life within the meaning of Article 8. The allowance thus falls inside the scope of that provision. It follows that Article 14, taken together with Article 8, is applicable.

It requires little imagination to see what consequences this may have when combined with the very broad understanding of the notion of 'private life' discussed above. Certainly, a municipality or a State requiring all public buildings to be made accessible to persons with limited mobility, would thereby demonstrate their respect for private life within the meaning of Article 8. This is not to say that such measures would be required under Article 8 but, rather, that an authority which chose to take such measures would be brought within the scope of Article 8 and hence Article 14. Thus, if a State adopted legislation requiring that work stations should be adjusted so as to meet the needs of certain categories of disabled people but not others, Article 14 could be invoked in conjunction with Article 8, on the basis that this constituted a discriminatory implementation of Convention rights.

Were Article 14 to be given such an expanded scope, there would still be an issue as to whether it could be interpreted so that the requirement of non-discrimination included an obligation to accommodate disabled people. Certain new developments are encouraging in this regard. The case of *Thlimmenos* is particularly significant. It concerned a Jehovah's Witness who wished to become a chartered accountant, but was denied access to the profession because of a criminal conviction for refusing to serve in the armed forces for religious reasons. The Court famously stated that:

> [t]he right not to be discriminated against in the enjoyment of the rights guaranteed under the Convention [is violated not only when States *treat differently persons in analogous situations without providing an objective and reasonable justification*, but also] when States without an objective and reasonable justification *fail to treat differently persons whose situations are significantly different*.[43]

It found that the Greek authorities had discriminated against Mr Thlimmenos because they had failed:

> to introduce appropriate exceptions to the rule barring persons convicted of a serious crime from the profession of chartered accountants.[44]

[43] *Thlimmenos v Greece* (6 April 2000) Application No 34369/97 at para 44.
[44] *Ibid* at para 48. The Court follows the opinion expressed by the European Commission of Human Rights in its report of 4 December 1998:

> In the circumstances of the case, the Commission finds no objective and reasonable justification for the failure of the drafters of the rules governing access to the profession of chartered accountants to treat differently persons convicted for refusing to serve in the armed forces on religious grounds from persons convicted of other felonies. By failing to introduce such a distinction, ie by failing to introduce an exception to the rule barring from the profession of chartered accountants persons who have been convicted of felonies, the drafters of the rules violated the applicant's right not to be discriminated in the enjoyment of his right to manifest his religion (para 50).

Although the expression, as such, does not appear in the judgment, the language used by the Court is reminiscent of the notion of reasonable accommodation:

> The Court considers that, as a matter of principle, States have a legitimate interest to exclude some offenders from the profession of chartered accountant. However, the Court also considers that, unlike other convictions for serious criminal offences, a conviction for refusing on religious or philosophical grounds to wear the military uniform cannot imply any dishonesty or moral turpitude likely to undermine the offender's ability to exercise this profession. Excluding the applicant on the ground that he was an unfit person was not, therefore, justified …. It follows that the applicant's exclusion from the profession of chartered accountants did not pursue a legitimate aim. As a result, the Court finds that there existed no objective and reasonable justification for not treating the applicant differently from other persons convicted of a serious crime.

The importance of this case lies not only in its introduction of the concept of indirect discrimination into the case-law of the ECtHR, but also arguably in its contribution to the concept of reasonable accommodation. That is to say that a failure to take account of certain specific needs of an individual may now amount to discrimination; it may be unjustified to *refuse to create an exception to the general norm*, even where that norm is justifiable as reasonably related to a legitimate aim and proportionate to the fulfilment of that aim.

It is precisely because of this point that the prohibition against indirect discrimination and the obligation to provide effective accommodation must be recognised as distinct concepts: indirect discrimination occurs where an apparently neutral measure has a disproportionate impact or imposes a particular disadvantage on a certain category, and cannot be justified as a measure pursuing a legitimate aim by means both appropriate and necessary; the failure to provide effective accommodation is a failure to create an exception, where one would be required to take into account the specific situation of a category of persons, although the general rule is justified to the extent that it applies to the generality. In this sense, *Thlimmenos* is not a case about indirect discrimination, despite the fact that this is how it is usually presented (even, indeed, by the Court itself). It is, rather, a case about reasonable accommodation and its reasoning is, therefore, immediately useful to disability rights advocates.

4.6 The Obligation Not to Inflict Inhuman or Degrading Treatment or Punishment

In contrast with the Article 8 cases discussed above, the Court has been noticeably less reluctant to impose an obligation of reasonable accommodation where a disabled person has been deprived of his/her liberty by the State and where, consequently, the State authorities bear a special responsibility for ensuring that s/he is not placed in an environment which creates additional disadvantage or which causes distress or physical or psychological damage. The leading case in this area is *Price v UK*. There, the applicant, who experienced phocomelia due to thalidomide, was committed to prison for seven days for contempt of court.[45] She was allegedly prohibited from taking with her the battery charger for her wheelchair because this was considered to be a luxury item. Before she was taken to prison, however, she spent a night in a cell at a police station. According to the description given in the judgment of the ECtHR:

> This cell, which contained a wooden bed and a mattress, was not specially adapted for a disabled person. The applicant alleges that she was forced to sleep in her wheelchair since the bed was hard and would have caused pain in her hips, that the emergency buttons and light switches were out of her reach, and that she was unable to use the toilet since it was higher than her wheelchair and therefore inaccessible.[46]

Despite the fact that their attention was drawn to this situation by a doctor who was called during the night, at the request of Ms Price, the responsible police officers did nothing to ensure that she was removed to a more suitable place of detention. When she was moved to the prison the next day, she was detained in the prison's health care centre, because of her limited mobility. Her cell had a wider door for wheelchair access, handles in the toilet recess and a hydraulic hospital bed. The nursing staff, however, expressed their concern upon her admission about the problems that were likely to be encountered during her detention, including reaching the bed and toilet, hygiene and fluid intake, and mobility (if the battery of her wheelchair ran down). Nevertheless, the transfer of Ms Price to an outside hospital, as was recommended by these medical staff, did not occur. The ECtHR found that this amounted to a violation of Article 3. Despite the absence of any 'positive intention to humiliate or debase the applicant,'[47] the Court considered that:

> to detain a severely disabled person in conditions where she is dangerously cold, risks developing sores because her bed is too hard or unreachable, and is unable to go to the toilet or keep clean without the greatest of difficulty, constitutes degrading treatment contrary to Article 3 of the Convention.[48]

[45] As a result of the rules on remission of sentences however, she was in fact detained for three nights and four days.

[46] *Price v UK* (10 July 2001) Application No 33394/96.

[47] Although the presence of such an intention is one of the factors the Court takes into account in considering whether a particular treatment is 'degrading' within the meaning of Art 3 ECHR, 'the absence of any such purpose cannot conclusively rule out a finding of violation of Article 3' (*Price* (*ibid*) at para 24, citing *Peers v Greece* Application No 28524/95 paras 67–68 and 74, ECHR 2001–III).

[48] *Price* (*ibid*) at para 30.

It was the lack of any consideration of Ms Price's special needs, therefore, which led to the Court's finding that degrading treatment had taken place. As noted by Judge Greve in her separate concurring opinion, it is the failure to treat differently a person whose situation is significantly different that is degrading. Being a disabled person, in her view, made the applicant 'different' from other people so that treating her in the same way as them was both discriminatory and a violation of Article 3. Nowhere in the judgment does the Court allude to the fact that lack of resources could justify treatment which attains such a level of severity as to bring it within the scope of Article 3. This is significant because Ms Price had not attempted to bring an action in negligence against the Home Office precisely because, according to English case-law, the standard of care in a prison hospital is lower than would be required in an equivalent outside institution because of the shortage of resources.[49]

The judgment in *Price* is, of course, explained by the specific responsibility of prison authorities to provide the requisite medical care for detained persons and, more generally, to ensure that the detention is compatible with the health of those persons.[50] The State does not owe the same responsibility to individuals in the 'free world'. In this context, moreover, there is no 'floodgates problem'; the obligations imposed on the public authorities are clearly circumscribed and will not extend indefinitely. Further, if the State truly cannot take appropriate measures to ensure that the detention does not constitute degrading treatment, the disabled detainees could be released. We therefore cannot be confident that the *Price* doctrine, according to which the denial of reasonable accommodation may amount to a form of degrading treatment, will be applied to disabled people not detained in institutions.

Indeed, this position has been adopted since *Price* by UK courts. In *Bernard v Enfield LBC*[51], the applicant failed to convince the court that Article 3 had been violated. She had been obliged to live for twenty months in a house not equipped to meet her needs, which had resulted in severe inconvenience and a lack of independence, which of course also had a negative impact on other family members and on family life in general. Although the court concluded that the situation amounted to a violation of the right to respect for family life, *Price* was regarded as not applicable because, in the words of Sullivan J, 'the cases concerned with prisoners' rights [...] must be treated with great caution outside the prison gates.' Anna Lawson has explained this result thus:[52]

---

[49] See *Knight and others v Home Office and another* [1990] 3 All ER 237, cited in *Price* at para 19.
[50] See eg *McGlinchey and others v UK* (29 April 2003) Application No 50390/99 at para 57.
[51] [2002] England and Wales High Court 449.
[52] A Lawson, 'The Human Rights Act 1998 and disabled people: a right to be human?' in C Harvey (ed), *Human Rights in the Community* (Oxford, Hart Publishing, 2005).

The crucial factor may be that prisoners, unlike tenants, are subjected against their will to regimes controlled in every detail by others. On this basis, *Price* would apply equally to other institutions in which disabled people might be confined, such as psychiatric wards. Outside the institutional context, however, it would seem to be extremely difficult to establish a breach of Article 3 without proof of a positive intention to humiliate or debase.

5 REASONABLE ACCOMMODATION IN EMPLOYMENT

The future will reveal the extent to which *Thlimmenos* will be developed into a general obligation to accommodate the specific needs of members of religious groups and whether, from there, it will be extended to the claims of disabled people. Hitherto, the institutions set up to oversee the ECHR have been somewhat reluctant to require exceptions to rules of general applicability, even where those rules impose a particular disadvantage on the adherents to a particular faith.[53] In the well-known case of *Ahmad v UK*, a muslim schoolteacher was refused permission to be absent on Friday afternoons to attend mosque. He had to leave his job and accept a part-time position compatible with the requirements of his faith. The European Commission of Human Rights found that this did not amount to a violation of Article 9, as Mr Ahmad had freely accepted the obligations of his teaching position when he took up the job offer and had not requested any adjustment to his schedules during the first six years of employment.[54] According to this ruling, which stands in sharp contrast with the attitude of the Canadian Supreme Court to a very similar issue a few years later,[55] the freedom of an employee to manifest his/her religion does not impose any requirement to adjust the

---

[53] See generally C Evans, *Freedom of Religion under the European Convention on Human Rights* (Oxford, OUP, 2001) ch 9; and St Stavros, 'Freedom of religion and claims for exemption from generally applicable, neutral laws' (1997) 6 *European Human Rights Review* 607.

[54] *Ahmad v UK* (12 March 1981) DR 22 p 27.

[55] See *Ontarian Commission of Human Rights v Simpson-Sears Ltd* [1985] 2 Supreme Court Reports 536. In this case, Ms O'Malley, whose religion strictly obliged her to rest between sunset on Friday and sunset on Saturday, complained that her employer wished to see her work on Friday evenings and on Saturdays. The Court concluded that this constituted a form of discrimination, as the employer had neither sought to accommodate her religious practice by proposing other working hours, nor proved that any such accommodation would result in undue hardship for the undertaking. See also *Commission Scolaire Régionale de Chambly v Bergevin* [1994] 2 Supreme Court Reports 525 (a collective agreement not providing for a holiday on the day of the Yom Kippur produces a disparate impact on teachers of Jewish faith, and is thus discriminatory unless effective accommodation is provided by the employer, where this does not impose an unreasonable burden on the employer).

organisation of work on an employer.[56] This view has been affirmed in subsequent cases, all relating to the conflict between religious obligations and work schedules.[57] It is based on the proposition that, ultimately, leaving a job may be the price of exercising religious freedom. In other words, the imposition of professional constraints which are incompatible with the religion of an employee are acceptable because the employment has been voluntarily chosen by that employee at the beginning of the employment relationship and may be voluntarily ended by the employee if s/he attaches more value to her freedom of religion.

This approach has been reaffirmed by the Court even after the *Thlimmenos* decision,[58] thus raising a doubt as to the precise message to be drawn from that case. It may be that the Court will decide that the ECHR will require effective accommodation only where the person concerned has not implicitly consented to the restriction on his or her religious practices by, eg, entering into an employment contract containing the restrictive requirement.[59]

[56] See generally JT Gunn, 'Adjudicating rights of conscience under the European Convention on Human Rights' in JD Van der Vijver and J Witte (eds), *Religious Human Rights in Global Perspective* (The Hague/Boston/London, Martinus Nijhoff, 1996) at p 305; or G Quinn, 'Scope and limits of conscientious objection: conscientious objection in labour relations' in *Freedom of Conscience*, Proceedings of the Leiden Seminar, 12–14 November 1992 (Strasbourg, Council of Europe, 1993) at p 112; B Tahzib, *Freedom of Religion or Belief—Ensuring Effective International Legal Protection* (The Hague/Boston/London, Martinus Nijhoff, 1998) at p 326; P Frumer, *La renonciation aux droits et libertés. La Convention européenne des droits de l'homme à l'épreuve de la volonté individuelle* (Bruxelles, Bruylant, 2001) at pp 383–94.

[57] European Commission of Human Rights, *Konttinen v Finland* (2 December 1996) *DR* 87–B, at p 68; European Commission of Human Rights, *Stedman v UK* (9 April 1997) *DR* 89–B at p 104.

[58] See above, n 43.

[59] Indeed, in *Pichon and Sajous v France* Application No 49853/99, the Court, in an inadmissibility decision of 2 October 2001, agreed with the French authorities that the conviction of two pharmacologists for having refused to sell contraceptives to three women was compatible with Art 9 ECHR, despite the fact that they based their refusal on their religious convictions:

The Court notes that in the present case, the applicants, who are pharmacologists, have argued on the basis of their religious beliefs to refuse to sell, in their pharmacy, contraceptive pills. The Court considers that, as the sale of this product is legal, may only be sold upon medical prescription and exclusively in pharmacies, the applicants should not be allowed to impose their religious views on others to justify a refusal to sell this product, as these convictions may be manifested in many ways outside the professional sphere.

The outcome of *Pichon and Sajous*, however, can be explained by the fact that the exercise of religious freedom would have led to denying to women, who were prescribed the use of contraceptives by their physician, a medical product they required. This may be compared with a case (this time outside the professional sphere) where parents complained that they were denied the possibility of not sending their children to school on Saturdays, despite the fact that their religious belief imposed total rest on that day of the week. The Court considered the application manifestly ill-founded, as such an exemption would enter into conflict with the right of the child to education: see *Martins Casimiro and Cerveira Ferreira v Luxembourg* (27 April 1999) Application No 44888/98. It should be emphasised however that the Court does not seem to share the view of the national jurisdictions that any authorisation granted to parents not to send their child to school on Saturdays would result in such a disorganisation of the school system that it would ultimately threaten the rights of the other schoolchildren.

Despite these ambiguities, the following observations can be made about the presence (or absence) in the ECHR of an obligation on States to ensure that employers effectively accommodate the needs of their disabled employees unless doing so would constitute an undue burden.

First, it can be argued that the absence of national legislation requiring employers to adapt the working environment to the needs of an otherwise competent disabled person, presents such a direct and immediate link to the 'private life' of the individual concerned that Article 8 would apply. Such a case would be closer to *Marzari* or *Sentges* than to *Botta* or *Zehnalová and Zehnal*. In the past, the Court has recognised that, if respect for private life comprises a right to establish and develop relationships with others, there is no reason in principle why activities of a professional or business nature should not be included. Indeed, according to the Court:

> it is, after all, in the course of their working lives that the majority of people have a significant, if not the greatest, opportunity of developing relationships with the outside world.[60]

Assuming, then, that a refusal of the State to oblige employers to provide some form of accommodation for a disabled person falls under the scope of Article 8, will such a refusal be justifiable? The aims which might be invoked to justify such a restriction can be easily identified. Accommodations will be seen as costly; a point which should be balanced against the potential benefits of such adjustments, both to the employer (where it leads to the recruitment of the best candidate or where it increases the productivity of the worker),[61] and to society more generally. The ECtHR has accepted that the 'economic well-being of the country' and the 'rights of others' (both legitimate objectives under Article 8(2)) may justify restrictions on the rights of individuals where undue burdens would otherwise be imposed.[62]

Quite where this balance will be struck is a matter of speculation at present. It is clear from previous ECtHR decisions that it will not adopt the approach of the Irish Supreme Court, which ruled that the requirement to make reasonable accommodations violated the property rights of employers.[63]

[60] *Niemietz v Germany* (16 December 1992) Series A No 251–B, para 29.

[61] See, for the argument that a statutory duty to provide reasonable accommodation may promote efficiency on the labour market by reducings the risks entailed by the incomplete information of the employer and the asymmetry between the employer and the candidate employee as to the qualities of the latter: JH Verkerke, 'Is the ADA efficient ?' (2003) 50 *University of California Law Review* 903. A recent attempt to a systematic analysis of the relationship between reasonable accommodation of persons with disabilities and efficiency requirements is by MA Stein, 'The law and economics of disability accommodations' (2003) 53 *Duke Law Journal* 79.

[62] *Hatton and others v UK* (8 July 2003) para 121, see n 28.

[63] See further, C Gooding and C Casserley, 'Open for all? Disability discrimination laws in Europe relating to goods and services' ch 8 below. See also *Mellacher and others v Austria* (18 December 1989) Series A No 169, s 56 (concerning the compatibility with the right to property of Art 1 Protocol No 1 ECHR of legislation on rent control, even in the circumstance where the measure adopted by the Austrian legislature affected the further execution of previously concluded contracts).

However, whether a refusal to provide reasonable accommodation will be judged to strike a fair balance between all the interests involved, is a question to which only highly contextualised answers can be given. It could be argued, on the basis of the existing case-law , that this balance is upset wherever laws or practices of general applicability are imposed without the flexibility necessary to take into account the circumstances of people who are adversely affected because of particular personal characteristics. Indeed, the Court has on some occasions moved towards a requirement of proportionality, which would imply that any laws or practices of general applicability should allow for exceptions in specific situations where their application would lead to excessive hardship.[64] The requirement of proportionality would thus apply not only to the rule itself, but also to the absence of any provision for exceptions to the rule.

There are some traces of such a two-tiered understanding of proportionality in the case-law. In *Gaskin v UK*, the Court held that a requirement that access to personal records should be dependent on the consent of the persons who contributed the information was in principle compatible with Article 8. Nevertheless, the absence of any procedure for an independent consideration of the particular circumstances of each situation was held not to comply with the requirement that the restriction on the right of access to personal data must be 'necessary in a democratic society.' The Court observed that, while such a system could be regarded as compatible with Article 8 obligations, taking into account the State's margin of appreciation:

> under such a system the interests of the individual seeking access to records relating to his private and family life must be secured when a contributor to the records either is not available or improperly refuses consent. Such a system is only in conformity with the principle of proportionality if it provides that an independent authority finally decides whether access has to be granted in cases where a contributor fails to answer or withholds consent.[65]

No such procedure being available to the applicant, the Court found a violation of Article 8. This example is not isolated. In *Immobiliare Saffi v Italy*, the Court held that although:

> in principle, a system of temporary suspension or staggering of the enforcement of court orders followed by the reinstatement of the landlord in his property is not in itself open to criticism, having regard in particular to the margin of appreciation permitted under the second paragraph of Article 1 [of Protocol 1 ECHR]. However, such a system carries with it the risk of imposing on landlords an excessive burden in terms of their ability to dispose

---

[64] See S Van Drooghenbroeck, *La proportionalité dans le droit de la Convention européenne des droits de l'homme* (Brussels, Bruylant-Publ des FUSL) 2001, No 281–84.
[65] *Gaskin v UK* (7 July 1989) Series A No 160, para 95.

of their property and must accordingly provide certain procedural safeguards so as to ensure that the operation of the system and its impact on a landlord's property rights are neither arbitrary nor unforeseeable.

It observed that 'the Italian system suffered from a degree of inflexibility.' Indeed, no court had jurisdiction to rule on the impact which the delays caused by this system might have in a particular case so that the applicant company was deprived of any means by which to compel the government to 'take into account any particular difficulties they might encounter as a result of the delay in the eviction'. This led the Court to conclude that there had been a violation of Article 1 of Protocol 1.

It is only fair to say that case-law is not settled on this point. It is possible to identify cases that point in different directions. The case-law relating to freedom of conscience in the work environment has already been referred to, and the principle evident in those cases (that where the individual in question has made a choice, he or she cannot then require the adjustment of general conditions even where this imposes considerable hardship) can also be found in other contexts. In *Hatton*, only a very small segment of the population neighbouring Heathrow airport (representing 2–3 per cent of that population) suffered from the noise produced by aeroplanes flying at night. The Court commented that it considered it reasonable, in determining the:

> impact of a general policy on individuals in a particular area, to take into account the individuals' ability to leave the area. Where a limited number of people in an area … are particularly affected by a general measure, the fact that they can, if they choose, move elsewhere without financial loss must be significant to the overall reasonableness of the general measure.[66]

The implication is that, where a general policy is justified with respect to the generality of situations to which it applies, it will not need to be justified in its application to each individual case, at least where the individuals concerned could have chosen not to be affected by that policy.

This stands in sharp contrast to the contextualised requirement of proportionality identified in *Gaskin* or in *Immobiliare Saffi*, as well as to the notion that effective accommodation should be provided to take into account specific individual situations, at least where this does not result in the imposition of disproportionate burdens. These contrasting answers to the question of proportionality make it very difficult to anticipate whether the ECtHR will impose an obligation to provide reasonable accommodation in future employment cases beyond the scenario exemplified by *Thlimmenos*, where the exercise of religious freedom led to a prohibition on entering certain professions.

[66] *Hatton and others v UK* (8 July 2003) see n 28, para 127.

6 CONCLUSION

The concept of 'private life' has been interpreted broadly in the case-law of the ECtHR. In some cases this has led it to impose far-reaching positive obligations on the State parties to the Convention. Moreover, in *Thlimmenos*, the Court has demonstrated its willingness to move beyond a formal understanding of the requirement of non-discrimination. Despite these encouraging developments, however, the ECtHR has not yet affirmed an obligation to provide disabled people with effective accommodations, either in the sphere of employment or in other domains, which could contribute to their social integration. Nevertheless there are signs that the Court is moving towards such an affirmation. Three final remarks may be made about the conditions in which this development is occuring.

First, the current case-law of the ECtHR distinguishes between situations where the denial of effective accommodation for disabled people presents a direct and immediate link to their private and family life and other situations where, in the absence of such a link, Article 8 will be considered inapplicable. Although the sphere of employment would appear to fall within the former group of situations, the *Botta* line of cases confronts us with an implicit view that certain activities in life (eg travelling, going on vacation, having the choice of which chemist to visit) are less worthy of protection, because they are less essential to the fulfilment of one's personality. Perhaps we should question this hierarchy. Perhaps we should challenge both the practicability of such a distinction—as if housing or employment, for instance, can be distinguished from public transportation or access to services of general interest—and, especially, the underlying idea that it would be compatible with the requirement of autonomy to oblige a person to restrict him/herself to his or her immediate surroundings and deny him/her the opportunity of moving beyond them.

The centrality of employment to one's self-fulfilment may also be questioned, particularly if (as in the Council Directive 2000/78/EC) it results in an exclusive focus on employment as the sphere in which an obligation to make reasonable accommodation may be imposed. In fact, the professional sphere and other spheres are not easily separable. Citing the 1993 Standard Rules on the Equalisation of Opportunities for Persons with Disabilities (the purpose of which is to ensure that all disabled people 'may exercise the same rights and obligations as others'), the UN Committee on Economic, Social and Cultural Rights insists, in its General Comment no 5 of 1994, that disabled people, 'whether in rural or urban areas, ... have equal opportunities for productive and gainful employment in the labour market.' Equal access to employment requires, however, that the artificial barriers to integration are removed, not only in the workplace, not only in the working environment, but also in the general environment; as the Committee emphasises:

it is very often the physical barriers that society has erected in areas such as transport, housing and the workplace which are ... cited as the reason why persons with disabilities cannot be employed.[67]

Second, we have seen that even post-*Thlimmenos*, uncertainties remain around the question whether the duty to provide reasonable accommodation (which may, in certain cases, take the form of an exception to a general rule) will become part of the requirement of non-discrimination as formulated in the ECHR, and will benefit disabled people seeking access to employment or to remain employed, but facing architectural or other barriers. *Marzari* and *Sentges* show that the closer the link between the measures requested from the State and the everyday activities of the individual, the easier it will be to invoke the applicability of Article 8. Moreover, while the Court was hesitant about the large-scale consequences (including budgetary consequences) which a finding of violation in cases such as *Botta* or *Zehnalová and Zehnal* would have implied, such consequences are not to be feared where reasonable accommodation in work and employment is concerned. The scope of what an accommodation requires in order to be effective is well-defined in such cases: it must create the conditions which will make it possible for a competent individual with an impairment to perform the essential functions of the job. And whether such an effective accommodation must be provided will depend on whether it is reasonable; such a duty will not exist where it imposes an undue, or unreasonable, burden on the employer.

Finally, the ambiguity inherent in the relationship between the prohibition of indirect discrimination, on the one hand, and the obligation to provide effective accommodation, on the other, should be noted. Although the obligation to provide reasonable accommodation is a specific consequence of the general prohibition of indirect discrimination, it should not take priority over that prohibition or be seen as a substitute. A number of indicia show that a duty of reasonable accommodation could be read into the Convention. At the same time, it would be inadvisable to present this, without further reflection, as the preferred (or exclusive) solution to the exclusion of disabled people from the social or professional sphere. The duty of reasonable accommodation should be seen, rather, as subsidiary to the prohibition of indirect discrimination. Where a regulation or practice produces an adverse impact on disabled people, putting them at a particular disadvantage, it first has to be asked whether it may be objectively justified by the pursuance of a legitimate aim by the appropriate and least restrictive means. Only if the answer to this first question is in the affirmative must we then ask the further question: whether an effective accommodation would make it possible for the disabled person not to be excluded,

---

[67] *General Comment No 5* (11th session, 1994). *Report of the Committee on Economic, Social and Cultural Rights*, UN Doc E/1995/22, pp 99–109. The quotation is from para 22.

and whether it would be reasonable to impose a duty to provide such an effective accommodation.[68] Otherwise, the duty to provide reasonable accommodation would oblige the collectivity to make certain adjustments, here and there, to do what was needed in order to avoid excluding particular disabled people; but disabled people generally would remain inhabitants of structures conceived by and made for others—structures which, by their very nature, will render them forever strangers and outsiders.

---

[68] It has been pointed out that Directive 2000/78/EC of 27 November 2000 establishing a general framework for equal treatment in employment and occupation (OJ L 303 of 2.12.2000, p 16) creates an ambiguity in this respect. Under Art 2(2)(b) of the Directive:

> indirect discrimination shall be taken to occur where an apparently neutral provision, criterion or practice would put persons having ... a particular disability ... at a particular disadvantage compared with other persons unless: (i) that provision, criterion or practice is objectively justified by a legitimate aim and the means of achieving that aim are appropriate and necessary, or (ii) as regards persons with a particular disability, the employer or any person or organisation to whom this Directive applies, is obliged, under national legislation, to take appropriate measures in line with the principles contained in Article 5 in order to eliminate disadvantages entailed by such provision, criterion or practice.

This suggests that, provided the employer provides effective accommodation to the disabled employee, the employer will be authorised to maintain provisions, criteria or practices which put disabled people at a particular disadvantage. Ad hoc, individualised compensation measures risk becoming substitutes for wider scale modifications especially in the built environment or the organisation of work, despite the disincentive this could represent for disabled people. This danger is highlighted by L Waddington and A Hendriks, 'The expanding concept of employment discrimination in Europe: from direct and indirect discrimination to reasonable accommodation discrimination' (2002) 18 *International Journal of Comparative Labour Law and Industrial Relations* 403.

5

Hate Speech and Disabled People: Some Comparative Constitutional Thoughts

IAN CRAM*

1 INTRODUCTION

"'MOVE, BLIND LADY,' a man hissed at me as he twisted my arm and grabbed my cane. He threw my cane down the escalator, which was taking me to the subway in Washington, DC. He spat on me and growled, 'You people belong in concentration camps'. I knew that some people dislike those of us with disabilities, but before this encounter at the subway, I had no idea that this hostility could take the form of such rabid hatred."[1]

In this essay I consider the thorny constitutional question of permissible restraints on a form of politically controversial expression, namely expression which is targeted at an individual or group and which seeks to promote hatred on the basis of the victim's physical and/or mental impairment. I will treat such speech as belonging to the broader category of hate speech and raising constitutional issues akin to other forms of hateful speech (eg in the context of race, religion, ethnic origin, gender or sexual orientation). A central dilemma posed by hate speech is whether it is right to suppress speech which, whilst falling short of causing immediate physical harm to others, rejects the constitutional values of dignity and equal respect owed to all members of the community. Underpinning the sharp division of opinion on the matter is a theoretical dispute about the constitutive role (if any) that might be played by law in shaping and enforcing community values. On one view, found in libertarian thinking (and evident in much US First Amendment scholarship), the State is a threat to individual autonomy. Absent a demonstrable and causally linked risk of physical

---

* Senior Lecturer and Co-Convenor of the Human Rights Research Unit, University of Leeds.
[1] K Wolfe, 'Bashing the disabled: the new hate crime', *The Progressive* (November 1995) 59.

harm to others, the State simply has no business telling people which opinions they may receive and which they may not. The centrality of the autonomous individual in liberal thought makes expression intrinsically valuable as opposed to the contribution it makes to societal goals. Racial and religious harmony is but one vision regarding the optimal organisation of society. Individuals must be free to make up their own minds about whether they share this particular vision. The resort to law, then, can be seen as a coercive and improper attempt by the State to make dissenters join (or at least suppress signs of outward dissent from) a community of shared values.[2] In contrast to this libertarian tradition, much European thinking on freedom of expression has, in the main, tended to endorse hate speech restraints as defining rules of civility which, when enforced, can play an important role in 'constituting and subsequently maintaining a community committed to the principle of equality amongst its members'.[3] Indeed, the positive role envisaged for law in creating a community of political equals marks out European jurisprudence as closer (if not wholly congruent) to elements in civic republican thought. As used here, 'civic republican' is intended to refer to the school of thought in political philosophy that upholds the ideal of an inclusive community of political equals who search through open deliberation and dialogue for a reasoned understanding of the common good.[4] Deliberation in politics can only occur *inter alia* where there is freedom of expression on matters of politics and public affairs, as well as the right to vote.[5] The political equality of *all* participants requires elimination of the disparities in influence that different actors would otherwise have in deliberative structures. This may entail reducing the political influence of the powerful and affording a voice to weaker members of the community. Civic republicanism is committed to promoting genuine deliberation among a multitude of voices.[6] Controversially, its supporters hold out the possibility of mediating different approaches to politics and the public good through dialogue and deliberation to yield up a consensual 'common good' on some (though by no means all) important issues. Legal restrictions can thus be placed on

---

[2] B Neuborne, 'Ghosts in the attic: idealized pluralism, community and hate speech' (1992) 27 *Harvard Civil Rights—Civil Liberties Law Review* 371.

[3] M Chesterman, *Freedom of Speech in Australian Law—A Delicate Plant* (Aldershot, Ashgate, 2000) at 216.

[4] For an Aristotelian account of civic republicanism, see A Oldfield, *Citizenship and Community: Civic Republicanism and the Modern World* (London, Routledge, 1990). For the view that civic republicanism ideas derive from a world differing vastly from our own, see T Sandalow, 'A skeptical look at contemporary republicanism' (1989) 41 *Florida Law Review* 523. For trenchant criticism, see S Gey, 'The unfortunate revival of civic republicanism' (1993) 141 *University of Pennsylvania Law Review* 801; M Redish and G Lippman, 'Freedom of expression and the civic republican revival in constitutional theory—the ominous implications' (1991) 79 *California Law Review* 267.

[5] C Sunstein, 'Beyond the republican tradition' (1988) 97 *Yale Law Journal* 1539.

[6] *Ibid* at 1571.

expressive activity where that activity hinders progress towards the common good.[7] On a civic republican approach, viewpoint restrictions of the sort encountered in the regulation of hateful expression can be supported because they suppress 'bad answers' to societal problems and deter minority groups from participating in community affairs as equal citizens. On this account, the freedom to engage in expressive activity is instrumental; it exists only inasmuch as it advances the common good. Viewed in this way, speech that induces hatred of minority groups can only ever be peripherally connected to the core reasons why freedom of expression is valuable. Accordingly, the claims of this 'low-value' speech to constitutional protection can more easily be overridden by competing societal interests. Civic republicans, it should be noted, do not share the faith of liberals that reasoned discourse will always reveal the flaws in the claims of racist and other hateful speakers. They point to the successes of Nazi propaganda to show that at times of pressure and hardship the individual can be swayed, and even swept away, by hysterical, emotional appeals.

In what follows, I examine some issues of principle raised by the regulation of hateful expression, contrasting the constitutional rationales offered for tolerating extremist speech in the United States with countervailing arguments which inform much of European regulation. Attention is then focused on international and domestic legal constraints on hate speech. The absence of specific restraints on anti-disability expression is considered in this part. In the final substantive section, dealing with US First Amendment doctrine, I shall argue that the obstacles erected by the Supreme Court in *RAV v St Paul*,[8] and placed in the way of States and local authorities who wish to control extremist expression, are difficult to reconcile with the Court's previous jurisprudence. By way of conclusion, the compatibility of any future anti-disabled expression restraints in domestic law with European Convention norms is considered. To begin with, however, it is important to gain a sense of the problem of hatred manifested against disabled people. In the next section, the little empirical evidence concerning hate crimes against disabled people that does exist is considered. Most of our current information comes from the US, although there are signs that some police forces in the UK are beginning to monitor this matter more closely. Nonetheless, for reasons provided below, the real likelihood of the under-reporting of such crime should make us wary of drawing too many conclusions from the apparent low levels of criminal activity directed against disabled people. Surveys of such people may provide a more accurate indicator of the nature of the problem.

---

[7] A leading account is to be found in C Sunstein, above n 5.
[8] 505 US 377 (1992).

2 HATE CRIMES AGAINST DISABLED PEOPLE—A STATISTICALLY INSIGNIFICANT PROBLEM?

Following the passage into US law of the Hate Crimes Statistics Act 1990, the FBI became obliged to collect statistics on reported hate crime. Since 1997 this obligation has extended to reports of crime where the victim's disability appeared to be a factor which, in part or whole, accounted for the perpetrator's actions. In 2001, some 9,730 hate crimes were reported to the FBI. 14.3 per cent or 1,391 of these were connected to the victim's sexual orientation. Only 39 (or about 0.4 per cent) were motivated by disability bias, however. Equivalent figures for the longer 1997–2001 period reveal a similar percentage: 44,265/133 = 0.3 per cent.[9] The low visibility of disability-based crimes may be a product of the fact that federal law recognises only race-based hate violence. Currently some 30 US States, on the other hand, have hate crime statutes which make reference to disability-based crimes.[10] These statutes fall into two broad categories: those that create a new, stand-alone offence of using violence against targets selected on grounds of race, colour, gender, or disability;[11] and those that empower a sentencing court to increase the penalty attached to an existing crime if the perpetrator was motivated by hatred of the victim's race, colour, gender or disability.[12] Supporters claim that these criminal measures are justified because they send out the strong signal that society, as well as the individual, is the victim of hate crime. The prevalence of violence directed at minority groups questions a society's very commitment to the values of tolerance and pluralism.

In Europe, physical attacks on disabled people by members of extreme right political groups are, sadly, not a new phenomenon. As is widely known, during the 1940s the Nazis engaged in a policy of murdering newly-born (and other) disabled people. The programme seems to have been developed almost by chance after a request sent by the father of a five month old blind and 'deformed' boy to Hitler that his son be 'put to sleep'. The son was given a lethal drug by doctors personally instructed by Hitler. The cause of death was falsely recorded as 'heart failure'.[13] In 2003, the

---

[9] See further the Los Angeles County Crime Commission *Summary of 1998 Hate Crime Report* which takes the view that disability hate crimes occur in much greater numbers than are actually reported.

[10] Figures produced by the Anti-Defamation League—a US anti-Semitism monitor and published at http://www.adl.org/learn/hate_crimes_laws/map_frameset.html.

[11] A good example is to be found in the New York State Consolidated Laws Penal s 485.05, where hate crime is defined as specified offences committed against persons intentionally selected 'because of a belief or perception regarding the race, color, national origin, ancestry, gender, religion, religious practice, age, disability or sexual orientation' of those persons.

[12] Eg Wisconsin's penalty enhancement statute, which was upheld by the US Supreme Court in *Wisconsin v Mitchell* 508 US 47 (1993).

[13] See the evidence of Dr Karl Brandt during his Nuremberg trial in *Trials of War Criminals before the Nuremberg Military Tribunals under Control Council Law No 10, Nuremberg* (New York, William S Hein and Co, 1997) vols I and II.

German Government published a report on the euthanasia programme, code-named T4, set up a month after this murder in August 1939. Hitler's Interior Ministry oversaw T4, which was responsible for the deaths of up to 8,000 children. At its height, some 296 clinics in Germany, Austria, Czechoslovakia and Poland were engaged in the drugging, gassing or starving of children and adults deemed 'unworthy of living.' Doctors at the clinics worked under false names and sent relatives false accounts of their loved ones' deaths.[14] In Germany today, evidence that the Nazi National Democratic Party (NPD) was implicated in a spate of physical attacks on disabled people and immigrants prompted Chancellor Schroeder's Social Democratic Government to have the NPD banned. Although the ban was agreed by the Bundestag, it was overturned by the Constitutional Court in March 2003 when doubts arose about the reliability of the evidence provided by a leading witness.[15] During parliamentary debates evidence emerged that, accompanying these physical attacks, victims had in recent years frequently endured crude verbal outbursts that demeaned disabled people and their value to society. Wheelchair-users had been spat upon, beaten up and told by their attackers that 'Under Hitler you would have been gassed.'[16] In another incident, neo-Nazis reportedly staged a mock execution of disabled persons.[17]

In the UK, few police forces record incidents targeted at disabled people, although several divisions of the Essex Police have begun to monitor them (putting them on a par with homophobic and racial incidents). A NACRO Report, published in September 2002, revealed that the types of crime particularly feared by disabled people were, in descending order: *hate crimes*, especially being verbally harassed or physically attacked because of being disabled; followed by *crimes against the person*, especially being mugged or pick-pocketed; and finally *property crimes*, especially being burgled or having property vandalised.[18] 11 out of the 14 disabled participants in the two NACRO focus groups stated that they had been victims of verbal harassment, many of them having experienced this form of victimisation repeatedly.[19] Furthermore, national research conducted by Mencap in 1999 revealed that 9 out of 10 people interviewed with learning difficulties were harassed in 1998–99 alone.[20]

[14] *Sunday Telegraph*, 12 October 2003. See also M Burleigh, *Death and Deliverance, 'Euthanasia' in Germany, 1940–1945* (Cambridge, CUP Cambridge University Press, 1994).

[15] See further BBC News World Edition available electronically at http://news.bbc.co.uk/2/hi/europe/2859851.stm.

[16] *Newsletter No 4* (London, 1993) Disability Awareness in Action.

[17] *Newsletter No 31* (London, 1995) Disability Awareness in Action.

[18] S Cunningham and S Drury, *NACRO* Community safety briefing (London, NACRO, 2002).

[19] One focus group consisted of people with learning difficulties who were members of the Camden Society, whilst the other included people with physical impairments who were members of a disability action group.

[20] Mencap, *Living in Fear: The Need to Combat Bullying of People with a Learning Disability* (London, Mencap, 1999).

There are, of course, some forceful explanations for the fact that the recorded statistics for crimes against disabled people may seriously understate the true picture. In the first place, victims may require the assistance of a third party to relay the information to the police authorities. Some victims (especially those with learning difficulties) may not fully realise that they have been the victim of an offence. In other situations, the police station may simply be inaccessible to crime victims with physical impairments. Another reason for under-reporting may lie in the fact that the perpetrator is a caregiver upon whom the victim depends. In other instances, the police and the media may not consider the crime victim's disabled status to be as relevant as other descriptors. This happened recently, and most notoriously, in the murder of James Byrd in Texas. Byrd, a black, disabled man, was chained to the back of a pick-up truck and dragged along roads for three miles. Most news reports focused on the victim's racial status, omitting to mention his disability altogether or giving it a low profile.[21]

In addition, the 2002 NACRO study found anecdotal evidence that when people with visual impairments took a complaint to the police, the matter was not pursued because of perceived problems of assailant identification.

At bottom, there may be a lack of confidence that police will meet the needs of disabled crime victims. A 1995 study by the Joseph Rowntree Foundation indicated that disabled people who reported incidents of harassment, verbal abuse and insult to the police, felt that these public order offences were not taken seriously and claimed that none of the reported crimes resulted in charges being brought.[22]

3 'STICKS AND STONES MAY BREAK MY BONES BUT NAMES SHALL NEVER HURT ME'—ISSUES OF PRINCIPLE RAISED BY THE REGULATION OF HATEFUL WORDS

Children who are the victims of name calling incidents at school or in the street are often told to remember the old adage, 'sticks and stones may break my bones but names shall never hurt me.' When adults are on the receiving end of abusive words (unaccompanied by physical violence), on account of their membership of a minority group, some would doubtless say that they should be expected to show the same degree of fortitude we seek to instil in our children. Words, it seems, are different to physical

[21] See the CNN/Associated Press Report, '3 Suspects arraigned in "racial" killing' (9 June 1998). The first mention of Byrd's disabled status occurs in the final section of the article. There is a good discussion of the low visibility of anti-disability crimes by M Sherry, 'Don't ask, tell or respond: silent acceptance of disability hate crimes' available electronically at http:///www.farnorthernrc.org/mylifemychoice/Hate%20Crimes-Mark%Sherry.pdf (M Sherry is a post-doctoral research fellow at the University of California).

[22] *Crime Against People with Learning Disabilities,* Social Care Research 70 (York, Joseph Rowntree Foundation, 1995).

conduct. Unless used to convey a threat of immediate unlawful violence,[23] we should be prepared to put up with the expression of views with which we disagree. Indeed, to suggest that minority target groups need special assistance from the criminal law, might indicate that members of the group in question are less able to defend themselves.[24]

Hate speech, which is typically defined as speech targeted at an individual or group which seeks to promote hatred on the basis of the victim's race, religion, ethnic origin, gender or sexual orientation,[25] has been said to be 'deeply problematic' for liberal democratic societies.[26] On the one hand, the high value placed by such societies on expression that challenges the political consensus, would seem to require that special importance be attached to the free articulation and dissemination of unpopular or controversial viewpoints. Speakers and audience, individuals and society, may all benefit when comfortable orthodoxies are held up to challenge. This is a dominant theme in US First Amendment jurisprudence where the State's motives when suppressing speech on contents grounds have to be viewed with intense scepticism. After all, the State may be trying to drive notions from the 'marketplace of ideas' simply because it finds them uncomfortable or inconvenient. As members of the audience, we should resist the temptation to acquiesce in the official suppression of views with which we disagree, or loathe or find offensive for the additional, selfish reason that, on a subsequent occasion, the targeted speech may be our own, or that of people with whom we agree. More abstractly, others have pointed to the trait in human character that tends towards maintaining a sense of shared beliefs and values as a force for general intolerance and, consequently, the suppression of views outside, or in contradiction to, prevailing values. Judicial protection of forms of expression at this periphery against populist calls for regulation helps maintain a 'buffer zone' inside which more intrinsically valuable speech is insulated.[27] This insulation works by a conscious refusal to allow the value of a particular exercise of freedom of speech to be legally relevant to the question of whether it is constitutionally protected. Apart from its function of buffering more valuable forms of speech, toleration of objectionable speech has separately been advocated by Lee Bollinger, in *The Tolerant Society*,[28] on the ground that this type of expression is particularly suited to the inculcation of the virtues of self-discipline,

---

[23] Where immediate unlawful violence is the likely result, even US law permits restraints on expressive activity: *Terminiello v Chicago* 337 US 1 (1949).

[24] This, of course, may be true for disabled people but not for able-bodied black people, members of religious minorities, gays, lesbians and others.

[25] This definition is under-inclusive failing, as it does, to acknowledge abusive expression directed at disabled people.

[26] LW Sumner, 'Hate propaganda and Charter rights' in WJ Waluchow (ed), *Free Expression—Essays in Law and Philosophy* (Oxford, Clarendon Press, 1994).

[27] See further the fortress model of L Bollinger, *The Tolerant Society* (Oxford, Clarendon Press, 1986); he refers to the problematic 'impulse to excessive intolerance' at pp 86–90 ff.

[28] *Ibid.*

restraint and open-mindedness.[29] Although necessarily tempered by a recognition of human frailty, freedom of speech for extremist viewpoints can be justified in terms of building up positive human characteristics. On this view, however, the limits of toleration are reached when the bonds that normally hold society together come under serious threat of destruction. This is a judgment to be made by each society. There is also an informational gain to be made in allowing the expression of hateful opinion. By being made aware of the presence of this sort of discontent (and possibly its extent) we are better able to decide whether the grievances that may lie behind it merit a policy response in terms of improving education, employment, housing conditions etc. It is better for disruptive individuals or groups to operate in public, where a sense may be gained of the presence of disease within the body politic, rather than in private where, conversely, false beliefs might circulate more or less unchallenged.

Outside the US, however, these reasons for refusing to suppress hateful communications have not prevailed. In particular, mistrust of the State's purposes in regulating hateful expression is less common.[30] Accordingly, in the UK, Canada, and much of Europe, domestic authorities are given considerably greater latitude to regulate expression on grounds of content.[31] Far from being concerned that certain unpopular viewpoints will be excluded from public discourse, many liberal democracies have sought to silence speech considered to incite racial and even religious hatred. This is hardly surprising. The impetus for the protections enshrined in the Council of Europe's Convention on Human Rights was, after all, the hatred and intolerance shown towards Jews, Gypsies, homosexuals and others in the concentration camps of the Second World War. Libertarian opponents of restraints tend to restrict their analysis of speech regulations solely to the damage they do, or do not do, to *speech*.[32] In contrast to this exclusive focus, defenders of legal restraints—whilst acknowledging the 'silencing' effect upon the expressive activities of the victims of hateful speech—point to other significant *non-speech* injuries and costs including the physiological symptoms and emotional distress (including post-traumatic stress disorder, hypertension and psychosis) experienced by the victims of hate speech.[33] There are important social consequences too. Not only may others be persuaded to think less of individual group members, but they may

---

[29] *Ibid.* Precisely why self-restraint should be the pre-eminent justification for free speech, when the type of expression it protects is likely to open up the prospect of inter-communal strife, is a central question raised by this work.

[30] An interesting comparative discussion is offered by M Rosenfeld, 'Hate speech in constitutional jurisprudence: a comparative analysis' (2003) 24 *Cardozo Law Review* 1523.

[31] For an indication of the type and range of legal techniques used in recent years in different jurisdictions, see J Magnet, 'Hate propaganda in Canada' in WJ Waluchow (ed), *Free Expression* (Oxford, Clarendon Press, 1994).

[32] *Ibid* at 73.

[33] MJ Matsuda, 'Public response to racist speech: considering the victim's story' (1989) 87 *Michigan Law Review* 2320.

be watching to see how the target responds. This anticipation is sensed by the target who can never fully disconnect his/her own feelings towards him/herself from the feelings others have towards him/her.[34] Some are driven to reject their identity as a victim-group member. As Matsuda has put it, 'to be hated, despised and alone is the ultimate fear of all human beings.'[35] What is more, the definition of the *community* itself is called into issue when hateful expression occurs. The response of dominant forces within a community to hateful expression, their willingness to act against more overt forms of hatred, will assume a symbolic importance to beleaguered minorities. In this sense, the imposition of legal restraints can serve as the expression of a community position on the issues raised by the speaker and, in so doing, forge a social identity which uncompromisingly rejects, as a value, the unequal status of individuals that is being urged by the speaker.

Where, by contrast, the will to protect individuals or groups is absent, a lessening of societal coherence cannot be far behind. Even where the message is resisted by victims and well-meaning members of the dominant racial group, there are costs to inter-communal relations. Victim-group members may come to view all dominant group members with suspicion, whilst the latter experience an ambivalent relief that they do not belong to the target group and thereby become distanced from victims.

4 INTERNATIONAL, REGIONAL AND DOMESTIC HUMAN RIGHTS-BASED REGULATION OF HATEFUL EXPRESSION

4.1 International Human Rights Controls

In international law, commitment to the fundamental and pervasive notions of equality and the inherent dignity of all human beings is well established. Norms found in both international treaties and the UN Charter are premised on the legitimacy of limits on the freedom to engage in forms of hate expression. Thus, the International Covenant on Civil and Political Rights (ICCPR) provides in Article 19(2) that everyone has the right to seek, receive and impart information and ideas 'of all kinds'. The exercise of these rights may, however, be restricted by law when necessary for the respect of the rights or reputations of others,[36] or for the protection of national security, public order, public health or morals.[37] In practice, hate speech, as an issue in international law, has tended to be conceived of in terms of expression which is hostile to racial or ethnic groups. Far less

---

[34] 'The interconnections between the individual self and social perceptions is true for groups as well as for individuals which, of course, is why racial and religious slurs are so hurtful'; L Bollinger, *The Tolerant Society* (above n 27), at 66.
[35] See Matsuda article (above n 33) at 2338.
[36] Art 19(3)(a).
[37] Art 19(3)(b).

prominent has been the issue of protecting disabled people from hateful expression.

4.2 Regional Human Rights Controls—The European Convention on Human Rights

4.2.1 Article 10 ECHR

At the level of regional human rights instruments, the ECHR provides the framework of human rights protection in Council of Europe Member States. Article 10 provides qualified protection from interference with free expression (including, but not limited to, speech). It provides that:

1. Everyone has the right to freedom of expression. This right shall include the freedom to hold opinions and to receive and impart information and ideas ... This article shall not prevent States from requiring the licensing of broadcasting, television or cinema enterprises.
2. The exercise of these freedoms, since it carries with it duties and responsibilities, may be subject to such formalities, conditions, restrictions or penalties as are prescribed by law and are necessary in a democratic society in the interests of national security, territorial integrity or public safety, for the prevention of disorder or crime, for the protection of health or morals, for the protection of the reputation or rights of others, for preventing the disclosure of information received in confidence, or for maintaining the authority and impartiality of the judiciary.

Described as a core guarantee of the Convention, Article 10 was said in one of the earliest cases to reach the Court, *Handyside v UK*, to constitute 'one of the basic conditions for the progress of democratic societies and for the development of each individual'.[38] The democracy-enhancing and individual-developing functions of freedom of expression have since been reiterated on numerous occasions, notably in *Lingens v Austria*[39] and *Oberschlick v Austria*.[40]

The purposes for which expression may be legitimately interfered with are expressly stated in Article 10(2).[41] The range of derogations extends to safeguard both collective interests (such as public safety, national security and the authority and impartiality of the judiciary) and individual interests (the rights of others). In addition to showing that expression has been curtailed for a legitimate purpose, the State must satisfy the Court that the interference is 'necessary in a democratic society'—a phrase interpreted to

---

[38] *Handyside v UK* (1979–80) 1 EHRR 737.
[39] (1986) 8 EHRR 407, 418.
[40] (1995) 19 EHRR 389, 421.
[41] Thus contrasting with the US and Canadian Constitutions, to name but two jurisdictions where the legitimacy of a purpose behind limitations on freedom of speech/expression have had to be judicially developed.

correspond to a 'pressing social need and ... proportionate to the legitimate aim pursued'.[42]

In interpreting Article 10 ECHR the Strasbourg Court, whilst notionally tolerant of expression which shocks and offends,[43] has tended in practice to subordinate the interests of offensive speakers to the wider societal goals of tolerance and community harmony. In *Otto Preminger Institut v Austria,* somewhat controversially, expression that merely offended the sensibilities of a religious group (Roman Catholics) was found to fall outside the protective ambit of Article 10.[44] More recently, in a domestic context, the House of Lords declined to interfere with the BBC's refusal to show a party election broadcast which contained images of aborted foetuses.[45] The refusal was justified by reference to paragraph 5.1(d) of the *Licence and Agreement* and the broadcaster's obligation not to include material that is offensive. The obligation itself was deemed consistent with Article 10 even though its impact was to curtail political speech during an election.

4.2.2 *Article 17 ECHR*

Speakers who engage in extremist forms of speech which communicate threats to, or incite hatred of, others may find any Article 10 protection removed by Article 17. This provides that:

> Nothing in this Convention may be interpreted as implying for any state, group or person any right to engage in any activity aimed at the destruction of the rights and freedoms set forth herein or at their limitation to a greater extent than is provided for in the Convention.

In *Glimmerveen & Hagenbeek v Netherlands* Article 17 was invoked by the Strasbourg authorities against racist expression to dismiss, as 'manifestly ill-founded,' an allegation of unlawful interference with Article 10 rights. The applicant, Glimmerveen, had been sentenced to two weeks' imprisonment for possession of leaflets likely to incite racial hatred, and was removed from a list of candidates seeking election to public office after openly calling for the repatriation of non-white immigrant workers. The Commission ruled that the applicant's words actively promoted racial discrimination in direct contradiction to norms set out in the Convention and elsewhere in international law and that, accordingly, they fell outside the protection of Article 10.[46] More specifically, in the case of challenges to holocaust denial

---

[42] *Olsson v Sweden* (1988) 11 EHRR 259.

[43] *Oberschlick v Austria* (1995) 19 EHRR 389.

[44] Note the joint dissenting judgment of Judges Palm, Pekkanen and Makarczyk which maintained, with some force, that '[t]here is no point in guaranteeing this freedom only as long as it is used in accordance with accepted opinion' (1995) 19 EHRR 34, 61.

[45] *R (On the Application of Prolife Alliance) v BBC* [2003] *Entertainment and Media Law Review* 23.

[46] *Glimmerveen and Hagenbeek v Netherlands* Application Nos 8348/78 and 8406/78, 18 *Decisions and Reports of the Human Rights Commission* 187.

laws, the Court has stated that the negation or revision of clearly established historical facts (such as the Holocaust itself) is also removed from the
protection of Article 10 by virtue of Article 17.[47] In justifying these sorts of
speech restrictions the Court has made reference, at various times, to the
values of tolerance,[48] pluralism, equality and individual dignity, which
underpin the Convention.

The upholding of restraints on hateful expression via Articles 10 and 17
may point up underlying civic republican concerns in Convention jurisprudence that certain expressive activities offer 'bad solutions' to societal problems and may deter minority groups from participating in community
affairs as equal citizens. Convention jurisprudence does not, it seems, share
the faith of more libertarian schools of thought that reasoned discourse will
always expose the vileness of hateful speakers and secure the triumph of
non-hateful alternatives. Europe's history provides a forceful reminder that
States' failure to signal their rejection of eugenic theories can, under the
appropriate socio-economic conditions, have devastating human rights consequences.

4.3 Domestic Human Rights Law

The focus of domestic regulation of hate speech in the UK has changed since
its earliest inception. From an initial concern, evident in the 17th century,
to outlaw seditious libel in order to protect the security of the government
of the day, subsequent regulation (in the form of the Race Relations Acts
1965 and 1975) sought to control speech which incites hatred among the
non-target audience towards others.[49] Today, Part III of the Public Order
Act 1986 criminalises speech that is targeted at minority groups, or individuals belonging to minority groups, and is intended or likely to stir up
hatred. The minority groups to which these laws apply are those defined by

---

[47] *Lehideux and Isorni v France* (1998) 5 British Human Rights Cases 540. See further *H,
W, P and K v Austria* Application No 12774/87, 62 *Decisions and Reports of the Commission
on Human Rights* (1989) 216 and discussion by J Cooper and AM Williams, 'Hate speech,
holocaust denial and international human rights law' (1999) 6 *European Human Rights Law
Review* 593.

[48] That is an enforced toleration on the part of the racist speaker, not forbearance from listeners in having to endure racist expression.

[49] The Act remains in force and applies typically to publications written by members of racial
supremacy groups for consumption by other members. The RRA 1965 made it an offence to
'publish words which are threatening, abusive or insulting' and which are intended to incite
hatred on the basis of race, colour or national origin.' The Act was used to convict blacks *R v
Malik* [1968] 1 All ER 582 where the defendant, in front of other blacks, asserted that 'whites
were nasty and vicious people … If you ever see a white man lay his hands on a black woman,
kill him immediately …' It also sometimes led to the acquittal of whites. In *R v Kingsley John
Reid* 6 January 1978, unreported, the defendant had, at a public meeting, responded to news
of the death of an Asian youth in Southall with the comment 'one down, a million to go'. His
speech also contained references to 'wogs, coons and niggers'. He was acquitted after the judge
told the jury to allow toleration and freedom to the individual 'otherwise we are all caught up
in a vice of dictatorship, repression or slavery.'

race, colour, nationality and ethnicity. Incitement to hatred of disabled people is not an offence under Part 3 of the 1986 Act.[50]

Generic restraints on the use of 'threatening, abusive or insulting' words or conduct, which might provide the basis of criminal liability for disability hate speech, are to be found in ss 4, 4A and 5 of Part I of the Public Order Act 1986. Section 4 is the most serious offence and is committed where the words or conduct are directed at another and are intended or likely to cause fear of immediate unlawful violence. At the less serious end of the spec-trum, s 5 requires that the threatening, abusive or insulting words be uttered 'within the hearing or sight of a person likely to be caused alarm, harassment or distress.'[51] There is no need for alarm or distress actually to be caused, but the defendant must either intend, or be aware, that his conduct is threatening, abusive or insulting.[52] A serious limitation on the practical use to which these provisions may be put in the case of disabled persons arises from the fact that the Act expressly excludes criminal liability in respect of words uttered inside a dwelling to another who is also inside that or another dwelling.[53]

An alternative basis of criminal liability, risked by persons who engage in abusive epithets directed at disabled people, is to be found in the Protection from Harassment Act 1997. Section 1 provides that a person must not pursue a course of conduct which amounts to harassment of another and which he knows, or ought to know, amounts to harassment of another. 'Conduct' is defined to include speech, and 'harassment' to include causing a person alarm or distress.[54] A 'course' of conduct requires there to have been at least two occasions on which the relevant conduct has occurred, preventing isolated instances of abusive conduct from coming under the Act's ambit.[55] Unsurprisingly, a search of a number of legal databases in June 2004 failed to reveal a single case of disability hate speech being prosecuted under the 1997 Act. Less predictably, however, the same search produced no reported prosecutions under the 1986 legislation in respect of speech which was threatening, abusive or insulting to a person on

---

[50] Public Order Act 1986, s 17.

[51] Rather than directed at somebody as is the case with s 4 of the 1986 Act.

[52] The intermediate offence, in terms of seriousness, is intentional harassment, alarm or distress laid down in s 4A, Public Order Act 1986. This states:

> (1) A person is guilty of an offence if, with intent to cause a person harassment, alarm or distress, he (a) uses threatening, abusive or insulting words or behaviour, or disorderly behaviour, or (b) displays any writing, sign or other visible representation which is threatening, abusive or insulting, thereby causing that or another person harassment, alarm or distress.

[53] Ss 4A(3), 5(3) 1986 Act.

[54] S 8(3), Protection from Harassment Act 1997.

[55] Note also D Tausz and D Ormerod, 'Harassment: whether leaving three abusive and threatening phone calls on the victim's voice mail, which were listened to at one time, capable of constituting a course of conduct' [2003] *Criminal Law Review* 45, commenting on *Kelly v DPP* [2002] EWHC 1428.

account of their disability. Nevertheless, latest indications suggest that the Act's potential value, as a check on insulting expression, is understood. In January 2004, the Queen's Bench Division in *Hammond v DPP*[56] upheld the decision of magistrates to convict an evangelical Christian, under s 5 of the 1986 Act, in respect of a sign that equated homosexuality and lesbianism with immorality. Magistrates had been entitled to find that the sign was 'insulting' within the meaning of s 5; a conclusion reinforced by the factual finding that the defendant had been made aware, on a previous occasion, of the adverse reaction produced by his sign.[57]

4.4 The Likely Impact of ECHR Jurisprudence on Future Domestic Disabled Hate Speech Law

It is interesting to speculate whether broadening current legal protection beyond the incitement of racial, religious or ethnic origin, to cover disability hate speech would infringe domestic human rights law. As is well known, s 2 of the Human Rights Act 1998 (HRA) requires English judges to take account of the jurisprudence of the European Court of Human Rights when construing domestic legislation. Plainly, restrictions upon the speech of those who would inflame or incite others against minority groups directly engages the protection for freedom of expression under Article 10 ECHR,[58] and, in accordance with the interpretative duty laid down in s 3(1) HRA, a judge would have to read and give effect to domestic legislation in a way 'which is compatible' with Article 10. In the case of restrictions on racist speech we know, from *Jersild v Denmark,* that national authorities may criminalise abusive racial expression without breaching Article 10.[59] This suggests that abusive speech directed at disabled people might also be curtailed without infringing the Convention. The rarely invoked Article 17 might also be pleaded by Member States to justify a proportionate restriction on hateful expressive forms. In conclusion, then, whilst not the subject of specific protection in domestic law, prosecutors may act against the individual perpetrators of disability hate speech under existing generic laws (such as s 5 of the 1986 Public Order Act) without fearing an adverse reaction from Strasbourg. On the other hand, if the UK Parliament was to introduce specific protection for victims of disability hate speech, the European

---

[56] 14 January 2004 (Lawtel), *The Times,* January 28 2004.

[57] In the case of harassment of disabled people in the workplace, it is worth noting that the Employment Framework Directive discussed by Lisa Waddington in this book will require EU Member States to prohibit such treatment (though not necessarily via the criminal law).

[58] HRA, s 1(1)(a).

[59] (1995) 19 EHRR 1. The broadcast remarks of members of the 'Greenjackets' included the statement 'A nigger is not a human being, it's an animal, that goes for all the other foreign workers as well, Turks, Yugoslavs and whatever they are called.' The highly abusive nature of the anti-immigrant/anti-ethnic remarks were stated by the Court to be more than insulting to members of the targeted groups and outside the protection of Article 10.

Court would, in any challenge to the legislation's compatibility with Article 10, need to be convinced that the additional restrictions on expression corresponded to a pressing social need. This would require evidence *inter alia* of a deliberate targeting of disabled persons on a scale previously unacknowledged. In view of the problem of the underreporting of crimes against disabled persons, it is far from certain that such evidence currently exists.

5 THE (OVERLY) TOLERANT SOCIETY? THE UNITED STATES AND HATEFUL EXPRESSION

5.1 First Amendment Themes

The consensus in domestic and international law about the importance of eliminating forms of hateful expression may be contrasted with judicial hostility in the US to state legislatures' attempts to curb the expressive activities of hateful speakers. In the final section of this chapter, attention is paid to the distinctive contribution made by First Amendment jurisprudence to the on-going debate in this area.

According to the First Amendment of the Bill of Rights 1791, 'Congress shall make no law ... abridging the freedom of speech, or of the press.' This command is well known, but what are the overriding themes and prevailing values that have informed First Amendment jurisprudence? Three main overarching principles or doctrines may be identified: first, hostility to content and viewpoint-based regulation of speech; second, the hierarchy of speech types; and, third, the doctrine of over-breadth.

The first principle is that the State may not, as a general rule, regulate speech based upon hostility or favouritism towards the underlying message expressed. Allowing the State to regulate particular topics or communications, on a selective and discriminatory basis (eg to prohibit newspaper advertisements attacking the Government), would plainly violate viewpoint neutrality as it might result in certain disfavoured ideas being removed from public discourse altogether.[60] Such restrictions are said to be presumptively invalid.[61] The self-interested motives of government for suppressing such speech forms provide a strong reason for maintaining strict judicial oversight.[62]

A second principle that commands widespread support is the proposition that not all speech forms enjoy the same level of protection from state

---

[60] *Simon and Schuster Inc v Members of New York State Crime Victims Board* 502 US 105, 116 (1991).

[61] *RAV v City of St Paul Minnesota* 505 US 377 (1992).

[62] See eg *New York Times v Sullivan* 376 US 254 (1964); *New York Times v US* (Pentagon Papers case) 403 US 713 (1971) and see the academic work of F Schauer, *Free Speech—A Philosophical Inquiry* (Massachusetts, Cambridge University Press, 1982) and TM Scanlon, 'A theory of freedom of expression' (1972) 1 *Philosophy and Public Affairs* 204.

interference.[63] On this view, the First Amendment is predicated upon a tiered system of speech forms, in which 'political' speech is accorded greater protection than lower value speech forms, such as purely commercial or artistic expression.[64] Indecent, though non-obscene, sexually explicit speech has been treated as falling into this lower tier category of protected speech. Significantly, however, obscene speech and child pornography, involving the use of actual children, have been cast outside the protective ambit of the First Amendment altogether on the basis that the value of the expressive conduct to society is *de minimus*.[65] This hierarchy of speech protection may be traced back to the Constitution's distinctive emphasis upon popular sovereignty. The author of the First Amendment, James Madison, famously contrasted the British system of government, where sovereignty rested with the King in Parliament, with that established under the US Constitution, where 'the People, not the Government, possess the absolute sovereignty.'[66] To function effectively, popular sovereignty requires public access to information and opinions so as to ensure that decisions are appropriately informed. If this is granted it would seem to follow that political speech, ie speech 'intended and received as a contribution to public deliberation about some issue',[67] ought to be the central concern of the First Amendment and accorded the highest level of protection from governmental interference. Thus, restrictions on political speech must satisfy an especially heavy standard of proof; namely, clear and compelling evidence of substantial and imminent harm to a legitimate State interest.[68] Moreover, they must not be overbroad and strike at otherwise protected expression.[69] Consistent with this view, speech falling outside the definition of political speech (eg commercial advertising, artistic expression or non-obscene sexually explicit

---

[63] See the Supreme Court rulings in *Chaplinksy v New Hampshire* 315 US 568 (1942); *Dennis v US* 341 US 494 (1951); *Gertz v Robert Welch Inc* 418 US 323 (1974); *Virginia Pharmacy Board v Virginia Consumer Council* 425 US 748 (1976); *Dun and Bradstreet Inc v Greenmoss Builders Inc* 472 US 749 (1985). See further C Sunstein, *Democracy and the Problem of Free Speech* (New York, Macmillan, 1993); G Stone, 'Content-neutral restrictions' (1987) 54 *University of Chicago Law Review* 46.

[64] Attempts at line drawing between 'political' and 'commercial' or 'artistic' speech forms may not always, of course, be convincing or command universal agreement but this fact alone does not mean that the distinction is without force.

[65] This is despite the fact that the categorisation of obscene speech as morally offensive or corrosive is plainly content-based. See respectively *Miller v California* 413 US 15 (1973) and *New York v Ferber* 458 US 747 (1982). Other examples of unprotected content-based categories of expression include defamation of private figures (*Gertz v Robert Welch* 418 US 323 (1974)) and 'fighting words' (*Chaplinsky v New Hampshire* 315 US 568 (1942)).

[66] Report on the Virginia Resolution, January 1800, Vol 6 *Papers of James Madison*, p 385.

[67] This is the definition preferred by C Sunstein, *Democracy and the Problem of Free Speech* (above n 62), p 130.

[68] See thus the test of 'clear and present danger of imminent and serious evil' adopted by the Court in *Bridges v California* 314 US 252 (1941) applied to restrictions on speech pertaining to court proceedings.

[69] *Broadrick v Oklahoma* 413 US 601 (1973).

speech) belongs to the lower tier of protected expression. However, even this lower value speech is deemed worthy of some protection and may be regulated only where the restriction advances a substantial government interest, in a proportionate manner, without inadvertently chilling political speech.[70]

The third theme to inform First Amendment jurisprudence is that of over-breadth. Under the over-breadth doctrine an entire statute regulating speech may be invalidated, despite having a lawful objective, if the methods chosen by the legislature to achieve that object 'sweep unnecessarily broadly and thereby invade the area of protected freedoms.'[71] Thus, in *Globe Newspapers v Superior Court for the County of Norfolk*, a challenge was mounted against a Massachusetts statute which automatically excluded the press and the public from the courtroom during the testimony of minor victims in sex offence trials.[72] It was held that, while it would have been permissible to allow closure in particular cases in order to protect the welfare of the child, automatic closure in every case could not be justified and, accordingly, the provision in question was struck down.[73] Over-breadth is strong constitutional medicine; it can be used to strike down legislative provisions even where the person challenging the statute has not been able to point to any interference with his/her rights to free expression. In the past, the courts have tended to use the doctrine sparingly. After all, as Blackmun J observed in *Illinois Board of Elections v Socialist Workers Party*, all but the most unimaginative of judges can find an alternative, slightly less restrictive rule, in almost any situation, which enables them to strike down almost any legislation.[74] A related, though distinct, ground for impugning the validity of a statute regulating speech is vagueness. Here it is asserted that the statute in question is lacking in clarity and that, in the words of Justice Brennan, persons 'of common intelligence must necessarily guess at its meaning and differ as to its application.'[75] Thus, a prohibition on three or more persons meeting on the pavement and acting in a manner 'annoying' to persons passing by was held, in *Coates v City of Cincinnati*, to be constitutionally invalid on vagueness grounds.[76]

---

[70] *Central Hudson Gas and Electricity v Public Service Commission* 447 US 557 (1980).

[71] *NAACP v Alabama* 357 US 449 (1964) per Harlan J and also *Schaumberg v Citizens for a Better Environment* 444 US 620 (1980), *Broadrick v Oklahoma* 413 US 601 (1973). There is however an issue about how far the Court should strain to find potential applications of a statute which may invade the area of protected freedoms.

[72] 457 US 596 (1983).

[73] Note the similar conclusion of the Ontario Court of Appeal in *Canadian Newspaper Co v Attorney General* (1985) Ontario Reports (2d) 557 where a mandatory publication ban in respect of the identity of a sexual offence complainant imposed by s 442(3) of the Canadian Criminal Code was deemed to violate ss 1 and 2 of the Canadian Charter of Rights and Freedoms.

[74] 440 US 173, 188 (1979).

[75] *Zwickler v Koota* 389 US 241, 250 (1967).

[76] 402 US 611 (1971).

5.2 *RAV v St Paul*—The Assault on the Tiered View of Speech Types[77]

In recent years the view that some expressive forms are entitled to a lesser level of judicial protection under the First Amendment, or are altogether outside its protection, has come under challenge from sections of the Supreme Court. This re-write of received First Amendment wisdom began in *RAV v City of St Paul, Minnesota*, which concerned the so-called 'fighting words' doctrine first enunciated by the Court in *Chaplinsky v New Hampshire* in 1942.[78] These are words 'which by their very utterance inflict injury or tend to incite an immediate breach of the peace.'[79] Chaplinksy had been convicted for calling a city marshall a 'God damned racketeer' and a 'damned fascist'. His remarks, whilst plainly of a political nature and though addressed to a public official who might reasonably have been expected to show a measure of self-restraint, were nonetheless held to be outside the protective ambit of the First Amendment. The Supreme Court reached this conclusion because the words made an extremely slight contribution to the exchange of ideas, posing instead a considerable danger of public disorder. It seems the Court feared that law-abiding persons of reasonable fortitude and forbearance would have been provoked into a violent response by the defendant's words. Chaplinsky's conviction was accordingly upheld.

In *RAV v City of St Paul, Minnesota*, a unanimous Court struck down, for sharply divergent reasons, a city ordinance which purported to outlaw the burning of crosses which could reasonably be anticipated to arouse anger, alarm or resentment in others, on the basis of race, colour, creed, religion or gender.[80] Justice Scalia, joined by Rehnquist CJ and Kennedy, Souter and Thomas JJ, cast aside the idea that fighting words and other forms of *de minimus* expression were entirely invisible to the Constitution and laid down what one commentator was later to call 'an ambitious reconceptualisation and synthesis of First Amendment doctrine'.[81] Fighting words, we learned, were entitled to a considerable degree of First Amendment protection where, as here, the State was purporting to impose a contents-based restriction on expression. In other words, St Paul's selection of particular subsets of 'fighting words' meant that speakers who wished to air their views on *disfavoured* subjects would be caught by the ordinance, whilst others who provoked anger, alarm or resentment on the bases of political affiliation, disability, trade union membership or homosexuality would be

---

[77] For commentary, see I Cram, 'Hate speech, cross-burning and the First Amendment' (2003) 8 *Communications Law* 389.

[78] 315 US 568 (1942).

[79] *Ibid* at 572.

[80] 505 US 377 (1992). The ordinance had been read down by the Minnesota Supreme Court to reach only those symbolic expressions of hate which constituted fighting words. The US Supreme Court proceeded on the basis of this limiting construction.

[81] AR Amar, 'The case of the missing amendments' (1992) 106 *Harvard Law Review* 124, 127.

outside its sweep. Race-based fighting words (or symbolic acts such as cross-burning) were thus to be treated differently from other sorts of fighting words. Somewhat paradoxically, the ordinance failed to pass First Amendment scrutiny because it did not seek to ban enough speech and this under-inclusivity was judged fatal to its constitutionality. In the eyes of the majority, the State appeared to be trying to restrict, on a selective basis, the airing and receipt of racist, bigoted and sexist opinion.

5.3 Letting Local Communities Decide—Civic Republican Concerns in *RAV*'s Minority Opinion

St Paul's content-based ordinance appeared to be based upon a judgment that harms caused by racial, religious and gender-based invective were qualitatively different from, and more serious than, harms caused by other forms of fighting words. Doubtless, St Paul's ordinance would have survived constitutional scrutiny under the European Convention on Human Rights and in many other liberal democracies. For the Supreme Court minority, St Paul had been entitled to engage in the selective proscription of unprotected expression directed at particular groups, provided that it had *reasonably* determined that the harm caused by the regulated expression was more serious than the harm caused by the unregulated expression.[82] As Stevens J pointed out, the ban was fairly narrow;[83] it did not outlaw all cross-burnings, only those which were threatening because directed at an individual or group. Neither did it prevent the espousal of views of racial superiority. As Blackmun J put it:

> I see no First Amendment values that are compromised by a law that prohibits hoodlums from driving minorities out of their homes by burning crosses on their lawns, but I see great harm in preventing the people of St Paul from specifically punishing the race-based fighting words that so prejudice their community.[84]

Present in these separate minority opinions are more obviously civic republican concerns. References to the history and practice of cross-burning as a method of intimidating and silencing a section of the community (as well as causing other harms to society), and an inclination to read the ordinance as a legitimate means of lifting a barrier to black participation in societal affairs, seem to rest upon a conception of the common good.[85]

[82] In *Ginsberg v New York* 390 US 629 (1968) the harms caused to minors by obtaining obscene publications justified a law prohibiting sale of such materials to minors.
[83] 505 US 377, 436 (1992).
[84] 505 US 377, 416 (1992).
[85] For an indication of the conceptual problems to which *RAV* has given rise, see I Cram, above n 77, where the Supreme Court ruling in *Virginia v Black* 262 *Virginia* 764 (2003) is discussed.

Notwithstanding such sentiments, the implications of the majority's reasoning in *RAV* for any attempt to proscribe the expression of anti-disability opinion remain stark. The pre-eminence of a libertarian mistrust of State regulation, and unwillingness to undermine individual autonomy to utter and receive all manner of expression falling short of provoking immediate unlawful violence, mean that disabled people on the Washington DC subway must continue to accept the abusive epithets of their fellow travellers.

6 CONCLUSION

This essay has sought to contrast different approaches to the problem of hate speech. Outside the US, a degree of consensus exists in international, regional and UK domestic human rights instruments that hate speech must invariably give way to the opposing claims of individual dignity and community cohesion. As the European jurisprudence makes clear, hateful expression is considered to threaten the very foundations upon which the Council of Europe was built. By contrast, the prevailing (though by no means unanimous) view of free speech under the First Amendment demonstrates that the speaker's interest in communicating his/her extreme views (including in symbolically dramatic ways) are to be prioritised over and above any offence caused to listeners. Underpinning this stance lies a genuine concern that the power of the State ought not to be used to coerce a community of shared values, no matter how worthy those values may be.

As far as domestic law is concerned, the UK presently lacks a specific criminal prohibition on anti-disability expression. The lack of any serious political impetus for legal reform is unlikely to change whilst there remains little in the way of statistical information about instances of anti-disability expression or crimes against disabled people more generally. Were domestic reform to be attempted, the major Convention issue to arise would, doubtless, centre on the proportionality of any future law. The onus would fall on UK authorities to show that the restriction corresponded to a pressing social need. Although the goal of achieving an inclusive society, committed to the dignity and equality of all its citizens would presumably constitute a legitimate purpose for restriction, the Strasbourg Court would additionally require evidence that any new law was necessary in order to curtail a significant problem. Unless new efforts are made to encourage the reporting and official recording of anti-disability expression to render it more visible, this is likely to prove a major hurdle to ensuring Article 10 compliance. In the meantime, however, individual instances of anti-disability expression that occur outside of private dwellings can be made subject to public order sanctions in the criminal law.

Part III
Anti-Discrimination Laws

6

Disability Discrimination Law:
A Global Comparative Approach

THERESIA DEGENER*

1 INTRODUCTION

ALTHOUGH THE FOCUS of this book is on European disability law, this chapter will extend beyond European perspectives by providing a global view on recent developments in disability discrimination law. The bulk of the research on which it draws was carried out during a research and lecturing year at Berkeley Law School in 1999–2000. Laws from 42 countries of all regions of the world were compared. In this updated version, laws from 45 countries are considered.[1]

The study was restricted to federal statutes. It did not consider regional or local laws or collective agreements (even though in some countries collective agreements have the same legal status as statutes). This decision was based on the assumption that federal statutes would be more likely to be published in international compilations or on the internet than would regional or state laws or collective agreements.

Another methodological decision was to leave out all anti-discrimination laws which did not explicitly mention disabled people, even where they contained an open clause such as 'any other status.' In the context of equal rights, disabled people have until recently been a forgotten minority. Consequently, it was assumed (based on experience of German and international law) that an anti-discrimination statute which did not expressly mention disability (or health status)[2] would probably not, in practice, be applied for the protection of disabled people.

This chapter, then, aims to provide a global overview of the current state of anti-discrimination law for disabled people. First, the US Americans

---

* Professor of Law, Administration and Organisation at the University of Applied Sciences, Bochum, Germany.

[1] See Appendix I for a list of the laws analysed. Note that some of the names of the laws may not be the official name. Translation in some cases by the author.

[2] Health status was included because there is no consensus on the definition of disability or on the terminology.

With Disabilities Act 1990 (ADA) and the UN Standard Rules on the Equalization of Opportunities for Persons with Disabilities 1993 (Standard Rules) will be outlined. They provided a source of legislative inspiration around the world. Second, the chapter will identify the different legal contexts (constitutional law, criminal law etc) in which disability discrimination law is to be found. Third, I will examine the groups protected by different laws; some cover more than one group vulnerable to discrimination whereas others are disability-specific in nature. I will then compare the equality and/or discrimination concepts at play before going on to describe enforcement mechanisms.

2 THE ADA AND THE STANDARD RULES: A GLOBAL TEMPLATE

At the domestic level, disability law in many countries has undergone significant change over the last few decades. More than 40 out of 189 UN Member States have now adopted some kind of anti-discrimination law for disabled people. For a number of reasons comparing and analysing these laws globally is a difficult enterprise. First, not only do these countries have different historic, economic and political backgrounds, but they are also characterised by different legal systems, notably the common law tradition or the civil law tradition. The role played by the judiciary in the common law tradition (heavily influenced by precedent and case-law) is very different from that played by them in the civil law tradition. Second, disability law as a branch of legal research is a fairly recent development in most countries. Thus, relevant legal literature and comparative studies are still somewhat rare.[3] Most of the comparative legal literature that exists concerns European countries.

With these reservations in mind, some observations can be made about anti-discrimination laws for disabled people around the world. Most such laws have been enacted in the last decade, though some were enacted in the

---

[3] L Waddington, 'Legislating to employ people with disabilities: the European and American way' (1994) 1 *Maastricht Journal of European and Comparative Law* 4; G Quinn, M McDonagh and C Kimber, *Disability Discrimination Law in the United States, Australia and Canada* (Dublin, Oak Tree Press, 1993); M Jones and LA Basser Marks (eds), *Disability, Divers-Ability and Legal Change* (The Hague, M Nijhoff, 1999); M Hauritz, C Sampford and S Blencowe, *Justice for People with Disabilities: Legal and Institutional Issues* (Sydney, The Federation Press, 1998); M Rioux, 'The place of judgement in a world of facts' (April 1997) *Journal of Intellectual Disability Research* 102–11; P Thornton and N Lunt, *Employment Policies for Disabled People in Eighteen Countries—A Review* (York, Social Policy Research Unit, University of York, 1997); M Carley, 'International equality at work. Disability, employment and the law in Europe—part one' (1994) *Industrial Relations Review 251*; E Besber, 'Employment legislation for disabled individuals: what can France learn from the Americans With Disabilities Act?' (1995) 16 *Comparative Labour Law Journal* 399; B Gutow, 'Survey of rights of workers with disabilities: comparison of the United States with the European Community' (1998) 11/2 *New York International Law Review* 101; L Waddington and A Hendriks, 'The expanding concept of employment discrimination in Europe: from direct to indirect discrimination to reasonable accommodation' (Winter 2002) 18/3 *The International Journal of Comparative Labour Law and Industrial Relations*, 303–427.

1980s. Exceptionally early was the Rehabilitation Act 1973, one of the first US pieces of anti-discrimination legislation for disabled people. US law, especially the ADA, has been instrumental in the evolution of disability discrimination law in many countries. Indeed, the ADA has had such an enormous impact on foreign law development that one might feel inclined to say that its international impact has been larger than its domestic effect.[4]

Another incentive to enact disability discrimination legislation came from the UN Standard Rules. According to Rule 15:

> States have a responsibility to create the legal basis for measures to achieve the objectives of full participation and equality for persons with disabilities ... States must ensure that organizations of persons with disabilities are involved in the development of national legislation concerning the rights of persons with disabilities, as well as in the ongoing evaluation of that legislation ... Any discriminatory provisions against persons with disabilities must be eliminated. National legislation should provide for appropriate sanctions in case of violations of the principle of non-discrimination ...[5]

The history of disability discrimination law in a number of countries reveals that the ADA, the Standard Rules, or both served as a model for domestic developments. With respect to the Standard Rules, this is an interesting example of the impact a soft law can have internationally if taken seriously by governments. The fact that these governments took disability seriously as a discrimination issue is due to the work of the disability movement in each country. Anti-discrimination laws for disabled people are the result of an organised social movement of disabled people and disability advocates around the world. This movement demanded human rights instead of laws based on pity or charity, reflecting the paradigm shift in disability policy nationally and internationally.

A more recent incentive to adopt disability discrimination laws emerged from the European Union in the shape of the Framework Employment Directive,[6] concerning the equal treatment in employment and occupation of several minority groups, including disabled people. According to this, Member States were obliged to transpose the directive into domestic law by December 2003.[7] Thus, a number of EU countries have recently adopted new discrimination laws, or reformed existing ones,[8] and several more bills are in the pipeline.[9]

---

[4] Within the US legal literature there is today no consensus whether the ADA has been successful. See the ADA Symposium Issue (2000) 21/1 *Berkeley Journal of Employment and Labour Law*. The Symposium was called 'Backlash Against the ADA.'

[5] GAOR, 45th Sess, Supp No 40, UN Doc A/45/40 (1990).

[6] Council Directive 2000/78/EC of 27 November 2000, OJ L 303/16.

[7] Member States can also ask for an extension of three more years for transposition.

[8] Such as Germany, Luxembourg, The Netherlands and Portugal.

[9] Austria, France and Spain at least.

3 A GLOBAL COMPARISON OF ANTI-DISCRIMINATION LAWS

3.1 Overview

The relevant laws in the countries analysed[10] differ widely in their scope, their conceptions of discrimination and equality, their definitions of the protected groups, their enforcement mechanisms and in numerous other ways. Some laws define and clearly prohibit disability-based discrimination; others leave the question of what constitutes discrimination to the courts or other monitoring bodies. Some uphold the principle of equality but provide no clear picture of what needs to be changed in society in order to reach this goal. While these questions are often dealt with in separate regulations supplementing the primary legislation, the language and the structure of the statute may reveal legislative intent. Some laws give the impression that, though they contain some anti-discrimination language, they are in reality social welfare laws fostering programmes that are not necessarily aimed at the complete social equality and integration of disabled people.[11] However, it is important to note that disability discrimination law is truly a new development in social policy around the world. It is a manifestation of the paradigm shift from the medical model to the social model of disability. To treat disability as a legally recognised discrimination category implies an acknowledgement that disabled people are people with rights, not problems.[12] Some of these anti-discrimination laws are strong; others appear to be 'toothless tigers.'

Disability groups, which fought hard for equality laws, have often not been satisfied with the legislation finally enacted.[13] The history of US discrimination law reveals that the legislative battle for equality is long and more than one statute needs to be passed in order to achieve the goal of comprehensive protection against discrimination. Between the first attempts to include disability in the Civil Rights Acts of 1964 and the

---

[10] The research was carried out in preparation for a conference which took place in October 2000 in Washington, DC: 'From Principle to Practice—An International Disability Law and Policy Symposium,' organised by DREDF (Disability Rights Education and Defense Fund). See ML Breslin and S Yee (eds), *Disability Rights Law and Policy: International and National Perspectives* (New York, Transnational, 2002).

[11] Eg the Korean laws (see Appendix I). Each statute's prohibition on discrimination takes place in a kind of vacuum. There is no bestowal of individual rights, or any mechanism that allows disabled people to complain or enforce the prohibition. While the laws contain the potential for actual reform, the main legal emphasis is on discretionary and welfare-oriented disability programmes that have led to exclusion in the past.

[12] G Quinn, 'The human rights of people with disabilities under EU law' in P Alston (ed), *The EU and Human Rights* (New York, Oxford University Press, 1999), pp 281, 290.

[13] In the UK, disability groups had fought for more than a decade to achieve anti-discrimination legislation. They had prepared their own draft which was defeated in the parliament. When the Disability Discrimination Act was passed in 1995 many disability rights activists were disappointed. BJ Doyle, *Disability Discrimination: The New Law* (Bristol, Jordan, 1995); C Gooding, *Blackstone's Guide to the Disability Discrimination Act 1995* (London, Blackstone Press, 1996).

passage of the ADA in 1990 several decades went by and at least five federal disability discrimination acts[14] were passed by Congress.

As mentioned at the outset, significant differences in approach can be identified in current disability laws. These will be considered in the remainder of this section. The first issue to be examined is the different legal contexts in which anti-discrimination for disabled people is located. Such legal protection may be placed in the context of criminal law, constitutional law, civil rights law or social welfare law. These will now be examined in turn.

3.2 Different Legal Contexts

3.2.1 Criminal Law

France,[15] Finland,[16] Spain[17] and Luxembourg[18] prohibit discrimination against disabled people through their criminal law. The Spanish law prohibits disability-based discrimination in the context of recruitment or in the course of employment if the disabled worker is capable to do the job.[19]

Luxembourg and France outlaw disability-based discrimination in employment, business activities and in the provision of goods and services to the public. The punishment is a maximum of two or three years' imprisonment or a fine. The Finnish Penal Code punishes employment-related discrimination and discrimination in the provision of goods and services to the general public.

Other States which have adopted not criminal but civil or social law statutes regarding disability discrimination also provide for criminal or administrative penalties within these civil or social laws. For instance, the Australian discrimination statute provides that the incitement of unlawful discrimination or harassment is an offence punishable with six months' imprisonment or a fine. Victimisation of a person who exercises his or her rights under the Act is also declared an offence.[20] Similar provisions are to be found in the Hong Kong Discrimination Ordinance. A person who incites hatred towards, serious contempt for or severe ridicule of disabled people commits a serious offence of vilification and is liable to a fine or two

---

[14] Architectural Barrier Act 1968, 42 USC ss 4151–7; Rehabilitation Act 1973, 29 USC s 791, 793, 794; Individuals With Disabilities Education Act (IDEA), 20 USC ss 1400–85 (enacted under another name 'Education For All Handicapped Children Act' in 1975); Voter Accessibility Act 1984, 42 USC ss 1973ee, 1973ee–1 to 1973ee–6; Fair Housing Act as amended in 1988, 42 USC ss 3610–3614, 3614a.

[15] Art 225 Penal Code, Loi 90–602 de 12 juillet 1990.

[16] Penal Code 1995, chapter 11(9) and chapter 47(3).

[17] Art 314 Criminal Code (Organic Law 10/1995, 23 November).

[18] Ss 454–57 Criminal Code as modified in 1997.

[19] However, some more extensive legislative protection will be contained in the proposed employment discrimination bill in order to transpose the EU Framework Employment Directive.

[20] Disability Discrimination Act 1992, ss 42 and 43.

years' imprisonment.[21] The law of Mauritius punishes certain violations of the anti-discrimination rules with a criminal or administrative fine.[22] The same is true for the relevant Acts of Israel,[23] the Philippines,[24] Zambia[25] and Zimbabwe.[26]

While Finland and Spain also have anti-discrimination provisions in other fields of their legal systems, France and Luxembourg stand out in that they regulate disability-based discrimination exclusively through their criminal codes. Disability-based discrimination is thus prohibited only if it constitutes a criminal offence and this requires that the perpetrator acted with deliberate intent.

In reality, however, much disability-based discrimination is carried out by people for what they might consider to be benevolent motives. The restaurant owner who does not serve wheelchair users because the entrance is inaccessible will generally have no hostile feelings towards disabled people and will not conceive of him/herself as a discriminator. Though there is no statistical evidence, it seems that criminal anti-discrimination law is rarely enforced.

3.2.2 Constitutional Law

Several countries have constitutional anti-discrimination provisions which explicitly cover disability. These are: Austria,[27] Brazil,[28] Canada,[29] Finland,[30] Fiji,[31] the Gambia,[32] Ghana,[33] Germany,[34] Malawi,[35] New Zealand,[36] South Africa,[37] Switzerland[38] and Uganda.[39] These clauses generally prohibit discrimination against disabled people without defining what exactly constitutes discrimination. Some mention direct and indirect forms of discrimination.[40] The equality clause of Fiji's constitution is exceptionally broad, covering unfair direct and indirect discrimination and, in addition, stating:

---

[21] Discrimination Ordinance 1995, s 47.
[22] Training and Employment of Disabled Persons Act 1996, s 18.
[23] Equal Rights for Persons With Disabilities Law, ss 15 and 19(d).
[24] Magna Carta for Disabled Persons 1992 Title IV, s 46.
[25] Persons With Disabilities Act 1996, s 32.
[26] Persons With Disabilities Act 1992, s 10(c).
[27] Federal Constitutional Law as amended in 1997, Art 7.
[28] Constitution of the Federative Republic of Brazil, as of 1993, Art 7.
[29] Charter of Human Rights and Freedoms 1982, s 15.
[30] Constitution as amended in 1995 and in 2000, s 6.
[31] Constitution as of 1997, s 38.
[32] Draft of a Constitution for the Second Republic of Gambia of 1996, s 31. It is not certain that the Constitution has been adopted yet. The draft was released for publication in 1997.
[33] Constitution as of 1992, Art 29.
[34] Basic Law of the Federal Republic of Germany as amended in 1994, Art 3.
[35] Republic of Malawi (Constitution) Act 1994, s 20.
[36] Human Rights Act of 1993, s 21.
[37] Constitution as of 1996, s 9.
[38] Constitution as amended in 1999, Art 8.
[39] Constitution of the Republic of Uganda as of 1995, Art 21.
[40] Fiji: s 38(2); South Africa: ss 9, 3,4; Gambia: s 33; New Zealand: s 65.

Every person has the right of access without discrimination on a prohibited ground [such as disability] to shops, hotels, lodging-houses, public restaurants, places of public entertainment, public transport services, taxis and public places.[41]

The constitutions of Austria, Brazil, Canada, Germany, Ghana, Malawi, South Africa, Switzerland and Uganda also enable or entrust the legislature to take affirmative action to combat disability discrimination. Affirmative action means preferential treatment in the form of quotas or other means of positive discrimination. Affirmative action thus targets structural or institutional discrimination, which is one of the major obstacles to the equalisation of opportunities for disabled people.

In the employment area, many States have introduced quotas designed to benefit disabled people. These were introduced into disability policy after World War II and require employers to hire a certain percentage of disabled workers. They represent classic welfare measures, being founded on the idea that people with disabilities cannot compete in the real world.

With the rise of civil rights movements in the context of race and gender, quota policies gained a new equality-related dimension. This in turn influenced quota schemes in the disability field. In this respect, it is interesting to note that some of the constitutions provide for quota schemes in the field of employment,[42] whereas others provide for quotas in the area of political representation. The constitution of Malawi, for instance, provides that the Senate (a legislative body) shall include representatives of various interest groups including disability groups.[43] Similarly, the constitution of Uganda requires that the parliament shall consist of a certain number of representatives of disabled people.[44] Meanwhile, the Ugandan Parliament has five seats reserved for representatives of the disability community and the first minister for disability (and women and the elderly), Florence Nayiga Sekabiro, was herself a disabled person. Drawing on the affirmative action clause of the constitution, Uganda's legislators passed several statutes designed to increase the representation of disabled people in the public sphere. An example is the Local Government Act 1997 according to which a certain number of seats in elected political bodies at all levels are allocated to disabled people. As a result, there are now more than 2,000 disabled elected officials at all levels, from the parish to the district level.[45] Another interesting characteristic of those constitutions that have been amended to include disability in the prohibition of discrimination is that

---

[41] S 38(4).
[42] Brazil with respect to public employment, Art 37 of the Constitution.
[43] S 68(2)(i).
[44] Art 78(1)(c).
[45] These numbers were given by Mrs Nayiga at an international human rights seminar for young disabled women in New York, 1–7 June 2000.

they recognise the right to use sign language. The constitutions of Finland,[46] South Africa[47] and Canada[48] contain such provisions.[49]

Constitutional anti-discrimination clauses seem to be more effective in achieving social change than do criminal anti-discrimination clauses. Because the constitution is generally the highest law of the land, constitutional amendments receive more public attention and may render lower law unconstitutional and void. Furthermore constitutional amendments must be observed by the judiciary and may thus lead to reform in disability case law. Yet, for several reasons, constitutional disability discrimination law has had only limited effect.

First, some constitutions give no substantive rights to citizens, which means that a disabled person may not enforce the anti-discrimination clause in court. Second, constitutional rights are applicable only in public or 'vertical law.' Constitutional provisions protect disabled people only from discrimination by state entities, not by private employers or private providers of goods and services. Finally, constitutional provisions tend to be broad and vague. None of the constitutional provisions (apart from those of New Zealand)[50] define either disability or discrimination. This leaves vast discretion to the courts. Court rulings are very much determined by the legal culture. In Germany, for example, where there is no history of civil rights legislation and litigation, the constitutional anti-discrimination clause has been rendered a toothless tiger by a decision of the Federal Constitutional Court in 1996. In a case filed by a girl who used a wheelchair and who was denied access to a mainstream school, the Court decided that the constitutional anti-discrimination clause was not violated by the school authorities.[51] The reasoning of the Court is reminiscent of a case that was decided more than 150 years ago by the US Supreme Court upholding racial segregation in schools. Like the court in *Plessy v Ferguson* in 1896,[52] the German Court reasoned that educational segregation of disabled children is not discriminatory because it is separate but equal. The separate but equal ruling of *Plessy* was struck down in the US in 1954 with the groundbreaking decision of *Brown v Board of Education of Topeka*[53] in which the Supreme Court finally acknowledged that separate educational facilities in the context of race are inherently unequal. The German Federal Constitutional

---

[46] S 17.

[47] S 6.

[48] S 14 confers the right to an interpreter to any deaf party or witness in legal proceedings.

[49] Though Portugal's constitution has no anti-discrimination clause which explicitly includes disability, it should be mentioned here that the right to use sign language was amended in 1997: Art 74.

[50] Because the Human Rights Act 1993 is an entire statute dealing with discrimination. The Constitution of New Zealand consists of several legislative acts.

[51] Bundesverfassungsgericht, Urteil vom 8 October 1996, Europaeische Grundrechtszeitschrift 1997, s 586.

[52] 163 US 537 (1896).

[53] 349 US 294 (1955).

Court, however, was very reluctant to consider exclusion from education as potential discrimination. While it acknowledged that it would be discriminatory to deny admission to a disabled student who did not need any accommodations or special services, it was unwilling to extend this to disabled students who needed ramps, lifts, sign language interpreters, alternative reading formats or any kind of special education services. Thus, the medical model of disability was reinforced by this first decision on the new German anti-discrimination clause for disabled people.

Whilst the German experience testifies to the potential weakness of anti-discrimination constitutional clauses at the mercy of judicial interpretation, the experience of Ireland illustrates what can happen in the absence of strong constitutional anti-discrimination provisions. Because the equality clause in the Irish Constitution of 1937 is exceptionally weak, the Irish Supreme Court was able to strike down two pieces of discrimination legislation in 1997 which covered disability as well as other grounds. The Court found that the statutory requirement to engage in reasonable accommodations violated the property rights of employers.[54] The laws had to be redrafted and were weakened with respect to disability. Thus, where countries have written constitutions it is important that they have strong equality clauses which can serve as a firm foundation for statutory anti-discrimination laws.

Finally, a positive example of how to interpret vague constitutional equality clauses is provided by a 1997 decision of the Supreme Court of Canada. *Eldridge v British Columbia*[55] concerned the failure of British Columbia to provide medical interpretation services to deaf patients. Robin Eldridge had been unable to communicate with her physician, and John and Linda Warren had undergone the ordeal of giving birth to their twins without being able to fully comprehend what their doctors and nurses were telling them. The plaintiffs framed their action under the equality clause (s 15 of the Charter), claiming that provincial hospitals legislation discriminated against deaf people by failing to provide for sign language interpretive services when effective communication is an inherent and necessary component of the delivery of medical services. Though the lower courts rejected their claim, the Supreme Court of Canada held that the equality clause had been violated. By interpreting the equality clause so as to recognise that certain groups may need some accommodation in order to enjoy equality, *Eldridge* at least creates the possibility that s 15 of the Canadian

---

[54] *In the Matter of Article 26 of the Constitution of Ireland and in the Matter of the Employment Equality Bill,* judgment of the Supreme Court, May 1997; *Re Article 26 and the Equal Status Bill,* judgment of the Supreme Court, May 1997. See G Quinn, *From Charity to Rights—The Evolution of the Rights-Based Approach to Disability: International and Irish Perspectives,* CPI Handbook of Services (Dublin, 2000), available at www.enableireland.ie/accesswest/intros/essayindex.html (last viewed 3 March 2002).
[55] *Eldridge v British Columbia (Attorney General)* (1997) 151 DLR (4th) 577 (SCC).

Charter requires governments to take positive and substantive steps to ensure that disabled people (and other groups who experience discrimination) receive the 'equal protection and equal benefit' of the law. However, despite encouraging obiter comments, the Supreme Court has continued to leave open the issue of positive obligations under the equality clause.[56]

3.2.3 Civil Rights Laws

A third approach is to enact civil rights anti-discrimination laws for disabled people. A number of countries have adopted such laws and more are about to do so.[57] Countries with a civil rights oriented disability discrimination law are: Australia,[58] Belgium,[59] Canada,[60] Chile,[61] Costa Rica,[62] Ethiopia,[63] Finland,[64] France,[65] Germany,[66] Ghana,[67] Guatemala,[68] Hong Kong,[69] Hungary,[70] India,[71] Ireland,[72] Israel,[73] Korea,[74] Madagascar,[75] Malta,[76] Mauritius,[77] Namibia,[78] the Netherlands,[79] Nigeria,[80] the Philippines,[81] Portugal,[82]

---

[56] *Vriend* v *Alberta* [1998] 1 SCR 493. For more comprehensive analysis see B Porter, 'Beyond *Andrews*: substantive equality and positive obligations after *Eldridge* and *Vriend*' (1998) 9/3 *Forum Constitutionnel* 71–82; DM Lepofsky, 'The Charter's guarantee of equality to people with disabilities—how well is it working?' (1998) 16 *Windsor Yearbook of Access to Justice* 155–214; M Jackman, '"Giving real effect to equality": *Eldridge v British Columbia (Attorney General)* and *Vriend v Alberta*' (1998) 4/2 *Review of Constitutional Studies* 352–71.

[57] Eg, Austria, Germany, The Netherlands, Portugal, Switzerland.

[58] Disability Discrimination Act 1992.

[59] Act to Combat Discrimination and to Amend the Act of 15 February 1993 to Establish a Centre for Equal Opportunity and to Combat Racism (adopted 25 February 2003).

[60] Canadian Human Rights Act, RSC 1985, c H–6.

[61] Act No 19.284 of 1994.

[62] Law 7600 for Equalization of Opportunities for Persons with Disabilities (1996).

[63] The Rights of Disabled Persons to Employment, Proclamation No 101/1994.

[64] Ch 2 s 1 Employment Contracts Act (55/2001).

[65] Labour Code Art 1.122–45 and a bill is in the pipeline.

[66] S 81(2) Social Law Code, Book Nine of 2001 (SGB IX) and Act on the Equalization of Persons with Disabilities (BGG) of 2002.

[67] Persons with Disabilities Act 1993.

[68] Act for the Protection of Persons with Disabilities, Decree No 135–96 (1996).

[69] Disability Discrimination Ordinance 1990.

[70] Act No XXVI of 1998 on Provision of the Rights of Persons Living with Disability and their Equality of Opportunity (hereinafter cited as Act No XXVI).

[71] The Persons with Disabilities (Equal Opportunities, Protection of Rights and Full Participation) Act 1995.

[72] Employment Equality Act of 1998, Equal Status Act of 2000 and National Disability Authority Act 2000.

[73] Equal Rights for People with Disabilities Law, 5758–1998 (hereinafter cited as ERPWDL).

[74] Act Relating to the Employment Promotion, etc of the Handicapped, Law No 4219 (1990) and Special Education Promotion Law (1994).

[75] Labour Code as of 29 September 1994.

[76] Equal Opportunities (Persons with Disability) Act of 10 February 2000.

[77] Training and Employment of Disabled Persons Act (Act No 9 of 1996).

[78] Labour Act as amended in 1992.

[79] Act on Equal Treatment on Grounds of Disability and Chronic Disease of 2003.

[80] Nigerians with Disability Decree 1993.

[81] Magna Carta for Disabled Persons 1992.

[82] Labour Code as of 2003.

South Africa,[83] Spain,[84] Sri Lanka,[85] Sweden,[86] Switzerland,[87] the UK,[88] the US,[89] Zambia[90] and Zimbabwe.[91] With the exception of the law of Chile, all of these statutes cover employment-related discrimination against disabled people. Some are labour laws and thus only cover employment discrimination.[92] The laws differ markedly in their coverage of other areas. The most comprehensive disability discrimination laws are to be found in Australia, Canada, Hong Kong, Malta, the Philippines, the UK and the US.

The Australian Disability Discrimination Act 1992 prohibits discrimination in the areas of work, housing, education, access to premises, clubs and sports and other facilities, land possession and the provision of goods and services.[93] The Canadian Human Rights Act 1985 covers discrimination in the provision of goods, services, facilities or accommodation that are available to the general public (including transportation). Further, it prohibits discrimination in employment, the provision of commercial premises or housing.[94] The 1995 Disability Discrimination Ordinance of Hong Kong covers employment, education, premises, goods and services, facilities for the general public, barrister chambers, clubs and sports, and government activities.[95] The 2000 Equal Opportunities (Persons with Disability) Act of Malta contains anti-discrimination provisions in the areas of employment, education, public premises and goods and services as well as housing. The 1992 Magna Carta for Persons with Disabilities of the Philippines prohibits disability-based discrimination in employment, transportation, public accommodation and goods and services.[96] The British Disability Discrimination Act 1995 covers discrimination in employment, in the provision of goods, facilities and services and, to some degree, also covers the area of education and public transportation.[97] Finally, the ADA prohibits

[83] Employment Equity Bill 1998 and Skills Development Bill 1998.

[84] Statute of Workers' Rights (Royal Legislative Decree 1/1995, 24 March). A more comprehensive disability discrimination bill was introduced into Parliament in May 2003 (Law on Equal Opportunities and Non-Discrimination against people and universal accessibility for disabled people (PLIO)).

[85] Protection of the Rights of Persons with Disabilities Act, No 28 of 1996.

[86] Prohibition of Discrimination Against Persons With Disabilities in Employment Act, SFS No 1999–132, 1999.

[87] Federal Act on the Elimination of Discrimination against Persons with Disabilities of 13 December 2002.

[88] Disability Discrimination Act 1995 and Disability Rights Commission Act 1999.

[89] Americans With Disabilities Act 1990, which needs to be read together with other disability discrimination laws enacted earlier (see n 14 above).

[90] Persons With Disabilities Act 1996 (Act No 33 of 1996).

[91] Disabled Persons Act 1992.

[92] Canada (Employment Equity Act 1994–95), Ethiopia, Germany (s 81(2) Social Law Code No 9 of 2001), Ireland (Employment Equality Act), Korea (Act Relating to the Employment Promotion, etc), Madagascar, Mauritius, Namibia, Portugal, Spain (Statute of Workers' Rights 1995), South Africa (Employment Equity Bill of 1998) and Sweden.

[93] Ss 3, 15, 22–30.

[94] Ss 5–11.

[95] Ss 11–20, 24, 25–9, 33–7.

[96] Title III, ch I–III.

[97] Ss 4, 19, 22, 29, 30, 32–9, 40–7.

discrimination in the area of employment, state and local government activities (including education, transportation and social services), public accommodations (goods and services) and telecommunication.[98]

The civil rights laws of the other countries are also broad in scope in that the legislation covers a wide range of areas, not all of which are covered by anti-discrimination provisions. For instance, the 1996 Act on Equal Opportunities for Persons with Disabilities of Costa Rica covers access to education, employment, public transport, public services, information and communication, and cultural, sports and leisure activities. However, discrimination is explicitly prohibited only in relation to employment, public health services and participation in culture, sports and leisure activities.[99]

The Indian Persons With Disabilities (Equal Opportunities, Protection of Rights And Full Participation) Act 1995 differs from the other civil rights laws in that it has rather weak non-discrimination provisions but instead provides for quotas in various areas. Non-discrimination provisions cover transportation, roads, built environment and government employment (excluding recruitment).[100] Duties to enable access for disabled people apply only 'within the limits of ... economic capacity and development' and are thus relatively easy to evade. A three per cent quota scheme applies to government employment, government-aided educational institutions and poverty alleviation schemes.[101] The government employment quota system reserves one per cent to persons with certain types of impairment, notably visual, hearing and physical impairments.[102] Of interest is that any vacancy under the three per cent quota scheme in government employment will be carried forward to the next year.[103] Theoretically, this might lead to a situation where a government agency can only hire or promote employees who are disabled. Many other countries have quota provisions, particularly in the public employment field.

Compared to criminal and constitutional anti-discrimination laws, civil rights disability discrimination legislation is more detailed as to its scope. Most of the laws also provide a definition of what constitutes discriminatory practice or equality. In addition, all the civil rights disability discrimination laws have provisions on enforcement mechanisms. The concepts of both discrimination and equality, and the different enforcement mechanisms, will be discussed below.

3.2.4 Social Welfare Laws

Finally, some countries tackle the issue of disability discrimination through social welfare laws relating to disability. These countries are: Bolivia,[104]

---

[98] Title I–IV.
[99] Arts 24, 31 and 55.
[100] Ch VIII, ss 44, 45, 46 and 47.
[101] Ch VI, ss 33–40.
[102] Ch VI, s 33 (i)–(iii).
[103] Ch VI, s 36.
[104] Act No 1678 on the Person with Disability (1985).

China,[105] Costa Rica,[106] Germany,[107] Korea,[108] Nicaragua,[109] Panama,[110] Spain[111] and the US.[112]

In these laws, anti-discrimination provisions are found alongside more traditional provisions on prevention of disability and rehabilitation. Non-discrimination provisions in social welfare legislation tend to be vague and limited to one area—eg public employment or public education. For instance, the Spanish Act on the Social Integration of the Disabled 1982 deals with the prevention of impairment; diagnosis and assessment; the system of benefits in cash and kind; medical and vocational rehabilitation; and community services and integration at work. The only anti-discrimination provision in the Act states that any disability-based discriminatory provision in labour regulations, collective agreements, individual contracts or unilateral decisions shall be null and void.[113]

The German Social Law Code, Book I (SGB I) and Social Law Code, Book X (SGB X), as amended in 2001, address the issues of accessibility in social administration and discrimination against deaf or hearing impaired people. Section 17(2) of SGB I and s 19(1) of SGB X provide that deaf people have the right to use German sign language when communicating with social administration. Section 17(1)(lit4) prescribes that social agencies must ensure that their offices and their services are barrier-free in relation to architecture and communication. Social Law Code, Book IX (SGB IX) of 2001 prohibits (in Article 81(2)) employment discrimination against severely disabled people in the public and private spheres.[114]

The Chinese Law of the People's Republic of China of 1990 contains a general prohibition clause regarding disability discrimination[115] but does not specify what this means for the organisation of society. A textual analysis of the law gives the impression that the traditional medical model of disability (institutionalisation and segregation) provides the framework of the Act. Article 29, for instance, lays down the rule of concentrated employment for disabled people as a guiding principle. This means that

---

[105] Law of the People's Republic of China on the Protection of Disabled Persons (1990).

[106] Decree No 119101–S–MEP–TSS–PLAN of 1998.

[107] Social Law Code (SGB) Ninth Book (IX) (Rehabilitation and Participation of People with Disabilities).

[108] The Welfare Law for Persons with Disabilities, Law No 4179 (1989) and The Special Education Promotion Law as of 1994.

[109] Act No 202 Regulations and Politics Regarding Disabled in Nicaragua/Act for the Prevention, Rehabilitation and Equalization of Opportunities for Persons with Disabilities in Nicaragua (1995).

[110] Family Law Code, Act No 3 as amended in 1994.

[111] Law on the Social Integration of the Disabled (1982).

[112] Rehabilitation Act of 1973.

[113] Title VII, s 38(2).

[114] Thus, s 81(2) SGB IX is rather an employment discrimination law and should be characterised as a civil rights law rather than a social (welfare) law. However, the law (SGB IX) as a whole clearly belongs to the area of social welfare law.

[115] Ch I, Art 3.

employment opportunities are offered by special welfare enterprises and institutions. Within these special institutions, discrimination against disabled people in relation to recruitment, employment, promotion, determining professional or technical titles, payment, welfare and other aspects is prohibited.[116] Given that this is the only detailed anti-discrimination provision in the whole Act, it seems that the law conveys a rather peculiar concept of equality. The medical model approach of the law is also evident in some provisions regarding the obligations of disabled people. According to Article 10, Chinese disabled people 'should display an optimistic and enterprising spirit,' which implies the notion that impairment leads to negative attitudes and depression.

Some countries, such as the Philippines, have laws that could be characterised as both social welfare and civil rights laws. The Magna Carta of the Philippines, however, contains a clear statement which manifests the legislature's intent to move from the medical model to the human rights model of disability. Title I ch I s 2(b) states that 'Persons with disabilities' rights must never be perceived as welfare services by the Government.'

The history of US disability discrimination law shows that anti-discrimination provisions for disabled people often appear initially in social law. This is the area of law where disability law tends to be developed. The US first prohibited certain forms of discrimination against people with disabilities in the 1973 Rehabilitation Act. The famous s 504 provides that every entity which receives federal financial assistance or is conducted by any federal agency must not discriminate against an 'otherwise qualified' disabled person. The 1988 amendment of the Fair Housing Act, which prohibits discrimination in housing matters, was the first step towards including disability in general civil rights legislation in the US. The final step was taken with the enactment of the ADA. Similarly, Costa Rica and Spain have disability discrimination provisions within social welfare legislation as well as civil rights laws.

In sum, discrimination provisions in social welfare legislation tend to be less comprehensive and reform-oriented. The paradigm shift from the medical model of disability to the human rights model of disability seems to be less obvious in this kind of legislation.

3.3 Different Protected Groups: The Disability-Specific Approach or the Trans-Group Approach

Some of the anti-discrimination laws covering disabled people protect them as part of a wider group (group laws), whereas others focus exclusively on disability. The group law approach protects other minorities or groups which historically have been the targets of discriminatory practices (such as

---

[116] Art 34.

women, homosexuals, children, the elderly, linguistic or religious minorities). With the exception of Ghana,[117] all of the constitutional discrimination provisions protect disabled people as part of a wider group. The same is true for discrimination provisions in employment law[118] as well as criminal law. Disability discrimination laws that are designed as civil or social laws tend to be aimed exclusively at disabled people.

As well as protecting people who are currently disabled, some laws also protect those who have been disabled in the past,[119] those who may become disabled in the future,[120] or those who are wrongly regarded as being disabled.[121] Furthermore, some laws also protect family members or other associates of disabled people,[122] and people who are victimised because they make a complaint about an act of discrimination or exercise other anti-discrimination rights.[123]

Most discrimination laws which take the form of civil rights or social welfare legislation contain a definition of disability. Commonly, the definition is medically oriented in that disability is defined as a physical or mental impairment which results in some significant functional limitation. The issue of disability definitions is not discussed in detail in this chapter because it has been done amply elsewhere.[124]

3.4 Different Equality and Discrimination Concepts

The underlying equality concepts to be found in the disability discrimination laws under review vary. Some laws support a more formal equality model, in that they guarantee equality rights on the condition that a disabled person adapts fully to the non-disabled culture and society. Some constitutional anti-discrimination clauses can be viewed this way, as shown by the German education case.[125]

Other laws explicitly state that, in some circumstances, disability may provide a legitimate basis on which to discriminate. For instance, the 1992

[117] The constitutional equality clause (Art 17) does not cover disability, which is dealt with by a special provision (Art 29).

[118] Except for Germany's s 81(2) Social Law Code IX, which only covers severely disabled employees.

[119] Australia, Canada (Human Rights Act), Hong Kong, New Zealand, the Philippines, the UK and the US.

[120] Australia, Belgium, Hong Kong and Sweden.

[121] Australia, Hong Kong, the Netherlands, New Zealand, the Philippines and the US.

[122] Australia, Hong Kong, Malta, New Zealand, the Philippines and the US re public accommodations, goods and services (Title III) of ADA.

[123] Australia, Canada (Human Rights Act), New Zealand and the UK.

[124] Eg A Hendriks, 'Different definition—same problem—one way out?' in M Breslin and S Yee (eds), *Disability Rights Law And Policy* (Ardsley, Transnational, 2002) 195; R Luckasson, 'Terminology and power' in S Herr *et al* (eds), *The Human Rights of Persons With Intellectual Disabilities* (Oxford, New York, Oxford University Press, 2003) 49; A Dundes Renteln, 'Cross-cultural perceptions of disability: policy implications of divergent views' in S Herr *et al* (eds), *ibid* 59.

[125] Bundesverfassungsgericht, Urteil vom 8 October 1996, Europaeische Grundrechtszeitschrift 1997, s 586.

Labour Act of Namibia provides that a person shall not be regarded as having been unfairly discriminated against if, because of his/her disability, s/he is unable to perform the job.[126] The 1992 Persons With Disabilities Act of Zimbabwe provides that disability may be a legitimate reason for employment discrimination,[127] and the denial of any public service or amenity seems to be excused if it is 'motivated by a genuine concern for the safety of the disabled person.'[128] While the Korean Special Education Promotion Law (as amended in 1994) prohibits discrimination against disabled students in all schools, only heads of special schools

> should take appropriate measures to provide appropriate convenience for entrance examinations and schooling for children with disabilities based on types and degree of disability.[129]

Thus, the liability of heads of mainstream schools for discriminatory omissions is implicitly limited.

About a quarter of the laws reviewed here, however, are based on a structural equality concept. This includes a commitment to the view that society must change in order to guarantee true equal opportunity for disabled people. The key phrase in this respect is 'reasonable accommodations' or 'reasonable adjustments,' or 'effective accommodations' which have to be undertaken by the employer, the service provider, government or any other entity under anti-discrimination obligations. The laws of the following countries include such a duty, even though it does not always apply to all areas covered by the anti-discrimination rule: Australia,[130] Belgium,[131] Canada,[132] Germany,[133] Hong Kong,[134] Hungary, [135] Ireland,[136] Israel,[137] Malta,[138] the Netherlands,[139] New Zealand,[140] the Philippines,[141] Sweden,[142] the UK,[143] the US[144] and Zimbabwe.[145]

---

[126] S 107(2)(b).

[127] S 9(2)(b).

[128] S 10(b)(ii).

[129] Art 13.

[130] Eg, s 5(2) and s 45.

[131] Art 4.

[132] S 5 of the Employment Equity Act.

[133] S 81 (4)(lit 4) of Social Law Code IX. The failure to provide reasonable accommodations is, however, not explicitly recognised as a form of discrimination.

[134] In various provisions, eg ss 12, 24–6.

[135] Ss 5–8.

[136] S 16(3)(b) of the Employment Equality Act 1988 and s 4(1) of the Equal Status Act 2000.

[137] S 8(e).

[138] S 7(2)(d).

[139] Art 2 (effective accommodation).

[140] Eg ss 29, 35, 43, 56, and 60.

[141] Title II, ch 1–7 (ss 5–31).

[142] Ss 3 and 6.

[143] Eg ss 6, 21, 32.

[144] Eg s 504 of the Rehabilitation Act, and Title I s 102, Title II s 202 and Title III s 302 of the ADA.

[145] Ss 7 and 9.

Another indicator of a structural equality concept in discrimination law may be found in affirmative action provisions because they imply that positive action has to be taken in order to achieve true equality. At least sixteen countries[146] have affirmative action provisions, most of them relating to quota schemes.

The main focus of the majority of discrimination laws is on employment discrimination. This might be explained by the fact that this is the field where discrimination law relating to groups more generally (eg race and gender) has been developed. Thus, it makes sense to follow that path for disabled people. However, it should be taken into account that this is the realm of economic, social and cultural human rights; the set of human rights traditionally applied to disability, whereas civil and political rights have generally been neglected in disability policy. In this regard, it is remarkable that some of the disability discrimination statutes explicitly guarantee non-discrimination in relation to civil and political rights for disabled people.[147] Others, however, do not explicitly mention such rights because they are covered by the anti-discrimination provisions relating to public premises, services and accommodations.

The concept of discrimination may be derived from the definition of disability-based discrimination and the areas covered by the discrimination prohibitions. The latter issue has already been discussed in this chapter. The focus here will therefore be on the definition of discrimination; a point dealt with in half of the reviewed statutes.

The majority of statutes define discrimination as unfavorable treatment on the basis of disability,[148] whereas a minority define discrimination as unjustified differentiation.[149] Some laws distinguish between direct and indirect forms of discrimination[150]—the latter commonly defined as the application of requirements or conditions with which it will generally be more difficult for disabled people to comply. The aforementioned key phrase 'denial of reasonable accommodations' is contained in the discrimination concept of the laws in 16 countries.[151] Interestingly, some discrimination

---

[146] Canada (Human Rights Act), Germany (Social Law Code IX), Ghana, Ethiopia (but very weak), India, Israel, Mauritius, Nigeria, Philippines, Portugal, South Africa (Employment Equity Act, but specifically excluding quotas), Spain, Uganda, US, Zambia and Korea.

[147] The Nigerians With Disability Decree has provisions on the right to vote and the right to information (ss 12 and 13). The Magna Carta of the Philippines has provisions on the rights to vote, to assembly and to organise (ss 29–31).

[148] Australia (s 5), Canada (HRA, ss 5–11), Fiji (Art 38), Germany (Art 3), Guatemala (Arts 35 and 44), Hong Kong (s 6), Ireland (s 16 EEA, s 3 ESA), Namibia (s 107), Mauritius (s 16), New Zealand (ss 22, 37, 42, 53 ff), Philippines (s 32), South Africa (s 9), Sweden (s 3), UK (s 5) and Zambia (s 19).

[149] France (Art 225–1), Ethiopia (s 3), Luxembourg (Art 454), Netherlands (Art 1), Uganda (Art 21).

[150] Australia (s 6), Fiji (Art 38), Namibia (s 107), New Zealand (s 65), the Philippines (s 32), South Africa (s 9), Sweden (ss 3 and 4) and Zambia (s 19).

[151] Australia, Belgium, Canada, Germany, Hong Kong, Hungary, Ireland, Israel, Malta, Netherlands, New Zealand, Philippines, Sweden, UK, US and Zimbabwe (see nn 122–37 above).

Acts have provisions on access to public places, buildings and transport, but inaccessibility is not defined as a discriminatory practice.[152] Where access is not formulated as an individual right, it seems to be provided as a welfare service.

Some of the discrimination laws treat acts of harassment and victimisation as prohibited forms of discrimination.[153] The Canadian Human Rights Act additionally outlaws discriminatory public communications, publications and hate messages.[154] Another interesting finding is that a significant number of discrimination laws also address the issue of exploitation or abuse of disabled people.[155]

While few discrimination statutes support the principle of segregated education for disabled students,[156] only a minority of the Acts convey a clear statement that separate education is inherently unequal and a classic form of disability discrimination.[157] The most comprehensive definitions of disability discrimination can be found in the laws of Australia, Belgium, Canada, Hong Kong, Malta, New Zealand, the Philippines, the UK and the US. These laws define discrimination in relation to every area covered, such as employment, public accommodation, goods and services. With regard to each area, the definitions consist of long lists of acts that are considered discriminatory, such as denial of participation, participation under unequal conditions, or separate benefits. Some of the laws explicitly mention auxiliary aids, guide dogs and interpreters as illegitimate reasons for discriminatory treatment (eg Australia and Hong Kong).

3.5 Different Enforcement Mechanisms

Generally the enforcement of legislation is the task of public administrative agencies and courts. Legislation which aims to transform society to some extent, such as human rights and discrimination legislation, usually establishes some kind of special enforcement body. This might be a human rights or an equal opportunity commission, an ombudsperson, a national council or an agency. Of the disability legislation under review, only the civil rights or social welfare law statutes include provisions for enforcement or monitoring.

Thus, the Australian Disability Discrimination Act establishes a Human Rights and Equal Opportunity Commission and a Disability Discrimination

---

[152] Brazil, China, Costa Rica, Ghana, Guatemala, Israel and Nicaragua.
[153] Australia (ss 35–40), Canada (HRA, s 14) Hong Kong (s 7), Israel (s 10), Portugal (Art 24) Sweden (s 9), UK (s 55).
[154] Ss 12 and 13.
[155] Costa Rica (Law on Equal Opportunity, Art 4), Ghana (Constitution, Art 29) and Panama (Art 520).
[156] Eg Brazil and Nigeria.
[157] In my opinion the laws of the following countries can be read this way: Australia, Canada, Hong Kong, Hungary, the Philippines, US and Zambia.

Commission.[158] The Canadian Human Rights Act is enforced by a Human Rights Commission and a Human Rights Tribunal.[159] The Equal Rights for Persons With Disabilities Law of Israel entrusts various ministries with the enforcement of the law and additionally establishes a Commission for Equal Rights.[160] In the UK, a Disability Rights Commission is the watchdog for the Disability Discrimination Act.[161]

A significant number of acts entrust representatives of disability organisations with the task of monitoring implementation. For instance, the Law of the People's Republic of China on the Protection of Persons With Disabilities establishes the China Persons with Disabilities' Federation, which is responsible for representing and protecting the rights and interests of disabled people in China.[162] The Hungarian Discrimination Act establishes the National Disability Affairs Council in which disability organisations have to be represented.[163] The Indian law established a multi-sector planning and monitoring mechanism. There is a Central Coordination Committee with the Chief Commissioner for Persons with Disabilities and several State Coordination Committees, which are focal points of disability matters at the State level. The law requires that a certain number of seats in each committee be filled by disabled people.[164] The Nigerian discrimination law establishes a National Commission of Persons with Disabilities, whose chair must be disabled and in which all the major disability groups must be represented.[165] Similarly, the Persons With Disabilities Act of Ghana establishes the National Council on Persons with Disabilities in which six seats are reserved for representatives of disability organisations. The law of Zimbabwe establishes a Disability Board in which half of the seats must be filled by representatives of disability organisations.[166] Similar provisions can be found in the law of Malta with respect to the National Commission of Persons with Disabilities.[167] The same holds true for the Zambian Agency for Persons with Disability, which is the enforcement body of the Zambian discrimination law.[168]

---

[158] Ss 67 and 113.
[159] Ss 26 and 48.
[160] Ss 20–25.
[161] Established by the Disability Rights Commission Act 1999. This new body replaces the former National Disability Council which was established by the DDA but was much weaker. S Minty, 'Introducing the UK Disability Rights Commission' available at http://www.disabili tyworld.org/June-July2000/Governance/UKDisabilityRights.htm.
[162] Art 8.
[163] S 24.
[164] Ss 3, 9, and 13. The disability movement in India is rather disappointed with the slow implementation of these provisions. A Mohit, 'Governance & legislation: initiatives of the Government of India to advance Asia & Pacific Decade of Disabled Persons' available at http://www. disabilityworld.org/April-May2000/Governance/India.htm.
[165] S 14.
[166] Ss 4, 5, and 7.
[167] S 21.
[168] Ss 6 and 25.

The functions of these monitoring bodies are manifold and range from advisory and information-gathering for the government and raising awareness among the general public to investigation and complaint filing. The Disability Board in Zimbabwe and the Zambia Agency for Persons with Disabilities also have the mandate to issue 'adjustment orders,' requiring specific action from owners whose premises or services are inaccessible to disabled people.

4 CONCLUSION

Disability discrimination laws around the world vary widely. Disabled people may be protected against discrimination by constitutional, criminal, civil rights or social welfare law. The most comprehensive legal method of preventing disability-based discrimination seems to be the civil rights approach. However, it should be noted that the principal method used here for evaluating these laws was a textual analysis of the relevant pieces of legislation. The few cases cited indicate that the impact an anti-discrimination law may have on society depends, to a large extent, on the attitude of the judiciary rather than on the text of the legislation itself.

Today there is no universal definition of disability-based discrimination and no universal concept of equalisation of opportunities for disabled people. Definitions of discrimination range from unjustified differentiation to direct or indirect unfavourable treatment, to detailed lists of discriminatory practices. However, it can be concluded that modern disability discrimination laws adhere to the principle of desegregation, de-institutionalisation and the duty to provide reasonable accommodations, and thus to the active tackling of structural discrimination. In addition to a strong definition of discrimination, the law needs to provide clear and effective enforcement mechanisms through which disabled people, individually or as a group, should play a major role.

7

Implementing the Disability Provisions of the Framework Employment Directive: Room for Exercising National Discretion

LISA WADDINGTON*

1 INTRODUCTION

THE ADOPTION OF the European Community Framework Employment Directive,[1] which prohibits employment discrimination on the grounds of religion or belief, disability, age and sexual orientation, has already resulted in much academic commentary and analysis.[2] The Directive, both as a whole and as a set of individual articles, has been

* EDF Chair in European Disability Law, Maastricht University. I am grateful to Marianne Gijzen for commenting on an earlier version of this paper and for providing background information, to Mariken Lenaerts for editorial assistance, and to the following colleagues who provided background information on national legislation: Ulrike Davy, Theresia Degener, Nikos Gavalas, Paul Lappalainen, Philip Scott, Pilar Villarino and Silvia Yee. This paper was written within the framework of the Aspasia project sponsored by the Netherlands Organisation for Scientific Research (NWO) on 'The Emerging Equality Principle in EU Law'. The author gratefully acknowledges the support of NWO. The usual disclaimers apply.
[1] Council Directive 2000/78/EC of 27 November 2000 establishing a general framework for equal treatment in employment and occupation, [2000] OJ L303/16.
[2] A non-exhaustive list of relevant literature in English includes: M Bell, 'Article 13 EC: the European Commission's anti-discrimination proposals' (2000) 29 *Industrial Law Journal* 79–84; Lord Lester, 'New European equality measures' [2000] *Public Law* 562–67; L Waddington, 'Article 13 EC: setting priorities in the proposals for a horizontal employment directive' (2000) 29 *Industrial Law Journal* 176–81; P Skidmore, 'EC framework employment directive on equal treatment in employment: towards a comprehensive community anti-discrimination policy?' (2001) 30 *Industrial Law Journal* 126–32; S Fredman, 'Equality: a new generation?' (2001) 30 *Industrial Law Journal* 145–68; U O'Hare, 'Enhancing European equality rights: a new regional framework' (2001) 8 *Maastricht Journal of European and Comparative Law* 144–65; L Waddington and M Bell, 'More equal than others: distinguishing European Union equality directives' (2001) 38 *Common Market Law Review* 587–611; C Barnard, 'The changing scope of the fundamental principle of equality?' (2001) 46 *McGill Law Journal* 955; M Bell and L Waddington, 'Reflecting on inequalities in European Community equality law' [2003] *European Law Review* 349–69.

critically reviewed and commentators have reflected on how various provisions might be interpreted, as well as on the relationship between the Directive and other Community equality instruments. Five years on from its adoption, the time seems ripe to take the discussion a step further and to begin considering the impact which the Directive is having on the non-discrimination laws of the Member States and, in the context of this book, national disability non-discrimination legislation in particular. This is especially so given that the deadline for implementing the Directive was 2 December 2003. However, as will be seen below, by no means have all—or even most—Member States fully respected this deadline.

Like all Community directives, the Framework Employment Directive allows a considerable margin of discretion to Member States in deciding how to achieve the set aims and goals. Different national approaches to securing implementation are therefore to be expected, and these will reflect the various choices made by the national legislators as well as the differing legal climate and set of traditions existing in each Member State. In light of this permitted room for variation, this chapter seeks to consider the impact the Framework Employment Directive is having on disability non-discrimination legislation in the Member States. The chapter will identify some of the areas in which Member States have (considerable) room for exercising national discretion when implementing the Directive, and consider how the choices made might impact on the effectiveness of the implementation legislation. This discussion will be illustrated with examples from implementation measures in selected Member States.

The chapter first provides a brief introduction to the Directive and considers the extent of the obligations imposed on Member States. A general overview of the kinds of national responses the Directive has prompted, in terms of implementation measures, is then provided. The bulk of the chapter consists of an examination of six areas which are covered in the Directive and which leave room for the exercise of national discretion at the transposition stage. Both the relevant provisions of the Directive and the legislative responses of selected Member States are considered, and the chapter reflects on the room for differing interpretations provided by the Directive and the consequences of the legal choices made by certain Member States when implementing the measure.

2 THE FRAMEWORK EMPLOYMENT DIRECTIVE

2.1 Content

It is not my intention to give a detailed overview of the Framework Employment Directive; this has been done amply elsewhere.[3] It will suffice

---

[3] See *ibid* for a list of relevant literature.

at this stage simply to mention some of the main elements of the Directive and to note that specific provisions are discussed in more detail later in the chapter.

The Framework Employment Directive was adopted in November 2000 and was the second so-called 'Article 13 Directive,' following on from the Race Directive adopted in June 2000.[4] It prohibits employment related discrimination (including that related to vocational training) on grounds of religion or belief, age, sexual orientation and disability.[5] Most of the Directive consists of 'common' provisions which apply equally to all grounds. In addition, a few provisions confer extra levels of protection, or deny the 'standard' level of protection, to certain grounds.

Discrimination is defined as including: direct discrimination; indirect discrimination; harassment; and an instruction to discriminate.[6] The broad employment-related scope is defined in Article 3. In addition, employers are obliged to provide a reasonable accommodation to disabled people, unless this would amount to a disproportionate burden.[7] Given that this protection is restricted to disabled people, it confers on them an additional level of protection not provided to other victims of discrimination under Community law.

Member States are allowed to adopt certain forms of positive action for all groups. With regard to disabled people, they are also permitted to adopt provisions relating to the protection of health and safety at work, or to safeguard or promote the integration of disabled people into the working environment.[8]

The Directive provides for relatively detailed enforcement provisions and sets certain requirements with regard to remedies and sanctions.

2.2 Obligations Imposed on Member States

As noted in the introduction, EC directives set goals which Member States are obliged to achieve within a given period, but leave Member States free to select the most appropriate means of achieving those goals.[9] Member States are therefore able to consider the existing relevant legal framework, national legal traditions and even to use means other than legislation (eg collective bargaining agreements).[10] Furthermore, the directive presently under discussion is a framework directive; it only sets the general

---

[4] Council Directive 2000/43/EC of 29 June 2000 implementing the principle of equal treatment between persons irrespective of racial or ethnic origin, [2000] OJ L180/22.

[5] Art 1.

[6] Art 2.

[7] Art 5.

[8] Art 7.

[9] See P Craig and G de Búrca, *EU Law, Text, Cases, and Materials* (Oxford, Oxford University Press, 1998), pp 108–09.

[10] Subject to the limits set by the ECJ regarding implementation by collective bargaining agreements.

parameters of the national implementation measures, leaving Member States a large amount of discretion when deciding how to implement it.

Some provisions in directives attain a relatively high level of specificity; meaning that Member States have less room for manoeuvre when implementing those provisions than with regard to those where little or no elaboration is given. Such a higher level of precision is, arguably, reflected in Article 2 of the Framework Employment Directive. This Article contains definitions of direct and indirect discrimination which, to a limited extent, build on already existing definitions in earlier legislation and in case-law of the European Court of Justice (ECJ).[11] Member States must define direct and indirect discrimination in line with these European definitions; although, as will be seen, even here there is some room for manoeuvre. Whilst some Member States have simply copied the definitions in the Directive, others have developed their own national definitions. The alternative definitions must nevertheless be in accordance with the meaning of the definitions in the Directive.

In contrast to the definitions provided for direct and indirect discrimination, there is no definition in the Directive of 'on the grounds of disability',[12] leaving Member States, at least initially, a great deal of discretion when deciding how to define the personal scope of the national implementation legislation.

It is possible that common European definitions and concepts will ultimately be developed in these relatively undefined areas. This is most likely to result from preliminary questions asked of the ECJ by national courts, which will require the Court, probably in a piecemeal manner, to develop EU-wide definitions and tools of interpretation.[13]

In addition to the text in the articles, each directive also contains a preamble. The paragraphs in the preamble, whilst not legally binding, can also contain elaboration on what is meant by certain phrases or requirements in the main body of the directive. This is the case, for example, with regard to the reasonable accommodation provision.[14] Preamble para 20 elaborates on the kinds of measures that can be taken to make a reasonable accommodation and para 21 provides some guidance on when making a reasonable accommodation will amount to a disproportionate burden.[15] However,

---

[11] See eg Case 43/75 *Defrenne v Sabena* [1976] ECR 455 and Case 129/80 *MacCarthys Ltd v Smith* [1980] ECR 1275 (both direct sex discrimination); Case 170/84 *Bilka-Kaufhaus GmbH v Weber von Hartz* [1986] ECR 1607 (indirect sex discrimination); and Case 237/94 *O'Flynn v Adjudication Officer* [1996] ECR I–2617 (indirect nationality discrimination). However, none of the definitions of direct and indirect discrimination developed by the ECJ in these cases completely match the definitions found in the Framework Employment Directive.

[12] Art 1.

[13] The gradual emergence of a set of EU-wide rules for interpretation is envisaged. An example of this approach can be found in the ECJ's ruling in Case C–13/94 *P v S* [1996] ECR I–2143 (see below).

[14] Art 5.

[15] See section 3.4 below.

given the relative brevity of this preamble (and, indeed, the main body of this Directive) this guidance is also necessarily limited.

2.3 National Responses to the Framework Employment Directive

Whilst the deadline for implementing the Directive was 2 December 2003, the Directive in fact allowed Member States to opt for a maximum of three additional years to take action to prohibit discrimination on the grounds of disability (and age).[16] It seems that only three Member States have requested such an extension. As a result there should, in theory, now exist a rich body of European national disability non-discrimination legislation, at least partially inspired by the Framework Employment Directive, available for analysis and discussion. Reality presents a somewhat different picture.[17]

At the time of completion of this paper (January 2004), four different national responses to the (disability) provisions of the Directive could be identified. First, some Member States (eg Austria)[18] have simply failed to

[16] Art 18 of the Directive. In order to make use of this possibility Member States were obliged to inform the Commission of their intention, and to give reasons for the delayed implementation. Member States which had neither implemented the disability provisions of the Directive by 2 December 2003 nor requested an extension by that date are regarded as being in breach of the Directive by the Commission, and the Commission has previously expressed its intention to initiate non-compliance procedures against these States. A Commission Press Release of 3 December 2003 noted that Denmark had requested a full three year extension, the UK was expected to ask for one additional year to implement the disability provisions and three years regarding the age provisions, whilst Belgium was expected to ask for three additional years to implement the age provisions. Memo/03/250, European Day of People with Disabilities, 1.

[17] The European Social Platform reported that only four Member States—the UK, Spain, France and Belgium—had fully implemented the Framework Employment Directive by the 2 December 2003 deadline. In fact it is questionable whether even these four States have fully implemented the Directive, with Belgium and the UK being reported elsewhere as having requested an extension, Spain having adopted a law designed to implement the disability provisions of the Directive on 31 December 2003 (ie after the deadline) and doubts being raised as to the compatibility with the Directive of pre-existing national legislation in France, where a bill to implement the disability provisions of the Directive is before Parliament (Projet de Loi pour l'égalité des droits et des chances, la participation et la citoyenneté des personnes handicapées).

[18] The Austrian Secretary of State for Social Security published a tentative draft for a bill on equal treatment of people with disabilities, inviting a number of other departments, the *Länder* (states), political parties, the social partners, and disability groups to participate in consultations. The January 2004 draft was in fact composed of three different draft bills: a bill on equal treatment of disabled people (*Behindertengleichstellung*), a bill on the establishment of an arbitration committee (*Schlichtungsstelle*) and an ombudsman, and a bill to amend the BEinstG 1969 (*Änderung des BEinstG*). The draft bill on equal treatment of disabled people launches a truly far reaching political initiative: the draft proposes to introduce a general prohibition of discrimination on account of disability and goes far beyond what is required by the Framework Employment Directive. When enacted, the prohibition of discrimination will extend to all possible areas other than employment (*Arbeitswelt*). Disability discrimination in employment and occupation will be addressed by a number of provisions to be inserted in the BEinstG 1969, as proposed by the draft bill to amend the BEinstG 1969. Finally, the draft bill on an arbitration committee is basically confined to rules on organic structures and functions of the committee and an ombudsman, as well as to procedural rules. I am grateful to Ulrike Davy for providing this information.

adopt any relevant legislation. The reasons for this inaction vary, and may include a lack of awareness of the extensive nature of the requirements set under the Directive, or political disruption caused by changes in government.[19] Second, some Member States (eg Italy,[20] Luxembourg[21] and Greece[22]) have essentially taken sections of the relevant language version of the Directive and either simply transformed them into national law or used them in modelling draft legislation. This approach is arguably an inappropriate means of implementing a framework directive, and it remains to be seen how national employers, workers and courts will respond to such generally phrased legislation. Third, in some Member States where disability non-discrimination legislation already existed (eg Germany[23] and Sweden[24]) the authorities have amended the relevant statutes in an attempt to fill identified lacunae so as to comply with the Directive. Finally, a small number of Member States (including Belgium and the Netherlands) have adopted completely new legislation which is designed, *inter alia*, to implement the disability provisions of the Framework Employment Directive.

The impact of the Directive on national legislation has, arguably, been greatest in those Member States which have adopted the last approach and, for this reason, much of the discussion in this chapter focuses on the implementation measures adopted in Belgium and the Netherlands,[25] with the aim of throwing light on how national choices concerning implementation

[19] In a more general context, the Commission has noted that delays in transpositions are often not the result of a deliberate refusal to act on the part of the Member State, but of domestic administrative problems and in particular problems of understanding often complex Community legislative texts. Commission Communication on Better monitoring of the application of Community law, COM(2002) 725 final, 7.

[20] Decreto Legislativo 9 July 2003, no 216 Attuazione della direttiva 2000/78/CE per la parità di trattamento in materia di occupazione e di condizioni di lavoro. Gazetta Ufficiale della Republicca Italiana, 13 August 2003, Serie generale–no 187. The definitions of direct and indirect discrimination in particular are clearly modelled on the Directive.

[21] At the time of writing, a bill, large sections of which were clearly closely modelled on the Framework Employment Directive, was before Parliament. It is expected to be adopted in 2004. See Projet de Loi portant transposition de la directive 2000/78/CE du Conseil du 27 novembre 2000 portant création d'un général en faveur de l'égalité de traitement en matière d'emploi et de travail.

[22] In November 2003 the Greek government published a bill on the application of the principle of equal treatment regardless of racial or ethnic origin, religious or other beliefs, disability, age or sexual orientation. Sections of this bill, such as Art 10 on reasonable accommodation, Art 12 on positive action, Art 14 on the burden of proof, and Art 15 on victimisation are all identical to, or very closely modelled on, the Framework Employment Directive. The bill is expected to come before the Parliament in 2004.

[23] Germany currently has a wealth of disability non-discrimination law, consisting of constitutional provisions, federal statutory law and state law. The disability provisions of the Framework Employment Directive have been partially implemented through an amendment to s 81(2) of the Social Law Code IX 2001 (*Sozialgesetzbuch* IX 2001).

[24] The prohibition of Discrimination in Working Life of People with Disability Act (1999:132) (Lag (1999:132) om förbüd mot diskriminering i arbetslivet av personer med funktionshinder) was amended by Act (2003:309).

[25] It is unclear how many other Member States have also opted for the adoption of wide ranging new legislation designed to implement the disability provisions of the Framework Employment Directive.

can influence the effectiveness of the adopted measures. Occasional reference will also be made to implementation measures adopted in other Member States.

The implementation measures considered[26] are the Belgian Act to Combat Discrimination and to Amend the Act of 15 February 1993 to Establish a Centre for Equal Opportunity and to Combat Racism[27] and the Dutch Act of 3 April 2003 to Establish the Act on the Equal Treatment on Grounds of Disability or Chronic Illness.[28]

In both Member States other, pre-existing legislation and instruments are also relevant to disability discrimination and, in particular, to positive action and employment policy. However, this chapter focuses only on the legislation recently adopted to implement the disability provisions of the Framework Employment Directive.

3 IMPLEMENTING THE DIRECTIVE—NATIONAL CHOICES

3.1 A Symmetric or Asymmetric Approach to Disability Discrimination

3.1.1 The Directive

Non-discrimination law generally adopts a symmetric approach. This means that the starting point for the legislation is a prohibition of all forms of discrimination with regard to the covered ground, and that members of both the majority or advantaged group and the minority or disadvantaged group are equally protected from discrimination. However, such a starting point does not, at least in Europe, necessarily exclude possibilities for positive action in favour of disadvantaged groups although this has been the tendency of some forms of non-discrimination legislation in the US.

EC non-discrimination law likewise adopts a symmetric approach. This can be seen in the gender equal treatment directives which prohibit discrimination against both men and women, and which have been relied upon before the ECJ by both men[29] and women. This approach is also reflected

---

[26] All translations into English are unofficial and have been provided by the author.

[27] Wet ter Bestrijding van Discriminatie en tot Wijzinging van de Wet van 15 februari 1993 tot Oprichting van een Centrum voor Gelijkheid van Kansen en voor Racismebestrijding.

[28] Wet van 3 april 2003 tot vaststelling van de Wet gelijke behandeling op grond van handicap of chronische ziekte.

[29] See eg the well-known Case C–262/88 *Barber v Guardian Royal Exchange Assurance* [1990] ECR I–1889, concerning the right of men to claim an occupational pension at the same age as women. However, this case is only one of many which had been brought by men. It is interesting to note that many of these cases have not resulted in men acquiring the sought benefit in the same way or at the same age as women, but in women having to meet the same (harsher) access conditions as men in order to claim the benefit. A prime example is Case C–408/92 *Smith v Advel* [1994] ECR I–4435, in which the ECJ held: 'Article 119 of the Treaty does not preclude measures which achieve equal treatment by reducing the advantages of the persons previously favoured,' para 21.

in Article 141 EC, which uses gender-neutral language by referring to the use of 'specific advantages' to benefit the 'under-represented sex.' A symmetric approach is, in addition, reflected in the latest Article 13 EC equality directives: the Race Directive, which was adopted a few months prior to the Framework Employment Directive, prohibits discrimination 'on the grounds of racial or ethnic origin',[30] and thus covers racial and ethnic minorities as well as members of the dominant racial or ethnic group.

The Framework Employment Directive prohibits discrimination 'on the grounds of religion or belief, disability, age or sexual orientation'.[31] There is little doubt that followers of all religions (and followers of no religion), people of all ages, and heterosexuals and homosexuals are all protected from discrimination under this provision.

However, the symmetry may not apply with regard to disability discrimination. An asymmetric approach to disability discrimination implies that only people who have been discriminated against *on the grounds of disability* would be protected from discrimination, whilst those who have been discriminated against on the grounds that, for example, they do not have a disability, or are not assumed to have a disability, or are not associated with a disabled person, would not be protected.

At least two commentators have argued that the disability provisions of the Framework Employment Directive are asymmetric. Catherine Barnard has noted that:

> There can be no direct discrimination [against non-disabled people] because the Directive does not provide for the non-disabled to make a claim.[32]

Paul Skidmore has argued that:

> ... with regard to disability the Directive does not operate in the same symmetrical fashion as provisions on sex and race do. It is only discrimination on grounds of disability and not 'non-disability' which is prevented by the Directive.[33]

It is indeed clear that the definition of indirect discrimination in the Directive is asymmetric with regard to disability. The Directive states:

> [I]ndirect discrimination shall be taken to occur where an apparently neutral provision, criterion or practice would put persons having ... *a particular disability* ... at a particular disadvantage.[34]

---

[30] Art 1.
[31] Art 1.
[32] C Barnard, above n 2, at 972, fn 107.
[33] P Skidmore, above n 2, at 131.
[34] Art 2(2)(b).

As a consequence, only those who have 'a particular disability' can claim protection. However, this concept could in fact be defined in national legislation to cover those who do not actually have an impairment but who, for example, have a disabled family member and experience discrimination as a result. The concept would nevertheless remain asymmetric.

On the other hand, the definition of direct discrimination may be open to an alternative interpretation. The Directive provides:

> The purpose of this Directive is to lay down a general framework for combating discrimination on the ground ... of ... disability.[35]

> Direct discrimination shall be taken to occur where one person is treated less favourably than another is, has been or would be treated in a comparable situation, on any of the grounds referred to in Article 1.[36]

These provisions could be interpreted as embracing a *symmetric approach* to disability discrimination, in other words as protecting an individual from discrimination on the grounds that they are disabled as well as discrimination on the grounds that they are not disabled. This interpretation would be more in keeping with the approach to discrimination on other grounds under EC law, but clearly goes against the line adopted with regard to indirect disability discrimination in the Directive. Alternatively, inspired by the definition of indirect discrimination in the Directive, an asymmetric interpretation could also be applied to the concept of direct discrimination.

3.1.2 Implementation

Disability anti-discrimination law at the national level frequently adopts an asymmetric approach. Existing legislation, for example in the UK[37] and the US,[38] follows this line, as does German legislation[39] and the recently adopted Spanish disability non-discrimination statute.[40]

Interestingly, however, the Dutch implementation legislation follows a symmetric approach according to which non-disabled people are also protected from discrimination they experience on the grounds that they have no impairment. This is clear from a reading of the legislation, in combination with the Explanatory Memorandum. The definition of discrimination in the Dutch Act does not result in protection being conferred only on those who have experienced discrimination on the grounds of disability, but also

---

[35] Art 1.
[36] Art 2(2)(a).
[37] Disability Discrimination Act 1995 (DDA).
[38] Americans With Disabilities Act 1990 (ADA).
[39] S 81(2) Social Law Code IX 2001 (*Sozialgesetzbuch* IX 2001).
[40] A Law for Equal Opportunities and Against the Discrimination of Disabled Persons (Texto Ley 51/2003 de igualdad de oportunidades, no discriminación y accesibilidad universal de las personas con discapacidad) of 2 December 2003. This Act is not designed to implement the Framework Employment Directive.

covers those who have experienced discrimination on the grounds that they are not disabled. Direct discrimination is defined as:

> b. differentiation between people on the grounds of a real or supposed disability or chronic illness. [41]

Indirect discrimination is defined as:

> c. differentiation on the grounds of traits or behaviour other than those described in section b which results in direct differentiation. [42]

The Explanatory Memorandum accompanying the legislative proposals for this Act made it clear that protection from direct and indirect discrimination extended not only to those people with a disability or chronic illness, but to everyone regardless of whether or not they were disabled. [43] The existence of symmetry is also reflected in the fact that positive action measures, in favour of people with a disability or chronic illness, are treated as an exception to the non-discrimination principle and not as an element thereof; and by the fact that the prohibited act is described as 'differentiation', which is a symmetrical concept in Dutch law, rather than 'discrimination', which is an asymmetrical concept in Dutch law. [44] By contrast, Dutch legislation does adopt an asymmetric approach to reasonable accommodation, which is available only to disabled people.

This is not a hollow discussion, as is hinted at by the Dutch treatment of positive action in favour of disabled people. If an asymmetrical approach is adopted, it will not be possible for an individual who has been discriminated against on the grounds that they are not disabled to bring a complaint. This means that all forms of positive action and reasonable accommodation designed to benefit disabled people cannot be challenged on the grounds that they exclude people who are not disabled. Given the large scale employment quota systems existent in some Member States, including Germany and France, [45] the implied protection from legal challenges (from disgruntled non-disabled people who feel they have lost out) is not insignificant. By contrast, Dutch courts and the Dutch Equal Treatment

---

[41] Art 1(b): 'onderscheid tussen personen op grond van een werkelijke of vermeende handicap of chronische ziekte.'

[42] Art 1(c): 'onderscheid tussen personen op grond van andere hoedanigheden of gedraginen dan die bedoeld in onderdeel b, dat direct onderscheid tot gevlog heeft.'

[43] Memorie van Toelichting, Tweede Kamer, 2001–2002, 28 169, no 3, p 9. See also M Gijzen, 'Het nieuwe gelijkebehandelingsrecht voor gehandicapten en chronisch zieken' in *Oordelenbundel* (Utrecht, CGB, 2003), 101.

[44] See further section 3.3 below.

[45] See L Waddington, 'Reassessing the employment of people with disabilities in Europe: from quotas to anti-discrimination laws' (1996) 18 *Comparative Labor Law Journal* 62–101 and L Waddington, 'Legislating to employ people with disabilities: the European and American way' (1994) 1 *Maastricht Journal of European and Comparative Law* 367–95.

Commission[46] may have to engage in a delicate balancing act, should positive action in favour of disabled people be challenged by a non-disabled person, in order to determine whether such measures fall within the permitted
exception to the non-differentiation principle.

3.2 The Definition of Disability and Protection from Discrimination on Grounds of Disability

3.2.1 The Directive

The Framework Employment Directive does not contain a definition of disability. Neither does it elaborate on what is meant by discrimination 'on the
grounds of disability.' This absence of a definition of the ground protected
from discrimination is a characteristic common to all Community equality
directives. The Equal Treatment Directive prohibits discrimination on
'grounds of sex,' without elaborating on what is meant by 'sex.' This concept, which may seem relatively straightforward when compared with
other grounds covered by Community equality directives (eg racial or ethnic origin, religion, or disability) has nevertheless been the subject of case-
law before the ECJ. The Court has been called upon to determine whether
discrimination on the grounds of having undergone transgender surgery
amounted to discrimination on the grounds of sex.[47] Likewise, there is a
possibility that the Court will be asked to develop, probably through a
piecemeal approach, a European definition of the other undefined grounds
(including disability) covered by the equality directives. One could even
envisage the unhappy situation where an almost unending series of preliminary questions are referred to the Court asking if individuals, each with a
slightly different impairment, are covered by the Directive.

In the meantime, however, Member States will have a relatively free hand
in determining what definition of disability, if any, to include in implementation legislation and to determine who should be protected from discrimination on the grounds of disability. With regard to the former point, the
variety of possible approaches, ranging from a strictly medical conception
of disability to a social model of disability, has been widely covered in the
literature.[48] The latter point has perhaps received less attention in the
literature and it is worth noting that many people, other than those who
currently have a (work-related) impairment, can experience employment-
related discrimination on grounds of disability. A concise overview of the
categories of people who may face discrimination on grounds of disability

---

[46] The Commission is a semi-judicial body charged with hearing cases of alleged discrimination.

[47] Case C-13/94 *P v S and Cornwall County Council* [1996] ECR I–2143.

[48] See eg J Swain *et al* (eds), *Disabling Barriers—Enabling Environments* (London, Sage
Publications, 1992).

can be found in Article 2(7) of the Disability Specific Directive which has been proposed by the European Disability Forum (EDF).[49] This reads as follows:

> For the purposes of this Directive, a person shall be regarded as having a disability if they currently have a disability, they have had a disability in the past, they may have a disability in the future, they are associated with a person with a disability through a family or other relationship, or they are assumed to fall into one of these categories.

It is possible that Member States could opt to provide an equally broad coverage when implementing the Framework Employment Directive or that the ECJ, faced with an appropriately worded preliminary reference, could interpret the Directive as covering some or all of these categories. However, given the silence of the Directive—a silence which is not surprising given the difficulties involved in reaching agreement amongst fifteen Member States on this controversial topic[50]—neither of these possibilities is certain, and implementation and interpretation could equally result in a narrow definition and personal scope.

At this point it may be worth noting an interesting comparison with British race discrimination law, where terminology similar to that found in the Framework Employment Directive concerning discrimination 'on the grounds of disability' has been given a broad interpretation. The Race Relations Act 1976 defines direct discrimination as follows: 'a person discriminates against another ... if he treats that person less favourably ... on racial grounds'.[51]

This has been interpreted by courts and tribunals to mean that a person may complain of discrimination on grounds of *somebody else's race*. In *Showboat*[52] the Employment Appeals Tribunal held:

> ... the words 'on racial grounds' are perfectly capable in the ordinary sense of covering any reason for an action based on race, whether it be the race of the person affected *or of others* ... The only question in each case is whether the unfavourable treatment afforded to the claimant was caused by racial considerations.

---

[49] The EDF, an umbrella group representing the interests of disabled people in the EU, has produced a proposal for a directive designed to combat disability discrimination in areas beyond employment, based on Art 13 EC. The proposal is designed to be a lobbying tool to prompt the EU institutions to take action in this field. The text of the EDF proposal can be found at http://www.edf-feph.org/en/policy/nondisc/nond_pol.htm.

[50] Indeed, it is highly likely that, had the Commission and Council been determined to include a definition of disability or the personal scope of the Framework Employment Directive with regard to discrimination on grounds of disability, the whole project would have failed. In that sense, the decision to steer clear of a definition may well have been the price paid for the inclusion of disability (and perhaps the other grounds) in the Directive.

[51] S 1(1)(a).

[52] *Showboat Entertainment Centre Ltd v Owens* [1984] IRLR 7.

This approach was subsequently confirmed by the Court of Appeal in 1999 in *Weathersfield*.[53] By contrast, the UK Sex Discrimination Act 1975 prohibits discrimination 'on the ground of her [or his] sex',[54] which has been interpreted as not covering instances of discrimination on grounds of someone else's sex.[55]

3.2.2 Implementation

Both the Dutch and the Belgian implementation legislation mirror the Directive by failing to provide a definition of disability.

The Belgian implementation legislation, which goes far beyond an implementation of (the disability provisions of) the Framework Employment Directive, provides protection from discrimination on a wide variety of grounds, including: 'current or future state of health, disability or a physical characteristic'.[56]

During the Parliamentary discussions in the Belgian Senate and House of Representatives, an amendment was proposed which would have included a broader definition of disability. It defined a disability, for the purposes of the non-discrimination law, as:

> [A] physical or psychological disturbance or restriction that forms a hindrance to a normal access to and/or participation in the diverse aspects of life.[57]

Both Houses of Parliament rejected this amendment, preferring to leave the term undefined. The Senate supported this position by arguing that any definition would result in an exclusion of that which was not mentioned.[58] However, the Parliamentary discussion did make it clear that the intention was to interpret the concept of disability very broadly. Kim Van den Langenbergh has argued that, given this intention, it would have been more appropriate to have included a definition, or legislative guidance, on this point so as to ensure that the term 'disability' was not interpreted in the way common in 'daily use.'[59] Nevertheless, Van den Langenbergh notes that the lack of a broad definition may be less problematic in practice, given that

---

[53] *Weathersfield Ltd v Sargent* [1999] IRLR 94.
[54] S 1(2)(a).
[55] I am grateful to Marianne Gijzen for providing this information.
[56] Art 2(1): 'de huidige of toekomstige gezondheidstoestand, een handicap of een fysieke eigenschap.'
[57] 'een fysieke of psychische stoornis of beperking die een belemmering vormt voor een normale toegang tot en/of participatie aan de diverse aspecten van het leven.' *Parl St* Senaat 2001–2002, no 2-12/14, 3. See also K Van den Langenbergh, 'Discriminatie van gehandicapten bij aanwerving: een verkennende analyse' in *Vrijheid en Gelijkheid, De horizontale werking van het gelijkheidsbeginsel en de nieuwe antidiscriminatie wet* (Antwerp, Maklu, 2003), 573 at 597.
[58] *Parl St Senaat* 2001–2002, no 2–12/14, 3–4 and Van den Langenbergh, *ibid*.
[59] Van den Langenbergh, *ibid*, p 597.

the relevant statute also provides protection from discrimination on grounds of physical characteristics.[60] One should note, though, that the reasonable accommodation duty is confined to those regarded as having a disability under the statute, and a limited interpretation of the term may result in reduced access to accommodations. Further, it is unlikely that the Belgian legislation can offer protection from discrimination to people associated with a disabled person.

As noted above, the Dutch implementation legislation also fails to provide a definition of disability. The legislation covers discrimination on the grounds of 'a real or supposed disability or chronic illness'.[61] Like the Belgian legislation, therefore, the Dutch measure goes beyond the Framework Employment Directive in covering discrimination on grounds of chronic illness or state of health.

The Dutch Act is also interesting in that it provides protection for those who are 'supposed' or 'assumed' to have a disability or a chronic illness. This covers one of the additional groups mentioned in the disability-specific directive proposed by the EDF. Given the desire to interpret the concept of disability broadly in the Belgian legislation, it is possible that the Belgian courts will also interpret their implementation legislation in this way. However, because criminal sanctions can be applied to cases of discrimination under the relevant legislation, the principle of legal certainty may prevent such an interpretation.[62]

A further comparison may be made with the Maltese Equal Opportunities (Persons with Disability) Act 2000.[63] This Act, although not adopted to implement the Directive (to which Malta became subject on 1 May 2004), does go a long way towards complying with its obligations.[64] The Equal Opportunities (Persons with Disability) Act 2000 covers individuals with a disability and individuals who are known or believed to have a relationship or association with such a person.

By contrast, German implementation legislation[65] protects only those people who have been classified as 'severely disabled' ('*schwerbehinderter*'). Such a status can only be obtained through registration, and it is conferred on those people whose disability grade is judged to be at least 50 per cent. In addition, at the discretion of the registration office, those individuals with a disability grade of at least 30 per cent can also be registered as severely disabled where their disability hampers their opportunity to obtain

---

[60] *Ibid*, p 598.
[61] Art 1(b): 'een werkelijke of vermeende handicap of chronische ziekte'.
[62] Van den Langenbergh, above n 57, p 598.
[63] Act No I of 2000, 19 January 2000.
[64] However, the Maltese Equal Opportunities (Persons with Disability) Act 2000 does not amount to a complete implementation of the disability provisions of the Framework Employment Directive.
[65] Implementation has been partially achieved through amendments to existing legislation. The provision in question is the Social Law Code, s 81(2).

employment. It is, in fact, questionable whether this provision amounts to full implementation of the Directive's prohibition of discrimination on grounds of disability. The Directive refers to disability generally and is not restricted to those with severe impairments. It therefore does not appear compatible with the limited interpretation embraced in German law. Arguably, the limits of the scope for exercising national discretion have been exceeded in this instance.

3.3 The Definition of Discrimination

3.3.1 The Directive

The Framework Employment Directive prohibits four kinds of discrimination in Article 2: direct discrimination, indirect discrimination; harassment; and an instruction to discriminate. Of the four forms of discrimination covered in Article 2, the definitions of direct and indirect discrimination have attracted most attention from commentators.[66] The terms are defined as follows:

> [D]irect discrimination shall be taken to occur when one person is treated less favourably than another is, has been or would be treated in a comparable situation.
>
> Indirect discrimination shall be taken to occur where an apparently neutral provision, criterion or practice would put persons having a ... particular disability ... at a particular disadvantage compared with other persons unless that provision, criterion or practice is objectively justified by a legitimate aim and the means of achieving that aim are appropriate and necessary, or as regards persons with a particular disability, the employer or any person or organisation to whom this Directive applies, is obliged, under national legislation, to take appropriate measures in line with the principles contained in Article 5 [referring to reasonable accommodation] in order to eliminate disadvantages entailed by such provision, criterion or practice.

A couple of points are worth noting, before considering how these provisions can be, and have been, implemented by Member States. Whilst indirect discrimination can be justified where the measure in question serves a 'legitimate aim and the means of achieving that aim are appropriate and necessary', no such broadly phrased justification can be applied to direct discrimination. Direct discrimination can generally be justified only in cases where there is a 'genuine and determining occupational requirement' which justifies the exclusion of members of certain groups, covered by the Directive, from the specific employment in question.[67] Second, whilst the

---

[66] See eg L Waddington and M Bell, above n 2, pp 590–95.
[67] Art 4.

Directive contains an obligation to make a reasonable accommodation for disabled people in Article 5, a failure to make an accommodation is not classified as a form of discrimination.

3.3.2 Implementation

Whilst Member States have the option of simply copying the Directive's definitions of direct and indirect discrimination, neither Belgium nor the Netherlands have taken this route.

The Belgian implementation legislation defines direct discrimination in the following way:

> [A] difference in treatment that cannot be objectively and reasonably justified, directly based on ... the current or future state of health, a disability or a physical characteristic.[68]

This definition seems to permit an open system for the justification of direct discrimination; a system which would be in conflict with the stricter approach found in the Directive. However, Article 2(5) of the Belgian statute specifies that, with regard to employment (ie the field covered by the Directive), an objective and reasonable justification can only exist in the case of a genuine and determining occupational requirement. This position was confirmed in Parliamentary debates by the Minister for Employment and Labour.[69] However, the legislative text is not altogether clear as to whether the 'objective and reasonable justification' requirement found in Article 2(1) is only illustrative or exhaustive, and the provision could be interpreted so as to allow for an open system of justification.[70]

Unlike the Directive, the Belgian statute defines a denial of a reasonable accommodation as a form of discrimination:[71]

> The denial of a reasonable accommodation for a person with a disability is discrimination in the sense of this statute.[72]

Dutch implementation legislation adopts a different approach to the definition of direct and indirect discrimination. Indeed, the word 'discrimination'

---

[68] Art 2(1): 'een verschil in behandeling dat niet objectief en redelijkerwijze wordt gerechtvaardigd, rechtstreeks gebaseerd is op ... de huidige of toekomstige gezondheidstoestand, een handicap of een fysieke eigenschap.'

[69] *Parl St* Kamer 2001–2002, no 1578/008, 40. Van den Langenbergh, above n 57, p 593.

[70] Van den Langenbergh, above n 57, p 593.

[71] Art 4.

[72] Het ontbreken van redelijke aanpassingen voor de persoon met een handicap vormt een discriminatie in de zin van deze wet. 'This point is discussed more fully in the following section.'

does not actually appear in the Dutch implementation legislation at all; rather 'differentiation'[73] is the key concept.[74]

In order to understand why the Dutch authorities have chosen to implement the Framework Employment Directive in this way, it is important to consider how Dutch legislators and academics regard the concept of discrimination. It has been argued that Dutch legal theory perceives the term 'discrimination' as an asymmetrical and group-oriented concept, and that the combating of 'discrimination' is regarded as a tool to be used to target and benefit disadvantaged social groups (ie a substantive concept of equality).[75] However, Dutch equal treatment law, including the well-known General Equal Treatment Act,[76] does not adopt this group-based perspective but, instead, takes an individualistic and symmetrical approach (ie a formal approach to equality).[77] The term discrimination (in Dutch, '*discriminatie*') is therefore a highly loaded and pejorative term, and carries much greater weight than the identical term in English or, indeed, than the same term in Dutch/Flemish in Belgium. Instead, the General Equal Treatment Act uses the term differentiation, which is regarded as a neutral concept. The question of whether the new Dutch disability statute should also adopt this terminology, or follow the Dutch language version of the Directive which does refer to discrimination, prompted discussion in the Netherlands. Ultimately the decision was made to follow the approach favoured under the General Equal Treatment Act, and to refer to differentiation rather than discrimination. However, the Council of State (*Raad van State*)[78] and the Ministerial Inter-department Commission on European Law[79] both advised the Government to follow the terminology found in the Directive, whilst the Dutch Equal Treatment Commission advised against a change in approach.[80] Marianne Gijzen argues that, because the term '*discriminatie*'

---

[73] Translating the relevant term ('*onderscheid*') is, in fact, problematic. The Dutch Equal Treatment Commission translates the term as 'discrimination' on its home page (in a translation of the General Equal Treatment Act). This translation seems incorrect, in light of the discussion elaborated in this paper.

[74] See section 3.1.2 for the full text of the relevant provision.

[75] T Loenen, *Het Gelijkheidsbeginsel* (Nijmegen, Ars Aequi Libri, 1998). See also R Holtmaat, 'Stop de inflatie van het discriminatiebegrip' (2003) 23 *Nederlands Juristenblad* 1266–276.

[76] Algemene Wet Gelijke Behandeling.

[77] See M Gijzen, above n 43, p 101.

[78] Advies van de Raad van State en Nader Rapport, Tweede Kamer, 2001–2002, 28 169 B, p 5–6. See also M Gijzen, above n 43, p 102.

[79] Interdepartementale Commissie Europees Recht, advies implementatie richtlijnen op grond van Artikel 13 EG Verdrag, ICER 2001/54, 22 June 2001. See also M Gijzen, above n 43, p 102.

[80] Commentaar van de Commissie Gelijke Behandeling inzake implementatie van de gemeenschappelijke bepalingen van de EG Kaderrichtlijn (Rightlijn 2000/78/EG van 27 november 2000) en de EG anti-rassendiscriminatierichtlijn (Richtlijn 2000/43/EG van 29 juni 2000). To be found at: http://www.cgb.nl/adviezen/2001egkaderrichtlijn.html. See also M Gijzen, above n 43, p 102.

in EU law has far less negative connotations than the same term in Dutch law (specifically, Dutch criminal and constitutional law), the approach followed by the Government was appropriate and compatible with the Directive. Indeed, she even argues that the term 'differentiation' is broader than discrimination because the former is a symmetrical all-encompassing concept, and that the introduction of narrower discrimination based terminology may have been in conflict with the non-regression clause found in Article 8(2) of the Directive.[81]

One further interesting point is that the Dutch legislature has opted not to apply the 'genuine and determining occupational requirement' exception to instances of direct disability discrimination.

Dutch law, like the Belgian implementation legislation and unlike the Directive, also defines the failure to make a reasonable accommodation as a form of discrimination.[82]

3.4 The Definition of Reasonable Accommodation

3.4.1 The Directive

Article 5 of the Framework Employment Directive creates the obligation for employers to make reasonable accommodation for disabled people:

> In order to guarantee compliance with the principle of equal treatment in relation to persons with disabilities, reasonable accommodation shall be provided. This means that employers shall take appropriate measures, where needed in a particular case, to enable a person with a disability to have access to, participate in, or advance in employment, or to provide training for such a person, unless such measures would impose a disproportionate burden on the employer. When this burden is, to a sufficient extent, remedied by existing measures as an element of disability policy in the Member State, it should not be considered disproportionate.

Given the many intricacies involved in establishing and assessing reasonable accommodation requirements, this provision is perhaps relatively brief. By contrast, the Americans With Disabilities Act 1990 (ADA) contains a far more detailed set of provisions on reasonable accommodation, and is accompanied by lengthy explanatory guidance.[83] However, a limited amount of further information is provided in the non-binding, but influential preamble to the Framework Employment Directive. Preamble para 20 expands on the kinds of measure which could amount to a reasonable accommodation:

---

[81] M Gijzen, above n 43, p 102.
[82] See following section.
[83] Equal Employment Opportunities Commission (EEOC) regulations to the Act, 29 CFR s 1630.2 (o).

> Appropriate measures should be provided, ie effective and practical measures
> to adapt the workplace to the disability, for example adapting premises and
> equipment, patterns of working time, the distribution of tasks or the provi-
> sion of training or integration resources.

Some guidance is also given with regard to assessing whether any particular accommodation amounts to a disproportionate burden in preamble
para 21:

> To determine whether the measures in question give rise to a disproportion-
> ate burden, account should be taken in particular of the financial and other
> costs entailed, the scale and financial resources of the organisation or under-
> taking and the possibility of obtaining public funding or any other assistance.

As noted above, the ADA imposes an obligation on employers[84] (and others) to make reasonable accommodations for disabled people. It is submitted that this US statute directly influenced the drafting of Article 5 of the
Framework Employment Directive. In particular, it is submitted that the
term 'reasonable accommodation,' first used in the US Rehabilitation Act
of 1973 and adopted in the ADA, was determinant of the terminology used
in Article 5. A conscious choice was made to use the term 'reasonable
accommodation' in the Directive because of the level of familiarity with this
particular element of the ADA amongst relevant Commission staff,
Member States, and disability NGOs. Furthermore, the term 'reasonable
accommodation' in the Directive was, arguably, intended to convey the
same meaning as it has in the ADA, or at least the meaning the term had
when the Act was originally adopted.[85] In this context, a 'reasonable accommodation' with regard to the Directive should be seen as a modification or
adjustment that is effective in enabling an individual with a disability to
perform the 'essential functions' of a particular job. The reasonableness of
the accommodation does not refer to its limited cost or inconvenience to the
employer, but rather to its potential to provide equal opportunity, reliability, and efficiency. The question of reasonableness, as understood in this
way, is therefore quite separate from the analysis relating to existence of an
undue hardship or disproportionate burden for the employer.[86] However,

---

[84] In S 101(9).

[85] The meaning of the term 'reasonable' in this context may have changed as the result of a
recent Supreme Court decision. In 2002 the US Supreme Court addressed the issue of reasonable accommodation under the ADA in *US Airways v Barnett*, 122 S Ct 1516 (2002). The
majority of the Court gave independent significance to the term 'reasonable', regarding it as a
modifier to the duty to make an accommodation. The majority opinion of Justice Breyer stated: 'in ordinary English the word "reasonable" does not mean "effective". It is the word
"accommodation", not the word "reasonable", that conveys the need for effectiveness'. See
also A Meyerson and S Yee, 'Reasonable accommodation after Barnett', Paper for the National
Council on Disability, www.ncd.gov.

[86] For further commentary on the original interpretation of the reasonable accommodation
provision under the ADA, see L Waddington, *Disability, Employment and the European
Community* (Blackstone, 1995), 164–67.

this interpretation does not seem to have been made explicit in the Directive or its Preamble, and this may create confusion at the implementation phase.

3.4.2 Implementation

As noted above, both Belgian and Dutch implementation legislation define a failure to make a reasonable accommodation as a form of discrimination. However, neither statute specifies whether such a failure should be regarded as direct discrimination, indirect discrimination, or as a third form of *sui generis* discrimination.[87] Furthermore, as with the Directive, both statutes are noticeable for their brevity when creating this obligation.

There was an initial reluctance to include any reasonable accommodation provision in the federal statute implementing the Framework Employment Directive in Belgium. A proposal to include such a provision, the wording of which was heavily based on Article 5 of the Directive, was rejected. One of the reasons given for this, by the Minister of Employment, was that the proposal amounted to a form of positive action whilst the national statute in question was only an anti-discrimination measure.[88] The Belgian Federal Government does not have competence to legislate on positive action, and this perception of reasonable accommodation therefore constituted a significant hurdle to legislation at the federal level (although it would not restrict implementation at other levels of government).[89] Eventually, the inclusion of the following Government amendment provided a way round this impasse:

> The denial of a reasonable accommodation for a person with a disability is discrimination in the sense of this statute.

---

[87] See L Waddington and A Hendriks, 'The expanding concept of employment discrimination in Europe: From direct and indirect discrimination to reasonable accommodation discrimination' (2002) 18 *International Journal of Comparative Labour Law and Industrial Relations* 403–27.

[88] *Parl St* Senaat 2001–2002, no 2–12/15, 149–152. Further reasons included the future adoption of specific legislation on this topic, and the need to discuss the measure with the social partners. See also Van den Langenbergh, above n 57, pp 601–04.

[89] The Belgian constitutional structure divides the task of promoting equal opportunities for disabled people between: the Federal level, which has the responsibility for defining non discrimination requirements in criminal and labour law and by regulating the contract of employment; the Regional level, which has the responsibility for promoting the professional integration of disabled people in employment policy; and the Communities, which have the responsibility for promoting the rehabilitation and vocational training of disabled people. However, some recent developments have brought about more coherence at the Regional and Community level.

A reasonable accommodation is an accommodation that does not create a disproportionate burden, or where the burden is sufficiently compensated for by existing measures.[90]

Van den Langenbergh has commented that this provision does not amount to an obligation to make an accommodation, but it does make it clear that a refusal to take account of the situation of a disabled person, by refusing to make an accommodation in their favour, is a form of discrimination. She argues that the provision should not be regarded as a form of positive action and hopes, in this way, to avoid the aforementioned competence problems. She is, however, doubtful as to whether the Belgian Constitutional Court will accept such a position.[91]

One can see from the second part of Article 2(3) of the Belgian statute that an accommodation is judged to be reasonable if it does not create a disproportionate burden for the employer. This interpretation conflicts with the aforementioned US inspired understanding of the notion of reasonable accommodation, which regards an employment related accommodation as reasonable if it is effective in allowing an individual to carry out a specific job. The preparatory texts relating to the Belgian statute, in fact, make it clear that when determining whether any accommodation amounts to a disproportionate burden (or, in the terminology of the Belgian Act, whether it is reasonable), three criteria have to be considered:

(1) Are any accommodations possible which would allow a specific person with a disability to effectively participate in an equal way in a specific activity?

(2) Do these accommodations amount to a disproportionate burden for the person who must make them?

(3) Do there exist any measures that significantly reduce the burden on the person who is under the duty to accommodation?[92]

Only the last two criteria have been included in the statute, however, and Belgian law (unlike the Directive and the Dutch implementation provision) does not impose an obligation to make an accommodation to meet the particular needs of an individual.

On the other hand, Belgian law does go beyond the Directive in a number of respects. Most notably, the obligation to make an accommodation is not confined to employment but applies to all fields covered by the law.[93] In

---

[90] Art 2(3): 'Het ontbreken van redelijke aanpassingen voor de persoon met een handicap vormt een discriminatie in de zin van deze wet. Als een redelijke aanpassing wordt beschouwd de aanpassing die geen onevenredige belasting betekent, of waarvan de belasting in voldoende mate gecompenseerd wordt door bestaande maatregelen.'

[91] Van den Langenbergh, above n 57, p 603.

[92] *Parl St* 2001–2002, no 1578/008, 30–1. See Van den Langenbergh, above n 57, pp 604–5.

[93] See section 3.6 below.

addition, a failure to make an accommodation is a form of discrimination and therefore potentially subject to criminal sanctions.

Dutch implementation legislation also defines a failure to make an accommodation as a form of discrimination or differentiation in Article 2:

> The prohibition on differentiation also means that the person on whom this prohibition is imposed is obliged to make effective accommodations where needed in a particular case, unless this would impose a disproportionate burden on them.[94]

The first point to note is that the Dutch legislation shies away from the term 'reasonable accommodation' ('*redelijke aanpassingen*'), in favour of the term 'effective accommodation' ('*doeltreffende aapassingen*'). In doing so, the Dutch legislature has, arguably, followed the US inspired interpretation of the reasonable accommodation provision in the Directive, and separated the issue of the effectiveness of the accommodation from the question of undue hardship or disproportionate burden. The Dutch Government opted to use the term 'effective accommodation' because this emphasised that the specific accommodation had to achieve the desired effect.[95] This is judged according to the 'suitability' or 'appropriateness' ('*geschiktheid*') and 'necessity' ('*noodzakelijkheid*') of a specific accommodation.[96] The second, and separate, stage of the assessment involves a consideration of whether the accommodation amounts to a disproportionate burden. This involves a balancing of the interests of the employer and the disabled person, inter alia, through the application of standard 'open norms' of Dutch civil law (ie the duty to act as a good employer and the notion of 'reasonableness').[97]

This clearly defined two stage process will arguably promote clarity and understanding, rather than resulting in a difficult merging of the separate issues of the effectiveness of the accommodation and the extent to which making that accommodation amounts to a disproportionate burden.

One should also note that the requirement to make an accommodation is not confined to employers, as is the case under the Directive, but applies to all parties who are prohibited from discriminating under the statute.

---

[94] 'Het verbod van onderscheid houdt mede in dat degene, tot wie dit verbod zich richt, gehouden is naar gelang de behoefte doeltreffende aanpassingen te verichten, tenzij deze voor hem een onevenredige belastig vormen.'

[95] Memorie van Toelichting, Tweede Kamer, 2001–2002, 28 169, no 3, p 25. See also M Gijzen, above n 43, p 105.

[96] Memorie van Toelichting, Tweede Kamer, 2001–2002, 28 169, no 3, pp 25–6. See also M Gijzen, above n 43, p 105.

[97] Memorie van Toelichting, Tweede Kamer, 2001–2002, 28 169, no 3, p 25–30. See also M Gijzen, above n 43, p 105 and A Hendriks, *Gelijke Toegang tot de Arbeid voor Gehandicapten* (PhD Universiteit van Amsterdam, 2000), 185–7.

3.5 A Disability Specific Statute or a Statute covering a Variety of Grounds

3.5.1 The Directive

The European Community has adopted a number of directives in the field of equality. The Framework Employment Directive was preceded by a race specific directive and by a set of long-standing gender specific equality directives. This combination of ground specific directives and the mixed Framework Employment Directive can be explained by a variety of factors including, most significantly, the system of legal competencies provided for under the EC Treaty, and diverse political factors which influenced the decision to adopt a race specific directive and a mixed ground Framework Employment Directive. These factors are, for the most part, not reflected within the legal systems of the Member States, which consequently have a much freer hand when determining whether to adopt ground specific or mixed non-discrimination laws.

The Framework Employment Directive takes a neutral stance with regard to the adoption of a disability specific or mixed non-discrimination statute. The only requirement under Community law is that the goals set out in the Directive are achieved through national implementation provisions.

A number of consequences may follow from a decision to opt for a single or multi ground implementation measure. A set of single statutes may allow for the ring fencing of funds to support enforcement, monitoring and information; and ensure that less prominent or less 'popular' grounds do not lose out financially once legislation has been adopted. Such an approach may also allow for the elaboration of specific measures which are of particular relevance to certain kinds of discrimination. One could consider whether this is the case for disability discrimination, which has a number of distinguishing characteristics.

By contrast, a multi ground statute would serve to emphasise the common nature of discrimination and stress the unacceptability of all forms of covered discrimination. Such a statute might also facilitate a co-ordinated response to multiple discrimination, which would seem to be far more difficult to address through a series of single statutes.

3.5.2 Implementation

The Belgian authorities opted to implement both the Race Directive and the Framework Employment Directive in a single statute. In addition the decision was made to include a large number of grounds which are not addressed in current Community equality directives. The legislation therefore covers discrimination on grounds of:

[S]ex, race, skin colour, origin, nationality or ethnic origin, sexual orientation, civil status, birth, wealth, and age, religion or belief, current or future state of health, disability or physical characteristic.[98]

This approach would seem to have many of the benefits of a multi ground statute referred to above.

The Dutch have taken a somewhat more complicated path. Implementation of the disability provisions of the Framework Employment Directive is likely to occur through a three stage process in the Netherlands. The first stage, which has already been completed, involved the adoption of a statute dealing specifically with disability discrimination which implemented some, but not all, of the provisions of the Directive. This statute primarily implements those provisions in the Directive which specifically relate to disability, and is not only an EC implementation measure, but also an elaboration of Article 1 of the Dutch Constitution, which deals with equality. This is the statute that has been referred to in this chapter. The second stage involved the implementation of the so-called 'common provisions' of the Directive, namely those provisions which apply to all grounds covered in the Framework Employment Directive and the grounds of racial and ethnic origin covered in the Race Directive. This was achieved through an amendment to the General Equal Treatment Act and through an amendment to the aforementioned disability statute. Article I of the Bill to amend the General Equal Treatment Act[99] covers the common provisions and addresses all grounds covered in that Act, including those grounds not covered under the EC equality directives. Article II implements the common provisions relating to the aforementioned disability statute.

The adoption of an amended General Equal Treatment Act should be sufficient to completely implement the Race Directive and the provisions dealing with sexual orientation, religion or belief and disability in the Framework Employment Directive.[100]

---

[98] Art 2(1): 'het geslacht, een zogenaamde ras, de huidskleur, de afkomst, de nationale of ethnische afstamming, seksuele geaardheid, de burgerliche staat, de geboorte, het fortuin, de leeftijd, het geloof of de levensbeschouwing, de huidige of toekomistige gezondheidstoestand, een handicap of een fysieke eigenschap.'

[99] Wet van 21 februari 2004 tot wijziging van de Algeme wet gelijke behandeling en enkele andere wetten ter uitvoering van rightlijn nr. 2000/43/EG en richtlijn nr. 2000/78/ EG (EG-implementatiewet Awgb) [Act of 21 February 2004 concerning amendments to the General Equal Treatment Act and some other Acts which implement Directives 2000/43/EC and Directive 2000/78/EC]. *Staatsblad* 2004, 120.

[100] The provisions relating to age discrimination in the Framework Employment Directive will also be implemented through a staged process. The Parliament has recently adopted a law to prohibit age discrimination (Wet gelijke behandeling op grond van leeftijd bij de arbeid). The next step might be the integration of this Act within a single General Equal Treatment Act. The reason for this staged implementation is that neither disability nor age currently fall under the General Equal Treatment Act. However, 'disability' legislation is being fast tracked as a result of political urgency. See M Gijzen, above n 43, fn 9.

The third stage of the implementation process is likely to involve the incorporation of the disability specific statute within the General Equal Treatment Act, thereby also achieving a broad multi ground non-discrimination statute. The Dutch Parliament wishes to further investigate the possibilities for an integral approach to equality through a single General Equal Treatment Act, and the Government is expected to commit itself to research on this in the near future. A single equality act would, arguably, enhance the transparency of Dutch equality legislation.

3.6 Material Scope

3.6.1 The Directive

The material scope of the Framework Employment Directive, as its title suggests, is restricted to the widely defined area of employment. This is in contrast with the Race Directive which has a significantly broader material scope. The Framework Employment Directive covers, insofar as the areas fall under the competence of the Community, the public and private sectors with regard to:

(a) conditions for access to employment, to self-employment or to occupation, including selection criteria and recruitment conditions, whatever the branch of activity and at all levels of the professional hierarchy including promotion;
(b) access to all types and to all levels of vocational guidance, vocational training, advanced vocational training and retraining, including practical work experience;
(c) employment and working conditions, including dismissals and pay;
(d) membership of, and involvement in, an organisation of workers or employers, or any organisation whose members carry on a particular profession, including the benefits provided for by such organisations.[101]

The problems associated with confining a non-discrimination obligation to the field of employment are obvious and, whilst academics and the disability community have, on the whole, welcomed the Framework Employment Directive, a broader approach which seeks to tackle the many other areas of daily life where disabled people experience discrimination has been called for. This is reflected most obviously in the proposal for a disability specific Directive which has been put forward by the EDF.[102]

Whilst Member States are obliged to prohibit employment-related disability discrimination under the Framework Directive, there are in fact no legal impediments to the introduction of more wide-ranging national non-discrimination legislation, and both Belgium and the Netherlands have gone beyond the material scope of the Directive in their implementation legislation.

[101] Art 3.
[102] See above n 49.

3.6.2 Implementation

It has already been noted that the Belgian implementation legislation has a far broader personal scope than that found in current Community equality directives, and this breadth is also reflected in the material scope of the adopted legislation. In addition to the employment related areas provided for in the Framework Employment Directive, the Belgian implementation legislation covers:

— the provision or availability of goods and services provided to the public;
— ... unpaid work ...;
— an announcement in an official text or in an official report;
— the distribution, the publicising or the making public of a text, a notice, a drawing or any other means including a discriminatory expression;
— access to and participation in, and any other expression of an economic, social, cultural or political activity accessible to the public.[103]

In addition, the Belgian legislation contains detailed provisions regarding criminal liability. Chapter III of the statute describes the offences relating to acts of discrimination (as defined in Article 2 of the statute). These offences concern:

(a) those who publicly incite discrimination, hatred or violence against a person, group, community or the members of a community on the basis of one of the covered grounds;

(b) those who give publicity to their intention to commit discrimination, or

(c) public servants who commit discrimination in the exercise of the public functions.[104]

Certain offences will result in a higher level of punishment (fine or imprisonment) where they appear to be motivated by hate or hostility against a person because of the existence of one of the covered grounds (hate crimes). Specifically, sexual assaults, a refusal to assist a person in danger, the deprivation of liberty, harassment, attacks against the honour or the reputation of an individual, arson, and destruction or deterioration of goods or property may result in a higher tariff being imposed upon conviction where a discriminatory intent is established.[105]

Dutch implementation legislation also goes somewhat further than the Directive, extending to public transport and travel information. Article 8 of the Statute provides:

---

[103] Art 2 (4): '—het leveren of het ter beschikking stellen van goederen en diensten aan het publiek;
— ... onbetaalde arbeid ...;
— de vermelding in een officieel stuk of in een proces-verbaal;
— het verspreiden, het publiceren of het openbaar maken van een tekst, een bericht, een teken of enig andere drager van discriminerende uitlatingen;
— de toegang tot en de deelname aan, alsook elke andere uitoefening van een economische, sociale, culturele of politieke activiteit toegankelijk voor het publiek.'
[104] Art 6.
[105] Arts 7–14.

1. Differentiation is prohibited in:
   a. granting access to the buildings and infrastructure associated with public transport which is required in order to travel;
   b. offering public transport services and travel information;
   c. concluding, executing or terminating contracts relating to public transport.[106]

A timetable for providing accessible public transport and related infrastructure is to be specified in secondary legislation, resulting in a long implementation period. In Parliamentary debates, an implementation deadline of 2010 has been proposed for bus transport, and 2030 for the rail network.[107]

4 CONCLUSION

Given the very nature of Community framework directives, Member States have a great deal of scope for exercising discretion when deciding how to implement the Framework Employment Directive and whether to address other related areas in the implementation legislation. Indeed, the Com-munity legislature's intention was, no doubt, the establishment of only a minimum level of protection against employment-related disability discrimination, with the anticipation that many Member States would utilise this opportunity to go beyond this level and provide higher degrees of protection against discrimination generally and against disability discrimination more specifically. An examination of Belgian and Dutch legislation implementing the Directive has revealed that this has indeed happened and that, in many areas, the relevant national legislation sets higher standards than those required by the Directive.

On the other hand, one can argue that the Framework Employment Directive has had a restrictive effect on Dutch legislation prohibiting disability discrimination. The Dutch legislature had committed itself to enacting such legislation before the Directive was adopted. The initial draft of this legislation, which preceded the Directive, was broader in certain respects than the statute that was subsequently adopted. Parliamentary documents make it clear that, as soon as the Government found itself obliged to implement the Framework Employment Directive, it decided to do no more than was required to discharge the obligations imposed by that Directive.[108] On the other hand, in the absence of the Directive, the Dutch legislature might well still be prevaricating on this matter, with no concrete changes to the statute book in sight.

[106] '1. Onderscheid is verboden bij:
   a. het verlenen van de voor het reizen vereiste toegang tot de bij het openbaar vervoer behorende gebouwen en infrastructuur;
   b. het aanbieden van openbaar-vervoersdiensten en reisinformatie;
   c. het sluiten, uitvoeren of beëindigen van overeenkomsten met betrekking tot openbaar vervoer.'

[107] Memorie van Toelichting, Tweede Kamer, 2001–2002, 28 169 no 3, 1 at 5.

[108] See M Gijzen, above n 43, fn 30.

This chapter also reveals the importance of national 'peculiarities,' which can result in unusual and unconventional approaches to the implementation of specific provisions of the Framework Employment Directive. The competence restrictions experienced by the federal legislature in Belgium regarding positive action, and the Dutch antipathy to the use of the term 'discrimination,' are two such examples. The flexibility of the legislative approach permitted by Community directives is specifically designed to make room for such national idiosyncrasies. What is clear from this analysis is that, in spite of the existence of Community legislation on disability employment discrimination, diverse approaches will continue to be found throughout the EU in this field. The history of Community sex discrimination legislation indicates that some of these diversities will be addressed and, perhaps, removed through case law of the ECJ. However, many will remain and, beyond that, in the absence of a wide-ranging disability specific directive,[109] no minimum level of protection against disability discrimination in areas beyond employment will exist within the EU.

Postscript

Since this article was completed, the Belgian Constitutional Court has annulled certain provisions of the Law of 25 February 2003 and established a restrictive interpretation of other provisions (Judgment 157/2004 of the Court of Arbitration, 6 October 2004). The judgment limits the scope of the criminal provisions of the non-discrimination law, but extends the scope of its civil provisions to cover a broader personal scope. As a consequence, some of the provisions of criminal law referred to in this chapter have been annulled (Articles 2(4), (5) (the distribution, publicising or making public of a text, a notice, a drawing or any other means including a discriminatory expression), 6(1) (those who give publicity to their intention to commit discrimination) and 6(2) (public servants who commit discrimination in the exercise of public functions)). The only remaining criminal sanctions in the statute concern public incitement to hatred or discrimination.

With regard to civil law, the judgment has resulted in an extension of the personal scope of the legislation to cover discrimination irrespective of the ground on which it was based. The list of enumerated grounds previously found in Article 2(1) has been deleted and direct discrimination is now simply defined as a difference in treatment that is not objectively and reasonably justified. The definition of indirect discrimination, found in Article 2(2), is now also completely open-ended. Other provisions of the statute, including Article 4 concerning positive action, have been interpreted in line with the constitution, and on occasions this has limited their scope.

---

[109] Or binding relevant legislation at the level of the Council of Europe (an unlikely prospect at present).

8

Open for All?
Disability Discrimination Laws in Europe Relating to Goods and Services

CAROLINE GOODING and CATHERINE CASSERLEY*

1 INTRODUCTION

T HE FIRST GENERATION of civil rights laws for disabled people (the Americans With Disabilities Act 1990 (ADA), the Australian Disability Discrimination Act 1992 and the New Zealand Human Rights Act 1993) adopted a comprehensive approach to disability discrimination. Discrimination was addressed not only in relation to employment but also in relation to a broad range of services and public facilities. Within the EU, by contrast, although there is a European Directive covering disability discrimination in employment and occupation (the Framework Directive)[1] there is as yet no Directive covering goods and services. The articulation of a draft Disability Directive by the European Disability Forum (EDF)[2] has, however, begun to act as a catalyst for debate.

There are, nevertheless, instances of anti-discrimination legislation within various European countries relating to disabled people which extend beyond the employment sphere. This legislation is very recent, and has received surprisingly little attention given the complexity and importance of the areas covered. This chapter seeks to lay the foundation for future analysis by providing a broad overview of four statutes: the UK Disability Discrimination Act 1995 (DDA), the Irish Equal Status Act 2000 (ESA), the German Law on the Equalisation of Disabled Persons 2002 (LEDP) and the Spanish Law For Equal Opportunities and Against the Discrimination of

---

* Caroline Gooding is the Special Adviser to the Disability Rights Commission. Catherine Casserley is the Senior Legislation Adviser to the Disability Rights Commission.
[1] European Directive on Employment (Council Directive 2000/78/EC of 27 November 2000 Establishing a General Framework for Equal Treatment in Employment and Occupation OJ L303/16).
[2] Set out in Appendix III below.

Disabled Persons 2003 (LEODDP).[3] The one aspect of these laws which we do not address is their definitions of disability. There is no space within this chapter to do justice to this critically important subject.

Anti-discrimination laws do not simply provide a framework within which individuals or groups who experience discrimination can seek redress. They also provide an important declaration of public policy. This symbolic role of the law is as important as its instrumental role. A law which contains an unequivocal endorsement of the principles of equality can play an important role in changing social attitudes, as well as providing clear guidelines for compliance—whether voluntary or through litigation. Setting out the purpose or aim of the statute as an introduction to its more detailed provisions is one way of providing a clear signal to society at large about the principles underlying the legislation. The Spanish LEOD-DP sets out laudable aims and describes the broad principles of inclusivity that underpin it:

> ... we know that the disadvantages experienced by a disabled person may have their origins in his/her own personal difficulties but above all they arise from the obstacles and limiting conditions presented by a society that is constructed around the standard of an average person.

The German LEDP expresses its aim as remedying and preventing

> the disadvantage of disabled persons and ensure[ing] the equal entitlement to the participation of disabled persons in the life of the community and provid[ing] them with autonomous existence.

By contrast, the UK and Ireland have no tradition of including a 'purpose clause' as a preamble to legislation, and their statutes are the poorer for this.

The manner in which a law articulates the principles of disability equality in its provisions is, of course, as important as whether or not it contains a clear statement of its aims. In this chapter we will examine the extent to which the four statutes express clear principles of equality in their drafting. As we will see, the detailed provisions of the Spanish LEODDP are broadly consistent with its laudable aims.[4] The other three statutes, on the other hand, fail in varying degrees to establish a strong and principled articulation of equality for disabled people.

---

[3] The British, Spanish and German laws are all specific to disability. However, the Irish ESA prohibits discrimination on nine grounds including Disability: Race; Gender; Sexual orientation; Family status; Marital status; Age; Travellers; and Religion.

[4] With the significant exception of its definition of disability which seems more fitted to a social welfare statute; Art 1 defines disabled people as those receiving certain specified state benefits, and all those 'who have a degree of handicap of 33 per cent or above.'

We will also consider the effectiveness of these four statutes in offering legal redress to those who have experienced discrimination; a consideration which will include some analysis of their enforcement mechanisms. In addition, we will examine their potential for tackling the structural or institutionalised forms of discrimination that confront disabled people in all areas of society. Before doing so, however, we would like to add a word of caution. All of these statutes are very recent. Indeed, the most recent of them, the Spanish LEODDP, establishes a framework which is to be implemented over a number of years by subsequent detailed regulations. The oldest and most firmly established is the UK DDA, which has progressively come into force since December 1996. For this reason, we will devote most attention to the DDA. Further, we should add that we will not consider the interaction of disability specific legislation with other domestic legislation such as penal laws. Finally, it should be noted that the translations of the German and Spanish laws are privately commissioned and may therefore not reflect an official interpretation.

2 COMPREHENSIVE COVERAGE?

2.1 Overview

All four statutes fall short of providing comprehensive rights across all areas of services. The scope of the legislation in relation to goods, facilities and services is broadly similar in the UK, Spain and Ireland. A range of private and public services are covered but some important exclusions are made. The UK DDA is, notably, the only one to exclude discrimination in relation to transport. The German LEDP, by contrast, focuses primarily on services provided by the public sector.

Comprehensive coverage is of critical importance, in both practical and symbolic terms. Practically speaking, legislating for equality in the health field will be of little benefit if the transport system is so inaccessible that disabled people cannot travel to obtain any healthcare which is available to them. In symbolic terms, narrowness of coverage suggests that the objectives of inclusion and equality are less important than other considerations. Thus, for example, the German LEDP conveys the message that equal treatment of disabled people is too onerous a burden to be imposed on private businesses.

2.2 The UK

The DDA prohibits discrimination by a provider of services. This is defined as a person who is 'concerned with the provision in the United Kingdom of services to the public or to a section of the public; and it is irrelevant whether a service is provided on payment or without payment.[5] 'Services' includes the provision of any goods or facilities.[6] The Act provides a non-exhaustive list of examples of services to which the relevant sections apply.[7]

Whilst the scope of the DDA is fairly wide, significant areas are excluded or treated separately. All of these exclusions will be addressed by the Disability Discrimination Bill, which is currently before Parliament.[8]

Case law under the Race Relations Act 1976 (RRA) (which will almost certainly be applied to the DDA) established that what are in essence 'private clubs' do not constitute services to the public.[9] To amount to a private club, however, a club must have a genuine selection procedure (eg, the requirement of a proposer and seconder) and thus be in no way open to the general public.

Other RRA cases[10] have raised questions about whether a broad range of 'public functions' (eg the actual arrest of an individual) constitute a 'service' to the particular member of the public concerned. Such functions may therefore be outside the current scope of the DDA.

Transport is inadequately covered. Any service which 'consists of the use of a means of transport' is excluded.[11] However, the transport infrastructure (eg train stations and airports) does not fall within this exemption and therefore remains protected by the DDA.[12] In addition, DDA regulations specify minimum access standards for buses and trains.[13]

Education was initially excluded from the goods and services provisions, but it is now the subject of specific provisions (in Part IV DDA) following the passing of the Special Educational Needs and Disability Act 2001 (SENDA). Many of the principles in the education provisions are the same as those relating to goods facilities and services (eg the anticipatory nature of the reasonable adjustment duty).[14]

---

[5] DDA s 19(2)(b).

[6] DDA s 19(2)(a).

[7] S 19(3).

[8] See the Report of the Joint Committee on the Draft Disability Discrimination Bill, Volumes 1 & 2, House of Lords and Commons, 2004.

[9] *Dockers Labour Club and Institute Limited v Race Relations Board* [1976] AC 285.

[10] See *R v Immigration Appeal Tribunal ex p Kassam* [1980] 1 WLR 1037; *R v Entry Clearance Officer ex p Amin* [1983] 2 AC 818; and, more recently, *Brooks v Metropolitan Police Commissioner* [2002] EWCA Civ 407, which saw the Court of Appeal take a broader interpretation of service than hitherto.

[11] S 19(5) (although this exemption will be removed with the passage and implementation of the Disability Discrimination Bill).

[12] Code of Practice on Rights of Access (London, DRC, 2002), para 2.36. See also *Ross v Ryanair and Stansted Airport Ltd* [2004] EWCA Civ 1751.

[13] GB Regulations: SI 1998/1970, SI 2000/3318, SI 1998/2456, SI 2000/3215, SI 2000/2990 and Northern Ireland: Rail Vehicle Accessibility Regulations (Northern Ireland) 2001 (Statutory Rule 2001 No 264); Public Service Vehicles Accessibility Regulations (Northern Ireland) 2003 (Statutory Rule 2003 No 37); Disability Discrimination (Taxis) (Carrying of Guide Dogs etc) Regulations (Northern Ireland) 2001 (Statutory Rule 2001 No 169).

[14] See J Schoonheim and D Ruebain, ch 9 below.

There have been several cases on the scope of the DDA's goods and services provisions. In one,[15] relating to education (prior to the implementation of SENDA), the District Judge took a purposive approach and interpreted the exclusion of education as narrowly as possible. In two further cases, relating to transport,[16] it was determined that assistance in a station fell within the scope of the DDA but that booking particular seats on a plane did not.

Finally, the sale, rental and management of premises is dealt with by a separate, more restricted part of the DDA. Sections 22–24 prohibit less favourable treatment in this context but do not require reasonable adjustments of any form. This not only means that landlords can refuse to adapt their flats or houses (or even to permit such adaptation by tenants) but also that they can refuse guide-dogs under a general 'no pet' rule, or refuse to communicate with tenants in accessible formats. Again, this will be addressed by the Disability Discrimination Bill.

Please note whilst the DDA applies to all parts of the United Kingdom the Disability Discrimination Bill will not apply to Northern Ireland, nor does SENDA apply in that jurisdiction.

2.3 Ireland

Section 2 of the ESA prohibits discrimination in the disposal of goods or in the provision of services to the public (whether generally or to a section of it), for consideration or otherwise. Like the DDA, it contains a non-exhaustive list of examples of services. Pension rights (within the meaning of the Employment Equality Act 1998 (EEA)) are specifically excluded, as are services or facilities to which the EEA applies.

Unlike the DDA, the ESA specifically covers transport. It also covers clubs, with special provisions (including a separate enforcement procedure) relating to registered clubs.[17] There are separate provisions covering those disposing of any estate or interest in premises or providing any accommodation or any services or amenities related to accommodation.[18] The provisions also cover any educational establishments.[19]

The question of whether 'public functions' are covered by the relevant anti-disability-discrimination statute has also arisen in Ireland. In *Donovan*

---

[15] *Thomas White v Clitheroe Royal Grammar School Preston County Court*, Claim no BB002640 29 April 2002.

[16] *McMurtry v Virgin Trains and Railtrack*, Claim No NE140154, Newcastle upon Tyne County Court 26 Sept 2001; and *Rimmer v British Airways plc* Great Grimsby County Court, Case No GG100921; see also the case of *Ross v Ryanair and Stansted Airport Ltd* [2004] EWCA Civ 1751 which, although scope was not an issue, did consider the issue of the exemption in relation to the provision of a wheelchair as a reasonable adjustment in going from check-in to departure.

[17] S 8.

[18] S 6.

[19] S 7.

v Garda Donellan,[20] which concerned a failure by the police to prosecute an individual, the Equality Officer considered various state services to be clearly covered by the ESA and that certain police services might also be included. However, relying upon comments in the Irish Parliament and on UK RRA cases on this matter, it was held that certain functions (such as arresting individuals) would not amount to services within the meaning of the ESA.

2.4 Spain

The LEODDP applies to telecommunications and information businesses; public spaces in urban areas, infrastructures, housing and buildings; public transport; goods and services for the general public; and state services.[21] Education does not appear to be specifically covered, as separate provision is made in the Educational Law of 1990, the Ley Organica de Ordenacion General del Sistema Educativo (LOGSE) (Law on the General Organization of the Educational System), for students with 'special needs'.

2.5 Germany

The LEDP aims to set 'barrier free' standards for access to buildings and other facilities, transport, technical items, information distribution systems, acoustic and visual information sources and communications facilities and other designed living areas.[22] However, the prohibition against discrimination applies only to 'public entities.' These are defined as follows:

> the departments and other sections of the federal administration, including direct governmental bodies, institutions and foundations under public law; state administrations, including direct governmental bodies, institutions and foundations under public law where these relate to Federal law.

3 PROTECTION FROM DISCRIMINATION

3.1 Overview

The 'bite' of anti-discrimination provisions depends both on the nature of the decisions the law chooses to scrutinise, and on whether or not the law allows any defences or exclusions. EU anti-discrimination law has historically categorised discrimination as either 'direct' or 'indirect.'[23] In relation

---

[20] Decision S2001-011, www.equalitytribunal.ie.
[21] Art 3.
[22] Art 4.
[23] European Directive on employment (Council Directive 2000/78/EC of 27 November 2000 Establishing a General Framework for Equal Treatment in Employment and Occupation OJ L303/16), and see also previous anti-discrimination provisions relating to gender.

to disability discrimination there is an additional, third concept—the duty to provide reasonable adjustments. This will be considered separately in the next section. Here we will examine only the extent to which the four statutes under discussion address direct and indirect discrimination.

Direct discrimination focuses on equality as consistency, identifying discrimination with hostility or prejudice. It scrutinises decisions where similarly situated individuals have been treated differently, with the aim of ascertaining whether the difference in treatment is caused by prejudice or stereotype. The Framework Directive thus prohibits direct discrimination on grounds of disability (in addition to religion, sexuality, and age), and defines this as:

> where one person is treated less favourably than another is, has been or would be treated in a comparable situation' on the grounds of disability.[24]

The concept of indirect discrimination was first developed in the US[25] in the context of race discrimination. It was founded on recognition of the fact that treating people in the same way, regardless of their differing backgrounds, can simply entrench inequality. The Framework Directive defines indirect discrimination as occurring:

> where an apparently neutral provision, criterion or practice would put ... persons with a particular disability ... at a particular disadvantage compared with other persons unless (i) that provision, criterion or practice is objectively justified by a legitimate aim and the means of achieving that aim are appropriate and necessary, or unless, as regards the persons referred to in (ii), the employer or any person or organisation to whom Article 3 applies, is obliged, under national legislation, to lay down appropriate measures in line with the principles contained in Article 5 in order to eliminate the disadvantages entailed by such provision, criterion or practice.[26]

In view of the fact that it is Article 5 which requires reasonable adjustments, this definition recognises that there is a potential overlap between duties to make adjustments and requirements not to indirectly discriminate.

A case under the Australian Disability Discrimination Act 1992 (DDA 1992) provides the only example, of which we are aware, of a case in which indirect discrimination has been established in relation to goods and services.[27]

---

[24] Art 2(2)a.

[25] In the seminal case of *Griggs v Duke Power* 401 US 424, 91 S Ct 849.

[26] Art 2(2)b.

[27] The indirect discrimination provisions of the Australian DDA are as follows: s 6 For the purposes of this Act, a person (*discriminator*) discriminates against another person (*aggrieved person*) on the ground of a disability of the aggrieved person if the discriminator requires the aggrieved person to comply with a requirement or condition: (a) with which a substantially higher proportion of persons without the disability comply or are able to comply; and (b) which is not reasonable having regard to the circumstances of the case; and (c) with which the aggrieved person does not or is not able to comply.

It illustrates the potential power of the concept of indirect discrimination in tackling structural discrimination. The Telstra Corporation provided standard headsets for telephones. However, it refused to provide any alternative telecommunications devices, such as the tele-typewriters (TTYs) which would make the telecommunications system accessible to people with hearing impairments. A complaint was lodged by Scott, who was profoundly deaf, and by a representative of the Disabled People's International (Australia) Ltd on behalf of all Australians who were deaf.[28] They argued that the refusal to supply them with TTYs amounted to discrimination and that, by this conduct, Telstra had denied them access to the telecommunications system while it provided access to hearing subscribers through the supply of the standard telephone. The Human Rights and Equal Opportunities Commission (HREOC) accepted that the service Telstra provided was communication over the network, and that the requirement that the network be accessed by standard handsets was clearly one with which a disproportionate number of people with profound hearing loss could not comply and which was patently unreasonable in the circumstances. The Commission concluded that the refusal to provide people with profound hearing loss with TTYs amounted to indirect discrimination under the DDA 1992.

In certain situations, potentially discriminatory treatment may conflict with other social priorities such as economic or social policy objectives. The scope of legal 'justifications' for potentially discriminatory treatment will be a powerful determinant of both the symbolic and instrumental efficacy of the law. As Sandra Fredman writes:

> The value that society places on equality is reflected both in the decision as to whether it is permissible to raise such a defence, and in the weight given to the defence relative to the discriminatory act.[29]

Historically, direct discrimination has not been capable of justification in EU law, although the Framework Directive does permit exclusion in very specific circumstances.[30] A consideration of potential justification is, however, intrinsic to the definition of indirect discrimination; the exact nature of the justification varying across the different directives. The nature of scrutiny to be applied to the question of justification in indirect discrimination cases has been the subject of much case law.[31]

All four jurisdictions make provisions for defences against claims of unlawful discrimination, framed either generically or specifically. In addition,

---

[28] *Geoffrey Scott v Telstra Corporation Ltd*, and *Disabled Peoples International (Australia) Ltd. v Telstra Corporation*, nos H95/34 and H95/51.

[29] S Fredman, *Discrimination Law* (Oxford, Oxford University Press, 2001), p 102.

[30] The Framework Directive provides three specific kinds of exceptions to the principle of equal treatment: Art 2(5) 'exceptions necessary in a democratic society', Art 4 'genuine occupational requirements', and Art 7 'positive action'.

[31] See S Fredman, *Discrimination Law* (above n 29) at pp 112–15 for a discussion of the European case law on this point.

the exclusion of treatment in specified circumstances from the application of non-discrimination principles can serve the same function as such defences, as is discussed in relation to the Irish legislation.

3.2 The UK

The DDA does not adopt the direct/indirect discrimination approach described above, though it is contained in the UK anti-discrimination statutes relating to sex and race.[32] Under the DDA, discrimination is defined as occurring in two ways. First, where a service provider treats the disabled person less favourably for a reason that relates to the disabled person's disability, than he treats or would treat others to whom that reason does not or would not apply, and he cannot justify that treatment. Secondly, where a service provider fails to comply with a reasonable adjustment duty imposed on him in relation to the disabled person, and he cannot show that his failure to comply with that duty is justified.[33]

In the leading case on the meaning of 'less favourable treatment' under the DDA (*Clark v TDG Ltd t/a Novacold*)[34] the Court of Appeal held that the test does not turn on a like-for-like comparison of the treatment of the disabled person with that of others in similar circumstances. Rather, it is based on a consideration of the reason for the treatment of the disabled person. Thus, in deciding whether an employee who was dismissed for disability-related sickness absence had been treated less favourably under the DDA, the comparison required was not with a non-disabled person who had had the same length of absence from work but, instead, with someone to whom the reason for the relevant treatment did not apply (ie someone who was not absent from work and who thus would not have been dismissed). In essence, less favourable treatment is established by showing that someone has been subjected to a detriment for a reason related to their disability. Once less treatment has been established, the issue becomes this: can this treatment be justified?

Although *Novacold* related to the employment provisions, it will apply equally to the goods and services provisions of the DDA where the same formulation of 'less favourable treatment' appears. Indeed, the Court of Appeal used a services analogy in their reasoning; that of individuals being refused entry because they are accompanied by a guide dog. The judgment makes reference to an example given by the Minister at the time of the passage of the Act. If no dogs are admitted to a cafe, the reason for denying access to refreshment in it by a blind person with his guide dog would be the fact that no dogs are admitted. That reason 'relates to' his disability. His guide dog is with him because of his disability.[35]

---

[32] Sex Discrimination Act 1975; Race Relations Act 1976.
[33] DDA s 20.
[34] [1999] IRLR 318.
[35] HL Deb, vol 566, col 267 (Lord Mackay of Ardbrecknish).

The reasoning in *Novacold* was adopted in the goods and services cases of *Thomas White v Clitheroe Royal Grammar School*[36] and *Glover v Lawford*;[37] as well as in a number of other cases where guide dog owners who were denied services because of an insistence that they leave their dogs outside (see the Disability Rights Commission website for further details). It was also adopted in the case of *Ross v Ryanair and Stansted Airport Ltd*,[38] and by the Court of Appeal in the housing case of *Manchester City Council v Romano and Samari*.[39]

Thus, the DDA's distinctive form of protection against less favourable treatment for a 'reason related to disability' is broader than direct discrimination. It is capable of addressing many of the issues tackled in other jurisdictions by the concept of indirect discrimination. Having said that, it is important to note that (unlike the majority of direct discrimination provisions) it is subject to justification.

The DDA sets out specific 'justifications', one or more of which must be established in order for potentially discriminatory treatment not to amount to unlawful discrimination (s 20(4)). There is a two-fold test: the service provider must have a genuine belief that one of the specified conditions exists, and it must be reasonable for the service provider to hold that belief. The conditions are that: the treatment is necessary for health and safety reasons; the treatment is necessary because the disabled person is incapable of entering into an enforceable agreement; the treatment is necessary to be able to provide the service to the disabled person or members of the public or to anyone at all; any difference in terms reflects the greater cost to the provider of the service (this latter justification is aimed at enabling service providers to charge for 'bespoke' services, such as the making of a specially designed bed to assist someone with back problems).

Regulations make specific provision for insurance cases.[40] According to these, the treatment is assumed to be justified if it is based upon information which is relevant to the assessment of the risk to be insured, is from a source which it is reasonable to rely upon, and is reasonable having regard to the information relied upon, and any other relevant factors.

The DDA's 'reasonable opinion' provision has attracted substantial criticism for potentially allowing prejudicial, but commonly held, views to

---

[36] Preston County Court, Claim No BB002640, 29 April 2002.
[37] 26 March 2003, Claim No MA26303.
[38] [2004] EWCA Civ 1751. That case also considered the treatment of disabled people with mobility impairments who were not wheelchair users, as against disabled people who were wheelchair users; the former were charged for wheelchair assistance, whilst the latter were not charged for any aspect of their assistance from check-in to boarding.
[39] [2004] EWCA Civ 834.
[40] For GB: Disability Discrimination (Services and Premises) Regulations 1996 SI 1996/1836 regs 1(2), 2(1) and (2) (a)–(c); For Northern Ireland: Disability Discrimination (Providers of Services) (Adjustment of Premises) Regulations (Northern Ireland) 2003 (Statutory Rule 2003 No 109).

justify discriminatory treatment.[41] There have been no cases at appellate level which have considered the justification issue in the context of goods, facilities and services. There has, however, been a premises case which dealt with the 'reasonable opinion' aspect of justification. This is highly relevant to the current discussion as the justification provisions for premises are similar to those for goods and services.[42]

In *Rose v Bouchet*,[43] Mr Rose (who was visually impaired) claimed discrimination in relation to the refusal of a landlord to let a flat to him for a week during the Edinburgh Festival. He had telephoned to enquire about renting the flat; when he explained that he was blind and asked whether there would be any objection to his guide dog, Mr Bouchet explained that the steps outside the flat did not have an adequate handrail. There was a drop of a few feet on either side of the steps. Mr Bouchet, having discussed the matter with his wife, refused to let the accommodation to Mr Rose on the grounds that the lack of a handrail would make the steps dangerous for a blind person. Thus, he accepted that, in refusing to let the premises to Mr Rose, he had treated him less favourably for a reason relating to his disability, but argued that he was justified in doing so on health and safety grounds. The sheriff dismissed the claim, accepting that Mr Bouchet had shown that his treatment of Mr Rose was justified because he had genuinely held the opinion that refusal was necessary in order not to endanger Mr Rose; and because it was reasonable, in all the circumstances of the case, for Mr Bouchet to hold that opinion. Mr Rose appealed unsuccessfully to the Sheriff Principal. It was held that the opinion reached by the defender [service provider], on the facts as then known to him, looked at objectively, was a reasonable one for him to reach. There was no duty on the defender to obtain more information before finalising his opinion.

A more stringent scrutiny of decision making (possibly because it related to a decision by a school rather than a small private landlord) was applied in *Thomas White v Clitheroe Royal Grammar School*.[44] The District Judge there held that the belief that the exclusion of a boy with diabetes from a school trip was justified could not be said to be based on a reasonably held opinion that it was necessary in order not to endanger his health or safety. There was no involvement of Thomas or his parents in the decision making process, the matters held against him were never put to him for an explanation and there was no serious attempt at a risk assessment, taking into account the nature of the holiday and the medical realities.

The Queen's Bench Division, in another housing case, considered the test of justification under the premises provisions. *North Devon Homes*

[41] The Disability Rights Commission has recommended that the wording of the justification provision be amended to provide an objective test for justifying potential discrimination in goods and services matters: *Disability Equality: Making it Happen* (London, DRC, 2003).
[42] DDA s 23.
[43] *Rose v Bouchet* [1999] IRLR 463.
[44] Preston County Court, claim No BB002640, 29 April 2002.

Ltd v Christine Brazier[45] concerned an order for possession which had been granted in respect of a tenant with a psychiatric disorder, despite the District Judge having found that the local authority had acted contrary to the DDA in seeking possession. Ms Brazier admitted persistent anti-social behaviour, including shouting at neighbouring tenants, keeping them awake and using foul language. The District Judge found that the eviction was not necessary in order not to endanger the health and safety of any person as, although the neighbours experienced a great deal of discomfort, neither their health nor their safety was alleged to be endangered. The decision was upheld by the Queen's Bench and the eviction order was quashed because, the necessity element of the justification defence not having been present, the eviction would amount to unlawful discrimination.

More recently, however, the Court of Appeal examined the issue of evictions for reasons relating to mental health in the case of *Manchester City Council v Romano and Samari*[46] and considered in particular the health and safety defence. It was held that 'health', in the case of the health and safety defence, bore the broad meaning ascribed to it by the World Health Organisation, whereby 'health is a state of complete physical, mental and social well-being and not merely the absence of disease and infirmity' (para 69 of the judgment) and thus that the decisions made in these cases to evict the tenants, as a result of the effect which their behaviour had on their neighbours, was not in breach of the DDA.

3.3 Ireland

The first point to note about the ESA is that it adopts a broad approach towards establishing the 'protected class,' covering those who are discriminated against on the basis of association with a disabled person and those who are discriminated against on grounds of future, past or imputed disabilities.[47]

The second point of note is that indirect discrimination is covered. This will occur where an apparently neutral provision puts a [disabled person] at a particular disadvantage compared with other persons, unless the provision is objectively justified by a legitimate aim and the means of achieving that aim are appropriate and necessary.[48]

---

[45] *North Devon Homes Ltd v Christine Brazier* (High Court QBD) BP200068 [2003] EWHC 574; [2003] HRR 59.
[46] [2004] EWCA Civ 834.
[47] S 2(1).
[48] S 3(c) as amended by the Equality Act 2004.

The use of the word 'reasonable' in the ESA's justification defence for indirect discrimination makes it relatively easy for service providers to claim that their conduct was justified. The Framework Directive refers instead to objective justification. It is not clear whether the ESA's reasonableness test would be an objective rather than subjective one and this issue does not appear to have been tested as yet.

The 'direct' discrimination provisions of the ESA, though not the subject of any decisions relating to disability, have been considered in relation to the other grounds. Early decisions[49] made it clear that a comparator would be needed in order to establish discrimination. This approach would therefore not extend to someone refused access because of a guide dog where others with dogs were also refused access, in contrast to the broader UK provisions.

The ESA allows no specific justifications for direct discrimination. However, it does provide for numerous circumstances in which neither the direct nor the indirect discrimination provisions will apply. In effect these provisions operate in the same way as justifications. Section 4(4) provides that where a person has a disability that, in the circumstances, could cause harm to the person or to others, treating the person differently to the extent reasonably necessary to prevent such harm does not constitute discrimination. Section 5(2) specifically disapplies the prohibition on discrimination in the provision of goods and services in relation to sporting facilities or sporting events to the extent that the differences are reasonably necessary having regard to the nature of the facility or event and are relevant to the purpose of the facility or event; or where the treatment is reasonably required for reasons of authenticity, aesthetics, tradition or custom in connection with a dramatic performance or other entertainment. There is also special provision in relation to financial issues. Section 5(2) permits differences in the treatment of persons in relation to annuities, pensions and insurance policies where the treatment is based on actuarial or statistical data from a reliable source or other relevant factors and it is reasonable having regard to the data or other factors.

Section 15 provides that nothing in the Act shall be construed as requiring a person to dispose of goods or premises, or to provide services or accommodation to a customer in circumstances which would lead a reasonable individual (having the responsibility, knowledge and experience of the person) to the belief, on grounds other than discriminatory grounds, that doing so would produce a substantial risk of criminal or disorderly conduct or behaviour or damage to property. In addition, action taken in good faith by or on behalf of the holder of a licence for the sale of

---

[49] Eg in *Conroy v Carney* DEC–2001–002.

intoxicating liquor, for the sole purpose of ensuring compliance with the provisions of the Licensing Acts 1833 to 1999, will not constitute discrimination.

Section 16(2) provides an exemption for discriminatory treatment where clinical judgment is being exercised in the health area or there is an inability to enter into a contract or to give informed consent. The former exclusion is likely to be of particular concern to disabled people as clinical judgment is often used to explain poorer treatment for those who have, for example, Down's syndrome.[50]

In sum, then, the ESA appears to set out a fairly extensive range of situations in which the disadvantageous treatment of a disabled person would not be unlawful. It is, of course, impossible to assess the exact parameters of such exemptions and justifications in the absence of case law.

The ESA also defines discrimination as including a refusal or failure by the provider of a service to do all that is reasonable to accommodate the needs of a person with a disability[51] (discussed below).

3.4 Spain

The Spanish LEODDP establishes a right to equal opportunities which is violated when either direct or indirect discrimination occurs. There is no definition of 'direct' discrimination (and it is worth noting that direct and indirect discrimination are already prohibited by Article 14 of the Spanish constitution).

Indirect discrimination will occur when a disabled person encounters some obstacle as a result of any legal provision or regulation, contractual clause, private pact, unilateral decision, criterion or practice or as a result of the design of public places, products or services, however apparently unbiased, where the purpose of those obstacles is neither just nor reasonable and the means used to achieve that purpose is neither satisfactory nor necessary.[52] This latter 'justification' appears to be modelled upon the definition of indirect discrimination in the Framework Directive. The LEODDP is progressive in its explicit recognition that non-inclusive design can be conceptualised as a form of indirect discrimination, and unusual (perhaps unique) in extending coverage to product design.

It is likely that enforcement of these provisions will be significantly affected by the accessibility standards which the LEODDP requires the Government to introduce.

---

[50] With respect to British experience see S Rutter and S Seyman *He'll Never Join the Army* (London Down's Syndrome Association 1999).

[51] S 4(1).

[52] Art 6.

3.5 Germany

The main focus of the LEDP is establishing targets for accessibility, an issue that will be considered in detail below. However, Article 7 prohibits discrimination by public entities, discrimination being defined as a disadvantage created where disabled and non-disabled persons are treated differently without cogent reason and thereby disabled persons are directly or indirectly impaired from participating in an equal manner in everyday life. This appears to allow for justification on the basis of a 'cogent reason', which would not be permissible in a case of 'direct' discrimination under the European Employment Framework Directive. Indeed, this has the potential to be a very broad justification which, depending upon how the courts treat these claims, could effectively render this aspect of the legislation meaningless.

4 CHANGING SOCIETY: REMOVING BARRIERS TO PARTICIPATION

4.1 Overview

Historically the environment, both physical and organisational, has been designed in a way which unthinkingly excludes and segregates disabled people. The concept of 'reasonable accommodation' as a legal mechanism for dismantling these societal barriers was first introduced by Regulations interpreting the Rehabilitation Act 1973 in the US.[53] The concept was subsequently employed, not only in the ADA, but in disability discrimination laws in Australia, New Zealand, South Africa and many other countries.

The reasonable accommodations provisions are, for many disabled people, the most important aspect of any disability discrimination legislation relating to goods and services. They oblige service providers to make changes to the way in which they deliver their services (including the physical environment) so that disabled people can access them. A right to such adjustments gives individual disabled people the power to achieve change. Framed in a way that permits case by case determination of 'reasonableness,' the concept provides flexibility so that large service providers with significant resources are expected to make more extensive adjustments than small, lower-resourced service providers.

However, to be effective the law needs to promote a systematic approach to dismantling environmental barriers and ensuring that new buildings/services are fully inclusive and not merely be dependent on enforcement by individuals. A duty to make reasonable accommodations for individuals is sometimes supplemented by accessibility regulations which set down specific standards. Standards provide far greater certainty about

---

[53] 28 CFR Part 41 (Department of Justice); 29 CFR Part 32 (Department of Labor); 45 CFR Part 84 (Department of Health and Human Services).

what is required in a specific instance than a requirement for 'reasonable adjustments'. This helps to promote greater conformity with requirements, without enforcement by individuals. Standards can prescribe the minimum requirements with which all new services might be expected to comply, thus avoiding the traditional scenario in which disabled people are not contemplated in the original design brief and are always subsequently playing 'catch up', requiring alterations to the 'normal' way of delivering services. However, there is a danger that standards are set too low, applying a 'lowest common denominator' according to which large multi-nationals are required to do only what is required of a small corner-shop. Above all, where standards are applied, they need to be designed with the full involvement of disabled people and other interested parties.

The Australian Disability Discrimination Act 1992 contains an early example of a more proactive approach to dismantling institutional barriers: organisational self-regulation.[54] It makes provision for action plans to complement its anti-discrimination provisions. Action Plans are documents voluntarily developed by service providers which lay out the process by which the organisation proposes, over time, to eliminate practices discriminating against disabled people. The purpose of Action Plans is to encourage service providers to investigate the barriers that produce inequality of access for disabled people and devise plans to overcome them, instead of doing nothing until a complaint is made.[55]

Action plans are not in themselves enforceable. Conversely, neither the existence of an Action Plan nor evidence of compliance with its terms confers immunity from liability under the DDA 1992. The success of an Action Plan as a defence to a complaint of discrimination will depend on how good the Action Plan is judged to be.[56] There are a number of incentives to encourage organisations to develop Action Plans. These range from minimising the risk of having a complaint lodged against the organisation, to improving the organisation's chances of receiving government funding.[57]

---

[54] Ss 59–64 DDA 1992.

[55] The minimum requirements of an Action Plan are specified in s 61 of the DDA: The action plan of a service provider must include provisions relating to: (a) the devising of policies and programs to achieve the objects of this Act; and (b) the communication of these policies and programs to persons within the service provider; and (c) the review of practices within the service provider with a view to the identification of any discriminatory practices; and (d) the setting of goals and targets, where these may reasonably be determined against which the success of the plan in achieving the objects of the Act may be assessed; and (e) the means, other than those referred to in paragraph (d), of evaluating the policies and programs referred to in paragraph (a); and the appointment of persons within the service provider to implement the provisions referred to in paragraphs (a) to (e) (inclusive).

[56] S 11 of the Act specifies that an Action Plan given to the Commission under s 64 is one of the factors to be taken into account when determining whether remedying the discrimination would constitute an unjustifiable hardship to the organisation.

[57] For a broad discussion of the Australian DDA see M Jones and LA Basser Marks, 'The limitations on the use of law to promote rights: an assessment of the Disability Discrimination Act 1992' in C Sampford, M Hauritz and S Blencowe (eds), *Justice for People with Disabilities* (Sydney, Federation Press, 1998).

In the remainder of this section we will consider the approach to reasonable adjustments adopted in the four countries, focusing on the purposes of the relevant duties, their triggers, their conceptions of reasonableness and the extent to which they are anticipatory in nature. We will also examine the extent to which the four countries have supplemented these duties with alternative means of dismantling the structural barriers that exclude disabled people.

4.2 The UK

The DDA creates a freestanding duty to make adjustments.[58] Three broad categories of adjustment may be required: reasonable steps to change practices, policies and procedures which make it impossible or unreasonably difficult for disabled people to use a service; reasonable steps to change physical features of premises, where they make it impossible or unreasonably difficult for disabled people to use a service; and reasonable steps to provide an auxiliary aid or service (such as information on tape, or the provision of a sign language interpreter) where this would enable or facilitate the use of a service by disabled people.

These provisions have been brought into force gradually. Those relating to practices, policies and procedures, auxiliary aids and services, and the provision of a reasonable alternative method of service, came into force in October 1999[59] and the remaining duties relating to physical features came into force in October 2004.[60] They are known collectively as 'the duty to make reasonable adjustments.'

Because the wording of the duty refers specifically to 'disabled persons,' it is said in the statutory Code of Practice to be 'anticipatory':[61] service providers are said to owe duties to disabled people as a whole and, as a result, should ensure that they have considered and taken steps to ensure the accessibility of their services in advance of disabled customers notifying them of problems. This has been regarded as immensely significant in Britain: as a major driver in encouraging service providers to think in advance about removing barriers experienced by disabled customers or potential customers. It helps to avoid a situation in which a provider claims that, because they did not know in advance that an adjustment was required, it was not reasonable to provide one. As a result of the anticipatory duty, for example, a conference provider should ask delegates in advance about what adjustments they need.[62]

---

[58] DDA s 21.
[59] Commencement order SI 1999/1190.
[60] S 19(1)(b) and see commencement order SI 2001/2030 (England, Wales and Scotland) and SR 2001/439 (Northern Ireland).
[61] Para 4.14.
[62] See *Roads v Central Trains Ltd*, CA [2004] EWCA Civ 1541.

The trigger of 'impossible or unreasonably difficult', however, is a potentially high one to meet; it means that, in effect, a service can be reasonably difficult to use and a disabled person may have no remedy.[63] This trigger has been the subject of criticism and the DRC has highlighted the need for it to be changed.[64] These concerns appeared to be substantiated by two negative decisions by county courts. *Alistair Appleby v Department for Work and Pensions* (DWP)[65] concerned a man who had a hearing impairment and who applied for a national insurance number, which required his attendance at a DWP office. His claim of discrimination included a claim that there had been a failure to make a reasonable adjustment. The visual display unit in the office was out of order with the result that he could not tell when it was his turn to go into the office. Staff refused to notify him directly when his turn arose. Instead, he had to rely upon members of the public to assist him. The court held that the practice of having to ask a member of the public to notify him of when it was his turn did not make it 'unreasonably difficult' for Mr Appleby to use the service. The District Judge observed that:

> Indeed with commendable imagination and improvisation he enlisted without apparent difficulty the help of two members of the public who, it would appear, were more than willing to assist, and he was thus able to ascertain when it was his turn.

This demonstrates the danger of this trigger being interpreted so as to allow service providers to continue to provide a second-class service, which leaves the onus on the disabled person to cope with it.[66]

Baggley v Kingston-upon-Hull Council[67] saw a similar approach taken in relation to a wheelchair user who was unable to attend a pop concert. However, the Court of Appeal, in the case of *Roads v Central Trains Ltd*[68], stated that the policy of the DDA is what it was held to be by Mynors Ch in *Re Holy Cross, Pershore* [2002] 1 Fam 105: 'to provide access to a service as close as it is resonably possible to get to the standard normally offered to the public at large.' This aproach will hopefully guide courts on this issue in future.

---

[63] It contrasts with the trigger used in both the employment and education provisions—that of substantial disadvantage, where substantial is said by the Employment Code of Practice to mean something 'not minor or trivial': para 4.17, Code of Practice for the Elimination of Discrimination in the field of employment against disabled persons or persons who have had a disability (London, Department for Education and Employment, 1996).

[64] *Disability Equality: Making it Happen* (London, DRC, 2003). This publication contains the recommendations of the Disability Rights Commission for changes to the DDA.

[65] Lambeth County Court, Claim No LB001649, 12 July 2002.

[66] It should be noted that other aspects of Appleby's case succeeded.

[67] *Baggley v Kingston upon Hull Council*, Kingston upon Hull County Court, Claim No KH101929, 21 Feb 2002.

[68] [2004] EWCA Civ 1541.

Adjustments are required only where they are 'reasonable'. Although the DDA itself provides no guidance on what might be reasonable, the Code of Practice lists some factors that may affect the reasonableness or otherwise of an adjustment. These are effectiveness, practicability, cost, disruption, resources, amount already spent on adjustments, and availability of other sources of assistance.[69] Claims to reasonable adjustments upheld by the courts have included: permitting a motorised golf cart to be used on a golf course in dry weather;[70] the provision of a wheelchair as an auxiliary aid and an alternative method of providing the service, and the alteration of a policy of charging for the provision of a wheelchair;[71] and the adjustment of a 'no pets' rule to allow entry to guide dogs.[72]

The reasonable adjustment duty is circumscribed by s 21(6), which states that nothing in the section requires a service provider to take any steps that would fundamentally alter the nature of the service in question or the nature of his trade, profession or business. Failure to make an adjustment is also subject to justification as discussed above.

There are specific provisions in the UK legislation for regulations to be made to prescribe, amongst other things, circumstances in which it is and is not reasonable for a provider of services to have to take steps of a pre-scribed description under different provisions.[73] Effectively, this enables the Government to prescribe accessibility standards. The regulations have been used to declare that changes will not be required where a physical feature meets the design considerations etc of Approved Document M of the Building Regulations[74] (or analogous requirements in Scotland), but no other regulations under these provisions have been made. As has already been mentioned, however, regulations relating to transport have been pro-duced.[75] Further, the Communications Act 2003 (a separate piece of legisla-tion, not explicitly linked to the DDA) lays down certain minimum propor-tions of programmes which should be produced with sub-titles, audio-description and sign-language interpretation.

Finally, it should be noted that the Disability Discrimination Bill, cur-rently before Parliament, would introduce a systematic approach to dismantling societal barriers. It would place a positive duty on the public sector to promote equality. The implications of such an approach are

---

[69] Para 4.22 Code of Practice, Goods, Facilities, Services, and Premises (DRC 2002).
[70] *Vernon Roper v Singing Hills Golf Course Ltd* Haywards Heath County Court, 26 April 2001.
[71] *Ross v Ryanair and Stansted Airport Ltd* [2004] EWCA Civ 1751.
[72] See further www.drc-gb.org
[73] DDA s 21(5)(a) and (b).
[74] SI 2001/3253.
[75] Above n 12.

extremely significant and are considered in more detail in Colm O'Cinneide's chapter.

4.3 Ireland

Section 4 of the ESA provides that discrimination includes a refusal or failure by the service provider to do all that is reasonable to accommodate the needs of a disabled person by providing special treatment or facilities if, without such treatment or facilities, it would otherwise be impossible or unduly difficult for the person to avail him or herself of the service. The trigger for adjustments is thus almost identical to that in the DDA—impossible or unduly difficult. In addition, what is required of the service provider is defined as 'special treatment.' This terminology undermines the principle of inclusivity. It detracts from the obligation to ensure access and focuses instead on a conception of disabled people as 'special' and, as such, in need of 'special treatment', rather than adjustments which may benefit the whole of society and which are required in the interests of broad inclusivity.

The duty in the ESA is not anticipatory as it is expressed as being owed to 'a person with a disability.'[76] Nor is there a specific provision addressing the issue of whether or not knowledge of an individual's impairment is required in order for the service provider to be in breach of his duty. In the absence of an anticipatory duty, however, it is difficult to see how a service provider would not require knowledge of disability and, in particular, knowledge of what treatment or facilities would be required in that particular case to ensure that that person could access the service. This adds to the reactive nature of the duty, depriving it of an ability to tackle systemic discrimination.

The ESA provides guidance as to what might be considered reasonable in relation to costs. According to s 4(2):

> A refusal or failure to provide the special treatment or facilities ... shall not be deemed reasonable unless such provision would give rise to a cost, other than a nominal cost, to the provider of the service in question.

This serious restriction of the duty was added following the reference of the Employment Bill and the Equal Status Bill to the Supreme Court by the Irish President, who queried their constitutionality. The Court held that, insofar as the reasonable accommodation provisions in those draft Bills required potentially costly adjustments, they were indeed contrary to the Irish constitutional provisions relating to property rights.[77]

---

[76] S 4(1).

[77] In the Matter of Article 26 and in the Matter of the Employment Equality Bill 1996 118/97; 15 May 1997—the provisions in the draft bill referred to costs not resulting in 'undue hardship.' However, following the implementation of the Framework Directive, this has now been amended in relation to employment to refer to 'disproportionate burden'.

Although the issue of 'nominal' cost has not been considered in relation to the goods and services provisions, it has been considered in relation to the employment provisions. The meaning of 'nominal' was considered in a case involving a claim that a local authority should have provided an employee with a professional job coach and a vocational assessment.[78] The comments of the legislature in debates during the passage of this provision were considered and it was held that in deciding whether a cost was 'nominal,' consideration should be given to the size and resources of the service provider.

Sections 17–19 also make provision for regulations to be made requiring: new road or rail passenger vehicles to be made accessible; operators of bus and rail stations to provide facilities at those stations so that they are readily accessible to and useable by persons with a disability; and a road authority, when constructing or altering or giving consent to the construction or alteration of any public footway or other public pavement, to provide or require the provision of ramps, dished kerbs, or other sloped areas at appropriate places at or in the vicinity of any pedestrian crossing or intersection used by pedestrians in that part of the footway or pavement. Thus it seems that the legislature has adopted an anticipatory, standards based approach for certain parts of the transport and mobility infrastructure.[79]

There have been very few cases brought under the ESA relating to disabled people and goods facilities and services. There appears to have been one case involving the reasonable adjustment provisions. This involved a guide dog owner who was not allowed to enter a pub with his guide dog.[80] The Equality Tribunal found that he had been discriminated against, contrary to s 4, in that the respondent had failed to provide special treatment to accommodate him on the grounds of his disability (ie by letting the guide dog in). 3000 euros were awarded in compensation and the respondent was ordered to display a notice stating that disabled people and guide dogs were welcome; and to ensure that all staff were trained in the ESA as well as in the food hygiene regulations and their application to guide dogs.

4.4 Spain

The LEODDP makes provision for both an individual reasonable adjustment duty, and for government regulations to determine accessibility criteria. Article 10 provides that the Government 'shall regulate basic conditions for accessibility and non-discrimination to guarantee standards for equal opportunities for all disabled citizens.' The regulations are to be established

---

[78] Office of the Director of Equality Investigations, Employment Equality Act 1998, Equality Officer's Decision No E/2002/4.

[79] It should be pointed out, however, that this makes no provision for tactile paving for those with visual impairments, which is a common feature of paving at crossings in the UK.

[80] *Roche v Alabaster Associates t/a Madigans*, DECS 2002–086.

progressively over time and 'shall also be progressive in the scope and reach of obligations imposed, and shall encompass all fields and areas as set out in Chapter I.'

The accessibility standards will be drawn up in relation to particular sectors. In particular, they are to include:

(i) Requirements for accessibility to buildings and public places, as well as to instruments, equipment, technology, goods and products used in the sector or area, and the removal of barriers to plants or factories and the adaptation of equipment or instruments.

(ii) The development and availability of public programmes for information, assistance and auxiliary services to enable adequate communication for use by people with different kinds of disability. This would include aural /visual communication systems, including support for oral communication and sign language, and other provisions that enable communication and access to information for people with a sensory impairment.

(iii) The adoption of in-house standards in companies or organisations that promote the removal of obstacles or discriminatory situations for disabled people.

The LEODDP sets out specific timings for the establishment of these accessibility standards. For example, over the course of two years from the establishment of the law, the Government will set out basic conditions for accessibility and non-discrimination in relation to public offices and public services, and also in relation to general government and the legal system.[81]

According to Art 7 LEODDP, 'requirements for accessibility' are 'requirements with which public places, products and services should comply, as well as conditions for non-discrimination in norms, criteria and practices, with special regard to the principles of universal access and design for all.'

The freestanding reasonable adjustment duty, set out in Article 7(c), requires that measures be taken to adapt the physical and social environment to the specific needs of disabled people in a practical and effective way, and without giving rise to disproportionate charges, so that accessibility and participation by disabled people are enabled on equal terms with able-bodied people. When determining whether a charge is disproportionate, the cost of making adjustments is to be considered as is the discriminatory effect on a disabled person if the adjustment is not made. In addition, the characteristics of the person, organisation or entity which has to make the adjustment will be considered, as well as the possibility of obtaining funding from public bodies or any other source. Article 7 also provides for the government to establish a system of public funding to contribute to the costs arising from the obligation to make reasonable adjustments.

---

[81] See Fifth Final Provision (1).

The provisions contained in the LEODDP appear to be very far reaching. They set a goal of participation on 'equal terms'. It seems that the reasonable adjustment duty is anticipatory, with its reference to 'disabled people' as opposed to a 'disabled person', although it does use the words 'specific needs,' which may imply an individual approach. Its emphasis is on the adjustments being practical and effective without incurring disproportionate cost. Although the term 'reasonable' is not used, the factors that need to be taken into account in considering whether the cost is disproportionate (eg, the effect upon the disabled person of not making the adjustment and the nature of the organisation) would appear to encompass many of the factors relevant to a broader concept of reasonableness.

In relation to housing, existing property law is amended to require shared owners of flats to pay up to the equivalent of three months' service charge to carry out access works to the common parts of the building for the benefit of disabled people.[82] This is extremely significant, given that this is a widespread form of dwelling.

4.5 Germany

Failure to provide a reasonable adjustment is not defined as a form of discrimination in the LEDP. Instead, a series of accessibility standards are created, and legal action can be taken by disabled individuals (and organisations representing them) if these standards are breached.

Specific regulations (to apply to public entities) are to be drawn up in relation to: the use of interpreters for hearing impaired people; the design of written decisions, general degrees, public contracts and forms; and access to information technology. Public entities must provide sign language interpreters on request 'where this is required to safeguard their rights in administrative proceedings.' There is thus no 'reasonableness' caveat in relation to this requirement. To date, three administrative regulations have been adopted in relation to the LEDP. These relate to: the use of sign language and other communication aids in federal administrative procedure; accessible documents for visually impaired people in federal administrative procedure; and barrier free information technology.

New civic buildings and extensions or conversions of them must be designed 'with freedom of access'. However, 'these requirements may be waived if freedom of access can be satisfied in the same extent using other means'.[83]

The distinctive feature of the LEDP, and the core of its approach, is its emphasis on groups of disabled people brokering agreements

---

[82] Third supplementary provision Law for Equal Opportunities, amending Article 10 Law 49/1960.

[83] S 2 article 8 (the 'waiving' here is similar to the provisions in the UKDDA which permit service by a reasonable alternative method as an alternative to removing physical barriers (s 21(2)).

('*Zielvereinbarungen*') with public or private enterprises. These agreements will contain detailed plans and timetables for achieving barrier-free access for disabled people. Agreements can be negotiated with regard to anything from restaurants, supermarkets and automatic machines to employment sites and conditions. It is up to German disability organisations to negotiate the terms of an agreement, and they have a right to demand the opening of negotiations. However, there appears to be no sanction or positive incentive to encourage organisations to conclude such agreements. This is a potentially fundamental flaw.

Article 5 states that agreements are to be reached between 'relevant' groups and enterprises. The relevant groups are those which are deemed to be permitted to take legal action in respect of a breach of the discrimination laws. These are specifically defined in Article 13 as organisations that 'permanently' promote the requirements of disabled people; that according to their composition are intended to represent the interests of disabled people at federal level; have been in existence for at least three years; carry out their role as set out in their constitutions (here the type and scope of their previous activities, their membership and their efficiency are to be considered); and that are not-for-profit. This would seem to allow the Government considerable scope in determining which organisations are to be involved in the drawing up of standards.

The LEDP has been described as playing a major role in future equal rights policy:

> Those directly involved are able to agree arrangements creating barrier-free environments which are adjusted to the respective circumstances and needs ... when such agreements are concluded the law is filled with life. Disabled persons will be able to contribute their goals and ideas here as a partner in negotiations with the business community independently and on their own responsibility. This is for them the clearest evidence of the paradigm change from an object to a subject.[84]

5 EFFECTIVE ENFORCEMENT

5.1 Overview

Rights that lack effective enforcement mechanisms cannot produce substantive change. We consider below whether the four countries under consideration allow groups of and for disabled people to take enforcement action, and whether there is a national independent body to promote and enforce

[84] 'Legislation to Counter Discrimination Against Persons With Disabilities', paper presented at Second European Conference of Ministers Responsible for Integration Policies for People with Disabilities, Malaga, May 2003. Working Group on legislation to counter discrimination against persons with disabilities in co-operation with Prof Dr Heinz-Dietrich Steinmeyer.

disability rights. We also outline sanctions for breach of the law which are, for example, required by the Framework Directive[85] to be 'effective, proportionate and dissuasive'.

5.2 UK

Claims relating to goods, facilities and services are enforced in the UK in the County Court in England, Northern Ireland, Wales, and the Sheriff's court in Scotland.[86] Compensation may include damages for injury to feelings (which are unlimited, although there is a limit to the amount which can be awarded by county courts).[87] Of the relatively few cases that have been brought to the courts, the highest compensation award was £3000 in *Thomas White v Clitheroe Royal Grammar School*.[88] In *William Purves v Joydisc*,[89] where a blind person was refused access to a restaurant with his guide dog, the Sheriff Principal upheld an appeal against the £350 compensation awarded at first instance. It was held that the sum of £750 was the least that that should be awarded for injury to feelings resulting from discrimination on the basis of disability.

Remedies ordinarily available in the courts may also be awarded, including a declaration of discrimination and an injunction.[90] The first injunction in a goods and services case was awarded in 2003.[91] This could prove to be a far greater deterrent than the relatively low amounts of compensation awarded.

Considerable difficulties relating to the enforcement of the goods and services provisions have been encountered in the UK. Comparatively few such cases have been brought. Research[92] indicates that only 53 cases were known to have been commenced by 1 February 2001. This is extremely low as compared with employment (8,908 employment tribunal cases between 2 December 1996 and 1 September 2000). The dearth of Part III cases is likely, in part, to be attributable to the complexities of this system and the lack of awareness of disability issues within it.[93] There have been

---

[85] Art 16.

[86] DDA s 25.

[87] Currently £50,000, though awards are generally much lower than this maximum.

[88] Preston County Court, Claim No BB002640, 29 April 2002.

[89] *Purves v Joydisc Ltd* [2003] IRLR 420.

[90] There is also a conciliation service which is funded and administered by the Disability Rights Commission, although it is operated by independent conciliators (as required by the provisions of s 28 DDA, as amended by s 10 DRC Act 1999). Referral to conciliation triggers a two-month time extension to the six-month limit.

[91] *Hutchings v D'Cruz*, Watford County Court, Claim No WD300805, 26 August 2003.

[92] S Leverton, *Monitoring the Disability Discrimination Act 1995, Phase 2* (London, Department for Work and Pensions, February 2002).

[93] N Meagre, B Doyle, C Evans, B Kersley, M Williams, S O'Regan and N Lackey, *Monitoring the Disability Discrimination Act 1995* (London, Department for Education and Employment, 1998).

calls for the enforcement of the services provisions to be transferred to the tribunal service.[94]

The DDA makes no direct provisions for group claims, nor does UK law in general facilitate such actions. However, there is some scope for Group Litigation Orders (Civil Procedure Rules, r 19.11).

Since 2000 an independent body, the Disability Rights Commission (DRC) has been funded by the Government to provide advice, information and legal support in relation to the DDA, as well as having powers such as the ability to conduct formal investigations into discrimination.[95]

5.3 Ireland

Claims under the ESA are brought to the Equality Tribunal and adjudicated by an Equality Officer.[96] The Equality Tribunal is an independent statutory body, established in 1999. It hears virtually all individual complaints of discrimination in both employment and service areas. The major sphere in which it does not adjudicate is in relation to registered clubs, claims in respect of which are heard by the District Court. The tribunal is inquisitorial, as opposed to adversarial, and has powers to seek evidence, to enter premises and obtain information and inspect work. It is an offence to obstruct an equality officer.[97]

Compensation of up to 6349 euros can be awarded by the tribunal.[98] There is also a mediation service available where neither party objects,[99] which is confidential to the parties and which, if unsuccessful, does not bar a return to the Equality Tribunal.

Referrals to the Equality Tribunal do not require payment of fees and it appears to be a much more accessible system, as well as having greater expertise, than a standard civil court. Nevertheless, very few cases relating to the disability ground in goods and services have been heard by Equality Officers.[100]

There is a separate enforcement system for registered clubs, which are dealt with in the District Court.[101] Their licenses may be suspended for breach of the provisions and this is potentially a very serious penalty.

The Equality Authority (EA) is an independent body set up under the Employment Equality Act 1998. The EA provides advice, information and

---

[94] *Disability Equality: Making it Happen,* above n 39. See also B Hepple, '*Equality: A New Framework Report of the Independent Review of the Enforcement of UK Anti Discrimination Legislation*' (London, Hart Publishing, 2000); C Casserley, *The Price of Justice* (London, RNIB, 2000).
[95] See N O'Brien, ch 13 below.
[96] Ss 75–9 Employment Equality Act 1998, s 21 ESA 2000.
[97] S 94 Employment Equality Act 1998.
[98] Based on the amount that can be awarded by a District Court—see s 27 ESA.
[99] S 24.
[100] See www.odei.ie for details of cases brought to date.
[101] Ss 8–10.

legal support in relation to the EEA and the ESA. It also has powers to ensure the development of a pro-active, equality conscious approach to equal opportunities in the workplace and in the provision of goods, facilities and services.

5.4 Spain

The LEODDP will be enforced, in part, through applications for arbitration. The Government is to establish an arbitration system (following consultation with interested parties and organisations for disabled people and their families), which will deal with claims brought by disabled people.[102] The procedure will be binding and enforceable for both parties.

Parties have to agree to participate in arbitration, and the adjudicators must include representatives from relevant sectors of society, from organisations for disabled people and their families and, where appropriate, from general government. This explicit involvement of disability organisations in decision-making is unique in the four countries we have considered here.

Claimants may also bring their cases to the civil courts. The LEODDP specifies that compensation will be unlimited and that it will be awarded even where there is no financial cost to the injured party. It is to be assessed according to the circumstances of the offence and the seriousness of the damage arising from it. Sanctions are also likely to be contained in the various regulations on accessibility which the Government is producing.

'Collective legitimate interests' are entitled to bring collective legal proceedings on behalf of a person authorising them to do so.[103]

Whilst there is no provision for a national independent body to promote and enforce disability rights, a National Disability Council has been established. Its role is to advise the Government and to promote equality of opportunity more generally. It brings together organisations of disabled people and the state administration.[104]

5.5 Germany

The LEDP makes specific provision for disability-related groups to take action relating to discrimination prohibited by the Act.[105] This right is limited, however, if an individual disabled person could have brought the action themselves, in that it can only be brought by the association if it is a matter of general importance (Article 13(2)). Claims are brought to the administrative or social law court, which may order the administrative agency to revoke its decision or to carry out a specified action. The target agreements

[102] Art 17.
[103] Art 19.
[104] Art 15.
[105] Art 12.

that are to be drawn up may also contain a contractual penalty agreement in the event of delay or failure to abide by the agreements.

There is no provision for a national independent body to promote and enforce disability rights. Nevertheless, a disability ombudsperson of the federal government has been created.[106] S/he has a right to participate in all legislative and administrative procedures as well as other important matters concerning disabled people. S/he has a right to information and inspection of records and all federal agencies have to support her/his work.[107]

6 CONCLUSION

It is clear from the considerations above that there is presently a great disparity in the disability discrimination provisions relating to goods and services in a number of European countries. Some, of course, have no legislation governing this aspect of life at all. It is clearly desirable not only to have legislation governing all aspects of life, but to have consistency in that legislation so as to ensure that disabled people have the same rights to societal participation regardless of where they live. To this end, we hope that the European Commission will soon introduce a European disability directive to address the key areas set out above, as the European disability movement had been urging.[108] Whilst the European Commission has not yet committed itself to doing so, the relevant Commissioner has expressed support for the initiative.[109] We hope that this consideration of concrete examples of legislative approaches to this area will encourage these deliberations.

---

[106] S 14 BGG.

[107] S 15 BGG.

[108] See Appendix III for the draft directive produced as the basis for discussion by the European Disability Forum.

[109] Statement by Employment and Social Affairs Commissioner Anna Diamantopoulou in Rome at the closing ceremony of the European Year of People with Disabilities on Sunday 7 December 2003.

9

Reflections on Inclusion and Accommodation in Childhood Education: From International Standard Setting to National Implementation

JACQUELINE SCHOONHEIM and DAVID RUEBAIN*

1 INTRODUCTION

INCLUSION HAS, OVER the course of the past twenty years, become a central component of the formulation of the right to education in international disability rights instruments. Nevertheless, few European Member States have incorporated this element into national legislation. The UK is an exception. Children are given a qualified right to education in the least restrictive environment, as well as to be free from discrimination in education at all levels. The requirement of reasonable adjustment contained in Part IV of the Disability Discrimination Act 1995 (DDA) entitles children to an accommodation, which schools must provide to enable disabled pupils to be included in mainstream facilities.

We will argue here that it is necessary to make positive efforts to guarantee non-discrimination in education. The removal of barriers to access requires more than opening doors to existing facilities; it also requires accommodations to enable the disabled child to participate effectively in the learning environment. In this regard, the disability-specific Shadow Directive proposed by the European Disability Forum (EDF) could, if adopted, provide other European countries (including the new Member States) with a framework within which to adopt inclusion and anti-discrimination

* Jacqueline Schoonheim, JD LLM is an instructor of private law at the Law Faculty of the Universiteit Maastricht, Netherlands and is conducting doctoral research on the right to education in the context of disability in a comparative perspective. David Ruebain is a solicitor in private practice in London and litigates on behalf of disabled children in the area of education law.

provisions in national legislation.[1] It will, very likely, take considerable time for the Member States of the EU to reach a consensus for adopting a wider disability-specific directive in the spirit of that proposed by the EDF.

This chapter will examine the nature of inclusive education and its adoption, in international disability rights instruments, as a primary means of equalising educational opportunities for all. An overview of relevant European developments will follow. The chapter will then focus, first, on how the right to inclusive education has been incorporated into relevant education and anti-discrimination legislation in the UK, and then on developments in the Netherlands, where the government is considering extending the scope of a disability-specific anti-discrimination law (recently enacted to implement the EU Framework Employment Directive)[2] to pre-18 education. The purpose of this analysis is to explore whether a right to inclusion can be conferred by anti-discrimination legislation, or whether a separate right to inclusion in mainstream educational facilities must be enacted in order to anchor the right to inclusive education. It is not clear that an expansion of anti-discrimination legislation alone necessarily translates into inclusion in mainstream facilities.

2 INCLUSION AT THE INTERNATIONAL LEVEL

2.1 Inclusive Education Defined

Three terms should be distinguished from each other in the context of education in special and in mainstream settings (assuming that 'special' and 'mainstream' require no further definition): '*integration*', '*inclusion*' and '*inclusive*'. Integration in mainstream educational settings is not the same as inclusion in facilities with an inclusive orientation. Integration refers to the admission of a pupil into a non-special, or mainstream, school without the curriculum being necessarily adjusted to their different abilities. Inclusion implies an environment in which a child will be able to learn in his or her own way, differently from other children, and still belong in the mainstream setting. In inclusive schools no enrolment criteria are set because it is assumed that everyone can be taught in the same environment, according to their particular learning needs. Inclusive education is a term used to describe the learning environment. UNESCO defines inclusive education as follows:

---

[1] The Directive is available at the website of the EDF: www.edf-feph.org/en/policy/nondisc/nond_pol.htm.

[2] Framework Employment Directive, 2000/78/EC of 27 November 2000 establishing a general framework for equal treatment in employment and occupation (2000) OJL L303/6 was transposed into Dutch law, Equal Treatment Act on the Ground of Disability and Chronic Illness (*Wet gelijk behandeling op grond van Handicap en Chronische Ziekte*), effective 1 December 2003.

Inclusive education is concerned with providing appropriate responses to the broad spectrum of learning needs in formal and non-formal educational settings. Rather than being a marginal theme on how some learners can be integrated in the mainstream education, inclusive education is an approach that looks into how to transform education systems in order to respond to the diversity of learners.[3]

The term 'inclusive education' refers to the kind of educational environment that is necessary to make inclusion in mainstream schools possible for children who have traditionally been excluded from them. These are students who have had no choice but to attend separate, special educational facilities, generally on the basis of referrals from the mainstream or regular setting, and subject to meeting qualifying criteria which are usually medical in nature.

Disability rights advocates and scholars, from a variety of disciplines, have amply documented the vital role of inclusion in promoting the participation rights of disabled children, traditionally confined to attending special schools.[4] Len Barton, a sociologist, defines inclusive education as a means to an end:

> It is about contributing to the realisation of an inclusive society with the demand for a rights approach as a central component of policy-making.[5]

This definition is, essentially, the same as international formulations of the right to education for disabled children, which aim for the full participation in society of all. Participation is a human right as well as a fundamental policy goal.

2.2 The Doctrine of Separate but Equal

In the landmark case of *Brown v Board of Education*,[6] the US Supreme Court held that even if schools were equal, as compared to one another, and students had access to equal facilities; equal protection of the law required that black students had access to the same schools as white students. It struck down the infamous 'separate but equal' doctrine which, for more than fifty years, had permitted separate educational facilities for black and

---

[3] UNESCO Education Towards Inclusion, Defining Inclusive Education, Website of UNESCO: http://portal.unesco.org/education/en/ev.php?URL_ID=11891&URL_DO=DO_TOPIC&URL_.

[4] See eg M Corker and JM Davis, 'Disabled children: (still) invisible under the law' in J Cooper (ed), *Law, Rights & Disability* (London, Jessica Kingsley Publishing, 2000); L Middleton, *Disabled Children: Challenging Social Exclusion* (Oxford, Blackwell Science, 1999); and G Hales (ed), *Beyond Disability, Towards an Enabling Society* (London, Sage Publications, 1996).

[5] L Barton, *Inclusive Education and Teacher Education, A Basis for Hope or a Discourse in Delusion*, Professional Lecture (Institute for Education, University of London, 2003) 13, available at www.leeds.ac.uk/disability-studies/archiveuk/archiframe.htm.

[6] 347 US 483 (1954).

white children. Segregated schools were held to be 'inherently unequal' and thus a violation of the Equal Protection Clause of the Fourteenth Amendment of the US Constitution.[7]

The Court, in *Brown*, assumed that race does not affect learning ability and thus does not provide a reasonable ground on which to differentiate between people for educational purposes. In the language of discrimination analysis, the children were 'similarly situated.' To the extent that functional impairment may, and in many cases does, affect learning ability, the situation of children segregated on grounds of learning impairment is obviously different from that of children segregated on grounds of race. The analysis of the Court, however, is not restricted to this point alone. It also takes into account 'intangible factors' which lead to a profoundly unacceptable result: lasting damage to and the marginalisation of a class of individuals. Significantly, it is in this sense, in the harm caused by separateness—the creation of feelings of inferiority and resulting social exclusion—that separate is inherently unequal, and thus inherently discriminatory.

Classic equality analysis, which *Brown* represents, does not prohibit segregation where material differences distinguish one group from another. Interestingly, the UN Convention against Discrimination in Education,[8] which stems from roughly the same period as the *Brown* case, identifies only three types of lawful segregation: separate schools on the basis of gender; separate schools for religious or linguistic reasons (in accordance with parental convictions); and private schools, provided that they do not aim to exclude any group.[9] Special educational facilities do not fall within these categories and would, therefore, seem to fall foul of the ban on 'separate educational systems or institutions for persons or groups of persons.'[10]

It is very likely that disabled children, having traditionally been 'invisible under the law,'[11] were simply not seen as a group relevant to the discussion about educational quality. Corker and Davis contend that:

---

[7] The Supreme Court observed that the doctrine of equality would be violated even if all quantifiable indicia of equality were satisfied: '… there are findings below that the negro and white schools involved have been equalised, or are being equalised, with respect to buildings, curricula, qualifications and salaries of teachers, and other "tangible" factors. Our decision, therefore, cannot turn on merely a comparison of these tangible factors in the negro and white schools involved … We must look instead to the effect of segregation itself on public education … To separate children (in grade and high schools) from others of similar age and qualifications solely because of their race generates a feeling of inferiority as to their status in the community that may affect their hearts and minds in a way unlikely ever to be undone.' 347 US 483, 492–94.

[8] Adopted by the General Assembly, Eleventh Session, 14 December 1960.

[9] Art 2.

[10] Art 1(c). It is unclear whether this argument has been pressed under the UN Convention (which provides no individual complaint mechanism), but modern anti-discrimination law provides a new way of redressing discriminatory treatment on the basis of disability, which is to define substantive discrimination as a failure to make a reasonable adjustment or accommodation, as will be discussed below in relation to the EU Framework Employment Directive and English education law.

[11] M Corker and JM Davis, above n 4 p 233.

[I]t remains the case that the dominant discourse of law in relation to disabled children is one that sees disability or children, but not disabled children, and views disability itself in terms of dependency. Thus the duty to 'care' or to provide 'reasonable accommodation' is put before a notion of disabled children's rights.[12]

Inclusive education, as set out in international disability rights instruments, does meet the challenge posed by Corker and Davis' analysis, by framing a right to inclusive *education* as a human right.

Conceptualising inclusive education as an educational response to difference invites a consideration of how the law must be formulated in order to make education systems responsive to the diversity of learners, including learners with impairments. If we understand disability as resulting from the interaction between an individual's functional limitations and his or her environment, it is obvious that schools and school curricula must be required to adapt to the learning needs of disabled children. These adaptations should be aimed at promoting participation in society generally. Since the near universal ratification of the United Nations Convention on the Rights of the Child, virtually all children can be said to have a right to education and should, accordingly, have access to meaningful and effective education.[13] The question is whether inclusion is an aspect of the substantive right to education. Regrettably, the Convention on the Rights of the Child does not answer this question directly. All international instruments concerning the rights of disabled persons do, however, stress the importance of inclusion in educational facilities as an essential aspect of the right to education.

2.3 The World Programme of Action (WPA)

The concept of inclusive education was introduced into the international disability rights context by the WPA Concerning Disabled Persons, adopted in 1982 by the UN General Assembly,[14] and later elaborated upon in the UN Standard Rules for Equalising Opportunity[15] (StRE) and the Salamanca Statement and Framework for Special Needs Education.[16] The UN General Assembly identified education as a key terrain in which to realise the

---

[12] *Ibid*. It is important to note that the concepts of 'care' and 'reasonable accommodation' are not the same and have differing ideological connotations. Care is closely associated with the medical model of disability, while reasonable accommodation derives from a human rights perspective toward disability.

[13] UN Convention on the Rights of the Child (New York 1989), Arts 28 and 29 concerning education specifically; and General Comment 1 on the Aims of Education, CRC/GC/2001/1.

[14] UN General Assembly Resolution 37/52 of 3 December 1982, UN Doc A/37/51.

[15] UN General Assembly Resolution 48/96 of 20 December 1993.

[16] UNESCO, *Salamanca Statement and Framework for Action on Special Needs Education*, World Conference on Special Needs Education: Access and Quality, Salamanca, Spain, 7–10 June 1994, ED 94/WS/18.

'equalisation of opportunities' and work toward the ultimate goals of achieving 'full participation' in social life and development, and 'equality.'[17] The equalisation of opportunities is presented as the third spear point of action in the WPA, following 'prevention' and 'rehabilitation.' Equalisation of opportunities for disabled persons is defined as a process, as opposed to a goal, in which immediate work is to be done in order to achieve the goal of accessibility for all. It is:

> [T]he process through which the general system of society, such as the physical and cultural environment, housing and transportation, social and health services, *education* and work opportunities, cultural and social life, including sports and recreational facilities, is made accessible to all.[18]

This aim of inclusion is strikingly similar to the concept of 'social inclusion', which has recently been suggested as a possible justification for positive action.[19]

> Social inclusion does not seek the same, or even broadly equivalent, outcomes for all citizens. Its focus is, not on relative disadvantage between groups, but rather on the absolute disadvantage experienced by particular groups. The objective is not some notion of equality of welfare, but one of securing a minimum level of welfare for every citizen.

Inclusion in the general system of society means securing a minimum level of access for every person, regardless of ability. The WPA provides a framework within which to consider the entire field of education, and within which to develop and formulate policies and laws at national level. It urges States to:

> [A]dopt policies which recognise the rights of disabled persons to equal opportunities with others. The education of disabled persons should as far as possible take place in the general school system.[20]

The WPA includes a monitoring and evaluation component, which has been carried out in five-year reviews.[21] The most recent review introduces new terminology to the framework for disability advocacy, calling for a 'rights-based approach' to development, 'systematic consideration of accessibility,' and application of the principle of 'universality.'[22] This review also places reliance on the more specific instructions provided by the UN StRE:

[17] WPA, Art 1, Objectives.
[18] WPA, Art 12.
[19] See eg H Collins, 'Discrimination, equality and social inclusion' [2003] *Modern Law Review* 21.
[20] WPA, Art 120.
[21] WPA, Art 195.
[22] UN Doc A/58/61–E/2003/5, Review and Appraisal of the World Programme of Action concerning Disabled Persons (WPA), http://www.un.org/esa/socdev/enable/disa5881el.htm.

With the adoption of the StRE, in resolution 48/96 of 20 December 1983, the initial frame of reference for policies and programmes was equalisation of opportunities for disabled people. *As the disability paradigm evolved*, attention focused on the contribution of the StRE in promoting equalisation of opportunities for all people, based on the principles of universality.[23]

2.4 The UN Standard Rules—StRE

The StRE were adopted by the UN General Assembly after two failed attempts to adopt an international convention on disability rights.[24] Their overriding purpose is to:

[E]nsure that girls, boys, women and men with disabilities, as members of their societies, may exercise the same rights and obligations as others.[25]

Education is designated as an explicit 'Target Area' for the equalisation of opportunities. Rule 6 requires the principle of equal education in 'integrated' or 'mainstream settings' to be introduced gradually if necessary, and defines it as follows:

In situations where the general school system does not yet adequately meet the needs of all persons with disabilities, special education may be considered. It should be aimed at preparing students for education in the same general system. The quality of such education should reflect the same standards and ambitions as general education and should be closely linked to it. At a minimum, students with disabilities should be offered the same portion of educational resources as students without disabilities. States should aim for gradual integration of special education services into mainstream education. It is acknowledged that in some instances special education may currently be considered to be the most appropriate form of education for some students with disabilities.

This paragraph recognises the reality of the difficulties in shifting from systems of segregated special education to education in integrated settings (now further evolved to integrated settings with 'inclusive education'). However, the intention of the framers of this paragraph is clear: States are expected to work toward breaking down the separation between special and mainstream education, often established in older educational systems,

---

[23] UN Doc A/58/61–E/2003/5, 3.

[24] 'Previous International Action' of the Standard Rules, Resolution 48/96, Arts 8 and 9. See generally T Degener, 'Disabled persons and human rights: the legal framework' in T Degener and Y Koster-Dreese (eds), *Human Rights and Disabled Persons* (Dordrecht, Martinus Nijhoff Publishers, 1995), p 12. Failure to adopt a convention is attributed to the belief of many UN representatives that existing human rights instruments fully include the rights of disabled persons.

[25] StRE, Art 15, 'Introduction.'

and to transform special education facilities into support centres for facilitating the transition of mainstream schools into inclusive schools equipped and able to teach all children, regardless of impairment.

Special Rapporteur Lindqvist observed in his first monitoring report of the StRE,[26] based on progress reports submitted by 83 governments and 163 NGOs, that:

> The recommendations in the Standard Rules are very progressive, and in the opinion of the Special Rapporteur, no country, not even among the most advanced countries, has fully implemented the rules. Nonetheless, there is no doubt that the rules, in the short time since their adoption, have been widely accepted and are being used as the main policy guidelines in the disability field both by Governments and non-governmental organisations.

With respect to education specifically, the Special Rapporteur endorsed the Salamanca Statement and use of the Framework for Action, urging governments to provide appropriate education for children (and adults) with special needs:

> That document, together with rule 6 on education, provides excellent guidance for educational policies in the disability field. UNESCO studies show that in many countries less than one per cent of children with special educational needs (SEN) receive education. In nearly 50 per cent of countries providing information, those children are excluded from education, either by law or for such reasons as severity of disability, lack of facilities, long distances and refusal by regular schools to accept children with SEN. When children with SEN receive education, most often it is through a separate system of education. An integrated approach, providing adequate support and accessibility in regular schools, seems far away in many countries.[27]

While subsequent monitoring has not focused explicitly on the implementation of Rule 6 concerning education, Lindqvist does point to several weaknesses in the StRE, including the lack of an adequate monitoring mechanism, which has led once again to the recommendation of the drafting of a specific disability rights convention.[28] The Ad Hoc Committee, formed to draft such a convention, summarised a final report of the Special Rapporteur as follows:

---

[26] UN Doc A/52/56, 52nd Session, Final Report of the Special Rapporteur on Monitoring the Implementation of the Standard Rules on the Equalisation of Opportunities for Persons with Disabilities, VI Conclusions and Recommendations, available at http:www.un.org/esa/socdev/enable/dismsre9.htm.

[27] UN Doc A/52/56, annex, paras 138–9.

[28] UN Doc A/58/118 & Corr 1, 3 July 2003, Summary of First Special Rapporteur on Disability, Ad Hoc Committee on a Comprehensive and Integral International Convention of Protection and Promotion of the Rights and Dignity of Persons with Disabilities (New York, 16–27 June 2003).

In his discussion on human rights and disability, Mr Lindqvist noted that general comment No 5 of the Committee on Economic, Social and Cultural Rights had analysed disability as a human rights issue and provided that persons with disabilities were entitled to the full range of rights recognised in the Covenant on Economic, Social and Cultural Rights. The question of human rights and disability could thus be characterised as an issue of approaches to follow to strengthen and improve the disability dimension in human rights monitoring and protection.[29]

The bodies established to monitor and protect those rights created by existing human rights treaties should also monitor the implementation of the human rights (including the right to education) of disabled people. They have not yet done so in any significant or vigorous way. The good intentions, expressed in international declarations, have yet to be translated into binding legal standards.

2.5 The Salamanca Statement and Framework

The Salamanca Conference[30] was the first international conference to focus on the specific educational requirements of disabled children. The Statement that resulted from the Conference is directed toward national governments and the international community and, in no uncertain terms, is a resounding endorsement of both integration in mainstream schools and, also, of 'inclusive education'.

> Regular schools with this inclusive orientation are the most effective means of combating discriminatory attitudes, creating welcoming communities, building an inclusive society and achieving education for all.[31]

Governments are called upon:

> [T]o adopt as a matter of law or policy the principle of inclusive education, enrolling all children in regular schools, unless there are compelling reasons for doing otherwise.[32]

This is a call for the recognition of a right of enrolment in a regular school, in the first instance; and not upon conditions of qualification, as are often required in societies with highly developed systems of special education.

The Framework for Action, which was adopted along with the Salamanca Statement, puts itself forward as an 'overall guide to planning

---

[29] *Ibid*, para 23.
[30] UNESCO, *Salamanca Statement and Framework for Action on Special Needs Education*, World Conference on Special Needs Education: Access and Quality, Salamanca, Spain, 7–10 June 1994, ED 94/WS/18.
[31] *Salamanca Statement*, Statement 2.
[32] *Salamanca Statement*, Statement 3.

action in special needs education.' To be effective, warn the drafters, the Framework must be 'complemented by national, regional and local plans of action inspired by a political and popular will to achieve education for all.'[33] Many changes are required, not least of which is 'new thinking in special needs education.' This new thinking requires:

— Developing a child-centred pedagogy capable of successfully educating all children, *including* those who have serious disadvantages and disabilities;
— Realising that human differences are normal and that learning must be adapted to the learning needs of the child, rather than the child being fitted to the learning environment;
— Understanding that inclusive schooling is the most effective means for building solidarity between children with special needs and their typical peers;
— Changing the role of special schools to that of providing support for developing inclusive schools, for providing early screening and identification of children with disabilities, and for serving as training and resource centres for staff in regular schools;
— Ensuring that all educational planning concentrates on education for all persons in all parts of a country and in all school sorts.

Teaching methods, methods of instruction, school curricula and materials, pupil-tracking systems, personnel training and support and the development of external support services must all receive attention from government, teacher training institutions, and related educational experts. These elements are stressed in the Framework, and suggest that it may be necessary to develop systems of educational 'governance' (to borrow a term from the world of medical service delivery).[34] Like a medical governance system, an educational governance system would bundle research on successful educational strategies, and develop and monitor the implementation of authoritative educational guidelines.

Aside from the guidance provided by the Salamanca Framework for breaking down segregated educational systems, Salamanca is also responsible for entrenching the term 'inclusive education' in our rights vocabulary. As reported in a follow-up of UNESCO activities since Salamanca, the appeal of inclusive education has gone beyond the community of disabled children:

While the concept of inclusive education grew in the early 1990s out of concerns about the exclusion of disabled learners from education and the segregation of all such learners into special education centres separate from mainstream schools, inclusive education now had begun to embrace the

---

[33] Framework for Action, ED–94/WS/18, Para 14.
[34] See eg V Harpwood, 'Clincial governance, litigation and human rights' (2001) 15 *Journal of Management in Medicine* 227–41.

participation of all learners who are vulnerable to marginalisation and exclusion, if at all possible, in the cultures, curricula and communities of local learning centres.[35]

This underscores the 'universality' of this aspect of education. From the concept of 'inclusive education' as an approach to education specifically, we seem to be moving more and more in the direction of claiming a right to inclusion, not only as an aspect of education, but also as a countermeasure to exclusion from many of society's institutions. This would make sense in the logic of the StREs, which view the equalisation of opportunities (in this case inclusion) not as an end-goal but as the process through which equality and participation in the larger society can be achieved. This is also in keeping with the aims of 'fourth generation equality laws,' where the emphasis in rooting-out discrimination has shifted from individual 'wrongdoers' to duties on public bodies to take positive action to promote equality of opportunity in carrying out public functions.[36]

3 EUROPEAN DEVELOPMENTS

3.1 The ECHR and the Right to Education

Article 2 of the First Protocol to the ECHR provides that no Member State may deny the right to education. The jurisprudence of the European Court of Human Rights (ECtHR) has not moved beyond recognising that a child must be able to benefit from the educational instruction provided in existing institutions:

> For the 'right to education' to be effective, it is further necessary that inter alia the individual who is the beneficiary should have the possibility of drawing profit from the education received, that is to say, the right to obtain, in conformity with the rules in force in each State, and in one form or the another, official recognition of the studies which he has completed.[37]

Although various cases have been brought to the ECtHR on behalf of disabled children alleging a violation of the right to education, none has been held admissible to date.[38]

We do not know, as yet, what is meant by an 'effective education' by the ECtHR in the context of disability. The ECtHR has interpreted States'

---

[35] ED–99/WS/43, *Salamanca 5 Years On, Review of UNESCO Activities in Light of the Salamanca Statement and Framework for Action*, http://www.unesco.org/education/educprog/snc.

[36] S Fredman, 'Equality: a new generation?' (2001) 30 *Industrial Law Journal* 165–6.

[37] *Belgian Linguistic Case*, Judgment of 23 July 1968, Series A, No 6, 31.

[38] No 36505/97, *Di Egido v Italy*, dec 6 April 2000; No 29046/95, *McIntyre v UK*, 21 October 1998; No 25212/94, *Klerks v the Netherlands*, 4 July 1995; No 18511/91, *Dahlberg v Sweden*, 2 March 1994; No 14135/88, *P and LD v UK*, 2 October 1989.

margin of appreciation widely in balancing conflicting policy interests. Requiring access to mainstream facilities is not something we can expect from the ECtHR in the very near future.

3.2 The EU Employment Framework Directive

The recent EU Framework Employment Directive,[39] mandating Member States to implement anti-discrimination legislation banning disability-based discrimination, extends to the areas of employment and employment training, but not to the areas of primary or secondary education. It stands to reason that, if one has not developed the skills required to participate in mainstream employment, one will have a difficult time entering the labour market at all. The EU is prepared to recognise the importance of banning race discrimination in many more aspects of community life (including that of primary education) than just that of employment.[40] It is, however, not yet prepared to do so with respect to other grounds of discrimination, including that of disability.[41]

3.3 EDF Disability-Specific 'Shadow Directive'

The disability-specific 'shadow directive,' proposed last year by the EDF, would extend the scope of disability-based anti-discrimination laws to many areas of public and private sector activity, including education.[42] It would require a presumption of mainstream education in national education legislation, as well as an educational accommodation requirement. Article 6 specifically applies to access to education and provides that:

> Member States shall ensure that all disabled children and adults in mainstream education and in special education benefit from reasonable accommodations covering their individual needs, including among others, tuition in Braille, special equipment, special educational material and assistive educational devices.

The general rule applying to education is 'participation in mainstream education' which, effectively, creates a presumption of mainstream education for all. In determining which form of education or training is appropriate for a given individual, 'the views of the person with a disability will be

---

[39] Council Directive 2000/78/EC of 27 November 2000 establishing a general framework for equal treatment in employment and occupation (2000) OJL L303/6.

[40] Council Directive 2000/43/EC of 29 June 2000 implementing the principle of equal treatment between persons irrespective of racial or ethnic origin, which extends inter alia to the areas of employment, social security, education and access to goods and services, Art 3(a)–(h).

[41] Sandra Fredman has described a 'hierarchy of directives' in this regard in 'Equality: a new generation?' (2001) 30 *Industrial Law Journal* 157–8.

[42] Above n 1.

considered as a significant factor.' The preference of the individual concerned would play a role in decisions about whether they were to attend mainstream or special facilities, although there would be a presumption of inclusion in mainstream facilities. This would impose upon mainstream schools a much clearer obligation to develop adaptive teaching methods, and accessible materials and environments, so as to be able to receive pupils with a wide variety of abilities.

Article 2 defines the failure to make a reasonable accommodation, necessary to enable participation, as discrimination:

> [T]he principle of equal treatment shall mean that there shall be no direct or indirect discrimination whatsoever on the grounds of disability and no discrimination in the form of a failure to make a reasonable accommodation.

It would seem that the requirement of reasonable accommodation, in combination with a presumption of participation in mainstream settings, is what is necessary to achieving inclusive education.

4 SPECIFIC COUNTRY EXAMPLES

4.1 England and Wales

Until the 1980s, many disabled children in England and Wales were prohibited from attending mainstream schools. Although there had been significant developments in the provision of education for disabled children after World War II, neither the law nor common practice promoted inclusive education. Instead, most disabled children were placed in one of eleven categories of special school, some of which related to particular kinds of medical conditions (eg blind and deaf) whilst others simply reflected prejudice (eg 'backward' and 'educationally sub-normal, severe').[43]

In April 1983, the law governing provision for disabled children was fundamentally reformed by the inception of the Education Act 1981. This radical piece of legislation emphasised a child-centred approach, by establishing a structure for assessing and determining a child's educational needs. There was also, perhaps for the first time, a general statutory 'encouragement' to educate disabled children in mainstream schools wherever possible. However, at that point, there was little recognition, nor any requirement, that mainstream schools would themselves have to change.

In 1993, the 1981 Act was replaced by Part III of the Education Act 1993, itself subsequently consolidated into Part IV of the Education Act 1996 (EA). That legislation enhanced the rights of disabled children in a number of ways. In particular,[44] it gave parents a right to choose mainstream

---

[43] The Education Act 1944 and the Education (Handicapped Children's) Act 1970.
[44] By s 316 EA.

provision unless this could not meet the needs of the child, constituted an inefficient use of resources, or would conflict with the efficient education of other children.

In January 2002, by virtue of amendments effected by the Special Educational Needs and Disability Act 2001 (SENDA),[45] the first two provisos were repealed. Now, when parents seek mainstream provision, their wishes must be acceded to unless that would be incompatible with the 'efficient education of other children.' Furthermore, local education authorities (LEAs) have a positive duty to take reasonable steps to remove any incompatibility with the education of other children.[46]

The EA requires, in addition, that for those children with more severe SEN, LEAs must draw up a Statement (a legally binding document) which sets out, amongst other things, all of the special educational provision (SEP)[47] that the LEA will arrange to meet the educational needs of the child.[48] A Statement, if properly drawn, affords children with SEN an absolute, unqualified right to receive extra or different provision, regardless of cost.[49] In that regard, it constitutes one of the strongest rights available to disabled children in the UK. In practice, since 1983, where a disabled child has required, for example, extra staffing or equipment or sometimes physical adjustments, they may obtain these through a Statement.

At present, about 100,000 children are educated in segregated special schools. This is some one per cent of the total school population, although the number is declining.[50] Of course, many (perhaps most) of these children are at such schools through the expressed preference or acquiescence of their parents but some are, as it were, 'compulsorily segregated.' Arguably, even where parents choose special schools, they do so not out of conviction but through fear that their child's needs will not be met in the mainstream.[51]

In recent surveys reported by the Disability Rights Commission (DRC), 36 per cent of young disabled people said they had been bullied at school; 20 per cent said that they had been discouraged from taking GCSEs; 36 per cent felt that they did not receive as much support from teachers and other staff as they needed because of their disability; 23 per cent of young disabled people said that they were discriminated against at school; and 48 per cent said they had missed out on PE or games at school because of their

---

[45] Part 1 SENDA.

[46] Ss 316 and 316(A) EA.

[47] Ie educational provision which is different from, or additional to, that available generally for children of that age in the area.

[48] Part IV EA.

[49] See s 324(5)(a)(i) EA 1996 and *R v London Borough of Harrow ex parte M* [1997] ELR 62.

[50] Department for Education and Skills, National Statistics Bulletin, Statistics of Education, Special Educational Needs in England: January 2003, Issue No 09/03 November 2003.

[51] Anecdotal evidence from David Ruebain and also from IPSEA (the Independent Panel for Special Educational Advice—a national organisation in England and Wales which supports families of children with special educational needs).

disability.[52] Meanwhile, the National Audit Office reported in January 2002 that disabled people aged 18 are only 40 per cent as likely as non-disabled people aged 18 to go into higher education.[53] According to the DRC's recent survey,[54] three in ten young disabled people felt that they were prevented from going on to further and higher education for a reason related to their disability. One quarter said that they were advised not to go on to further or higher education by their school.

With regard to anti-discrimination provisions for disabled people, the UK DDA was designed to afford some protection against some discrimination to some disabled people; primarily in the field of employment and the provision of goods and services. However, the provision of education (public and private) was expressly excluded from its scope; the then government arguing that provision of education for disabled students should remain within the exclusive domain of education, not discrimination, law. Following the May 1997 elections, the new government established a Disability Rights Task Force to examine and make recommendations on extending anti-discrimination provisions for disabled people. In its report, *From Exclusion to Inclusion*,[55] the Task Force stated:

> [I]nclusion of disabled people throughout their school and college life is one of the most powerful levers in banishing stereotypes and negative attitudes towards disabled people amongst the next generation.

Whilst Part IV of the EA 1996 provides the statutory framework for determining what additional educational provision disabled children should receive, and at which type of school, prior to September 2002 there was no direct anti-discrimination provision in UK domestic law. However, since then amendments to the DDA, effected by SENDA, have extended anti-discrimination protection for disabled students into schools and colleges.

As with the parts of the DDA dealing with employment and service provision, discrimination in education is defined as arising when a disabled person is treated less favourably than a non-disabled person for a reason relating to his/her disability without justification, and, also, where a reasonable adjustment is not made to arrangements for determining admission to a school and in the provision of education and associated services so as to prevent the disabled person being placed at a substantial disadvantage.[56] Discrimination is, however, permitted in circumstances where it is in accordance with a permitted form of selection to the school, or for a reason

[52] L-M Wilson, *Young Disabled People — A Survey of the Views and Experiences of Young Disabled People in Great Britain* (conducted by NOP) (London, Disability Rights Commission, January 2003).

[53] *Widening Participation in Higher Education in England* (London, National Audit Office, January 2002).

[54] See DRC Bulletins available at www.drc-gb.org/newsroom/bulletinarchive.ap.

[55] London, Department for Education and Employment, 1999, para 3, p 42.

[56] Ss 28A–28C DDA.

which is both material to the circumstances of the particular case and substantial.[57]

Discrimination is prohibited if it occurs in the context of admission arrangements; the terms on which admission is offered; the refusal or deliberate omission to accept an application for admission; the provision of education or associated services; exclusions; the victimisation of anyone who supports a disabled person in bringing a complaint; or in the failure to take steps to ensure that disabled pupils are not placed at a substantial disadvantage in comparison with non-disabled pupils. This requires changes to policies, practices and procedures which may otherwise be discriminatory. Factors to be taken into account in determining whether an adjustment is reasonable and, therefore, required include the need to maintain academic, music, sporting and other standards; the money available; the cost of the adjustment; the availability of provision through SEN law; the practicalities of making a particular adjustment; the health and safety of the disabled pupil and others; and the interests of other pupils.[58] A reasonable adjustment will be required only if the disabled child would otherwise be placed at a substantial disadvantage as compared with other pupils. A substantial disadvantage may include the time and effort that the disabled child might need to expend; the inconvenience, indignity or discomfort that the child might suffer; and the potential loss of opportunity, or lack of progress, of the disabled child.

In addition, since April 2003, LEAs and schools have been required to prepare accessibility strategies and plans with a view to increasing the extent to which disabled pupils can participate in a school's curriculum; improving the physical environment of schools for the purpose of increasing the extent to which disabled pupils are able to take advantage of education and associated services; and improving the delivery to disabled pupils, within a reasonable time and in ways which are determined after taking account of their disabilities and any preferences expressed by them or their parents, of information which is provided in writing for pupils who are not disabled.[59]

Where discrimination in schools has occurred, complaints may be brought to the Special Educational Needs and Disability Tribunal (SENDT) or to Independent Appeal Panels, depending on the nature of the complaint.[60] These do not have powers to order financial compensation but may order training for staff; guidance for staff; the involvement of an LEA equal opportunities officer in the school; changes to policies, practices and procedures; a replacement trip or additional tuition for a disabled child who has missed out on a school experience; the relocation of, for example,

[57] S 28B(6)–(7) DDA.
[58] Code of Practice on Disability Discrimination in Schools (London, Disability Rights Commission 2002).
[59] Ss 28D–28E DDA.
[60] Ss 28H–28L DDA.

the school library, to make it more accessible (short of requiring physical adjustments); the admission of a disabled child to a school; a written apology; or reinstatement to the school.

Thus far, few cases under the amended Part IV of the DDA have been decided. However, *Buniak v The Governing Body of the Jenny Hammond Primary School*[61] did examine the interface between Part IV EA 1996 (and its obligations to secure additional provision for a disabled child) and Part IV DDA (with its obligations not to discriminate against a disabled child). In that case, the mother of a six year old child with global developmental delay complained that his local mainstream primary school had discriminated against him in a number of ways. In particular, it had deliberately excluded him from a range of school activities, including participation in the Christmas Play, participation in a school trip and, generally, participation in the life of the school. In addition, she complained that the funding which had been made available to the school to secure an additional learning support assistant for his needs had not been used by the school to secure such support. The SENDT upheld the complaint. It found that the school had discriminated against the boy, both in excluding him from the various activities and also in failing to secure the additional staffing support required by his statement. The decision received a great deal of publicity in the UK but one point that was, perhaps, not fully understood was that the Tribunal (surprisingly perhaps) held that it had jurisdiction to consider discrimination in grounds of reasonable adjustments (in this case, extra staffing support) despite the fact that the general view amongst legal practitioners had previously been that questions concerning additional staffing and equipment would remain exclusively within the jurisdiction of the Education Law framework (ie Part IV EA) and not the Disability Discrimination Law Framework.

It would appear, then, that the anti-discrimination provisions governing disabled children in schools may impose requirements for reasonable adjustments by way of extra staff and equipment, notwithstanding the fact that they might also be sought through a statement of SEN. The hard boundaries of any legal distinction are not clear, but it is likely that children requiring extra support will continue to have to use the statement procedure and the EA, but that the precise nature of the support may be determined by the DDA. It is clear that the guarantees provided by both Acts together promote inclusion. How effective they will be in achieving this in practice remains to be seen. In addition, the proposed duty to promote equality, currently contained in the Disability Discrimination Bill (which has been the subject of scrutiny by a joint committee of the House of Lords and House of Commons)[62] may provide a strategic underpinning, to both of these legislative provisions, to further advance inclusion.

[61] Unreported, 22 October 2003.
[62] 'Report on the Draft Disability Discrimination Bill' (London, Stationery Office, 27 May 2004).

4.2 The Netherlands

In sharp contrast with England and Wales, but perhaps more representative of a number of other EU Member States, the Netherlands has no history of providing education to disabled children in the least restrictive environment, nor of individual entitlement to specific educational resources in mainstream schools. It does, however, have an official policy of mainstreaming which was adopted more than a decade ago and termed *Back to School Together*.[63] This policy was transposed into the national educational laws and took effect on 1 August 1998.[64] The basic aims of Dutch mainstreaming policy are to encourage children with mild learning disabilities or behavioural problems back into the regular schools, through extra support distributed to the regular schools for use as they see fit; and to support children with more severe learning difficulties and disabilities in the regular schools with pupil-specific funding.[65] Fourteen categories of special education have been reorganised into four clusters of special education, for which medical or psychological referral is required. This reconfiguration of the schools has resulted in some mainstreaming,[66] but the absolute numbers of children who are in segregated facilities is 214,000, constituting approximately five per cent of primary school children and 15 per cent of high school age children.[67] The percentage of disabled children in regular educational settings was estimated at 15 per cent in 1998, and the recently enacted pupil-specific financing for children who qualify for special schools is designed eventually to achieve a 25 per cent placement of all disabled children in regular schools.[68] No law, however, currently prohibits discrimination in education.

The Dutch Equal Treatment Act on the ground of Disability and Chronic Illness entered into force, in compliance with the EU Framework

[63] The contours of the policy were presented to the Parliament in a Government Paper entitled *Back to School Together* (*Weer Samen Naar School*) in October 1990, TK 1990/91, 21 860, nr 1.

[64] The Primary Education Act, Secondary Education Act and the Expertise Centres Act.

[65] The Expertise Centres Act provides that, as from 1 August 2003, a child who qualifies for placement in a Cluster school for special education is also entitled to receive a 'backpack' with financing to be used at the school of choice. This financing can be spent on four extra hours of individual remedial teaching per week and on specialist support for the teacher.

[66] *Fourth Progress Report on Policy Back to School Together* of Minister of Education, Culture and Science to the Lower House of Parliament, TK 2002–2003, 21 860, nr 68, p 4, Table 1, showing numbers of pupils in special and regular schools for the years 1997–2001, with a decrease of pupils in special schools for mild learning impairments, and a dramatic increase in pupils in special education facilities for more severe learning and/or behavioral impairments.

[67] C Hover and R Baarda, *Study of the Effects of Applying the Act for Equal Treatment on the Ground of Disability or Chronic Illness in Primary and Secondary Education* ('Effectstudie toepassing Wet gelijk behandeling op grond van handicap of chronische ziekte in primair en voortgezet onderwijs') (The Hague, October 2003), pp 15 and 75.

[68] N Poulisse, *A Shaky Balance, the Integration of Children with an Intellectual Disability in Regular Education* (*Een wankel evenwicht, de integratie van kinderen met een verstandelijke handicap in het reguliere onderwijs*) (ITS—Nijmegen, 2002), 7.

Employment Directive, on 1 December 2003.[69] Like the Framework Directive, its scope does not extend beyond employment and post-secondary education. Prompted by parliamentary pressure, the Dutch government announced its intention to consider extension of the Act to primary and secondary education as well.[70] To facilitate a decision as to whether anti-discrimination protection should be extended to childhood education, a study (the Hover and Barda Study) was commissioned by the Minister of Education into the potential legal and financial consequences of extending equality protection to primary and secondary education.[71] Drawing on parliamentary materials, produced in support of the Equal Treatment Act on the ground of disability, the authors make a number of observations as to the accommodations and changes schools will have to undergo in order to avoid discriminating. Under the Equal Treatment Act an 'effective accommodation' is required for those who come within the personal scope of the Act. An effective accommodation must be 'appropriate' and 'necessary' to relieve the barrier to participation. Once it is determined which accommodation is effective, this must be tested for reasonableness. To make this determination with respect to accommodation in post-secondary vocational education, the following factors would come into play:

— The size of the school in terms of numbers of pupils;
— The costs involved in making the accommodation;
— Available funding (from all available sources);
— The operational and technical feasibility of making the accommodation;
— The financial health of the educational facility.

The education-specific factors which also play a role[72] would include the potential disadvantage to other participants; and the presence and availability in the region of similar educational facilities.

The accommodations that would be required, were the Act to be extended,[73] would involve changes to buildings, equipment, school organisation (with respect to flexibility in scheduling and examination) and special needs support, including adaptive teaching and attention to individual care needs.

[69] Council Directive 2000/78/EC of 27 November 2000 establishing a general framework for equal treatment in employment and occupation (2000) OJ L303/6, enacted as *Wet gelijk behandeling op grond van handicap of chronische ziekte*, wet van 3 April 2003, S 2003, 206.

[70] *Equal Treatment Plan of Action for Persons with a Functional Limitation*, submitted by government on 18 December 2003 to the Lower House of Parliament, TK (2002–2003), 29 355, nr 1.

[71] Above n 67.

[72] Position Paper of government in parliamentary materials related to the Proposed Equal Treatment Act on the Ground of Disability and Chronic Illness, TK 2002, 28 169 (*Memorie van Toelichting*, nr 3, referred to in Hover and Barda Study, above n 67, pp 28–9.

[73] Hover and Barda Study, above n 67, pp 29–36.

It is significant that such accommodations would take place largely in regular schools so as to facilitate participation in mainstream facilities.

Extension of the scope of the Equal Treatment Act would affect the admission of disabled children to education in a number of ways, but only to a degree.[74] Regular schools are not required by law to admit children with impairments if they have a reasonable argument for denying admission. A decision to deny, in this sense, is currently subject to only marginal judicial review.[75] Judicial review would, arguably, provide closer scrutiny in the context of an anti-discrimination guarantee, since schools would then be prohibited from distinguishing on the basis of disability alone. It is important to note, however, that the Equal Treatment Act would allow the interests of the individual to be weighed against those of the group potentially adversely affected by the enrolment of a pupil displaying disruptive behaviour.[76]

If the Equal Treatment Act were extended to childhood education, the resources allocated to schools would take greater account of the needs of the individual pupil; there would be increased use of individual learning plans which would also stimulate the development of development-oriented and didactic standards; and there would be more flexibility in the use of personnel and material resources.[77] These are elements of inclusive education, as defined by the Salamanca Statement.

The conclusion of the study under discussion is that extension of an anti-discrimination guarantee to childhood education in the Netherlands could lead to some 40,000 legal claims of discrimination in education.[78] The majority of these claims, it is projected, would be brought by children with dyslexia, attention deficit and hyperactivity disorders (ADHD) and autism spectrum disorders, who currently qualify for no additional financial support, and most of whom attend regular schools.[79]

Thus, while implementation of anti-discrimination legislation will certainly improve the conditions for inclusion in the Dutch educational system by, for instance, encouraging the use of adaptive teaching techniques, it is not projected that children with more severe learning impairments will be affected. It would seem that without a legal presumption of enrolment in mainstream classrooms, the current two-track system will remain largely intact and non-inclusive.

---

[74] Hover and Barda predict that an increase could reach 30%, instead of the 25% now projected with enactment of pupil-specific funding: above n 67, p 42.

[75] See eg case from Zutphen of 17 November 2003, 57111/KG ZA 03–263 which concerned a mainstream high school's refusal to admit two brothers with behavioural issues on the ground that the money provided in their financial 'backpack' would not be enough to facilitate the kind of small group attention both boys needed according to the expert advisors consulted by the school.

[76] Hover and Barda Study, above n 67, p 41.

[77] *Ibid* pp 50–9.

[78] *Ibid* p 55, Table 14 specifying the nature and numbers of anticipated claims.

[79] *Ibid*.

5 CONCLUSION

International human rights standards have made a significant contribution to defining the right to education in terms of inclusion in mainstream settings. This is an aspect of the right to education which concerns the damage done to children by marginalisation and social exclusion, regardless of the learning abilities of an individual. As far as childhood education is concerned, the standards set out at the international level have not, as yet, made their way into the legal systems of most of the EU countries. The EU, in requiring anti-discrimination protection for disabled people, has targeted the fields of employment and vocational and higher education. Apart from the 'shadow directive' proposed by the EDF, no real activity is occurring to extend disability-specific protection beyond the limits of the Framework Employment Directive.

That the right to education has yet to be formulated and implemented as a right to inclusion in mainstream facilities, contrary to the thrust of international disability rights instruments, may be explained by a number of reasons. To begin with, education is a vast and complex area of employment for a considerable sector of society. Various professions are involved, from teachers to administrators to diagnosticians to makers of educational materials. Many persons, the vast majority non-disabled, have a professional interest in the organisation of educational facilities and approach education from an employment perspective.

Secondly, the right to education is not always viewed from the perspective of the child. If, however, the right to education is to be conceived as a human right and anchored in a human rights framework, it must be viewed from the perspective of the child. A growing body of international instruments, generated by the UN WPA in the 1980s, place the right to education squarely within the disability rights discourse as a fundamental human right belonging to the child.[80] Governments find it difficult to represent this perspective vigorously, not only because of obligations to regulate and protect significant sectors of the working population, but also because of their obligations to respect the often competing rights of school authorities and parents. The history of educational provision in western liberal states has seen the development of protection for parental rights to establish schools which conform to their religious convictions, now guaranteed in national laws and international treaties.[81] The right to education is thereby fraught with

---

[80] *World Programme of Action concerning Disabled Persons*, adopted by UN General Assembly Resolution 37/52 of 3 December 1982; UN Standard Rules on the Equalisation of Opportunities for Persons with Disabilities, adopted by the UN General Assembly A/48/627 on 20 December 1993.

[81] The Dutch Constitution protects both the right of establishment and the right to determine the religious or other tenor of a school in Art 23. The ECHR requires States to 'respect the right of parents to ensure such education and teaching in conformity with their own religious and philosophical convictions'. Protocol 1 Art 2.

competing interests and policy considerations. The ECtHR has described the right to education as a right which:

> by its very nature calls for regulation by the State, regulation which may vary in time and place according to the needs and resources of the community and of individuals.[82]

Access to the content of education, for purposes of legal or judicial scrutiny, has accordingly been circumscribed to a large extent. The child's right to education has by and large been conceived and defined as a right of access to existing facilities.[83] It has become obvious that a guarantee of access to existing facilities fails to change educational facilities, or to improve the opportunities for social inclusion of those attending existing separate facilities.[84] Competing policy considerations make it difficult to move beyond this limited conception, which has the result of maintaining status quo arrangements instead of pushing toward greater inclusion or flexibility in educational policy and educational facilities.

The trend throughout Europe today, at least in word if not in deed, is toward providing education in 'inclusive classrooms'.[85] The reality of most educational systems in Europe, however, remains two-track: special education facilities for children who need significant adjustments in order to benefit from education, on the one hand, and 'regular education' for those children who can manage without significant adjustments, on the other. The latter, though they may well be disabled, generally have no legal entitlement to resources to support their inclusion in mainstream educational facilities.

By contrast, England and Wales provide an example of how such protection may be effectuated in national legislation. Of particular significance is the fact that the right to inclusion in mainstream settings was provided in the law long before the DDA was enacted and subsequently extended to cover all levels of education. It would seem that achieving the right to inclusion in mainstream settings requires two guarantees, as evidenced in the legal systems of England and Wales and as proposed in the EDF directive: a general presumption of mainstream education for all, as well as an anti-discrimination guarantee in the form of a reasonable accommodation requirement. A brief study of the Dutch system, in which neither guarantee is contained in the education laws at this time, reveals a relatively low level of inclusion of disabled children in mainstream schools. Extending equal

---

[82] *Belgian Linguistic Case*, Judgment of 23 July 1968, Court Series A, Vol 6, ss 3–5, 30–2.

[83] 'The right to education is the right to avail oneself of the means of instruction existing at a given time.' *Belgian Linguistic Case (ibid)* 31.

[84] L Clements and J Read, *Disabled People and European Human Rights* (Bristol, Policy Press, 2003), pp 68–9.

[85] See eg C Meijer (ed), *Integration in Europe: Provision for Pupils with Special Educational Needs, Trends in 14 European Countries* (Brussels, European Agency for Development in Special Needs Education, 1998) and other publications of the agency at http//www.european-agency.org.

treatment law to childhood education alone would certainly help to create the conditions necessary for inclusion in adaptive classrooms, but, without a law creating an express presumption of mainstream education for all, anti-discrimination law may go only part of the way toward making schools accessible to all children.

10

Promoting Disability Equality after the Treaty of Amsterdam: New Legal Directions and Practical Expansion Strategies

AART HENDRIKS*

1 INTRODUCTION

U NTIL RECENTLY, THE law of the majority of European states did not prohibit discrimination on grounds of disability. Legislators and policy-makers commonly believed that disabled people were, instead, primarily in need of social security, care and assistance.[1] Many Europeans were proud of their generous social welfare laws and policies on disability and considered this type of approach superior to the civil rights model of disability adopted in the United States.[2] European and international law offered little to compensate for the lack of legal protection against disability discrimination at national level. In the last decade, however, the tide seems to have begun to turn.

The inclusion of Article 13 in the EC Treaty, by virtue of the Treaty of Amsterdam 1997,[3] and the subsequent adoption of the Framework Employment Directive 2000[4] represent significant milestones in

---

* Commissioner, Equal Treatment Commission, the Netherlands.

[1] AC Hendriks, 'From social (in)security to equal employment opportunities. A report from the Netherlands' in M Jones and LA Basser Marks (eds), *Disability, Divers-ability & Legal Change* (The Hague, Martinus Nijhoff Publishers, 1999).

[2] See generally L Waddington, 'Legislating to employ people with disabilities: the European and American way' (1994) 1 *Maastricht Journal* 367.

[3] The first paragraph of this Article reads as follows:

> Without prejudice to the other provisions of this Treaty and within the limits of the power conferred by it upon the Community, the Council, acting unanimously on a proposal from the Commission and after consulting the European Parliament, may take appropriate action to combat discrimination based on sex, racial or ethnic origin, religion or belief, disability, age or sexual orientation.

[4] Directive 2000/78/EC establishing a general framework for Equal Treatment in Employment and Occupation [2000] OJ L303/16. See generally D Schiek, 'A new framework

the history of the disability movement. These two instruments may eventually pave the way towards full recognition of the human rights of disabled people throughout (and indeed beyond)[5] the European Union—a recognition which would finally confer on them the right to be treated as the equals of non-disabled people. The advent of Article 13 and the Framework Employment Directive provide us with a unique opportunity to reconsider the foundations of European disability law and policy and to achieve a reconciliation between the solidarity-based social welfare model, traditionally associated with Europe, and the more individualistic civil rights approach, traditionally associated with countries such as the United States.[6]

The Framework Employment Directive prohibits disability discrimination in relation to employment and occupation, including vocational guidance and vocational training. It does not require Member States to outlaw disability discrimination in other fields, such as education, public transport and the provision of goods and services. The narrowness of the scope of the Directive will require organisations of disabled people and other disability rights advocates to be particularly careful when considering whether to pursue judicial or administrative procedures set up at the national level to implement the Directive.

What should disability organisations and advocates do to combat all forms of disability discrimination and to promote the establishment of more comprehensive laws protecting equal rights and equal opportunities for disabled people? How might they seek to expand the scope of the current Framework Employment Directive within a system which acknowledges the complementary nature of social welfare and non-discrimination measures? These questions will be addressed in this chapter. It will begin with an outline of the nature of protection afforded to disabled Europeans before the enactment of Article 13. This will be followed (in section 3) by a brief consideration of the new approach it heralds.

on equal treatment of persons in EC law' (2002) 8 *European Law Journal* 290 and R Whittle, 'The Framework Directive for Equal Treatment in employment and occupation: an analysis from a disability rights perspective' (2002) 27 *European Law Review* 303.

[5] Measures taken by EU institutions often have an impact far beyond the EU. Since the adoption of the Framework Employment Directive many non-EU countries have established disability-specific or single equality bodies. For a recent example, see the interview with Andreas Rieder (the newly appointed chair of the Swiss Federal Office for the Equal Treatment of People with Disabilities (EBGB)) in *Neue Züricher Zeitung*, 1 March 2004, p 11.

[6] See eg L Waddington and M Diller, 'Tensions and coherence in disability policy: the uneasy relationship between social welfare and civil rights models of disability in American, European and international employment law' in ML Breslin and S Yee (eds), *Disability Rights, Law and Policy* (Ardsley, NY, Transnational Publishers, 2000) and L Waddington, 'Article 13 EC: setting priorities in the proposal for a horizontal employment directive' (2000) 29 *Industrial Law Journal* 176.

2 COMBATING DISCRIMINATION BEFORE 'AMSTERDAM': THE SOCIAL WELFARE APPROACH

Prior to the inclusion of Article 13 in the EC Treaty, by virtue of the amending Treaty of Amsterdam, EC law did not offer legal protection against discrimination on grounds of disability. This was very much in line with other international, regional and national legal systems[7] (with the exception within Europe of the United Kingdom).[8] It should not, however, be inferred from the fact that there was very little explicit anti-disability-discrimination law that disabled people in Europe were necessarily denied any protection from discriminatory treatment before 1997.

The emphasis of national disability law and policy in Europe before Amsterdam was on ensuring that disabled people were provided with an income, with care and with assistance. These laws and policies typically built on the assumption that most disabled people were unable to generate an income through employment and that they were, almost by definition, dependent on care and assistance from others. It was only because of these laws and policies, reflecting the perceived solidarity between those who had incurred some kind of 'social risk' (such as unemployment, old age or disability) that people with impairments were, in any meaningful sense, able to live as human beings. For many people without impairments, solidarity with disabled people required, above all, the channelling of some tax money in their direction. The need to ensure equal treatment and equal opportunities in daily life was generally not recognised.

Nevertheless, in response to deep-rooted exclusionary mechanisms, states did, on occasion, impose solidarity inspired measures on employers, schools, housing associations and other providers of goods and services with the purpose of enabling disabled people to participate more fully in mainstream society. In the aftermath of war, many countries introduced laws and policies designed to increase the employment prospects of disabled people. These commonly established quota systems according to which a specified number or percentage of an organisation's workforce were required to be disabled.[9] Other measures focussed on the removal of barriers against the employment of disabled people by, for example, introducing tax benefits for employers, special education for disabled people and transportation and financial compensation schemes.[10]

The European social welfare systems, then, frequently did guarantee a basic income and essential care and assistance to disabled people. Seldom, however, did these laws and policies confer enforceable legal entitlements

---

[7] See generally T Degener and G Quinn, 'An overview of international, comparative and regional disability reform' in ML Breslin and S Yee (eds), *Disability Rights, Law and Policy* (Ardsley, NY, Transnational Publishers, 2002).

[8] The UK Disability Discrimination Act was enacted in 1995.

[9] L Waddington, 'Legislating to employ people with disabilities: the European and American way' (1994) 1 *Maastricht Journal* 367 at 368.

[10] See n 1 above.

on disabled people themselves. Where they contain enforcement mechanisms at all (such as sanctions to back up a quota system), decisions about
whether to implement them generally fell to public authorities, rather than
to the intended beneficiaries, and successful enforcement actions would,
in any event, rarely be to the advantage of a particular aggrieved disabled
person.

By no means, therefore, did the European social welfare laws and policies have the inevitable effect of securing equal rights and opportunities for
disabled people. Indeed, their result was, on occasion, to disempower and
segregate people with impairments from mainstream society through, for
instance, the operation of some forms of special education, sheltered
employment and special housing schemes. Further, the nature and scope of
compensation measures were constantly subject to change; often being
dependent on the state of the economy and the views of the dominant political parties on disability issues. This reinforced the idea that disability laws
and policies were largely charitable in nature, as opposed to responses to
the fact that disabled people should be treated as equals in human dignity
with full entitlements to equal rights.

3 COMBATING DISCRIMINATION AFTER 'AMSTERDAM': A MOVE TOWARDS CIVIL RIGHTS?

Against the legal and policy background outlined in the previous section,
Article 13 clearly stands out as an important landmark. Though it has no
direct effect within member states, its significance lies in the fact that it
provides a legal basis on which to ground rules requiring such countries to
adopt appropriate measures to combat discrimination on a number of
grounds, including that of disability.[11]

Against this background, then, the inclusion of disability as one of the
grounds protected by Article 13 should not come as a surprise. The drafters
of the Treaty of Amsterdam were, however, initially unconvinced of the
need to incorporate disability in this broad equal treatment provision.[12] It
was only because of intensive lobbying, at both the national and European
levels, that the removal of this ground from the draft treaty provisions was
prevented. Reluctance to include disability in Article 13 did not necessarily
stem from an objection to increasing protection for disabled people. Many
objectors were genuinely concerned that the adoption of disability non-discrimination laws would undermine the benefits of the European social welfare model and deter the development of positive equality duties.

European legislators, policy-makers and academics now increasingly
take the view that social welfare laws and anti-discrimination laws are not

[11] See n 3 above.
[12] See generally, on the history of Article 13 and its directives, U O'Hare, 'Enhancing
European equality rights: a new regional framework' (2001) 8 *Maastricht Journal* 133.

necessarily mutually exclusive but that they are, on the contrary, complementary to one another. A combined approach will, it is hoped, ensure that European disability law and policy do not fall into some of the pitfalls which have confronted the United States' civil rights model. The latter, with its unilateral focus on the concept of non-discrimination, is largely dependent on the willingness and ability (both financial and emotional) of individuals to file complaints.

Efforts to reconcile the two approaches are evident in the Framework Employment Directive. In Article 7 paragraph 2 on positive action, for instance, it is provided that:

> With regard to disabled persons, the principle of equal treatment shall be without prejudice to the right of Member States to maintain or adopt provisions on the protection of health and safety at work or to measures aimed at creating or maintaining provisions or facilities for safeguarding or promoting their integration into the working environment.

It should be noted, however, that provisions such as this are also open to abuse (whether intentional or unintentional) in that they may be relied upon to justify unnecessarily restrictive health and safety standards which may have the effect of impeding the integration of disabled people into the workplace.

In Article 5 of the Directive, on reasonable accommodation, there is some reference to the complementary roles of social welfare and non-discrimination measures. This reads as follows:

> This burden shall not be disproportionate when it is sufficiently remedied by measures existing within the framework of disability policy of the Member State concerned.

This clause will not render unreasonable an accommodation, which would facilitate the integration of a disabled person into the labour market, simply because there are no state subsidies or other public funds to compensate an employer for any associated costs. It will, however, make it much more difficult for employers to argue that an accommodation would create a disproportionate burden upon them where such subsidies do exist.

It should be remembered that many European countries (unlike, for instance, the United States) are obliged to guarantee economic and social human rights (including the right to work, to education[13] and to social security) by national constitutions, by international treaties (such as the European Social Charter, the International Covenant on Economic, Social and Cultural Rights and various conventions of the International Labour

---

[13] See eg the decision of the European Committee of Social Rights on the complaint by Autism–Europe against France (4 November 2003).

Organisation) and by the fundamental rights paragraph of the forthcoming European Constitution. In addition, outside the context of social and non-discrimination rights, the positive obligations arising from civil and political human rights can sometimes be invoked to further the equal rights and opportunities of marginalised groups.[14] As the European Court of Human Rights has demonstrated, it may be possible to use the civil and political human right not to be discriminated against in order to ensure that certain economic and social rights, available to some, are also made available to others.[15]

The social welfare model of disability, then, is firmly rooted in the European legal traditions. This model, however, should not be regarded as an end in itself but, rather, as a means of bringing us closer to a society in which the human rights of disabled people, as well as those of the members of all other disadvantaged groups, are fully realised. The recognition of the principle of equal treatment of disabled people by Article 13 and the Framework Employment Directive creates a unique opportunity for Europeans to reflect upon their disability law and policy largely based, as it is, on the traditional social welfare model and to identify changes which should be made in order to secure equality for disabled people. The challenge now, for EU institutions and Member States, is to ensure that their disability laws and policies do indeed further the equal rights and opportunities of disabled people. The challenge for organisations of disabled people and other disability rights advocates is to critically monitor the effects of such laws and policies and to campaign for improvements.

4 THE WAY FORWARD

4.1 The Need for Further Legislation

There are still a number of barriers obstructing the design of comprehensive equal treatment disability-related law and policy in Europe. At this moment, the most important of these relate to the Framework Employment Directive. The narrowness of the Directive's scope is problematic, as is the apparent inability or unwillingness of many Member States either to

[14] Although not always successful, see eg *Botta v Italy* (24 February 1998) *Reports and Decisions of the ECtHR* 1998–I, No 66 412; *Price v UK* (10 July 2001) App No 33394/96; *Zehnalová & Zehnal v Czech Republic* (14 May 2002) Appl No 38621/97; *Marzari v Italy* (4 May 2003) Appl No 36448/97; and *Sentges v the Netherlands* (8 July 2003) Appl No 27677/02. See also the judgment of the Court in *Koua Poirrez* (30 September 2003) Appl No 40892/98.

[15] See eg *Gaygusuz*, ECtHR (16 September 1996) *Report of Judgments and Decisions of the European Court of Human Rights* 1996–IV, No 14, p 1129; *Van Raalte*, ECtHR (21 February 1997), *RJD* 1997–I, No I, p 173; and *Van Kück*, ECtHR (12 June 2003), Appl No 35968/97. The UN Human Rights Committee has gone further still in its interpretation of Art 26 of the International Covenant on Civil and Political Rights; see eg HRC (9 April 1987), *Broeks v the Netherlands*, no 172/1984, UN Doc A/42/40, annex VIII, section B, pp 139–50.

implement its obligations swiftly or to interpret its provisions broadly. It is widely believed that it will be some time yet before any new, broad EC directive is adopted. The European Disability Forum (EDF) has drafted a disability-specific directive which would require member states to prohibit disability discrimination in most areas of life.[16] Alternatively, a case might be made for a new comprehensive non-discrimination directive, modelled on the Race Directive[17] but covering all the Article 13 grounds. This would have the advantage of guaranteeing an equally high level of protection from discrimination on the basis of all the relevant grounds.[18] This is an important consideration in view of the fact that many people (eg a disabled Muslim woman) are discriminated against on a multiplicity of grounds. Multiple-discrimination requires a comprehensive response from legislators, policy-makers and society at large. It goes without saying that the adoption of comprehensive non-discrimination laws would be an effective means of tackling the root causes of disability discrimination.

There is an important role to be played by organisations of disabled people and other disability rights advocates, both in the bringing about of legislative change and in the fullest possible development of such law as there currently is. A clear, well-balanced strategy for achieving these aims will be invaluable to such organisations and advocates. Such a strategy should, it is suggested, incorporate the three elements outlined in the next section.

4.2 Essential Elements of a Strategy for Expanding Disability Equality Law in Europe

4.2.1 Monitoring the Effects and Shortcomings of the Current Legal System

The effective promotion of the equal rights and opportunities of disabled people presupposes a good general grasp of the accomplishments, failures and shortcomings of the current legal system. In order to acquire such an understanding, it will be essential to gather evidence as to the types of discriminatory provisions, criteria, practices and other obstacles which continue to confront disabled people in their daily lives. The more evidence there is that existing laws and policies fail to offer adequate protection against discrimination, the easier it will be to persuade legislatures to introduce legal reform. The shortcomings of laws and policies can, as a general rule, be demonstrated most effectively by way of statistics (eg the number of complaints made) and by frequent or high-profile efforts to challenge a law or policy by way of a judicial or administrative procedure. Organisations of

---

[16] The text of the proposed directive is published on the EDF website at www.edffeph.org.
[17] Directive 2000/43/EC implementing the principle of equal treatment between persons irrespective of racial or ethnic origin [2000] OJ L180/22 (generally referred to as Race Directive).
[18] See generally M Bell and L Waddington, 'Reflecting on inequalities in European equality law' (2003) 28 *European Law Review* 349.

disabled people and other human rights advocates will often be well placed to gather this type of information and to publicise the consequent need for reform.

4.2.2 Identifying Litigation Priorities

An incremental expansion of non-discrimination law is most likely to be achieved if those seeking it begin by challenging barriers closely related to areas already clearly covered by existing law. Thus, inaccessible building design, or inaccessible public transport or education systems (which prevent disabled people enjoying equal employment opportunities) might be challenged in preference to discriminatory practices completely unrelated to employment (such as the inaccessibility of a beach in a small town in Kenya, affecting a European holiday-maker).[19]

An effective litigation strategy would promote solidarity between all groups of disabled people. Cases which involve challenges by people with one type of impairment to policies which treat them less favourably than people with another type of impairment (eg travel subsidies or parking cards offered to one group of disabled people but not to another) should, therefore, take a low priority. Preference should instead (at least initially) be given to supporting cases where no such potentially divisive comparisons need be made.

4.2.3 Developing Links with Other Grounds

The disability movement has many useful lessons to learn from the experiences of the feminist, anti-racist and gay rights movements. The development of close links with these other movements will, therefore, be invaluable. Further, in campaigns for enhanced anti-disability-discrimination laws, a powerful argument might be based on the fact that relevant protection has already been afforded to other grounds (such as sex or race) without causing major practical difficulties. Where possible, coalitions between disability groups and ones focussing on other grounds should be made. Together, campaigns for measures such as a new comprehensive equality directive, covering all grounds, are likely to be much stronger.

5 CONCLUSION

The adoption of the Framework Employment Directive is, without doubt, an important step forward in the recognition of the rights of disabled people. It heralds the beginning of a new era in European disability law. It provides us with a unique opportunity to develop civil-rights-based anti-discrimination

---

[19] This case should not be confused with the petition of Mr Botta, concerning the inaccessibility of beaches in his Italian holiday resort where there were laws which purported to guarantee their accessibility; *Botta*, ECtHR (24 February 1998), *Report of Judgments and Decisions of the ECtIIR* 1998–I, No 66, p 412.

measures without losing the benefits of our more traditional solidarity-based social welfare laws and policies. The law, however, does not yet go far enough. The European disability movement, alongside other equality movements, has a vital role to play in ensuring that protection is expanded further so that disabled people can genuinely be said to be entitled to equal rights and opportunities.

Part IV

Achieving Equality Through Law?

11

Disability Equality: A Challenge to the Existing Anti-Discrimination Paradigm?

SANDRA FREDMAN*

1 INTRODUCTION

D ISCRIMINATION LAW IN the UK has developed in distinct strands, through separate pieces of legislation for gender, race and disability, and the establishment of three independent Commissions. However, with the introduction of three new strands,[1] and the imminent creation of a single equality body responsible for all strands,[2] it is crucial to consider the extent to which a single concept of equality can be developed to cover all kinds of discrimination.

In this chapter, I examine the background concepts and controversies which have motivated discrimination law, contrasting trends in respect of race and gender with those in respect of disability. I argue that a possible way forward lies in the principle of social rights which impose positive obligations to promote equality. A duty to promote equality potentially bridges the gap between the two traditional approaches to tackling inequality: the legal strategy, via anti-discrimination legislation, and the social welfare strategy, which is sometimes seen as patronising and disempowering. The duty to promote equality, based on social rights, uses the force of legislation to encourage policy initiatives which are appropriate in that they further the aims of the equality agenda rather than obstructing it.

Gender, race and disability legislation have followed interlacing but essentially distinct paths. At the start, the gender and race anti-discrimination statutes were moulded according to the same basic structure. More recently, they have diverged. Gender legislation has been influenced primarily by EU

* Professor of Law, University of Oxford. I am indebted to Deborah Mabbett for her very helpful comments on earlier drafts. The errors are all my own.
[1] Religion, sexual orientation and age. See Council Directive 2000/78/EC of 27 November 2000 establishing a general framework for equal treatment in employment and occupation.
[2] Together with active steps to create single equality legislation in Northern Ireland.

law. Race laws, on the other hand, have developed primarily in response to domestic events. The revelation of widespread institutional racism in the police forces resulted in the Race Relations Amendment Act 2000, which heralds a new generation of discrimination law, focusing on a positive duty to promote equality. Although such legislation has been pioneered in the fair employment legislation in Northern Ireland, gender has yet to be incorporated into it.

Disability, however, has always been viewed as distinct from gender and race discrimination law. It was not until 1995 that it gained official recognition as a discrimination issue, in the form of the Disability Discrimination Act (DDA). Until then, disability had been largely seen as falling within the terrain of social welfare law with the isolated exception of the scarcely used quota system.[3] The DDA was given a different shape from that of the Race Relations Act 1976 (RRA) and the Sex Discrimination Act 1975 (SDA). Most importantly, it included a stringent threshold hurdle in the form of the definition of disability. In addition, it did not expressly prohibit indirect discrimination and it permitted direct discrimination to be justified. It also allowed employers under a certain size to discriminate against disabled people. On the positive side, the DDA foreshadowed the positive duty to promote equality by including a duty to make reasonable adjustments. Very soon, the courts were stressing that the model used in the DDA was different from that used in the established statutes.[4]

This insistence on a different model for disability has persisted despite the unified approach taken by the EU Framework Employment Directive,[5] which the UK was required to implement by the end of 2003. Even though the Directive uses a very similar model for disability as for the other strands, the amending regulations simply graft the changes on to the DDA, the aim being to disturb the existing model as little as possible.[6] For example, the Directive does not include a justification defence for direct discrimination;[7] rather than disapply the justification defence in relation to the existing form of discrimination contained in s 5(1) (less favourable treatment for a reason relating to disability), the regulations have 'carved out' what might be termed 'pure' direct discrimination and disapplied the justification solely to that.[8] Indirect discrimination, while specifically provided for in the directive, is not mentioned in the Regulations, the assumption being that it is covered by the existing duty to make reasonable adjustments. The only real innovations are the removal of the small employer exception, separate coverage of work placements and qualifications bodies, and the inclusion of a harassment provision.[9]

---

[3] Disabled Persons (Employment) Act 1944.
[4] *Clark v Novacold* [1999] 2 All ER 977.
[5] Above, n 1.
[6] DDA 1995 (Amendment) Regulations SI 2003/1673.
[7] Above, n 1; Art 2.
[8] Above, n 6; reg 4 inserting new s 3A (see, in particular, s 3A(4) and (5)).
[9] *Ibid*, reg 4 inserting new s 3B and reg 7.

Outside the UK, however, disability is not always viewed as necessitating separate legislation but is, instead, included as one of a number of listed grounds.[10] The most important example of this approach, for present purposes, is the EU Framework Employment Directive.[11] To what extent, then, are there overarching equality concerns common to disability discrimination, on the one hand, and to race and gender discrimination on the other? How can the lessons learned from each context be synthesised into a harmonious model for the future?

In this chapter, I take some tentative steps towards exploring this issue. I do so by examining the development of notions of equality and the parallels and contrasts between disability, race and gender legislation. Three main themes will be considered: the difference-equality debate, the move from individualism to minority group rights and then to universalism and, finally, the costs of equality. I then examine briefly how this has impacted on disability legislation, before making some very tentative proposals as to the way ahead.

2 DIFFERENCE vs EQUALITY

2.1 Difference as Inferiority

There are strong historical parallels between patterns of discrimination against women, blacks and disabled people. The right to equal treatment was extended only to those who were characterised as equal; but women, blacks and disabled people were, it was claimed, relevantly different. Aristotle, for example, characterised women as 'mutilated males'[12] and the view of women as weak, irrational and defective continued through feudalism and into the liberal era. The appeal to difference was the key way in which the contradictions between the liberal ideal of equality and the subordination of women were addressed. Rejecting a proposal to extend the suffrage to women in 1892, Asquith justified his position by arguing that '[Women's] natural sphere is not the turmoil and dust of politics but the circle of social and domestic life.'[13] Similar arguments were used to exclude women from higher education and the legal and medical professions and, more recently, to justify lower pay and poorer conditions.[14] There are strong

---

[10] See eg Canadian Charter of Rights and Freedoms s 15(1); Constitution of the Republic of South Africa s 9; South African Employment Equity Act 1998 s 6.

[11] Moving in the opposite direction, however, is the strong lobby within the United Nations to create a new international treaty on disability.

[12] Aristotle, 'The Generation of Animals' 737a 28, 775a 15 in J Barnes (ed), *The Complete Works of Aristotle* (Oxford, Oxford University Press, 1982); see generally S Fredman, *Women and the Law* (Oxford, Oxford University Press, 1997) 3ff.

[13] Asquith III Hansard Parl Deb 4th Series 27 April 1892, c.1513.

[14] See further S Fredman, *Women and the Law* (above n 12) chs 1–3.

parallels with the justifications offered for excluding and segregating disabled people and subjecting them to detrimental treatment.

Exclusion from participation in public life on equal terms did not always take the form of express stigmatic treatment. Some measures were characterised as 'special' or 'protective' measures, ostensibly aimed at helping or protecting the weaker sex or the disabled group. 'Protective legislation' which equated women with children, so far as limits on working hours or working underground were concerned, has aroused heated controversy.[15]

While these were measures which should have been extended to everyone, their restriction to women inevitably disadvantaged them in the labour market as well as characterising women as weak and in need of protection. This is even more apparent in respect of social security, where gender inequalities have been reinforced and even generated. Instead of treating women as autonomous individuals with self-standing social rights, benefits were frequently premised on the dependence of women on male breadwinners and on their role as homemakers. The result was not to achieve equality but to reinforce difference.[16]

Similarly, for many decades disabled people were depicted 'not as subjects with legal rights, but as objects of welfare, health and charity programs'.[17] The underlying social policy of exclusion and segregation was justified by the pervasive belief that disabled people were incapable of coping with social and other major life activities.

'Welfare' was given at the price of exclusion and loss of self determination. In the employment field the only measure was one establishing 'special protection' for disabled people. The Disabled Persons (Employment) Act 1944 required employers of a substantial number of employees to employ a set quota of people registered as disabled. Not only was compliance with the Act negligible, quotas were also based on the assumption that disabled people were less able and needed protection.[18]

Different treatment was so entrenched as a mindset that the major international human rights documents did not even mention disability as one of the grounds to be protected against discrimination. This is true both of the European Convention on Human Rights (ECHR) and the International Covenant on Civil and Political Rights (ICCPR).

2.2 Equality as Sameness

The logical response to the subordination of women, blacks and disabled people is to argue that they are not relevantly different and that they

[15] *Ibid* 67–74.
[16] *Ibid* 83–94.
[17] T Degener and G Quinn, 'A survey of international comparative and regional disability Law Reform' in *From Principles to Practice: An International Disability Law and Policy Symposium*, October 2000, 3.
[18] Degener and Quinn (*ibid*) 11.

accordingly qualify for equal rights. Early feminists therefore argued that women had equal rights because 'the nature of reason must be the same in all'.[19] Equality, however, meant no more than formal equality or a demand that like should be treated alike. This required the assertion that women or blacks should not be automatically assumed to be inferior, but should be treated as individuals on their own merit.

It soon became clear that equality as sameness, by requiring as a precondition for like treatment that two individuals could be shown to be relevantly alike, simply privileged the dominant norm. Clearly, treating two people alike, where one comes to the situation already burdened with disadvantage, will do no more than perpetuate the disadvantage. In Catherine McKinnon's memorable words, women rejected the difference paradigm only to find that equality meant conformity to a male norm.[20] The way forward was therefore a more substantive notion of equality, which reconfigured the norm itself.

A similar process is evident in relation to disability. Characterising disability as an irrelevant characteristic removes the underlying justification for detrimental treatment, but insisting on similar treatment simply reinforces a particular norm and perpetuates disadvantage. As in gender, this illuminates the sterility of the equality—difference debate itself. Instead of requiring disabled people to conform to existing norms, the aim is to develop a concept of equality which requires adaptation and change. Within disability discourse, this is reflected in the move from the medical to the social model of disability.

Thus a much richer, substantive notion of equality has developed, embracing a wide range of concepts such as equality of opportunity and equality of results. I consider below how this concept might be understood in the context of disability. First, however, it is necessary to follow the development of the second major current: that of the relationship of the individual to the group.

3 FROM INDIVIDUAL TO GROUP TO UNIVERSALITY

3.1 Individuals and Merit

Individualism is a fundamental tenet of liberal equality law. On this analysis, the chief mischief of discrimination is that a person is subjected to detriment because she is attributed with stereotypical qualities based on a denigratory notion of the group of people with similar qualities. Individualism requires that the individual be treated on her individual merits and regardless of her group membership. These aims have an immediate appeal.

[19] M Wollstonecraft, *Vindication of the Rights of Women* (Penguin Classics, 1983), 1.
[20] C McKinnon, *Feminism Unmodified* (Cambridge, Harvard University Press, 1987) 32–45.

It seems logical to respond to the identified problem of discrimination by requiring that each person be treated as an individual, according to her own merits.

However, the stress on individualism is problematic for three main reasons.[21] First, it buys into a liberal ethic which portrays individuals as primarily driven by their own rational self interest. Individualism therefore downgrades activities motivated by genuine care for others and fails to appreciate the value and importance of community and inter-relationships. Second, this approach assumes that discrimination is an individual problem, whereby an individual perpetrator causes detriment to an individual victim. Redress should therefore be sought against the individual at fault and take the form of an individual remedy. Yet much discrimination cannot be attributed to individual acts by specific perpetrators but flows, instead, from the institutions and structures of society. This is particularly true in the disability context.

The third problem of individualism is its assumption that individual merit can be quantified in an objective way, abstracted from the social context in which it is located. In fact, of course, merit is itself a social construct. Far from being abstract, it is judged in relation to the qualifications deemed necessary for a job, an educational opportunity, or other benefit. Only those relevantly qualified 'merit' selection. Yet individuals may lack the capability to achieve the relevant standard precisely because of entrenched social disadvantage or physical attributes, such as pregnancy or impairment. In addition, despite their apparent objectivity, merit criteria can incorporate the very discrimination they purport to eliminate. For example, the simple assumption that only non-disabled people can do a specific job incorporates discrimination into an apparently objective merit criterion. Equally importantly, a focus on 'merit' assumes that the individual should fit the job, rather than that the job should be adjusted to fit the worker. In fact, if equality is to make an impact, appropriate adjustments must be made to the environment to accommodate difference.

3.2 From Individualism to Minority Group Rights

Recognition of the limits of an individual merit analysis has led to important developments in the contexts both of gender and race equality and of disability equality. The analysis of racism moved away from an attempt to achieve a colour blind society based on individual merit. Instead, racism has been characterised according to a minority group rights analysis. This analysis recognises that black people as a group are a discrete and insular minority, who have suffered from a history of discrimination, who are relatively powerless politically and who are socially excluded. The parallels

---

[21] See Fredman (above n 12) 14–15.

with disability are clear; disabled people are also characterised as a discrete and insular minority, who have suffered from a history of discrimination and who are relatively powerless politically and are socially excluded.

Two aspects of the minority rights approach in respect of race seemed particularly apposite for disability: identity politics, and an analysis of dominance and subordination. Identity politics, as explained by Young, seeks to transform a historically stigmatised attribute, such as colour or race, into a positive aspect of group identity.[22] The analysis of dominance and subordination used by McKinnon in the feminist arena has similarly been used to support a minority rights analysis. Thus, Hahn argues:

> [F]eatures of architectural design, job requirements and daily life that have a discriminatory impact on disabled citizens ... support a hierarchy of dominance and subordination between non-disabled and disabled segments of the population that is fundamentally incompatible with legal principles of freedom and equality.[23]

The advantage of this analysis is to emphasise the political and social aspect of disability over the medical model. Disabled people call, not for charity, but for rights based on the need to redress unfair prejudice and a history of political, social and economic disadvantage. The analysis also stresses community relationships and the need for inclusiveness.

Strategically, this approach has been very productive. It was the central motivating force behind the Americans with Disabilities Act 1990[24] (ADA), which draws explicitly on the race discrimination model in the Civil Rights Act 1960. The ADA states expressly that:

> Individuals with disabilities are a discrete and insular minority who have been faced with restrictions and limitations, subjected to a history of purposeful unequal treatment and relegated to a position of political powerlessness in our society, based on characteristics that are beyond the control of such individuals and resulting from stereotypic assumptions not truly indicative of the individual ability of such individuals to participate in and contribute to society.[25]

Disability statutes in several other countries have expressly adopted this model, the best examples being the Australian Disability Discrimination Act 1992 and the UK DDA. Indeed, Bickenbach *et al* argue that, as a political strategy, this approach and the movements to which it has given rise 'can

---

[22] I Young, *Justice and the Politics of Difference* (Princeton, Princeton University Press, 1990).

[23] H Hahn, 'The political implications of disability definitions and date' (1993) 4 *Journal of Disability Policy Studies* 42 at 46–7.

[24] 104 STAT 327, 42 USC 1210.

[25] *Ibid* s 2(a)(7).

be credited with nearly every change in attitude and treatment of people with disabilities in the last two decades'.[26]

3.3 From Minority Rights to Universalism

But the minority group analysis also has problematic implications. Most importantly, the minority group analysis depends on viewing disability as a group-defining characteristic. This is problematic both socially and legally. Legally, it depends on identifying people as 'disabled', which has proved notoriously difficult, both in the field of discrimination law and in that of social security.[27] One of the biggest legislative stumbling blocks of the minority group approach has been the definition of disability itself. The ADA, for example, has been seriously limited by restrictive judicial inter-pretations of the threshold concept of disability.[28] Much litigation in the UK too has been devoted to this issue. This, argue opponents of the minority group analysis, is not just a technical legal difficulty. It reflects the social reality that disabled people do not form a discrete and insular group at all. On this view, not only are the reactions to different forms of impairments very diverse, but there is no sense of solidarity among disabled people. Nor, it is argued, are the leaders representative of the vast majority of disabled people.

Normatively, this approach has also meant a return to the equality dif-ference dichotomy. Instead of seeing impairment as a normal aspect of life, it emphasises distinctness. Furthermore, it has been argued that this approach unintentionally reinforces the medical conception of disability, necessitating a view of disability as fixed and dichotomous; either one has a disability or one does not. The ways in which an impairment impinges on one's life must be quantifiable once and for all.[29] Moreover, it leads direct-ly into conflict over the distribution of resources. As Zola (the foremost proponent of this critique) puts it:

> [S]eeing people with a disability as 'different' with 'special' needs, wants and rights in this currently perceived world of finite resources, they are pitted against the needs, wants and rights of the rest of the population.[30]

[26] JE Bickenbach, S Chatterji, EM Badley and TB Ustun, 'Models of disablement, universal-ism and the international classification of impairments, disabilities and handicaps' (1999) 48 *Journal of Social Science and Medicine* 1173 at 1180.

[27] D Mabbett, 'Why have disability categories in social security?' (2003) 11(38) *Benefits* 163–8.

[28] See eg *Sutton v United Airlines* 527 US 471 (1999); *Albertsons, Inc v Kirkingburg* 527 US 555 (1999); *Murphy v United Parcel Service* 527 US 516 (1999). See also M Lynk, 'A dream deferred' (1999) 15 *International Journal of Comparative Labour Law and Industrial Relations* 329.

[29] IK Zola, 'Towards the necessary universalizing of a disability policy' (1989) 67 *The Millbank Quarterly* 401; Bickenbach *et al* (above n 26) 1182.

[30] IK Zola (*ibid*) 406.

A minority group analysis can also create conflicts of interest over the criteria for distribution of resources. Mabbett argues that a skill or talent deficit caused by lack of educational facilities in a deprived area should qualify for the same priority as the capacity deficit of a person with impairments.[31]

Finally, many fear that in practice this means that policy-makers latch on to the minority group rights approach as a pretext for cutting social security benefits. This critique has led to a strong body of thought which argues that disability legislation needs to move away from the minority rights approach and instead promote a universalist view. Thus, rejecting the minority rights view, which tends to see persons with a disability as a vulnerable population group, the UN Ad Hoc Committee on the Rights of Persons with Disabilities insist that:

> the data suggest that disability is a normal aspect of life; all kinds of disabilities can happen to all types of people at all stages in their normal lifecycles.[32]

The universalist view sees disability as fluid and continuous:

> Disability is not a human attribute that demarks one portion of humanity from another; it is an infinitely various but universal feature of the human condition. No human has a complete repertoire of abilities.[33]

This does not mean that universalists call for normalisation. Rather, advocates of universalism call for a policy that 'respects difference and widens the range of the normal'. It is the social distinction which attaches to impairment, and not the impairment itself, which calls for political intervention. 'Disability policy is therefore not policy for some minority group; it is policy for all.'[34]

What, then, is the policy prescription of the universalist approach? Central is the call for justice in the distribution of resources and opportunities. From the universalist perspective, designing the environment only for people within a narrow range of ability is seen to accord special privilege to those who happen to fall within that range. Thus, policies should reflect a universal design, not just for buildings and transportation, but also for housing, workplaces and all other aspects of human activity, so that environments and tools are suitable to as many as possible.[35]

[31] D Mabbett, 'Some are more equal than others: definitions of disability in social policy and discrimination law in Europe', forthcoming in *Journal of Social Policy*.

[32] UN Ad Hoc Committee on a Comprehensive and Integral International Convention on Protection and Promotion of the Rights and Dignity of Persons with Disabilities (New York, 2003), 'Issues and Emerging Trends Related to Advancement of Persons with Disabilities' Doc A/AC.265/2003/1, paras 9–10.

[33] Bickenbach *et al* (above n 26) 1182.

[34] *Ibid.*

[35] *Ibid* 1183.

The non-binding UN Standard Rules on the Equalisation of Opportunities for Persons with Disabilities represent a significant attempt to give effect to this approach. As mentioned above, the approach has also been strongly endorsed by the 2003 Report of the Ad Hoc Committee on the Rights of Persons with Disabilities,[36] which stresses the concept of the 'new universe of disability'. Some proponents of this approach argue that universalism shows that disability is not genuinely a discrimination issue. 'To be sure there is a social evil, there is injustice and inequality; but of a different sort.'[37] A closer look demonstrates, however, that this is only because a narrowly formal and individualist notion of discrimination is used. Thus Bickenbach *et al* characterise 'discrimination' as a wrongful limitation of a person's negative freedom based on an irrelevant feature of the individual. They argue that the basis of discrimination law is an insult to individuals and, therefore, that discrimination law does not apply where disadvantage is created by neutral forces such as economic factors. In fact, as has been argued above, the equality agenda has moved beyond seeing discrimination as merely stigmatic or prejudiced treatment, towards a substantive notion of equality. The policy prescriptions of the universalist model in fact converge strikingly with the notions of substantive equality which have emerged in respect of gender and race.[38]

4 THE COST OF EQUALITY

A third major theme in equality law concerns costs, which constitute the hidden but powerful agenda behind much of equality policy and legislation. The ideals of equality and fairness are always tempered by a strong sense, among policy-makers, that equality should not impose 'burdens on business'. To this is added the view that public spending is a political rather than a rights-based issue, justifiably determined by notions of affordability. The rhetoric of burdens on business has changed significantly under New Labour, which has instead focussed on the benefits to business of discrimination laws.[39] Whether the rhetoric of burden or benefit is used, however, the ideal of equality remains firmly bounded by the business needs of employers and macro-economic policies towards public spending.

The role of costs is manifested in discrimination legislation both in the criterion of 'reasonableness' and in the justification defence. Thus discrimination may be excused if the employer can show it is justified for business reasons and the duty to make adjustments is bounded by what is reasonable to expect from employers. Underlying this is the policy prescription that

---

[36] A/AC.265/2003/1.
[37] *Ibid* 1181.
[38] See section 6 below.
[39] See further S Fredman, 'The ideology of new labour law' in C Barnard, S Deakin and G Morris (eds), *Liber Americorum Bob Hepple* (Oxford, Hart, 2004).

employers should not be expected to bear 'unreasonable' expenses or to suffer 'undue hardship' as a result of having to provide equality rights.

This has been particularly salient in disability legislation. Until 2004,
even direct discrimination could be justified under the DDA 1995, in stark
contrast to the sex and race discrimination legislation, where a justification
defence to direct discrimination has always been rejected. Moreover, the
courts were quick to hold that the standard required to establish the justification defence for less favourable treatment was low. The defence was
made out as long as the employer could show that the reason for the discrimination was material and substantial, and a reason would be substantial if the employer's decision did not fall outside the range of reasonable
responses to known facts.[40] The Court of Appeal itself in a subsequent case
admitted that the 'threshold of justification has been consistently recognised
as a surprisingly low one.'[41] As Lindsay P put it:

> [t]his is a conclusion which we do not reach with enthusiasm, ... but the rem-
> edy for the lowness of the threshold, if any is required, lies in the hands of the
> legislature and not the courts.[42]

A similar assumption permeated the structure of the duty to make adjustments. Here the employer had two bites of the cherry. First the duty was
only to make reasonable adjustments, and in determining whether adjustments were reasonable, the costs incurred by the employer and the extent
of the employer's resources are to be taken into account.[43] Even if the
adjustments were reasonable, the employer could still justify the failure to
make such adjustments.[44] The clear risk was that an employer could use the
same arguments in the justification defence as had been addressed to the
reasonableness of the adjustments.

This weighting in favour of the employer has been somewhat mitigated
by recent statutory changes and a softening of the judicial approach. Thus
recent amendments to the duty to make reasonable adjustment has removed
the justification defence, so that the weight of the employer's argument
must rest on the reasonableness of the adjustment.[45] The courts were in any
event showing themselves more willing to construe the justification defence
strictly in relation to reasonable adjustment.[46]

The defence to direct discrimination is more complex. EU legislation
requires Member States to introduce a provision outlawing direct discrimination without permitting a justification defence. However, the UK government

---

[40] *Jones v Post Office* [2001] IRLR 384, [2001] EWCA Civ 558 (CA).
[41] *Collins v Royal National Theatre Board Ltd* [2004] EWCA Civ 144 (CA).
[42] *Heinz v Kenrick* [2002] IRLR 144 (EAT), p 146 para 16.
[43] DDA, s 6(4).
[44] *Ibid* s 5(2)(b).
[45] *Ibid* s 3A.
[46] See above n 41.

remained reluctant to depart wholly from the overriding assumptions that employers should not be burdened. Thus instead of removing the justification defence entirely from the direct discrimination provisions, it introduced a second, narrower definition of 'direct' discrimination which cannot be justified, leaving the original, broader definition intact, including the justification defence.[47] The difference relates primarily to the width of the comparison. According to the first, original definition, an employer discriminates against a disabled person if, for a reason relating to disability, the employer treats him or her less favourably than others to whom that reason does not apply, and the employer cannot show that the treatment is justified.[48] The newer definition requires the complainant to find a comparator who does not have 'that particular disability and whose relevant circumstances, including his abilities, are the same as, or not materially different from, those of the disabled person'.[49] It is only this narrower version which does not have to be justified.[50]

Missing in this statutory framework is any express recognition that shifting the cost away from the employer will not make it disappear. Unless another cost-bearer is found, it falls on the individual disabled person. Within employment discrimination law, the debate is usually conducted as if the employer were the only cost-bearer. A similar debate occurred in respect of pregnancy discrimination,[51] the argument being that it was unreasonable to expect the employer to bear the costs associated with pregnancy. It was also argued that forcing employers to bear the cost would deter them from employing women in the first place.

The analysis needs to be broader than this. There are three potential cost-bearers: the employer, the individual and the State. As Humphries and Rubery argue:

> Many costs and benefits associated with economic well-being are not captured in the accounting framework adopted by single organisations; even at the national level, the tendency has been to sum up the estimated costs to individual employers without reference to the effects on other areas of economic and social life.[52]

The question should therefore be one of distributive justice; how can the cost fairly and efficiently be spread? In the case of pregnancy and parenthood, the key was to place the cost on the State in the form of Statutory Maternity

---

[47] Disability Discrimination Act 1995 (Amendment) Regulations 2003 SI 2003/1673 inserting s 3A(1).

[48] DDA 1995, s 5(1).

[49] Disability Discrimination Act 1995 (Amendment) Regulations 2003 SI 2003/1673 inserting s 3A(5).

[50] *Ibid* inserting s 3A.

[51] See S Fredman, 'A difference with distinction: pregnancy and parenthood reassessed' (1994) 110 *Law Quarterly Review* 106–23.

[52] J Humphries and J Rubery, 'Some lessons for policy' in J Humphries and J Rubery (eds), *The Economics of Equal Opportunities* (Manchester Equal Opportunities Commission, 1995) 399.

Pay. In the disability field, the State already bears a range of different costs, but this is not linked directly to the employer's duty not to discriminate or to make reasonable adjustments. The DDA does provide that, in determining whether it is reasonable for an employer to have to make a particular adjustment, regard should be had to the availability of financial or other assistance,[53] but there is no duty on the State to provide employers with such assistance (although the Access to Work scheme run by the Department for Work and Pensions does provide financial support for the needs of disabled employees in the workplace). Far more attention, then, must be given to redistributive questions if progress is to be made.

5 PIONEERING A NEW PARADIGM?

While the disability discrimination legislation has, in some respects, been more limited than race and gender laws the DDA has, in other respects, pioneered a substantive approach. In at least three ways it moves away from the 'equality as sameness' approach towards one based on minority group rights. First, it is expressly asymmetrical. Gender and race legislation deliberately do not target the disadvantaged group, but instead view any gender or race-based criterion as unlawful. This means that it is unlawful to use such criteria even where the goal is to benefit the disadvantaged group. The implicit aim is to achieve a gender neutral, colour blind society. By contrast, the DDA prohibits discrimination only against disabled people.[54] It thus aims, not at neutrality, but at redressing the disadvantage experienced by a specific group.

Second, the conformist tendencies of the direct discrimination concept in the race and gender legislation have been mitigated. The established concept of direct discrimination requires proof that a person has been less favourably treated than a comparator of the opposite race or gender. This is based on the principle of equality as sameness, requiring conformity to a white male norm as a precondition for protection. Although on its face the DDA appears to have a similar comparator requirement, from very early on, tribunals and courts found it difficult to identify an appropriate non-disabled norm to function as the comparator. In the seminal Court of Appeal case of *Clark v Novacold*,[55] Mummery LJ noted the:

> futile attempts of the … courts to find and identify the characteristics of a hypothetical non-pregnant male comparator for a pregnant woman in sex discrimination cases.[56]

He therefore deliberately distanced himself from the difficulties experienced under the race and sex discrimination legislation in identifying the

---

[53] S 6(4)(e).
[54] *Archibald v Fife Council* [2004] UKHL 32 (HL).
[55] [1999] 2 All ER 977.
[56] *Ibid* para 63.

characteristics of a hypothetical comparator. Instead, he held that the question was how a non-disabled person would be treated. The result is to minimise the role of the comparator, with the effect that it becomes unlawful simply to subject a person to detriment on grounds of their disability. It will be recalled, however, that the new provision on direct discrimination resurrects the focus on a comparator, requiring the complainant to find a comparator who does not have 'that particular disability and whose relevant circumstances, including his abilities, are the same as, or not materially different from, those of the disabled person'.[57]

Third, and most importantly, recognition that equality requires more than sameness results, in the form of the duty to make reasonable adjustments, in an explicit requirement that the norm be changed. This duty, modelled on the duty to make reasonable accommodations in the ADA, is in many senses a precursor to the positive duty to promote equality, or the fourth generation equality rights, allied to substantive equality.

However, to the extent that the DDA adopts a minority group rights approach, it also incorporates its major difficulty; that of defining the disabled group. A demarcating feature must be identified which sets the protected group apart from others. Thus, a person can benefit from the protection of the Act only if she:

> has a physical or mental impairment which has a substantial and long-term adverse effect on [her] ability to carry out normal day-to-day activities.[58]

Many applicants have been excluded by this definition.

At the same time, the DDA is not fully within the minority group rights paradigm. It is severely constrained by the continuing adherence to individualism. Thus, the DDA does not include a provision prohibiting indirect discrimination, disability being considered to be too individual a matter. This contrasts with legislation elsewhere. The ADA, for instance, has always had an indirect discrimination provision[59] and the EU employment directive has had little difficulty incorporating one. The Canadian Supreme Court has recently characterised disparate impact discrimination as the major form of disability discrimination.[60]

This individualism is reinforced by the duty to make reasonable adjustments, which, in the context of employment at least, is specifically formulated as an individual duty.

In this respect, it is far more limited than the positive duty found in fourth generation equality statutes. This too contrasts with legislation from other jurisdictions, where the group dimension of the accommodation duty

---

[57] Disability Discrimination Act 1995 (Amendment) Regulations 2003 SI 2003/1673 inserting s 3A(5).
[58] S 1(1).
[59] S 102(b)(3).
[60] *Eldridge v British Columbia* (1997) 3 SCR 624 (Canadian Supreme Court).

is stressed. Some have already generalised the duty of accommodation to embrace all grounds of discrimination. Thus, South African employment equity legislation places a duty on designated employers to take affirmative action, which includes making reasonable accommodation for blacks, women and disabled people.[61] Outside the employment field, the definition of unfair discrimination on grounds of race and gender as well as disability expressly includes the duty to take steps 'to reasonably accommodate the needs of such persons'.[62] The Canadian Supreme Court has taken this a step further, holding that:

> The principle that discrimination can accrue from a failure to take positive steps to ensure that disadvantaged groups benefit equally from services offered to the general public is widely accepted in the human rights field. It is also a cornerstone of human rights jurisprudence that the duty to take positive action to ensure that members of disadvantaged groups benefit equally from services offered to the general public is subject to the principle of reasonable accommodation.[63]

Finally, the inclusion of a justification defence for direct discrimination is based on an assumption that the individual should be treated on her merits, and that somehow a distinction should be drawn between limitations based on ability and limitations based on disability.

6 THE WAY FORWARD: SOCIAL RIGHTS AND SUBSTANTIVE EQUALITY

6.1 Substantive Equality

While the DDA makes some gestures towards substantive equality, it has been shown that these remain imperfect. Nor is it clear that a fully fledged minority group rights approach would be appropriate. Is it possible to achieve a new synthesis? In this final section, I briefly consider how such a synthesis might begin to be evolved, drawing on the insights gained from universalism and on the growing experience of the positive duty to promote equality.

As argued above, substantive equality moves beyond what was increasingly recognised as a sterile equality-difference debate. Instead, the concept of equality is reconfigured, so that the norm itself is refashioned to incorporate social diversity. In the case of disability, this means that the norm can include the wide range of impairments which might affect anyone during their normal life cycle, whether as a subject or a carer. In other words,

---

[61] Employment Equity Act 1998 s 15(2)(c).
[62] Promotion of Equality and Prevention of Unfair Discrimination Act 2000 ss 7–9.
[63] *Eldridge v British Columbia* (1997) 3 SCR 624 (Canadian Supreme Court) para 79.

impairment becomes a normal aspect of life.[64] Substantive equality therefore encapsulates the universalist analysis, according to which the aim is not different or special treatment, but universal access to all activities.

Substantive equality, understood in this way, requires that social institutions be restructured to reflect the widened norm. This in turn requires a radical departure from the established structure of discrimination law, which does not change institutions but gives compensation retrospectively to an individual who has been 'wronged' on proof of the 'fault' of another. Substantive equality requires a positive duty to promote equality, resulting in proactive structural change. In this way the duty to promote equality bridges the gap between the two traditional approaches to tackling inequality: the legal strategy, via discrimination legislation, and social welfare, via social security. Instead of being condescending and fostering dependence (difficulties often associated with social welfare), the duty to promote equality, based on social rights, uses the force of legislation to encourage policy initiatives which further the aims of the equality agenda. This also reflects the universalist approach. Thus mainstreaming, because it is proactive, makes provision for all potential beneficiaries.

What substantive values, then, does equality promote? In my recent paper for the Equal Opportunities Commission,[65] I argued that equality ought to encompass four central aims. First, it should break the cycle of disadvantage associated with out-groups. This means that it cannot be symmetrical. Treatment which imposes a detriment on a disadvantaged group is qualitatively different from treatment which imposes such a detriment on an advantaged group with the aim of redressing disadvantage. Second, it should promote respect for the equal dignity and worth of all, thereby redressing stigma, stereotyping, humiliation and violence because of membership of an out-group. Third, it should entail positive affirmation and celebration of identity within community. Finally, and closest to the goals expressed by the universalisation approach, is the stress on promoting full participation in society. Thus, according to the Disability Rights Commission's Annual Report:

> When disabled people participate—as citizens, customers and employees—everyone benefits. So we have set ourselves the goal of 'a society where all disabled people can participate fully as equal citizens'.[66]

Participation denotes full and active participation within the community or social inclusion. This is not confined to participation in the workforce but

---

[64] UN Ad Hoc Committee on a Comprehensive and Integral International Convention on Protection and Promotion of the Rights and Dignity of Persons with Disabilities (above n 32) paras 9–10.

[65] S Fredman, *The Future of Equality in Great Britain* (Manchester, EOC, 2002).

[66] Disability Rights Commission, *Annual Review 2001–2002* (Disability Rights Commission, London, 2002), p 2.

extends to participation in the community, which is particularly important for those who do not undertake paid work, whether because of disability, age or child-care obligations. Thus, participation is an important means of overcoming marginalisation and social exclusion. Participation also connotes inclusion in major social institutions, particularly decision-making bodies, from the legislature down to the workplace. Participation in this sense is an essential part of the positive duty. Positive duties are prospective, and must be fashioned to fit the problem at hand. They require a continuing process of diagnosing the problem, working out possible responses, monitoring the effectiveness of strategies, and modifying them as required. The participation of affected groups increases the likelihood that strategies will succeed as well as democratising the very process of achieving equality.

It could be argued that participation is not part of the universalist analysis, but reverts to the minority group approach, since fair representation or participation can only be measured if the group can be clearly identified. How can it be said that there is under-representation or lack of participation by disabled people unless those who are disabled can be clearly identified? Certainly, the link between participation and definitions of disability needs more consideration. Indeed, participation is itself a complex concept and far more work is needed on its role and meaning. While it is clear that autonomy requires participation in those decisions which affect one's life, the nature of that participation may range from the mere disclosure of relevant information, to consultation, to co-decision-making. Neither is it clear who the representatives of disabled people should be: a universalist approach might suggest a trade union whereas a minority rights view is likely to favour a specific lobby group. Finally, participation might bypass representative structures and concern the individual herself; the move towards personal budget systems providing a good example.[67] Rather than reject participation as an aim, more thought needs to be given to its possible structures and meanings.

6.2 Social Rights

A complementary approach is to pursue the equality agenda through social rights. Social rights can incorporate the universalist approach by according rights to all who can make use of them. For example, introducing rights to have the workplace, working hours or other working practices adapted, may benefit a variety of users. This is demonstrated by recently introduced rights for part-time[68] and fixed term[69] workers. Such rights to

---

[67] D Mabbett (above n 31).
[68] Part-time Workers (Prevention of Less Favourable Treatment) Regulations 2000 SI 2000/1337.
[69] Fixed Term Employees (Prevention of Less Favourable Treatment) Regulations 2002 SI 2002/62.

equal treatment do not need to be formulated for the specific benefit of a single interest group, but can benefit a variety of users, whether parents of young children, carers of older people, or disabled people. The right to request flexible working[70] introduced by the Employment Act 2002 should, on this view, not be confined to parents with children under five.

Social rights, as part of the positive duty, require economic and social programmes to be reoriented to facilitate participation and choice. For example, the European Social Charter states that everyone has the right to independence, social integration and participation.[71] This places a positive duty on the State to facilitate participation and choice, including government subsidies of supported employment and mainstreaming.

A good example of the way in which substantive equality based on social rights operates in respect of disabled people is the Canadian case of *Eldridge v British Columbia*,[72] which concerned a claim that failure to provide sign-language interpreters in hospitals infringed the rights of deaf people. In upholding the claim, the court stressed two key principles. First, it stated, this was not a claim for special treatment, but only for equal access to services that are available to all. Second, the equality right included a duty to take positive steps to ensure that disadvantaged groups benefited equally from services offered to the general public:

> To argue that governments should be entitled to provide benefits to the general population without ensuring that disadvantaged members of society have the resources to take full advantage of those benefits bespeaks a thin and impoverished vision of s 15(1).[73]

Restating the claim in terms of rights also has an important effect on the weight given to costs arguments. The respondents in *Eldridge* argued that recognition of the appellants' claim would:

> have a ripple effect throughout the health care field, forcing governments to spend precious health care dollars accommodating the needs of myriad disadvantaged persons.[74]

However, the Court had no difficulty in rejecting the argument:

> The respondents have presented no evidence that this type of accommodation, if extended to other government services, will unduly strain the fiscal resources of the state. To deny the appellants' claim on such conjectural

---

[70] Employment Rights Act 1996, ss 80F and 80G inserted by Employment Act 2002, s 47.
[71] European Social Charter para 15 Q36.
[72] [1997] 3 SCR 624.
[73] *Eldridge v British Columbia* (1997) 3 SCR 624 (Canadian Supreme Court) para 73.
[74] *Ibid*, para 91.

grounds ... would denude s 15(1) of its egalitarian promise and render the dis-abled's goal of a barrier-free society distressingly remote.[75]

Ironically, one of the locations in which a social rights approach has unex-plored potential to develop is that of the ECHR. This is probably because the equality guarantee in Article s14 is weak and dependent on other sub-stantive rights, and because disability is not expressly mentioned as a pro-tected ground. This has meant that disabled people have relied on other rights, one of the most fertile being the Article 8 right to respect for home and family life.

A particularly good example of the potential of Article 8 is found in the case of *Botta v Italy*,[76] which concerned the failure of an authority to ensure that a privately owned beach provided accessible facilities for wheelchair users. The Court itself held that there was no breach in this particular case (Italian law already required such facilities to be provided and the case in point was simply an 'occasional lapse'). However, the Commission in its opinion set out two important principles which have the potential to form the basis of a more fully-fledged social rights approach. First, the concept of private life in Article 8 was held to include the right to establish and develop relationships with other human beings. Second, as the concurring opinion of the Commission argued,[77] Article 8 can impose positive obliga-tions to ensure that disabled people are not deprived of the possibility of developing social relations with others. Such obligations include:

> appropriate measures to be taken, to the greatest extent feasible, to ensure that they have access to essential economic and social activities and to an appropriate range of recreational and cultural activities ... the crucial factor is the extent to which a particular individual is so circumscribed and so iso-lated as to be deprived of the possibility of developing his personality.

Social rights have the potential to add significant force to the substantive equality claims suggested above. Social rights refocus social welfare, not as a privilege, but as a right. Nor is this simply a negative right to be free of interference. As seen in both the ECHR and the Canadian cases, social rights give rise to positive duties on the State to ensure that all citizens have an equal opportunity to benefit from the right. In addition, social rights are afforded to individuals as human beings, not as members of a particular category. As the *Botta* case illustrates, there was no need for the applicant to argue himself into the 'disability' group because he was claiming a right which was owed to all people as people. The content of the duty on the

---

[75] *Ibid*, para 92.
[76] Application No 21439/9324 February 1998.
[77] Concurring opinion of Mrs J Liddy, Mrs GH Thune, Mm MP Pellonpää, N Bratza, D Sváby, A Perenic, HG Schermers.

State to fulfil the right was closely related to the fact of his disability but he did not have to prove his disability in order to benefit from it.

7 CONCLUSION

There is a strong tendency in the literature to portray different models as conflicting and mutually exclusive. The minority group model is contrasted with the universalist model. Similarly, the 'conflictual and adversarial' rights-based stance is set up in conflict with a participatory model; relational and distributional models are seen as mutually exclusive. However, as Bolderson and Mabbett show, there is no single approach that covers all issues. A universalist approach, which aims to provide accessibility to a widened range of 'normal', could be highly effective in public spaces and infrastructure. At the same time, individualised approaches are necessary to provide for other kinds of accessibility, such as education or care provision.[78]

Both of these approaches can be advanced within a framework of positive social rights furthering substantive equality.

---

[78] H Bolderson and D Mabbett, 'Non-discriminating social policy?' Paper given at the Stirling Conference *What Future for Social Security?*, 15–17 June 2000.

12

A New Generation of Equality Legislation? Positive Duties and Disability Rights

COLM O'CINNEIDE*

1 INTRODUCTION

A POSITIVE EQUALITY DUTY is a legal requirement that organisations promote equality in all aspects of their work in a manner which involves employees, employers and service-users. Such duties are often viewed as the 'next generation' of equality legislation.[1] In essence, they are attempts to require that organisations implement a proactive mainstreaming approach. It is probable that a positive 'disability duty' will soon be imposed on public authorities in the UK. The Disability Rights Task Force, in *From Exclusion to Inclusion*, recommended the introduction of such a duty;[2] a proposal accepted by the Government.[3] A Bill has now been introduced which provides for the introduction of such a duty.[4] Positive duties could also be applied to the private sector but no attempt has yet been made to take such a step in the UK.

The introduction of a public sector duty will represent a major new innovation in disability equality legislation. If implemented properly, such a duty would reinforce the development of a 'rights-based' approach to disability issues by requiring that public sector decision-making gives due weight to promoting the rights of disabled people. It can also be seen as an

---

* Lecturer in Law, University College London.
[1] B Hepple, M Coussey and T Choudhury, *Equality: A New Framework, Report of the Independent Review of the Enforcement of UK Anti-Discrimination Legislation* (Oxford, Hart, 2000), para 1.33. See also S Fredman, 'Equality: a new generation?' (2001) 30 *Industrial Law Journal* 163; B Hepple and C Barnard, 'Substantive equality' (2000) 59 *Cambridge Law Journal* 566; M Bell and L Waddington, 'Reflecting on inequalities in European equality law' (2003) 28 *European Law Review* 349, 357–8.
[2] (London, HMSO, 1999) available at http://www.disability.gov.uk/drtf/full_report/index.html.
[3] *Towards Inclusion—Civil Rights for Disabled People* (London, DWP, 2001) available at http://www.disability.gov.uk/drtf/towards_inclusion/index.html.
[4] Disability Discrimination Bill (December 2004) s 3.

attempt to respond to the 'social model' of disability, which focuses upon how social practices and norms cause people with impairments to be disadvantaged or treated unequally.[5] A positive duty would require, not only that public authorities treat disabled people fairly within the limited parameters of existing social practices, but also that they consider how their policies and practice across the full range of their functions should be altered to promote substantive equality.

Such duties are designed to encourage a focus upon the social circumstances that generate disadvantage and can be regarded as an extension of the principle underlying 'reasonable adjustment' requirements.[6] Both positive duties and reasonable accommodation rules are forms of positive action that require due regard to be given to changing social norms, practices and expectations which disadvantage disabled people. However, positive duties are designed to extend the 'reasonable accommodation' approach across the full range of policies and practices that an organisation implements, including areas such as procurement and policy development where reasonable accommodation requirements have not generally been applied. In addition, reasonable adjustment rules are often narrowly interpreted and conceptualised as requiring the alteration of existing inadequate practices and structures. However, positive duties are intended to be anticipatory in effect, ensuring that consideration for disability rights is mainstreamed in policy design and implementation from the outset. The design of a public transport system, policing, the provision of essential utility services and promotion strategies should all be influenced by the reasonable accommodation of the perspectives and needs of people with impairments: this is the aim of positive duties.

Positive disability duties, therefore, complement reasonable accommodation requirements and make sense in terms of theoretical approaches to disability issues. What, however, will be their practical effect and utility? In particular, what can the proposed new public sector duty contribute to combating institutional patterns of disability discrimination and what lessons can be learned, in the wider European context, from the design and nature of this duty? Understanding what public sector positive duties might and might not achieve in the disability context, their potential strengths and weaknesses and how to develop strategies to maximise their potential are all important issues.

---

[5] See C Gooding, *Disabling Laws, Enabling Acts: Disability Rights in Britain and America* (London, Pluto Press, 1994); JE Bickenbach, *Physical Disability and Social Policy* (Toronto, University of Toronto Press, 1993); JE Bickenbach, 'Disability and equality' [2003] 2 *Journal of Law & Equality* 7–15. See also the comments of Binnie J, writing for the majority of the Supreme Court of Canada, in *Granovsky v Canada (Minister of Employment and Immigration)* [2000] 1 SCR 703, 722.

[6] See DDA ss 3A, 5 and 6 for reasonable accommodation requirements relating to employment. See also DDA ss 19–21 for similar requirements in relation to access to goods and services.

Previous experience of the impact of public sector duties in the devolved regions of the UK and also in the context of race discrimination demonstrates the potential of such duties. It suggests that the introduction of such a duty would significantly assist disabled people's pressure groups in pushing for change. However, identifying the ways in which the existence of this duty will prove to be of most use to such pressure groups will be important. It is also timely to give due consideration to the possible usefulness, impact and design of private sector duties and to how they could best be introduced in the near future. Finally, the potential of positive duties should not be overlooked in developing a coherent EU approach to disability rights. These issues will now be explored in detail.

2 THE LIMITS OF EXISTING DISABILITY DISCRIMINATION LEGISLATION

Existing disability discrimination legislation, at national and European levels, is ultimately limited in impact. As Fredman argues in this book, in many ways, it diverges from and sometimes improves upon the standard approach (and deficiencies) of anti-discrimination law.[7] This is particularly evident in its reasonable accommodation requirements. Nevertheless, certain built-in limits are common to all forms of anti-discrimination law and disability discrimination legislation is no exception.[8]

Legal responses to discriminatory practices, in the main, aim to alter social attitudes by requiring compliance with a fixed legal standard of conduct, according to which all individuals are to be treated in a particular manner. These requirements are, traditionally, enforced by individuals or by equality commissions through legal proceedings. This is true of almost all anti-discrimination legislation within the EU, including the UK Disability Discrimination Act 1995 (DDA) and the EC Framework Equality Directive.[9] This approach is very effective at breaking down many visible barriers and overt forms of prejudice. It often proves inadequate, however, in dealing with more complex and deeply-rooted patterns of exclusion and inequality.[10]

The conventional anti-discrimination model is limited by the operation of four specific factors which, though common to all forms of discrimination, have particular force in the context of disability. First, the burden of enforcing disability legislation falls upon individual complainants

[7] See S Fredman, 'Disability equality: A challenge to the existing anti-discrimination paradigm?' ch 11 above.
[8] There are also some weaknesses specific to the DDA, often attributable to the lingering legacy of the 'medical' model of disability: eg the limited statutory definition of 'disability.' See generally on the 'medical' and 'social' models of disability, works cited in n 5 above.
[9] EC Council Directive 2000/78 establishing a general framework for equal treatment in employment and occupation, OJ L 303/16.
[10] See the Hepple Report (above n 1), para 1.33.

(sometimes supported by support groups) or upon the Disability Rights Commission (DRC) which has only limited funds.[11] Its implementation thus depends on the willingness and ability of individuals to bring actions or, at the very least, to approach the DRC.[12] This may be particularly difficult, or even impossible, for many disabled people.[13] Even if an action is brought, the focus is on remedying individual acts of discrimination after the event, not on the elimination of structures and patterns of behaviour that perpetuate discriminatory practices. Individual compensation does not necessarily guarantee change in practice.[14] The individual enforcement model also sets up a two-party winner-takes-all contest, which is confined in effect to the two parties concerned, leaving no room for best practice group settlements or the input of third parties.[15]

Second, the lack of clarity of the legislation, particularly as regards the extent of the reasonable adjustments duty and the limits of the justification defence, makes it difficult for individuals to ascertain their legal rights or to bring an action with confidence.[16] The residual focus of the legislation is still on the 'medical' nature of disabilities and on accommodating such 'departures from the norm' within existing structures.[17] This often results in low standards being set for justification and reasonable accommodation. It is also reflected in the perennial restrictiveness and lack of clarity in the definition of disability. Clarifying the nature and extent of these requirements may take decades of case law, perpetuating uncertainty that affects both complainants and employers.

Third, much of the prejudicial treatment faced by disadvantaged groups arises out of patterns of institutional discrimination, involving the neglect or lack of understanding of their specific needs. Very frequently, this neglect is due to the limited participation of members of these disadvantaged groups in decision-making processes and the inadequate consultation of their representatives. Disabled people have been particularly affected by

[11] For the perennial difficulties faced by equality commissions in deciding how to allocate resources to individual cases, see C O'Cinneide, *A Single Equality Body: Lessons from Abroad* (Manchester, Equal Opportunities Commission, 2002).

[12] See S Fredman, *Discrimination Law* (Oxford, Oxford University Press, 2001), p 165. See also S Fredman and E Szyszczak, 'Interaction of race and gender', in B Hepple and E Szyszczak, *Discrimination: The Limits of the Law* (London Mansell, 1992), p 216.

[13] This is especially true for DDA goods and services cases, which are heard by the courts and not tribunals. Between 2 December 1996 and 9 July 1998, only 9 such cases were lodged in England and Wales, whereas 2,456 were lodged in employment tribunals: see Meager and others, 'Monitoring the Disability Discrimination Act 1995', Research Report 119 (London, Department of Employment and Education, 1999); and C Casserley, *The Price of Justice* (London, Royal National Institute for the Blind, 2000).

[14] See Fredman, *Discrimination Law* (above n 12), pp 170–3.

[15] For the classic discussion of the limits of adjudication in such circumstances, see A Chayes, 'The role of the judge in public law litigation' [1976] *Harvard Law Review* 1281.

[16] See S Hannett, 'Equality at the Intersections: The legislative and judicial failure to tackle multiple discrimination' (2003) 23 *Oxford Journal of Legal Studies* 65–86.

[17] See M Oliver, *The Politics of Disablement* (Basingstoke, Macmillan and St Martin's Press, 1990), p 6. See also O Smith, 'Disability discrimination and employment: a never-ending legal story?' (2001) 23 *Dublin University Law Journal* 148–74, 152–3.

exclusion from decision-making processes and subjected to paternalistic 'assistance' by decision-makers. The anti-discrimination model imposes no requirement to consult with disadvantaged groups in developing strategies to eliminate discrimination or in improving performance, service delivery and general employee satisfaction.[18]

Finally, much of existing anti-discrimination law adopts a formal individualistic approach which requires that individuals be treated alike. This emphasis, on what Fredman has characterised as 'equality as sameness', ignores the fact that achieving substantive equality may actually require that the specific characteristics of groups be taken into account and positive steps taken to ensure their inclusion as equal participants in society.[19] It also glosses over the main thrust of the 'social model' of disability, which recognises that structural patterns of exclusion are often responsible for making particular impairments a source of disadvantage and that positive action to challenge these patterns is required.[20]

The reasonable accommodation requirement in existing disability discrimination legislation is an exception to this lack of emphasis on positive action, and a major step forward in the evolution of equality law.[21] However, there are serious limits to the scope of this requirement in practice, including the relatively wide extent to which a failure to accommodate can be justified.[22] Beyond its reasonable accommodation requirements, the DDA does little to encourage the taking of proactive steps to identify and eliminate practices that may have discriminatory impact.

This makes existing anti-discrimination law of limited use in combating institutional discrimination in both public authorities and private organisations.[23] Consequently, organisations tend to take defensive steps to meet their legislative obligations, which creates a culture of 'negative compliance'. There is also the additional consequence that practices amounting to

---

[18] See Fredman, *Discrimination Law* (above n 12), pp 22–3. The Hepple Report (above n 1), para 2.19, regarded, as a basic principle of anti-discrimination law, the need for 'opportunities for those directly affected to participate, through information, consultation and engagement in the process of change'.

[19] See Fredman, *Discrimination Law* (above n 12), pp 7–11.

[20] See Smith, 'Disability discrimination and employment: a never ending legal story?' (above n 17), pp 150–53; M Oliver, *Understanding Disability from Theory to Practice* (Basingstoke, Palgrave, 1996); G Quinn, 'Rethinking the place of difference in civil society—the role of anti-discrimination law in the next century' in R Byrne and W Duncan (eds), *Developments in Discrimination Law in Ireland and Europe* (Dublin, ICEL, 1997), pp 65, 75.

[21] The inclusion of the reasonable accommodation requirements is the major reason why the DDA can be seen as an advance on much existing discrimination legislation: see Fredman, ch 11 above. The Canadian equality legislation extends the 'reasonable accommodation' requirement across the full range of equality grounds.

[22] Note, however, the restriction on the extent to which a failure to make reasonable accommodation can be justified, effected by s 3A DDA, inserted by the Disability Discrimination Act (Amendment) Regulations 2003 (SI 2003/1673). See also *Collins v Royal National Theatre* [2004] EWCA Civ 114, 17 February 2004.

[23] Macpherson and others, *The Stephen Lawrence Inquiry* (London, Stationery Office, 1999), available at http://www.official-documents.co.uk/document/cm42/4262/4262.htm

institutional discrimination may appear acceptable, as they are outside the legally established definition of discrimination.[24] Deeply rooted discriminatory practices, particularly in the context of disability, benefit from this cloak of acceptability: if a practice is not prohibited by the DDA, then it will usually be socially accepted as 'normal' or 'reasonable', especially given the historical and persisting neglect of disability rights.

Disability discrimination legislation, such as the DDA or that required by the Framework Directive, can therefore only achieve so much in breaking down deep-rooted structural obstacles to equality. This is not to underestimate the importance of this legislation or the necessity to make sure that it is rigorously enforced and applied. Much of the prejudicial treatment faced by disabled people, however, arises from patterns of institutional discrimination or neglect of their specific needs, which remains untouched by existing legislation. If these problems are to be addressed, current anti-discrimination legislation must be supplemented with new strategies.

3 THE INGREDIENTS OF A NEW APPROACH

It is easy to identify, in general terms, what these new strategies should be designed to achieve. Individual-orientated complaint procedures and remedies need to be reinforced by measures which would remove group disadvantages, encourage positive action and break down patterns of institutional discrimination.[25] Reasonable accommodation is one example of positive action required by statute: the basic idea underpinning this needs to be strengthened, extended across the public and private sectors and given a wider scope. In the public sector, the new strategies should, in addition, be capable of working effectively with initiatives designed to combat social exclusion and improve service delivery.[26] The delivery of health services, for example, is distorted and undermined by patterns of inequality that affect disabled people in particular. In the private sector, enhancing diversity within workforces has to involve proactive action to eliminate obstacles to equality of opportunity.[27]

---

[24] Nicola Lacey has argued that the structure of existing equality law characterises behaviour defined as 'discriminatory' in legislation as *abnormal*, therefore establishing all other forms of behaviour, no matter how prejudicial in effect, as *normal* or, at least, less problematic. See 'From individual to group' in B Hepple and E Szyszczak, *Discrimination: The Limits of the Law* (above n 12), pp 102–3.

[25] See the Hepple Report, (above n 1). See also S Fredman, 'Equality: a new generation?' (2001) 30 *Industrial Law Journal* 163; B Hepple and C Barnard, 'Substantive equality' (2000) 59 *Cambridge Law Journal* 566; M Bell and L Waddington, 'Reflecting on inequalities in European equality law' (2003) 28 *European Law Review* 349, 357–8.

[26] See Audit Commission, *Equality and Diversity: Learning from Audit, Inspection and Research* (London, Audit Commission, May 2002), paras 87–113.

[27] See S Hardy, *Small Step or Giant Leap* (London, Work Foundation, 2001); *Equality and Excellence: The Business Case* (London, Opportunity Now, 2001). See, for a discussion of this in the race context, Cabinet Office Strategy Unit, *Final Report: Ethnic Minorities and the Labour Market* (London, Cabinet Office, 2003).

4 THE LIMITS OF MAINSTREAMING AND DIVERSITY MANAGEMENT

In general, the development of new proactive approaches to equality issues throughout the EU and elsewhere has taken the form of the piecemeal adoption of various forms of 'mainstreaming' strategies.[28] These policies are intended to ensure participation by disadvantaged groups in making policy and to encourage proactive policy-making to identify and, if possible, eliminate structural patterns of discrimination. Many UK public authorities have introduced various mainstreaming initiatives in the disability context, often as part of general equality mainstreaming initiatives.[29] Any disability rights activist will have a fair idea of the mixed impact of these initiatives. Some have produced impressively positive results, others have been under-resourced through insufficient support and training and an emphasis on procedure and 'tick-boxing' at the expense of outcomes.[30]

A persistent problem with such mainstreaming policies has been the failure to ensure sustained attention, and sufficient focus, upon disability issues. As mainstreaming initiatives are not legally enforceable, compliance is usually voluntary. This means that effective mainstreaming usually occurs only when the necessary ingredients of political good-will, organisational capacity, sustained leadership and expert advice are all in place.[31] In the absence of these conditions, initiatives tend, at best, to be procedure-orientated and, at worst, to lapse completely.[32] Lack of clarity as to the appropriate monitoring and evaluation tools is a recurring problem[33] and the nature and extent of participation by disability groups in policy-making has generally been very limited.

In the private sector, too, there are limitations to what can be achieved through the voluntary adoption of equal opportunities policies (which are

[28] See T Rees, *Mainstreaming Equality in the European Union* (London, Routledge, 1998); F Mackay and K Bilton, *Learning From Experience: Lessons in Mainstreaming Equal Opportunities* (Edinburgh, Scottish Executive Social Research, 2003), available at www.institute-of-governance.org/index.html.

[29] At the level of UK central Government, eg, the Policy Appraisal for Equal Treatment guidelines (PAET), reissued in 1998, set mainstreaming standards for race, sex, and disability. See C O'Cinneide, *Extending Positive Duties to Promote Equality* (London, Equality and Diversity Forum, 2004), Part 2.

[30] See for similar conclusions in the gender context, *Gender Mainstreaming: Conceptual Framework, Methodology and Presentation of Good Practices*, Final Report of Activities of the Group of Specialists on Mainstreaming (EG–S–MS (98) (Strasbourg, Council of Europe, May 1998).

[31] Eg the UK PAET guidelines were essentially voluntary in nature and, in the absence of political or organisational will, have frequently lacked impact. The Policy Appraisal and Fair Treatment (PAFT) guidelines were introduced in Northern Ireland in the early 1990s and had a similarly limited effect: see N Hutson, *PAFT in Northern Ireland—A Contribution to the Debate on Mainstreaming Equality* (Belfast, SACHR, 1996).

[32] See for a similar pattern in the gender context, AE Woodward, *Gender Mainstreaming in European Policy: Innovation or Deception?* Discussion Paper (Berlin, WZB Research Unit Organization and Employment, 2001).

[33] See *Equality and Diversity: Learning from Audit, Inspection and Research* (London, Audit Commission, 2002).

similar to mainstreaming requirements). What is required by 'best practice' in this area is very uncertain and the oft-cited term 'diversity management' covers a huge variety of practices, some of more utility and effect than others.[34] In addition, many businesses have simply not adopted any equal opportunities policies beyond those required to secure compliance with anti-discrimination law.[35] Even in a company which has a genuine and meaningful equal opportunities policy, unless it is given sufficient focus and attention, complacency is likely to result.[36] Sustainability, dependence on organisational good-will and the lack of enforcement mechanisms are, therefore, issues of concern in the private, as well as the public, sector.

Even with the growth in popularity of equal opportunities policies, and the existence of the legislative requirement to make reasonable accommodation, structural patterns of disadvantage remain deeply rooted in the private sector and are not breaking down at any appreciable rate.[37] In both the public and private sectors, mainstreaming and equal opportunities initiatives are delivering only mixed results and appear to be excessively dependant on institutional good-will.

5 EXISTING POSITIVE DUTIES

5.1 The Design of Existing Positive Duties

In the UK, positive duties have been developed in an attempt to rectify the deficiencies of mainstreaming initiatives. They impose various *legal* obligations to take proactive action to eliminate inequalities and aim to transform reactive negative compliance, or ad hoc mainstreaming initiatives, into proactive approaches informed by the perspectives of disadvantaged groups.[38] Their general structure is the same, irrespective of the area of equality policy in which they are applied. Thus, the proposed public sector disability duty appears similar to the existing race relations duty.

The crucial contrast between positive duties and the mainstreaming initiatives is that, unlike the latter, positive duties are legally binding and

---

[34] J Wrench, 'Managing diversity, fighting racism or combating discrimination? A critical exploration', paper delivered at Council of Europe and European Commission Research Seminar *Re-situating Culture—Reflections on Diversity, Racism, Gender and Identity*, (Budapest, June 2003).

[35] See the Hepple Report (above n 1), para 1.39 p 16, citing data from the ESRC Data Archive at the University of Essex. A recent survey conducted by the Confederation of British Industry (CBI) found that 83% of companies reported having written equal opportunities policies, but only 40% undertook regular monitoring and only 30% trained line managers on implementing the policy: CBI, *Employment Trends Survey: 2003* (London, CBI/Pertemps, 2003).

[36] For a good discussion of this, see D Jones, J Pringle and D Shepherd, 'Managing diversity meets Aotearoa/New Zealand' (2000) 29 (3) *Personnel Review* 364–80.

[37] See the Hepple Report (above n 1), paras 1.38–1.52 pp 16–20.

[38] *Ibid*, para 3.9 p 60.

intended to have real bite when conflicting priorities, or lack of internal will, might otherwise relegate equality to a subsidiary concern. The binding nature of the obligation is intended to ensure a degree of sustainability and internal commitment.

Duties may take different forms. In particular, those applying in the public sector are likely to differ from those applying in the private sector. All, however, require relevant bodies to adopt an *analytical* approach, to conduct their own monitoring and to implement mainstreaming strategies designed to identify and remove obstacles to equality. This approach is intended to ensure that organisations survey their own policies and practices and take the appropriate action to remove identified patterns of institutional discrimination, while also permitting them a considerable degree of flexibility in how to implement the duty. Thus, positive duties may be imposed upon a wide range of bodies and vary greatly in extent and duration.

Compliance is to be demonstrated by the publication of the steps taken by the body in question and its adherence to whatever procedural and reporting requirements are specified in the duty. In relation to public authorities, if it can be shown that there was a clear failure to give adequate weight to equality issues, the duty may be enforced by equality commissions, courts and auditing mechanisms. This regulatory model therefore relies on what the Hepple Report on the enforcement of UK anti-discrimination law described as 'enforced self-regulation':[39] the statutory enforcement of proactive duties is triggered as a last resort and only where bodies have failed to take the appropriate internal proactive steps.[40] However, given the degree of flexibility given to organisations and the fact that positive duties generally impose an obligation only to give 'due regard' to equality (ie to balance the importance of securing equality against other considerations), ensuring compliance with the spirit of the duty poses considerable difficulty.

5.2 Public Sector Duties

McCrudden has identified six core features underpinning the positive equality duty imposed upon public authorities in Northern Ireland:

— A clear positive statutory duty to promote equality of opportunity by public authorities across all areas of government policy and activities.
— The participation of affected groups in determining how this should be achieved.
— The assessment of impact of existing and future government policies on affected groups.
— Consideration of the alternatives which have less of an adverse impact.

[39] *Ibid*, para 3.3 pp 56–7.
[40] *Ibid*.

— The consideration of how to mitigate impacts which cannot be avoided.
— Transparency and openness in the process of assessment.[41]

The objective of positive duties is, therefore, to change how public authorities perform their functions by making equality a central goal of their day-to-day activities, and to prevent the sidelining of equality concerns.[42] This may involve alterations in service delivery, employment practices, access policies and policy formation in general. Positive duties can also extend across the full gamut of the functions of public authorities, including education authorities, central and local government, the police, health authorities and transport bodies.

In imposing this legal obligation to take proactive steps, legislation must make it clear that the positive duty will not be satisfied by compliance with existing non-discrimination obligations. Therefore, positive duties usually impose a legally enforceable obligation both to eliminate unlawful discrimination, as defined by current legislation (the 'negative' obligation), and to promote equality (the 'positive' obligation). Both elements are crucial parts of the duty.

Relevance and proportionality are also key concepts. The time and resources to be spent on implementing the duty, and the steps to be taken to eliminate or remedy discriminatory practices or policies, should be proportionate to the due importance of promoting equality, taking into account the other key functions and responsibilities of the bodies in question. Examples of initiatives that could be used to comply with the duty include policy impact assessment; the remedying or alteration of discriminatory policies; consultation with relevant groups; training initiatives; the development of access initiatives; the monitoring of educational attainment; surveys of user satisfaction of particular public services; and monitoring employee numbers from disadvantaged groups.

To be effective, the duties must be flexible and responsive to new circumstances, requiring a constant process of monitoring the impact of policies and equality strategies. The perspectives of the members of the disadvantaged groups themselves need to be integrated into this process.[43] Participation has to be recognised as a key value, and care must be taken to guard against paternalism and complacency.

5.3 The Race Relations Duty

A comprehensive positive duty has, to date, been imposed across Britain only in respect of race equality. Section 71 of the Race Relations Act 1976

---

[41] *Ibid*, para 3.11 p 60.
[42] *Ibid*.
[43] C McCrudden, 'Mainstreaming equality in the governance of Northern Ireland' [1999] *Fordham International Law Journal* 22.

(RRA) had imposed a duty on local authorities to make 'appropriate arrangements' to eliminate unlawful discrimination and to promote equality of opportunity and good relations between persons of different racial groups. This duty played a useful role in empowering local authorities to develop racial equality initiatives, including the network of local Race Equality Councils established in the 1970s. However, in the absence of any real enforcement mechanism, the duty was very limited in impact. The fatal flaw in the s 71 duty was its limitation to the making of 'appropriate arrangements'. This proved to be so vague as to deprive the duty of any meaningful content for enforcement purposes.[44]

The report of the Macpherson Inquiry into the racist killing of Stephen Lawrence, with its findings that institutional discrimination was prevalent in the Metropolitan Police, generated immense pressure for the UK government to reinforce and extend the s 71 duty.[45] In response to this, the Race Relations (Amendment) Act 2000 (RRAA) imposed a general positive duty on an extensive list of public authorities to pay 'due regard' to the need to eliminate racial discrimination. It also imposed a complementary positive obligation on them to promote equality of opportunity and good relations between people of different ethnic groups.[46] 'Due regard' is defined by the Commission for Racial Equality (CRE), in its code of practice, as meaning that 'the weight given to race equality should be proportionate to its relevance to a particular function', incorporating the requirements of relevance and proportionality discussed above.[47]

The general duty is supplemented by specific duties imposed by the Home Secretary on specific types of public authorities. Listed government departments, local authorities, police and health authorities, regulatory bodies, commissions and advice agencies are required to prepare and publish a Race Equality Scheme, setting out how they intend to fulfil the requirements of the duty. The Scheme is also to specify what race equality training initiatives the authority is putting into place, as well as the authority's arrangements for publishing their monitoring results and for ensuring that the public has access to public services and information on how the authority is complying with the duty. In addition, listed public authorities are under various specific duties to monitor the ethnic composition of their workforce; of the pool of applicants for posts, promotion and training; and

---

[44] See for a discussion of the limits of s 71 as an enabling mechanism for contract compliance mechanisms, PE Morris, 'Legal regulation of contract compliance: an Anglo-American comparison' (1991) 19 *Anglo-American Law Review* 87–144.

[45] Macpherson and others, *The Stephen Lawrence Inquiry* (above n 23).

[46] See s 71(1) RRA.

[47] CRE, *Statutory Code of Practice on the Duty to Promote Race Equality* (London, CRE, 2002). The code of practice also states that public authorities should 'consider' meeting the duty by identifying which of their functions are relevant to the duty, setting priorities for these functions based on their relevance to race relations, assessing how the implementation of these functions and related policies affect race equality, and considering how the policies and practices might be changed where necessary.

of those involved in grievance, disciplinary procedures and performance appraisals. A similar duty is imposed on educational bodies in respect of the ethnic composition and performance of their staff and pupils.

The CRE may issue a compliance notice to any public authority that is failing to comply with one of the specific duties, requiring it to take remedial steps. If, after three months, the CRE considers the authority is still in violation of the duty in question, it may seek an order from a county court requiring compliance. Compliance, with both the general and specific duties, may also be assessed by government audit mechanisms and judicial review. The introduction of the positive race duty has, generally, been warmly welcomed. The CRE commissioned an independent review of the responses to the duty in its first year.[48] This study was very limited in scope and yielded little meaningful information. However, it appears to show that thus far public authorities value the ways in which the duty has improved policy-making and service delivery and design.[49]

5.4 Northern Ireland: The Section 75 Equality Duty

The single most extensive positive duty imposed in the UK is that provided for by s 75 of the Northern Ireland Act 1998 (NIA), which imposes a duty on specified public authorities to have 'due regard to the need to promote equality of opportunity' across all the protected grounds, including disability, in carrying out their public functions.[50] Schedule 9 specifies the measures required to comply with the duty. In particular, it requires public authorities to prepare an 'Equality Scheme' which sets out the impact assessment, monitoring and consultation procedures they will undertake. The Northern Ireland Equality Commission (NIEC) has set out guidelines for drafting Equality Schemes and carrying out Equality Impact Assessments.[51]

The s 75 duty differs from the race duty in that it applies across all the equality strands and in that it has a more intrusive enforcement mechanism. It requires all equality schemes to be submitted to the NIEC for approval. If dissatisfied with a scheme, the NIEC can refer the authority in question to the Secretary of State for Northern Ireland, who may impose an alternative scheme if necessary. The Commission may investigate the extent of compliance with either the duty itself or with a specific scheme and, if

---

[48] Schneider Ross/CRE, *Towards Racial Equality* (London, CRE, 2003), executive summary available at www.cre.gov.uk. All information cited here is from this report.

[49] *Ibid.*

[50] See C McCrudden, 'The equal opportunity duty in the Northern Ireland Act 1998: an analysis', in *Equal Rights and Human Rights—Their Role in Peace-building* (Northern Ireland, Committee on the Administration of Justice, 1999), pp 11–23.

[51] For an excellent account of the origins and introduction of the s 75 duty, see C McCrudden, 'Equality' in CJ Harvey (ed), *Human Rights, Equality and Democratic Renewal in Northern Ireland* (Oxford, Hart, 2001), pp 75–131.

non-compliance is found, can also refer the matter to the Secretary of State.[52]

The NIEC prepared a progress report on the implementation of the duty up to March 2002. Its conclusions were generally positive, finding good levels of procedural compliance with the Schedule 9 requirements, despite extensive slippage in complying with timetables.[53] Public authorities were found to be integrating the requirements of the s 75 duty into corporate and business planning processes but many were prevented, by lack of resources, from delivering many of the requirements of equality schemes.[54] The progress report also identified examples of good practice and outcomes. Compliance with the duty had resulted in extensive equality training for public authority employees; the reform and overhauling of internal complaint procedures; the collection of hitherto unavailable data on the groups affected by policy decisions; the creation of special units within public authority structures; greater public access (especially for disabled people) to information and public services; and enhanced use of outreach initiatives.[55]

5.5 Devolution and Positive Duties

General positive duties have also been imposed upon the Welsh Assembly[56] and Greater London Authority:[57] both lack effective enforcement mechanisms, but have generated results similar to those in Northern Ireland.[58] The experience of positive duties in the devolved regions thus far, while limited due to their recent introduction, shows that they have the potential to serve as an effective tool in the implementation of tangible and demonstrable steps toward mainstream equality.[59] In particular, they have encouraged authorities to take tangible steps that can be cited as instances of compliance with the duty. However, the overall long-term impact of these duties remains to be seen. In all the devolved regions there has, hitherto, been considerable political support for equality initiatives and the value of the devolved

[52] A less intrusive mechanism was adopted for the race duty because it was felt that the size of Britain, in comparison with Northern Ireland, would preclude the CRE from approving each and every equality scheme.

[53] *Report on the Implementation of the Section 75 Equality and Good Relations Duties by Public Authorities 1 January 2000–31 March 2002* (Belfast, Equality Commission of Northern Ireland, 2003), available at www.equalityni.org/uploads/word/280503FinalFullS75Report.doc

[54] *Ibid*, pp 19–20.

[55] *Ibid*, pp 113.

[56] Government of Wales Act 1998 s 120.

[57] Greater London Authority Act 1998 s 33.

[58] See for discussion of the Welsh experience of the s 120 duty, P Chaney and R Fevre, *An Absolute Duty: Equal Opportunities and the National Assembly for Wales* (Cardiff, Equal Opportunities Commission, 2002), available at www.eoc.org.uk/cseng/abouteoc/ an_absolute _duty.asp; and, for a comprehensive summary of the GLA's equality initiatives undertaken in response to its s 33 duties, GLA, *Into the Mainstream: Equalities Within the Greater London Authority* (London, GLA, 2003).

[59] *Ibid*. See also C O'Cinneide, *Extending Positive Duties to Promote Equality* (above n 29), Part V.

positive duties will only be tested when they are applied in less favourable political waters.[60]

6 DISABILITY RIGHTS AND POSITIVE DUTIES

6.1 A Public Sector Disability Duty?

In accordance with this gradual rolling-out of positive duties, the UK Government, through s 3 of its Disability Discrimination Bill, will insert a new s 49A into the DDA. This provides for the introduction of a positive duty on public authorities to carry out their functions with due regard to the need to eliminate unlawful discrimination under the DDA, to eliminate unlawful harassment under the Act, to promote equality of opportunity between disabled and non-disabled people, and to take account of disabilities, even where that may involve more favourable treatment of disabled persons. As with much of the rest of the Bill, this was introduced to comply with the commitments made by the Government in response to the report of the Disability Rights Task Force.[61]

The explanatory notes accompanying the original draft Bill state that the duty is intended to ensure that bodies exercising public functions 'mainstream' disability rights issues. This means, in broad terms, that public bodies, when making decisions or when developing or implementing new policies, must treat the needs of disabled people as an integral part of the process and, in so doing, have regard to the need to eliminate discrimination and harassment against them and to improve opportunities for them.[62]

The DRC would be given similar enforcement powers to those of the CRE under the race duty and, as with the other positive duties, auditing mechanisms would also assist in implementation.

The duty contained in the Bill is therefore broadly similar to the race duty.[63] However, the Bill does not provide for the Secretary of State to draw

---

[60] Ibid.

[61] For the government's initial commitment, see Cabinet Office, Equality Statement, 30 November 1999.

[62] Draft Disability Discrimination Bill: Explanatory Notes Cm 6058–II (London, HMSO, 2003).

[63] The draft Bill represents a substantial improvement on the wording of the Private Member's Bill, the Disabled People (Duties of Public Authorities) Bill, introduced by Bridget Prentice MP into the House of Commons in 2003, which was a valuable attempt to put pressure on the UK Government to introduce a disability duty. The wording of this earlier bill provided that authorities 'must have regard to the following principles—(a) unlawful discrimination against and unlawful harassment of disabled persons must be eliminated; (b) equalisation of opportunity for disabled persons is to be pursued.' The use of 'due regard' in the draft Bill is a considerable improvement, as it implies that the necessary degree of proportionate attention to the equality issues must be taken into account: referring to 'regard' alone may mean that a public authority would only have to take disability issues into account, as distinct from treating these issues with due concern. In addition, providing that 'equalisation of opportunity must be pursued' is weaker than the race duty requirement that equal opportunities be 'promoted': 'equalisation' implies progressive steps rather than achieving full equality, and 'pursued' is weaker than 'promoted'.

up a list of public authorities to which the duty will apply. Instead, it would apply to bodies that fall within the same general definition of 'public authority' as that used in the Human Rights Act 1998 (HRA). There, public authorities are defined as bodies that perform certain functions of a 'public nature'.[64] This removes the necessity of listing each and every authority to which the duty applies.

The Secretary of State can exclude particular authorities from the scope of the duty.[65] This could pose the danger that such exclusions might be grounded solely on considerations of executive convenience. Admittedly, this has not been a problem thus far with the race duty. However, the strong political pressure that followed the Lawrence Inquiry ensured that it was applied to almost all public authorities. The pressure may not be so strong in the disability context and due vigilance will have to be exercised to ensure that unjustified exclusions are not introduced.

The use of the HRA definition, however, has the potential disadvantage of being linked to the definition of public authorities under the Act, which has already been given a relatively restrictive interpretation by the English courts.[66] As the HRA case-law develops, this may cause fluctuations and uncertainty as to which authorities are subject to the disability duty. Further, many private contractors providing public functions may fall outside the definition.[67] However, the disability duty, like the race duty, applies to the exercise of all the functions of a public authority, including the formation of private-public partnerships and the contracting-out of service-delivery. A failure to give due regard to disability equality in making such arrangements would, in all likelihood, constitute a breach of the duty. Nevertheless, the inclusion of a specific clause to this effect would ensure clarity and serious consideration should be given to replacing the use of the HRA definition with the 'list approach' used in the race duty.[68] The exercise of judicial functions would be exempt from the duty in order to ensure that there is no interference with the administration of justice. Parliament and recruitment to, and service in, the armed forces would also be exempt.[69]

---

[64] See new s 49B, inserted into the DDA by s 8 of the draft Bill.

[65] See new s 49B(3).

[66] See eg *R (on the application of Heather) v Leonard Cheshire Foundation* [2001] EWHC Admin 429; [2001] ACD 75; D Oliver, 'The frontiers of the state: public authorities and public functions under the Human Rights Act' [2000] *Public Law* 476.

[67] See the Hepple Report (above n 1), para 5.17 p 63, citing G Morris' response to the Review's options paper.

[68] The Joint Committee established to consider the Draft Bill recommended both the adoption of the race duty approach and the insertion of a clause making it clear that listed public authorities remain responsible for compliance with the duty even if functions are contracted out to private bodies. See the Report of the Joint Committee on the Draft Disability Discrimination Bill, *The Draft Disability Discrimination Bill* HL 82–I/HC 352–I, 27 April 2004, paras 208–22. The Committee also recommended extending the disability duty to include an obligation on public authorities to have due regard to promoting good relations between disabled and non-disabled people: again, this would parallel the approach taken with the race duty, even if it is as yet unclear what promoting good relations in the disability context would require. See paras 229–40.

[69] See s 49C as inserted by the draft Bill.

6.2 Potential Impact of the Disability Duty

A new positive disability duty is likely to have far-reaching consequences. Some outcomes will now be considered.[70]

A positive duty may lead to a re-orientation in the manner of delivery of certain health services (such as cancer screening, mental health and dental care), with greater emphasis being given to outreach to people whose impairments currently prevent them accessing such services. The inability of disabled people to access particular health services is often attributable to systemic failures in the design and delivery of those services.[71] A positive duty would require the collection of data from which patterns of non-access might be identified and would also require the taking of appropriate steps, within existing resources, to remove barriers to access.[72]

The new duty might also help to identify patterns of disadvantage and discrimination in public authority employment and to encourage greater efforts to set and meet recruitment and promotion targets. It may also ensure a greater emphasis on improved access to educational material and other information and bring about a re-orientation of focus to include the full range of needs of disabled people in education policy and provision.[73]

The duty could also result in considerably enhanced consultation of, and outreach to, all disabled people by public authorities, as demonstrated by some of the outreach initiatives implemented in Northern Ireland under the s 75 duty. The levels of discontent with public authority service delivery, experienced by disabled people, would be monitored and their views incorporated into the design of regeneration projects, the allocation of health expenditure and other decision-making processes.

Further, in requiring appropriate consideration to be given to disability and access considerations in funding allocation, the duty would encourage the improved design of facilities and internal work practices. By requiring

[70] I am grateful to Caroline Gooding for many of these examples.

[71] UK Department of Health, *Annual Statistics*, 1997.

[72] The Joint Committee recommended, eg, that the code of practice to accompany the duty (to be prepared by the Disability Rights Commission) should emphasise the importance of independent advocacy services and provide guidance on the circumstances under which the duty would require public authorities to ensure such services were available for disabled people. See n 68 above, paras 242–5.

[73] The duties already in place in the UK on educational authorities under the provisions of the Special Educational Needs and Disability Act 2001 do not adequately cover reasonable adjustments comprising auxiliary aids and services or physical features, and therefore miss a potentially crucial part of the anticipatory duty in relation to education. In addition, although SENDA does set out requirements on local education authorities and schools in England and Wales to draw up accessibility plans and strategies to improve access to education at schools over time, this duty does not require the tackling of systemic discrimination or the achievement of outcomes. It does not require schools and LEAs to set down a vision of full accessibility and how they will work towards that, as a positive duty would; instead, these educational authorities need only set out what they are going to do to improve accessibility and by when. A disability equality duty would clearly provide the outcome-orientated direction and impetus that is lacking, and provide an enforcement mechanism.

public authorities to monitor the impact of policies upon the disabled community, and the composition of their workforces, a positive duty will give a general legal impetus to the collection of up-to-date data on the numbers and characteristics of disabled people. There is, at present, a frustrating lack of such statistics.[74]

Which, if any, of these outcomes will materialise depends, largely, on how the duty is applied. However, given that disabled people have traditionally been neglected in policy design and service delivery,[75] a disability duty will, at an absolute minimum, represent an advance on existing mainstreaming initiatives. The mish-mash of existing public sector disability initiatives lacks the enforceability, weight and focus that a positive duty would provide, with its requirement that the public authority (at the very least) be seen to be treating disability equality as a core component of its functions. Such a duty will also constitute a powerful tool for disability groups, in persuading public authorities to take their concerns seriously. This, indeed, may prove its prime use. Even if it proves to have limited *internal* impact on the policies of particular public bodies, it opens up those authorities to *external* pressure to demonstrate compliance with the duty and progress in mainstreaming disability rights.[76]

6.3 Making a Disability Duty Work

This opening up of public authorities to scrutiny is an important new vehicle for inducing reform, which should not be neglected. Unless this new vehicle is appropriately utilised by disability rights activists, however, the same defects that have limited the impact of mainstreaming guidelines may well cause the positive duty, too, to remain little more than another rhetorical commitment. Its legally binding status may, in itself, make no difference if public authorities remain resistant to change. To date, there is no clear evidence that positive duties alone, in the absence of supporting political will, trigger substantial improvements.[77]

What will ensure that this duty will have real impact is its use, by disability rights campaigners, equality commissions and disabled people themselves, as a legal tool in pushing for reform with tangible outcomes. As with all forms of anti-discrimination legislation, the effectiveness of this provision will depend upon how it is utilised and enforced by pressure groups. In addition, it should not be forgotten that the existence of a duty will strengthen the hand of those within public sector organisations looking for

[74] See R Prasad, 'The fact vacuum', *Guardian Society*, 4 June 2003.
[75] See works cited at n 5 above.
[76] See O'Cinneide, *Extending Positive Duties to Promote Equality* (above n 29), Part IV.
[77] E Breitenbach, *Statutory Duties to Promote Equal Opportunities and Evidence of Their Impact—Briefing Note for the Strategic Group on Women* (Edinburgh, Scottish Executive, 2003), available at www.scotland.gov.uk/library5/social/bsng1-00.asp (last accessed 9 January 2004).

change and will ensure that disability rights are placed on the internal agenda. It will also ensure, at the very least, that some steps are taken to demonstrate some degree of compliance with the duty.

Another concern about positive duties is that compliance may take the form of basic 'process compliance', whereby authorities treat the duty as involving adherence to set consultation procedures rather than a requirement to focus on achieving effective *outcomes*. Process is important in ensuring the participation of disabled people in all decisions that concern them. It is not enough in itself, however. The disability duty should not become a mechanism that results only in multiple forms of consultation with disability groups, but which produces no real change. Excessive emphasis on procedural gains can create the illusion of progress: outcomes are what ultimately matter. One assessment of UK local authority and health care equality mainstreaming initiatives concluded that too much emphasis had been placed on 'the production of policies and protocols rather than service outcomes'.[78]

An approach designed to achieve substantive equality for disabled people should, therefore, require that the actual results of policies be assessed and monitored and that the emphasis be placed on securing effective outcomes that bring about real and meaningful equal treatment. Clear and committed central leadership and co-ordination, the adoption of 'best practice' models, pressure by NGOs and disability groups, extensive training and the efficient exchange of information between public authorities will all be necessary if the disability duty is to avoid the 'process' trap. Central Government, audit inspectorates, NGOs and equality bodies should all work with public authorities to guide their compliance with the duty towards an outcome-orientated focus.

However, it is sometimes difficult for disabled people to engage in the consultative process. The lack of financial and logistical support available to relevant groups wishing to participate has been identified as a problem with the Northern Ireland duty.[79] Similar concerns are inevitable in the disability context. If financial and logistical support for participation in the duty processes is absent, then there is a real danger that 'consultation' will be limited and ineffective in incorporating the full diversity of perspectives of disabled people.

6.4 Enforcing the Duty

A strong enforcement mechanism is also necessary to prevent positive duties becoming the latest equality policy to flounder on the rock of lack of

---

[78] U Khan, *Equality Standards in Health and Social Care* (London, Department of Health Equality Strategy Unit, 2001). See also C Collins, *Race and the Public Service Agenda: Policy Making in Whitehall* (London, Institute for Public Policy Research, 2002).

[79] See T Donaghy, 'Mainstreaming: Northern Ireland's participative-democratic approach', paper presented to the Jubilee Conference of the Australian Political Studies Association, October 2002, available at http://arts.anu.edu.au/sss/apsa/Papers/donaghy.pdf.

implementation.[80] However, positive duties do not readily lend themselves to individual enforcement. The positive disability duty does not confer specific rights to particular levels of resource allocation or to definite legal entitlements.[81] It requires simply that 'due regard' be given to achieving equality of opportunity. In other words, there is no need to achieve specified outcomes but the appropriate level of consideration, analysis and support must be given to disability issues. It would, for instance, be difficult to challenge a local authority's decision, having identified inadequacies in its service provision to particular groups of disabled people, not to rectify the situation on grounds of cost or competing priorities. Positive duties, therefore, are no substitute for enforceable social rights to a fixed minimum entitlement. Enforcing a requirement to give 'due regard', on the other hand, is a much more complex process, which has to focus upon the quality of the decision-making process as well as the achievement of measurable fixed outcomes.

Enforcing positive duties, then, raises difficulties, especially if the enforcement mechanism relies upon traditional forms of judicial enforcement. Judicial review is a potentially invaluable tool in securing compliance in cases of serious breach. However, it is both expensive and risky, as only an authority that acted in a clearly unreasonable manner in failing to give 'due regard' to the equality duty would be vulnerable to review.[82] Nevertheless, traditional remedies like judicial review could be combined with other forms of accountability mechanism to ensure an adequate focus upon compliance: enforcement need not be confined by traditional concepts of 'centralised' single-route accountability.[83] New accountability mechanisms, such as non-judicial auditing mechanisms using existing auditing bodies like the Audit Commission, may be developed.[84] The Independent Review recommended the design of a 'basket of indicators' which could show progress towards fair participation and fair access, across all the equality grounds, over a specific time period.[85] It suggested that these indicators should be built into the general performance management frameworks and audited by the general inspection and audit bodies.[86]

While the role of the audit inspectorates in enforcing the duty will be important, the DRC's enforcement role (as with the CRE's role under the

[80] See the Hepple Report (above n 1), para 3.11 p 60.

[81] Unlike statutory duties to provide appropriate education which, in certain circumstances, can give rise to a minimum level of entitlement, as recognised by the House of Lords in *Re T (A Minor)* [1998] UKHL 20.

[82] See for an illustration of how this would apply in the context of another statutory duty, *Meade v Haringey LBC* [1977] 1 WLR 637.

[83] See generally C Scott, 'Accountability in the regulatory state' (2000) 27 *Journal of Law and Society* 38–60.

[84] The CRE is working with the Audit Commission and other inspectorates to develop more sophisticated methods of auditing outcomes in the context of the race duty. See CRE, *Auditing for Equality* (London, CRE, 1999).

[85] These indicators might include the monitoring of employment, service delivery and studies of the comparative perception of public services. See the Hepple Report (above n 1), para 3.21 p 64.

[86] *Ibid.*

race duty) will be crucial. Audit mechanisms may lack 'bite' and transparency, and may also be operated by people lacking expertise in, and commitment to, equality issues. The DRC (or the proposed single equality commission), by contrast, would possess such expertise and commitment. It would, therefore, be well placed to work closely with authorities and audit inspectorates in giving effect to the duty.

The enforcement role of the DRC (contrary to the current proposal and the role of the CRE in relation to the race duty) should not be confined to ensuring compliance with the specific *procedural* requirements imposed under the duty. The commission should be able to trigger the enforcement mechanism for alleged non-compliance with any of the duty requirements.[87] This should not be confined to ensuring process compliance alone, as is currently the case.[88] This extension of enforcement powers need not result in a confrontational approach: recourse to enforcement mechanisms should remain a last resort, after advice, conciliation and 'naming and shaming' have proved unsuccessful.

Individuals and interest groups, such as trade unions and community groups, should also be able to bring enforcement actions. At present, under the Northern Irish s 75 duty, the race duty and the proposed disability duty, individuals and groups only have the option of referring allegations of non-compliance to the CRE[89] or NIEC,[90] or of seeking judicial review (which the commissions may also seek).[91] Given the limits of judicial review outlined above, and the possibility that the commissions will be unable or unwilling to take compliance action against particular public authorities, this severely restricts the ability of individuals to challenge public authorities. These limitations could be circumvented if a system of specialist administrative tribunals or internal independent review bodies were established to review and assess the application of the duty and to hear complaints from individuals. Internal review boards, for example, could be established within local authorities or central government departments to assess compliance: this would be a cheap internal remedy.

An external review mechanism, similar to an ombudsman system, could also be established, with a specific focus on the implementation of the equality duties and with specialist skills and expertise. Such review bodies

---

[87] For a more detailed analysis of the enforcement issues, see O'Cinneide, *Extending Positive Duties to Promote Equality* (above n 29), Part VII. The Joint Committee arrived at a similar conclusion: See above n 68, paras 246–53.

[88] *Ibid.*

[89] The CRE could take notice of an individual complaint in deciding to use its powers of formal investigation, or its powers to bring a non-compliance notice under ss 71D and 71E of the Race Relations (Amendment) Act 2000. It could also, in all likelihood, support an individual in bringing judicial review proceedings under its general power to assist individuals in legal action, conferred by s 66 RRA.

[90] As specifically provided for in Northern Ireland Act 1998 sch 9 para 10(1).

[91] The CRE and NIEC could probably bring judicial review as parties having a 'sufficient interest' in the implementation of the duty: see *R v Secretary of State for Employment, ex parte Equal Opportunities Commission* [1995] 1 AC 1

could apply a less restricted test than that used in judicial review and work to encourage authorities to enhance their performance. At present, no such bodies exist: serious consideration should be given to their establishment.[92]

Evidence of compliance with the general duty could also be made admissible in discrimination cases brought by individuals, and courts and tribunals given the power to draw appropriate inferences from it. This would substantially reinforce the impact of the duty, as non-compliance would be linked to the vulnerability of public authorities to legal challenge. This would have the effect of concentrating minds on compliance with the duty, and provide an external legal incentive to implement it properly. Positive duties are more concerned with culture change than the creation of enforceable legal rights: the use of effective and novel forms of enforcement can also ensure that positive duties and rights complement each other. Further, elected officials such as local councillors and MPs should be trained and encouraged to scrutinise the decisions of public authorities, bearing in mind the requirements of the duties.

6.5 Fitting a Disability Duty within the Framework of Existing Anti-Discrimination Law

Should a positive disability duty be introduced in isolation, or as part of a comprehensive equality duty? The latter option would reduce duplication of effort and improve the development of common best practice, but care would be required to ensure that disability was not neglected in the operation and enforcement of this general duty. Given the comparative newness of disability discrimination legislation, due care also needs to be taken to ensure that the introduction of positive duties will not divert attention or resources away from enforcing the new legislation. This will be a particularly important issue for the Disability Rights Commission or its successor. However, positive duties and anti-discrimination legislation should work hand-in-hand, if applied appropriately and with the provision of adequate resources.

7 POSITIVE DUTIES AND THE PRIVATE SECTOR

7.1 Private Sector Duties

The potential of positive duties is, by no means, confined to the public sector. They can also be applied to the private sector, in the form of legislative duties requiring proactive action on the part of private employers to eliminate discrimination. Such duties have similar potential for generating change as do public sector duties; in particular, by facilitating the

[92] See O'Cinneide, *Extending Positive Duties to Promote Equality* (above n 29), Part VII.

identification and elimination of obstacles to equality in relation to promotion, recruitment and training.

Nevertheless, some different considerations do apply in the design and
application of positive duties in the private sector. It is difficult to impose
consultation requirements on the private sector as many small businesses
will not have sufficient resources or access to consultative forums. Any positive duties will also have to centre upon employment: it would be difficult
to require private service providers to improve delivery of their services to
particular groups, once they have made reasonable accommodation, as this
would amount to directing their business operations. The diversity of private sector bodies also means that the design of positive duties needs to take
into account the differences in resources, facilities and sizes of workforce.
Bureaucratic load, and excessive cost imposition, must be avoided if the
duty is to be workable.

Nevertheless, positive duties requiring the monitoring of workforce composition and pay levels, the preparation of equality schemes providing for
the identification and elimination of obstacles to equal treatment and the
taking of proactive measures to promote equality of opportunity in training, employment and promotion may be imposed upon private bodies.
Indeed, this has occurred, with considerable success, in numerous jurisdictions. These obligations are no different, in principle, from legislative
prohibitions of discrimination in pay, promotion and recruitment, or the
reasonable accommodation requirement of the DDA (which can be seen as
a species of private sector duty). These duties, like their counterparts in the
public sector, are designed to be proactive, anticipatory and to promote
substantive equality.

Such positive duties also precisely mirror, in nature, form and content,
best human resources practice as developed across the private sector in
North America and by bodies such as the Employer's Forum on Disability
and other employers' organisations concerned with equality issues in the
UK.[93] As such, they should not, therefore, be regarded as an alien carry-over
from the public sector, but rather as giving legislative foundation to corporate best practice in the same way that the part-time work regulations have
done. Positive duties also have the immense advantage, for the private sector, of setting a clear minimum standard of good practice, compliance with
which would reduce the risks of exposure to anti-discrimination litigation
under the DDA.[94]

At present, the adoption of diversity best practice in the private sector is
frequently patchy, often at the mercy of fluctuations in internal commitment

[93] See eg Department of Trade and Industry, *Accounting for People* (London, DTI, 2003).
[94] They would also clarify the extent of permissible positive action that private firms are per-
mitted to adopt, which at present is often uncertain outside of the area of disability: see L
Barmes, 'Promoting diversity and the definition of direct discrimination' (2003) 32 *Industrial
Law Journal* 200; and L Barmes with S Ashtiany, *Diversity in the City: Initiatives in
Investment Banks in the UK* (London, Nabarro Nathanson, 2003).

and lacking in incentives to retain focus on implementation in the absence of strong backing from individual senior executives. The Hepple Report strongly argued that 'voluntarism' has consistently failed to deliver large-scale and widespread results in the private sector and suggested that voluntary initiatives would be effective only if reinforced by the backing of 'enforced self-regulation' (ie, the statutory enforcement of proactive duties where private sector organisations have failed to take appropriate voluntary steps themselves).[95]

This approach is consistent with that adopted, across the equality grounds, in Canada[96] and, for gender, in many EU countries. The Norwegian Gender Equality Act 2002 covers both public and private enterprises, and imposes a general positive duty upon employers to promote gender equality. This is reinforced by a requirement to report on progress in annual corporate reports or budgets, which must include detailed information on planned and implemented measures to promote gender equality and prevent differential treatment. This is supervised and monitored by the gender ombudsman and the company law authorities.[97]

South Africa has introduced employment equity legislation that relies upon a similar approach to the Canadian legislation and which applies to disability as well. It, however, imposes stronger enforcement requirements due to the South African historical experience, with employers working towards fixed targets and required to demonstrate clear evidence of interim progress and that 'due consideration' has been given to members of disadvantaged groups.[98] The Canadian and South African duties have generated very mixed results in the disability context, mainly because of their lack of a specific focus on disability and inadequate enforcement mechanisms.[99] To guard against this, any British duty must be designed so as to ensure that sufficient focus is placed upon disability and that an adequate enforcement mechanism is in place.

[95] The Hepple Report (above n 1), para 3.3 pp 56–7.
[96] Canadian Employment Equity Act 1986. See HC Jain, PJ Sloane and FM Horwitz, *Employment Equity and Affirmative Action: An International Comparison* (London, ME Sharpe, 2003), pp 22–7. The Canadian legislation has been the model for the Dutch employment equity legislation, which requires positive action to be taken by employers to recruit ethnic minorities, women and disabled persons and reporting on the steps taken: see FJ Glastra and others, 'Between public controversy and market initiative: the politics of employment equity and diversity in the Netherlands' in C Agocs (ed), *Workplace Equality: International Perspectives on Legislation, Policy and Practice* (London, Kluwer, 2003), ch 8.
[97] Sweden has similar legislation: see K Mile, 'Mainstreaming equality—models for a statutory duty', in *Mainstreaming Equality: Models for a Statutory Duty—Conference Report* (Dublin, Equality Authority, 2003), available at http://www.equality.ie/stored-files/PDF/Mainstreaming%20Equality%20-%20Conference%20Report%20-%20PDF %20version.pdff.
[98] See Jain, Sloane and Horwitz, *Employment Equity and Affirmative Action: An International Comparison* (above n 96), pp 34–41.
[99] See C Agocs, 'Canada's employment equity legislation and policy, 1986–2000: unfulfilled promises', in C Agocs (ed), *Workplace Equality: International Perspectives on Legislation, Policy and Practice* (above n 96), ch 4.

In determining how such positive duties can be designed to ensure 'enforced self-regulation', it should be noted that there are different varieties of private sector duties, with varying degrees of regulation and sanction. These different types of duties can be 'rolled out', and increasingly strengthened, if initial regulatory initiatives are not delivering results. In this way, private sector organisations are given an incentive to put their house in order. The 'Big Bang' introduction of a comprehensive scheme, as advocated by the Hepple Report, may be politically impossible at present. However, an incremental approach to introducing some forms of positive duties may be feasible, and have the advantage of educating employers as to what a proactive equality approach entails. Nevertheless, any such incremental steps should not be watered down so as to amount to a tokenistic requirement. Positive private sector disability duties will have to be designed effectively if they are to earn their spurs as cost-effective requirements that deliver real results for the disadvantaged groups.

7.2 Contract Compliance and Public Procurement

At a minimum, serious consideration needs to be given to ensuring that private bodies awarded public sector procurement contracts take proactive steps to promote equality and to eliminate unlawful disability discrimination. Contract compliance mechanisms are the appropriate route for ensuring progress on this front. Such mechanisms could be used to require that a private firm bidding for a public sector contract would have to show that it had taken, and was continuing to implement, appropriate measures for eliminating disability discrimination.[100] Appropriate measures might include pay audits, the assessment of training, promotion and recruitment strategies, the introduction of suitable human resources policies as regards work hours and time off, adequate monitoring of the composition of the workforce, consideration of what reasonable accommodation measures are necessary and the removal of unjustified obstacles to equal treatment. Failure to take the appropriate steps would result in exclusion from the tender process and the cancellation of existing contracts.

CRE guidance on complying with the race duty and best practice in public procurement,[101] as well as best practice initiatives developed in Wales under the general duty[102] and by local authorities as part of the 'best value' initiative, serve as initial outline models for any such schemes dealing with disability rights. These guidelines set out how local authorities should

---

[100] See PE Morris, *Legal Regulation of Contract Compliance: An Anglo-American Comparison* (1991) 1 *Anglo-American Law Review* 87–144.

[101] CRE, *Race Equality and Public Procurement: A Guide for Public Authorities and Contractors* (London, CRE, 2003).

[102] See P Chaney and R Fevre, *An Absolute Duty: Equal Opportunities and the National Assembly for Wales* (Cardiff, EOC, 2002), available at www.eoc.org.uk/cseng/abouteoc/an_absolute_duty.asp

consider the policies and practices of firms in awarding contracts for public procurement and service delivery. The Hepple Report, however, is correct in identifying considerable vagueness in existing schemes, and a lack of clear standards.[103] The Report also draws attention to the restrictive effect of EU public procurement rules in this area which, due to their uncertainty and lack of clarity, are acting as a deterrent to public authorities taking equality of opportunity best practice into account in awarding public procurement contracts.[104]

By contrast, both the US and Northern Ireland have developed extensive contract compliance mechanisms. In Northern Ireland, the Fair Employment Act 1989 (FEA) imposed a positive duty on employers to take measures to ensure fair proportions of Catholics and Protestants in their workforce.[105] The duty has been extended and modified by the Fair Employment and Treatment (Northern Ireland) Order 1998 (FETO). Employers are required to monitor the composition and pay scales of their workforce. If patterns of discriminatory treatment are identified, they are required to take appropriate measures, including the introduction of equality schemes and positive action measures. They must 'file' their monitoring returns and equality plans with the NIEC for approval, which can seek court orders to bring recalcitrant employers into line.[106] Employers failing to implement affirmative action policies may be excluded from

[103] The Hepple Report (above n 1), paras 3.62–3.65.

[104] *Ibid*, paras 3.71–3.73 pp 83–4. The EU public procurement rules are useful examples of policies which have been designed without due regard for the promotion of equal opportunities. Recent legislative modifications have clarified the position, and ECJ decisions have permitted the use of disability equality considerations in awarding public procurement contracts. However, the lack of clarity and precision in the wording of the public procurement directives has restricted the development of contract compliance initiatives and deterred public authorities from introducing such mechanisms, even though their use may be entirely legal under existing EC law. The implications for equality initiatives of this lack of clarity have often been overlooked or marginalised in framing and wording the relevant Directives—a classic example of a failure to mainstream. For a general overview of EC procurement rules, see C Bovis, 'The regulation of public procurement as a key element of European economic law' (1998) 4 *European Law Journal* 220–42.

[105] See C McCrudden, 'The evolution of the Fair Employment (Northern Ireland) Act 1989 in Parliament' in RJ Cormack and RD Osborne (eds), *Discrimination and Public Policy in Northern Ireland* (Oxford, Oxford University Press, 1991).

[106] The Commission can also launch investigations into employment composition and practices and this 'Art 55 review' continues to be the key mechanism for promoting equality in this area. The Commission can also enter into enforceable affirmative action agreements with employers. At the end of March 2001, the NIEC had agreed 301 affirmative action agreements with employers, 72 of which were legally enforceable: it also carried out formal reviews with 31 employers implementing such agreements during the year 2000–2001, and reported that 'the majority of the concerns had made good faith efforts to implement the programme and that there were some encouraging improvements in workforce composition'—see Equality Commission for Northern Ireland, *Annual Report 2000–2001*, p 25. See also PJ Sloane and D Mackay, 'Employment equity and minority legislation in the UK after two decades: a review' (1997) 23 *International Journal of Manpower* 18.

public sector tenders. The Northern Irish duties have proved largely successful,[107] but the extent of monitoring they require may make this model unworkable in the wider UK context.

US Executive Order 11246 requires government contractors to abstain from unlawful discrimination and to take positive action to increase the representation of racial minorities in their workforce.[108] The Office of Federal Compliance Programs enforces these contract compliance requirements by audits, enforceable conciliation agreements and, ultimately, by seeking judicial sanctions that can debar contractors from government work. It also requires contractors to file annual reports and to monitor the composition of their workforce. The Hepple Report concluded that these positive duties were most significant in influencing contracting organisations to develop good equality of opportunity policies.[109] Canada, South Africa and the Netherlands also make use of contract compliance initiatives, which extend to disability: these have again generated positive results, although the full impact and effectiveness of these measures is unclear, and patchy enforcement in Canada and the Netherlands has proved a problem.[110]

Drawing on this comparative experience, the Hepple Report recommended the use of comprehensive contract compliance initiatives as an integral part of the 'best value' process in governing public procurement.[111] This is a sound approach. By linking public procurement with the implementation of a proactive approach to disability issues, contract compliance can act as the first lever in encouraging private sector organisations to use proactive equality approaches more generally. The development of private finance initiatives over the last ten years has proceeded with little regard to the possibility of incorporating an equality dimension into the process. This has been a serious wasted opportunity, which should now be rectified. Enabling legislation and comprehensive codes of practice are required to ensure that public authorities introduce contract compliance initiatives. The expenditure of public money could, thus, reinforce equality of opportunity in the private sector.

---

[107] See Jain, Sloane and Horwitz, *Employment Equity and Affirmative Action: An International Comparison* (above n 96), p 31. See House of Commons Northern Ireland Affairs Committee Fourth Report (1999), para 48.

[108] Section 201, EO 11246 (30 FR 12319), as amended by EO 11375 (32 FR 14303) and EO 12086 (43 FR 46501). See Jain, Sloane and Horwitz (*ibid*), p 19.

[109] The Hepple Report (above n 1), paras 3.23–3.29.

[110] See C Agocs, 'Systemic discrimination in employment: mapping the issue and the policy responses' in C Agocs (ed), *Workplace Equality: International Perspectives on Legislation, Policy and Practice* (above n 96), ch 1, p 16; C Agocs, *Canada's Employment Equity Legislation and Policy* (above n 99); and Glastra and others, *Between Public Controversy and Market Initiative: The Politics of Employment Equity and Diversity in the Netherlands* (above n 96).

[111] Above n 1, paras 3.74–3.77.

7.3 General Private Sector Duties

Extending positive duties across the entire private sector, beyond the scope of contract compliance, will also have to be considered. The development of a set of positive private sector duties would seem to offer real benefits, provided that they are designed with a suitably light regulatory touch and that they take into account the varying sizes of private sector firms and the need for effective and credible promotion and enforcement mechanisms.

The 'Big Bang' duty, proposed by the Hepple Report for all equality grounds, would require a three-year periodic review of employment procedures, in consultation with interest groups; and, in the event of the discovery of significant under-representation, an obligation to take reasonable remedial action by means of an employment equity plan.[112] Such a plan would include provisions for reasonable adjustments to make progress towards a representative composition of the workforce at the appropriate level, and arrangements for appropriate consultation and for publication of the plan.[113] Employers with 10 or more employees would also be required to carry out a similar three-yearly periodic pay audit and take appropriate action via a pay equity scheme where discrepancies were identified.[114] The single equality bill recently introduced by Lord Lester and intended to give effect to the recommendations made by the Hepple Report made provision for such positive duties to be imposed upon employers across all the equality grounds, again including disability.[115]

However, despite the Hepple Report's optimism about the acceptability of such duties, the abolition of Ontario's employment equity scheme in 1996 by a newly-elected conservative state government shows that it may be very difficult, for the reasons discussed above, to introduce such a comprehensive scheme and to maintain political support for it.[116]

The Norwegian requirement for companies to include progress reports on achieving gender equality in their annual reports, with its accompanying supervision mechanism, may be a more appropriate and acceptable first step than the model advocated in the Hepple Report.[117] To ensure a specific focus upon disability issues, any reporting should have to contain a specific set of measures and initiatives relating to disability issues, including (but, crucially, not confined to) reasonable accommodation initiatives. In this way, reasonable accommodation requirements can be linked to wider disability-orientated positive action by private bodies.

---

[112] *Ibid*, para 3.37.

[113] *Ibid*, paras 3.37–3.40.

[114] *Ibid*, paras 3.41–3.50.

[115] See http://www.odysseustrust.org/equality.html

[116] See AB Bakan and A Kobayashi, 'Employment equity legislation in Ontario: a case study in the politics of backlash' in C Agocs (ed), *Workplace Equality: International Perspectives on Legislation, Policy and Practice* (above n 96), ch 5; and C Eboe-Osuji and E McIsaac, 'Repeal of the Ontario employment equity Laws: denial of equal protection of the law' in C Agocs (ed) (*ibid*), ch 6.

[117] See K Mile, 'Mainstreaming equality: models for a statutory duty' (above n 97).

The strength of the relevant enforcement provisions will be central to the effectiveness of any positive duties. Less than strict enforcement provisions have lessened the impact of the Ontario Pay Equity Act 1987, which imposed a statutory duty on employers with more than 10 employees to examine their pay structures for discriminatory pay patterns.[118] The Hepple Report proposed an active investigatory role for the Equality Commission in enforcing the duties recommended in the Report. It also suggests that evidence of compliance, or lack of compliance, should be admissible as evidence in discrimination actions and that tribunals should be able to draw appropriate inferences from it.[119] Both recommendations make sense and should be introduced as part of any set of positive duties applying across the private sector, even if such duties are initially less advanced than those in the Hepple model. It also makes use of latest regulatory theory by encouraging private methods of self-regulation (with statutory regulation as reinforcement) and linking the promotion of equality with the self-interest of employers.[120]

8 CONCLUSION

The Race and Framework Directives both state that 'the principle of equal treatment shall not prevent any Member State from maintaining or adopting specific measures to prevent or compensate for disadvantages [linked to the prohibited grounds for discrimination covered by the scope of the Directive]'.[121] The amended Gender Directive also adopts this broadly permissive, affirmative action, approach.[122] These provisions give leeway for positive duty approaches, especially in the disability context where positive discrimination has not been prohibited in EU or UK law. US-style affirmative action has, historically, been treated with suspicion in the EU[123] and has

---

[118] See A McColgan, 'Equal pay: lessons from Ontario's Pay Equity Unit', Working Paper No 5, Independent Review of the Enforcement of UK Anti-Discrimination Legislation (November 1999).

[119] See the Hepple Report (above n 1), para 3.40 p 71.

[120] *Ibid*, para 3.5 p 57, citing the research conclusions in N Gunningham, P Grabosky and D Sinclair, *Smart Regulation—Designing Environmental Policy* (Oxford, Clarendon, 1998). See also J Ayres and J Braithwaite, 'Responsive regulation: transcending the deregulation debate' (Oxford, Oxford University Press, 1992); Jain, Sloane and Horwitz, *Employment Equity and Affirmative Action: An International Comparison* (above n 96), pp 217–21.

[121] EU Council Directive 2000/43/EC of 29 June 2000 Art 5, implementing the principle of equal treatment between persons irrespective of racial or ethnic origin, OJ L 180/22; Article 7 EU Council Directive 2000/78 establishing a general framework for equal treatment in employment and occupation, OJ L 303/16.

[122] See European Commission, 'Proposal for a Council Directive on equal treatment between men and women outside the workplace', IP/03/1501, 5 November 2003.

[123] S Fredman, 'Reversing discrimination' (1997) 113 *Law Quarterly Review* 575; Case 450/93 *Kalanke v Freie Hansestadt Bremen* [1995] ECR I–3051, [1996] All ER (EC) 66, [1996] ICR 314; Case C–158/97, *Badeck v Landesanwalt beim Staatsgerichtshof des Landes Hessen*, Judgment of 28 March 2000, [2000] IRLR 432.

generated political controversy. These difficulties would be side-stepped by a positive duty approach. While positive duties encourage positive action, they are not dependent upon the utilisation of fixed quotas or the use of automatic preference for particular groups. They do, however, encourage the use of workforce targets and initiatives to remove obstacles to equality of opportunity. When combined with the leeway given to positive discrimination in the disability context, the introduction of positive duties would encourage the use of a wide range of tools to promote substantive equality for disabled people. In essence, such duties would extend the reasonable accommodation approach beyond access and work requirements to the full range of policies and practices that organisations implement.

Positive duties inevitably overlap with issues of human rights, social exclusion, access to social services and poverty, particularly in the disability context. It is, therefore, very important that initiatives under the disability duty be linked to existing anti-discrimination legislation, anti-poverty initiatives and human rights promotion. The importance of this cannot be underestimated. Compliance with positive duties will often overlap with compliance with the positive obligations imposed upon public authorities by the ECHR.[124] The threat of ECHR challenges may help ensure compliance with positive duties and positive duties, in turn, may represent an appropriate mechanism for helping public authorities to discharge their ECHR obligations. Similarly, positive duties could guide the development of social security and anti-poverty initiatives, ensuring that the diversity of disabled people is not overlooked.

Finally, the potential use of positive duties at the pan-European level should not be underestimated. We know, from the experience of sex and race discrimination, that the DDA and the Framework Directive will only take us so far down the path of equality: positive duties represent the next step. They are suitable for introduction at the level of the EU institutions themselves, to complement and reinforce the patchwork of existing mainstreaming initiatives that the Commission, in particular, applies. They can also be used throughout the EU, with suitable adjustment for the different legal systems of different Member States. Positive duties represent a new form of equality regulation. They are not a panacea but, in both private and public sectors, they can act as a lever for change. How effective they will be will depend upon enforcement and on resource allocation. However, even if comprehensive enforcement were not available, positive duties may still act as a point of pressure upon public and private bodies to take appropriate action to secure the rights of disabled people and of disadvantaged groups in general.

---

[124] See eg *R (Bernard) v London Borough of Enfield* [2002] EWHC Admin 2282; and *A v East Sussex County Council* [2003] EWCA Admin 167.

13

The GB Disability Rights Commission and Strategic Law Enforcement: Transcending the Common Law Mind

1 INTRODUCTION

I T IS TEMPTING to suppose that an equality commission will have as its primary enforcement function the support of litigation to remedy individual wrongs. Local redress for the violation of individual rights then becomes a major focus of activity and an equality commission itself emerges as a curious amalgam of law centre and legal aid provider.

Such a view gains credence from the success of the existing UK equality commissions in discharging precisely those functions since the 1970s. This has not, of course, been at the expense of all other activity (such as promotional and policy work) but has been a central preoccupation. High-profile cases attract media attention, clarify and, sometimes, change the law. They may also secure rights and a sort of justice.

There is, however, another, more ambitious account of the role of equality commissions which, for example, underpins the White Papers that preceded the Sex Discrimination Act 1975 (SDA) and the Race Relations Act 1976 (RRA).[1] On this view, precisely because of the limitations of individual litigation, equality commissions need other distinctive powers. The primary purpose of an equality commission would not be seen to lie in the replication of activities undertaken by individuals but, instead, in the promotion of social change by different and idiosyncratic means.

When, in 1975, the Government produced its White Paper in preparation for the SDA and the Equal Opportunities Commission (EOC),[2] it accepted the need for individual citizens to invoke the law to achieve redress for acts of discrimination across the full range of social and economic activity,

---

* Director of Legal Services, Disability Rights Commission. I would like to thank the DRC's librarian, David Sparrow, for his help in the preparation of this chapter.
[1] *Racial Discrimination* Cmnd 6232 (London, HMSO, 1976), and *Equality for Women: A Policy for Equal Opportunity* Cmnd 5724 (London, HMSO, 1975).
[2] *Equality for Women* (*ibid*).

and for a public enforcement agency or commission to support such individuals through what came to be known as 'complainant aid'. It stressed, however, that the special contribution of a commission would be the exercise of more 'strategic' legal enforcement powers, especially the new power to conduct formal investigations into individual persons and organisations and into entire social and economic sectors. The White Paper included a warning against the dangers of a commission becoming bogged down in the support of routine discrimination cases at the expense of activity that might have greater, and more distinctive, strategic impact.[3]

In the light of that warning, it is useful to reflect on the law enforcement experience of the Disability Rights Commission (DRC), which was established following the Disability Rights Commission Act 1999 (DRCA) and is the newest of the three equality commissions in Britain. Like the Commission for Racial Equality (CRE) and the EOC, the DRC is a government-funded non-departmental public body. It comprises fifteen non-executive commissioners (a majority of whom must be, or have been, disabled) and an executive staff of 180 employees based in offices in Manchester, London, Cardiff and Edinburgh.

According to s 2 DRCA, the general functions of the DRC are to work towards the elimination of discrimination, to promote the equalisation of opportunities, to encourage good practice and to keep the Disability Discrimination Act 1995 (DDA) and the DRCA itself under review. Enforcement, then, is not expressly included. A narrow, legalistic interpretation of that term (as used in the DRCA) might well confine it to formal investigations and non-discrimination notices.[4] The scope of this chapter, however, will not be so constrained. My aim here is to reflect on the impact of the DRC on the mobilisation of the law more generally[5] with due regard to the symbolic value of law, its capacity to express and direct social change, to embody and create value and to facilitate cultural transformation.[6]

---

[3] *Ibid* paras 81–124, esp paras 110, 117 and 118.

[4] The only point at which 'enforcement' is mentioned is in s 5, in the context of the new power to enter into agreements in lieu of enforcement action. There, 'relevant enforcement action' refers to a formal investigation or a non-discrimination notice. The DRC's discretion, under s 7, to assist individuals bringing legal proceedings under the DDA and, under s 10, to arrange conciliation of DDA disputes relating to goods, services and facilities, is not strictly an enforcement power.

[5] For the concepts of 'enforcement', 'invocation' and 'mobilisation', see R Cotterrell, *The Politics of Jurisprudence: A Critical Introduction to Legal Philosophy* (London, Butterworths, 1989).

[6] See eg M Cain and CB Harrington (eds), *Lawyers in a Postmodern World: Translation and Transgression* (Buckingham, Oxford University Press, 1994); P Fitzpatrick (ed), *Dangerous Supplements: Resistance and Renewal In Jurisprudence* (London, Pluto, 1991); and GR Rubin and D Sugarman (eds), *Law, Economy and Society: Essays in the History of English Law 1750–1914* (Oxford, Professional Books, 1984); S Fredman, *Discrimination Law* (Oxford, Oxford University Press, 2001); B Hepple and E Szyszczak (eds), *Discrimination: the Limits of Law* (London, Mansell, 1992); IM Young, *Justice and the Politics of Difference* (Princeton, Princeton University Press, 1990). On feminism and discrimination law, see N Lacey, *Unspeakable Subjects: Feminist Essays in Legal and Social Theory* (Oxford, Hart, 1998); and S Fredman, *Women and the Law* (Oxford, Oxford University Press, 1997).

I will, therefore, consider not just the DRC's forays into formal investigations and its support of litigation under the DDA but also its public law interventions; its provision of a formal conciliation service under Parts 3 and 4 DDA (goods, facilities and services, and education respectively); its encouragement of good practice by the promulgation of codes and guidance; and its work to establish better access for disabled people to the civil justice system. All these areas of activity represent important methods by which the law, broadly conceived, can be harnessed in the struggle to achieve equality for disabled people.

2 INDIVIDUAL LITIGATION

By the time the DRC was established in April 2000, a key question was how it could best engage in strategic enforcement work without either alienating the potential goodwill of business or defeating the often high expectations of individual disabled people, many of whom had campaigned long and hard for its creation.[7] Notwithstanding the legitimate expectations of campaigners for a new era of litigation-inspired activism, the advent of the DRC coincided with increased scepticism in the world at large about the efficacy of litigation by or on behalf of individuals as a means of dispute resolution and as a vehicle for achieving enduring social change. Hazel Genn concluded, from her research for the National Centre for Social Research,[8] that what people generally want from legal and associated services following a 'justiciable event'[9] is dispute resolution and not law enforcement; advice and information and not litigation.[10] If funded litigation is to form a significant part of an equality commission's work, it cannot therefore seek legitimacy in individualised outcomes alone. It must also attain strategic benefits that go beyond the contested benefits to the individual litigant whose case has been supported.

The particular climate in which the DRC has exercised its discretion to assist individual litigants is one characterised by the piecemeal introduction, since December 1996, of the DDA, and by continuing criticisms of the

---

[7] On the struggle for disability rights in Britain and America, see C Gooding, *Disabling Laws, Enabling Acts* (London, Pluto, 1994).

[8] H Genn, *Paths to Justice: What People Think and Do About Going to Law* (Oxford, Hart, 1999); H Genn and A Paterson, *Paths to Justice in Scotland: What People in Scotland Do and Think about Going to Law* (Oxford, Hart, 2001). For earlier investigations of similar issues, see, eg B Abel-Smith and R Stevens, *Lawyers and the Courts: A Sociological Study of the English Legal System 1750–1965* (London, Heinemann, 1967); and RL Abel, *The Legal Profession in England and Wales* (Oxford, Blackwell, 1988). For the mounting criticism of the inadequacy of legal services, see successive Annual Reports of The Legal Services Ombudsman for England and Wales, 1991–2003.

[9] *Ibid.* A justiciable event is defined on p 12 as 'a matter experienced by a respondent which raised legal issues, whether or not it was recognised by the respondent as being "legal" and whether or not any action taken by the respondent to deal with the event involved the use of any part of the civil justice system'.

[10] *Ibid* at pp 254–5.

limitations of the DDA itself, its definition of disability, its myriad exclusions and the centrality of the justification defence in the achievement of an unhappy juggling act between the rights of disabled people on the one hand and the demands of commerce on the other. Service providers felt the full weight of the Part 3 access provisions in October 2004, since which date they have been required to make necessary physical adjustments to their premises. The same date saw a major reform of Part 2 to bring it into line with the requirements of the Employment Directive under Article 13 of the Treaty of Amsterdam.[11]

Faced with inchoate legislation which was under-used by particular groups of disabled people, and by the relative neglect of entire clusters of rights, the DRC sought to target certain types of case for legal representation: Part 3 cases in general; cases involving people with particular impairments, especially those with learning difficulties and histories of mental ill-health; and Part 2 cases that would achieve clarification of, or at least probe, some of the more controversial legislative obscurities (eg the definition of disability and the threshold of the justification defence). These litigious interventions were to be complemented by the promotion of a conciliation service for Part 3 and 4 cases, in accordance with the discretion granted to the DRC by s 10 of the DRCA.[12]

At the end of its first three years, the DRC had arranged legal representation in 164 cases, 56 of which were Part 3 goods, facilities and services cases. It had also referred 328 cases to conciliation.[13] Of course, the most glittering prizes rest in the gift of the higher courts, especially the Court of Appeal and House of Lords. As a result of early collaboration with the Royal National Institute of the Blind, the DRC was able to support the first DDA case to go to the House of Lords.[14] The victory of the appellants in establishing that Part 2 of the DDA extends to post-contractual acts (such as the giving of references) not only established an important legal principle, but helped to put the DDA on the judicial map, especially given that similar issues were being raised under the SDA and RRA.

One of the most significant limitations of the DDA is its inability to touch many of the issues that most concern disabled people, issues that

[11] For an overview of the implementation of the DDA, see N Meager, B Doyle, C Evans, B Kersley, M Williams, S O'Regan and N Tackey, *Monitoring the DDA 1995, Department for Education and Employment, Research Report RR 119* (London, DfEE, 1999); S Leverton, *Monitoring the DDA 1995 (Phase 2), Department for Work and Pensions In-House Report 91* (London, DWP, 2002); J Hurstfield, N Meager, J Aston, J Davies, K Mann, H Mitchell, S O'Regan and A Sinclair, *Monitoring the DDA 1995 (Phase 3), Institute for Employment Studies* (London, DWP, DRC and Equality Commission for Northern Ireland, 2004).
[12] DRC Legal Strategy 2001–03, unpublished. On under-use of the DDA, see N Meager and others (above n 11).
[13] DRC Legal Bulletin, Issue 4, June 2003; and DRC statistics, unpublished.
[14] *Jones v 3M Healthcare* [2003] IRLR 484. For other cases supported by the DRC in the appeal courts, see eg *Kirton v Tetrosyl Ltd* [2003] IRLR 353; *Archibald v Fife Council* [2004] IRLR 197; *Paul v National Probation Service* [2003] IRLR 190; *Essa v Laing Ltd* [2004] IRLR 313.

are more easily seen as human rights breaches than as disability discrimination. Nearly 50 per cent of the calls taken by the DRC's helpline from disabled people concern matters such as welfare benefits, and community and social care issues, which generally lie beyond the DRC's express DDA remit.[15] Nevertheless, the DRC's residual power to intervene in judicial review and other proceedings, without being a party to those proceedings or funding one or other party, does enable it to have some limited influence on the law on such matters.

In *McNicol v Balfour Beatty Rail Maintenance Ltd*[16] the DRC intervened in an attempt to persuade the Court of Appeal that a condition known as 'functional or psychological overlay' should be treated as a physical rather than a mental impairment under the DDA. The point had significant implications for the approach to be taken to the meaning of disability. Importantly, the Court of Appeal recognised that the DRC did have a part to play in such proceedings, despite the fact that it was not formally supporting the disabled litigant and that the DRCA does not explicitly confer intervention powers of this sort.

Another significant development occurred in *R v East Sussex County Council ex parte A & B, X & Y*.[17] This case was not brought under the DDA at all but, nevertheless, the DRC intervened and made general policy submissions about the impact of EC-inspired manual handling regulations upon the welfare of many disabled people who, on dubious health and safety grounds, were being denied the necessary level of care. In that instance, an alliance of policy and legal initiatives, together with collaboration with the Health and Safety Executive, led to a High Court decision that has the potential to bring about real change for some of the most disadvantaged disabled people. Since then, the DRC has intervened in cases challenging the guidance offered by the General Medical Council regarding decisions to withdraw treatment and sustenance from patients; and questioning the decision of a London hospital to prescribe only limited ventilation to a severely disabled child who happened to have had an asthmatic attack, apparently on 'quality of life' grounds.

These instances of DRC activity in the courts demonstrate an increasing tendency, largely shared by the CRE and EOC, to focus legal resources on the attainment of 'added value'. With inevitably limited resources, a publicly funded equality commission faces hard choices in prioritising its activities. The aspiration, in the provision of legal services, must be that every case really counts as a significant contribution to the broader strategic agenda. By targeting particular groups, sectors or issues, by seeking clarification of technical obscurities in the higher appellate courts, and by intervening in public law actions that lie at the edge of, or even outside, the primary

---

[15] DRC statistics, unpublished.
[16] *McNicol v Balfour Beatty Rail Maintenance Ltd* [2001] IRLR 644.
[17] *R v East Sussex County Council ex parte A & B, X & Y* [2003] EWHC 167 Admin.

legislation of which the commission is custodian, an equality commission can bring an extra, and invaluable, 'public interest' dimension to the pursuit of litigation.

3 ACCESS TO CIVIL JUSTICE

As part of its strategic approach, the DRC has targeted some of the most disadvantaged disabled people, or at least those least likely to have had successful recourse to legal proceedings in the past. The nine cases brought on behalf of people with learning difficulties or histories of mental illness, for example, represent a significant proportion of the 56 Part 3 cases which have been funded.[18] One of those cases, concerning the exclusion of a young woman from a public house owned by a major brewery, disclosed what appeared to the DRC to be a pattern of discrimination and led to the first, albeit unsuccessful, attempt at negotiations aimed at reaching an agreement in lieu of relevant enforcement action under s 5 DRCA.[19]

Just as significant as the funding and outcome of cases brought on behalf of these disadvantaged groups have been the lessons learned about the 'access to justice' obstacles faced by many disabled people, especially those with cognitive impairments. These obstacles are not confined to the physical barriers to access, frequently encountered by those with mobility or sensory impairments, but extend to the more subtle, and ultimately more disabling, barriers thrown up by the judicial process itself; by its language, its assumptions, its way of working—in short, by its 'culture'.[20] The DRC has attempted to distil those lessons for more general application by feeding them into its work with the courts and tribunal services. In 2002 the DRC and the Council on Tribunals[21] jointly produced guidance for all major tribunals on the handling of disability matters.[22] For the civil courts, the Judicial Studies Board's Equality Handbook is similarly intended to raise awareness for judges and court staff of the way in which the legal process itself can unwittingly contribute to and reinforce the discrimination experienced by some of the most vulnerable litigants.

4 ALTERNATIVE DISPUTE RESOLUTION

It is salutary to recall that the idea that law and legal enforcement, as opposed to alternative dispute resolution mechanisms based on conciliation

---

[18] DRC statistics, unpublished. On Part 3 cases generally, see also N Meager and others (above n 11).

[19] *McKay v Scottish & Newcastle plc*, Central London County Court, Claim No IG100989 (unreported).

[20] DRC Legal Bulletin, Issue 3, December 2002.

[21] The President of which, Lord Newton, has been instrumental in promoting the guidance as part of a general re-examination of tribunal services.

[22] *DRC and Council on Tribunals, Making Tribunals Accessible to Disabled People: Guidance on Applying the Disability Discrimination Act* (November 2002).

and persuasion, should have a leading role in combating discrimination is, itself, relatively new and far from uncontested. As recently as 1966, the Race Relations Board in its first Annual Report to the Home Secretary, Roy Jenkins, still felt compelled to argue both that 'racial discrimination exists in this country' and that 'voluntary effort is insufficient in itself without legislation.'[23] Yet even then there was some prevarication:

> [L]egislation should not be thought of in terms of coercion. In America, in only a tiny proportion of many thousands of cases has it proved necessary to invoke the sanction of the law. This is because the process of conciliation is central to this type of legislation.[24]

The Race Relations Act 1965 was, in fact, limited in scope to discrimination 'in places of public resort', such as hotels, pubs and restaurants. Crucially, employment and housing were not covered by the Act. The Race Relations Board itself was charged with the creation of local 'conciliation committees' to resolve complaints received either by the Board or the committees themselves. Only in the event of conciliation failing, and of the Board identifying a course of discriminatory conduct which was likely to continue, did the possibility of legal sanction arise. The Board had discretion to report such conclusions to the Attorney General who, in turn, had discretion to apply to the court for a restraining injunction. In its first report, the Board noted that of 327 complaints received only 238 were in scope and that the majority of these concerned public houses. Only three complaints were not conciliated successfully.[25]

An interest in persuasion and conciliation has also emerged in the Government's recent consultation on the creation of a single Commission for Equality and Human Rights (which would cover age, sexual orientation and belief as well as race, gender and disability). In calling for a 'new emphasis' on 'raising awareness and stimulating debate', on 'mainstreaming' and 'providing advice and guidance to employers and service providers', the consultation paper published at the end of 2002 spoke of the need for 'flexible approaches to enforcement', with more emphasis on conciliation and other 'modern dispute resolution techniques'.[26]

The DRC is the newest of the domestic equality commissions. It is a feature of its modernity (albeit one which echoes the much earlier conciliation focus of the Race Relations Board), that its founding legislation makes express provision for alternative dispute resolution. As well as conferring on the DRC the sort of enforcement and funding powers shared by the CRE

---

[23] *Report of the Race Relations Board for 1966–67* (London, HMSO, 1967), p 21.
[24] *Ibid* at pp 21–2.
[25] *Ibid* at pp 6–10 and App III.
[26] *Equality and Diversity: Making it Happen—Consultation on Future Structures for Equality Institutions* (London, The Stationery Office, 2002).

and EOC, the DRCA[27] grants it the power to make arrangements for the provision of conciliation services in relation to consumer disputes under Part 3 DDA, to supplement the conciliation work of ACAS in relation to employment disputes under Part 2. The Special Educational Needs and Disability Act 2001 extended this power to disputes relating to education.

The conciliation process is capable of yielding results that go beyond the limited remedies available from the courts and tribunals. Free of charge to both parties, relatively quick and non-adversarial, conciliation is capable of achieving insight on the part of business; of producing change of policy; and of addressing issues that, although relevant to disabled people at large, do not necessarily form part of the original dispute. A good example of the potential of conciliation is provided by a dispute which arose after a wheel-chair-user booked a room in a hotel that was part of an international chain. He needed a bed for himself and another bed for his personal assistant. All the accessible rooms had only double beds and so an extra charge was incurred to accommodate his personal assistant in a separate room. Following formal conciliation, the hotel chain undertook to change its policy throughout Europe and provide better training on disability for its staff. It also agreed to look at its other policies affecting disabled people (eg its provision of shower facilities) and to pay compensation of £1,000.[28]

In its first year, and whilst making use of a service inherited from the Disability Access Rights Advice Service (DARAS), the DRC referred 156 Part 3 cases to formal conciliation. As many as 60 per cent of those cases reached settlement through telephone 'shuttle' conciliation, without recourse to the civil courts. In March 2001 the DRC entered into a three-year contract with Mediation UK (a community-based mediation network) to run a new Disability Conciliation Service from its offices in Bristol, drawing upon a specially recruited panel of 40 conciliators. By April 2003, nearly 170 further disputes had been referred to face-to-face conciliation. The average settlement rate in these cases was 54 per cent in the first year but rose to 70 per cent in the second year and to 79 per cent in the third. The average level of compensation received also increased; from £470 in the first year to £1,615 in the third.[29]

The 'modern' appearance of these conciliation arrangements reflects the contemporary interest, both domestic and international, in the use of alternatives to the courts to resolve disputes. In England and Wales, the reforms inaugurated by the report of Lord Woolf on civil justice in 1996 have translated that interest into practical necessity.[30] The Court of Appeal itself, has

---

[27] S 10.
[28] DRC data, unpublished.
[29] DRC Legal Bulletin, Issue 4, June 2003; and DRC statistics, unpublished.
[30] *Access to Justice: Final Report by the Right Honourable Lord Woolf, Master of the Rolls* (London, HMSO, 1996).

demonstrated in two recent decisions, that courts will impose cost penalties on parties who reject a proposal to mediate.[31]

Of course, conciliation (especially in the context of discrimination) has not received universal support. Beneath the expressions of scepticism lies a legitimate fear that justice will be made subordinate to administrative efficiency, that the radical force of reforming legislation will be tamed by the subterranean resolution of disputes at the convenience of one party and at the expense of the other.[32] It was, perhaps, such concerns that prompted commentators on sex discrimination in the 1990s to temper their endorsement of alternative, or 'appropriate', dispute resolution (ADR) with a call for any such conciliation to move beyond the ACAS model towards a 'rights-based' approach, the primary objective of which would be the promotion and enforcement of the SDA.[33] Under such a 'rights-based' approach, participation in ADR would be entirely voluntary; settlements, once achieved, would be binding and a matter of public record; and primary responsibility would rest on the mediators, who should have expertise in discrimination law and training on the handling of sex discrimination cases, to ensure that the parties were adequately informed about their rights. In this way, ADR might become, as Paul Miller (Commissioner at the US Equal Employment Opportunities Commission) puts it, a 'just alternative' rather than 'just an alternative.'[34]

In the present climate, the expansion of ADR seems inevitable. Its potential, in an anti-discrimination and human rights context, is yet to be fully explored. Where the litigation route for Part 3 and 4 cases takes applicants through either the small claims court, sheriff court or Special Educational Needs and Disability Tribunal, there is unexplored potential for rights-based conciliation to provide a significant alternative to litigation for those many disputants whose primary motivation, as identified by Genn, is to resolve the dispute and move on. In an environment where 'law' and 'legal enforcement' have traditionally taken centre-stage, it will require resolve, on the part of any equality commission, to persist with what many will regard as a fruitless and potentially dangerous experiment. Nevertheless, the facilitation of ADR, for those who wish to use it, remains a valuable

---

[31] *Dunnett v Railtrack plc* [2002] 1 WLR 2434; and *Frank Cowl & Others v Plymouth City Council* [2002] 1 WLR 803.

[32] For evidence of scepticism amongst users, see eg J Hurstfield and others (above n 11), pp 228–30.

[33] R Hunter and A Leonard, 'Sex discrimination and alternative dispute resolution: British proposals in the light of international experience' [1997] *Public Law* 293–314.

[34] P Miller, 'A just alternative or just an alternative? Mediation and the ADA' (2001) 62 *Ohio State Law Journal* 11–29. It is Miller's belief that justice has indeed been served by arrangements in the US that saw 7,544 discrimination cases (1,819 disability cases) referred to mediation in 1999 and a further 11,451 (2,646 disability cases) in 2000, at a settlement rate of 65%. In total, roughly 20% of all disability cases referred to the EEOC under the Americans With Disabilities Act 1990 (ADA) find their way to mediation.

component of the suite of services that an equality commission might seek to offer in support of its 'programme for change' agenda.

5 FORMAL INVESTIGATIONS

For the DRC, as for the other equality commissions, the chief enforcement alternative to litigation and conciliation, to the all-consuming dependence upon individual cases, is the formal investigation, whether named-party or general. Unlike individual cases, formal investigations can be initiated directly by the DRC; there is no need to identify an individual 'victim'; the process need not be formally adversarial; and the outcome of an investigation can be far-reaching and include the compulsion of change in policies, practices and procedures. Formal investigations thus hold out the prospect of an attractive alternative. Indeed, as the 1970s White Paper on the CRE observed, the main task of the commission would be:

> to identify and deal with discriminatory practices by industries, firms or institutions ... on their own initiative ... and whether or not there had been individual complaints about the organisation investigated.[35]

The history of the CRE's attempts to realise the White Paper's vision is, by now, well-known. An early flurry of investigative activity (as many as 16 investigations commenced in the first two years) halted by the imposition in the 1980s of judicial constraint. Lords Denning and Hailsham, between them, condemned the apparent licence of the formal investigation device as reminiscent of the Star Chamber or the Spanish Inquisition and considered it a thoroughly un-British sort of thing altogether.[36] The result was the effective emasculation of the formal investigation power, which became discredited by procedural density and delay and, consequently, fell into relative disuse. The formal investigation launched by the EOC in 2003 was, for these reasons, the first to be conducted by it for nearly a decade.[37]

Partly in response to the marginalisation of the formal investigation activity of the other commissions, the DRC has been the beneficiary of modified powers. Two distinctions stand out. First, the prescription of a very tight eighteen-month time limit. This, no doubt, is intended to focus minds and reduce the likelihood of long-drawn out investigations that, in some cases, have devoured as much as nine or ten inconclusive years.

---

[35] Cited by A McColgan, *Discrimination Law* (Oxford, Hart, 2000), p 293.

[36] See Lord Hailsham in the House of Lords debate on the Race Relations Bill, 373 HL Debs, 20 July 1976, col 745; and Lord Denning in *Science Research Council v Nasse* [1979] QB 144. See also *Hillingdon London Borough Council v CRE* [1982] AC 779; and *R v CRE ex parte Prestige Group plc* [1984] ICR 472.

[37] G Appleby and E Ellis, 'Formal investigations: the CRE and EOC as law enforcement agencies' [1984] *Public Law* 236–76; A McColgan (above n 35) ch 5; C Bourn and J Whitmore, *Anti-Discrimination Law in Britain* (London, Sweet & Maxwell, 1996) ch 9.

Secondly, the appearance of a formal power to enter into binding, but voluntary, agreements in lieu of commencing or continuing enforcement action by way of formal investigation or the imposition of a non-discrimination notice.[38]

Both these innovations have the potential to encourage a pragmatic approach to formal investigations and to reduce the risk that they become either excessively confrontational or lacking in direction. Yet, neither innovation decisively dispels the shadow of the CRE experience in the 1980s. The fear remains that, first, the need to establish a relatively high level of suspicion of unlawful conduct at the outset and, secondly, the need to prescribe tight terms of reference to which the investigation must adhere, will continue to make the named-party formal investigation a delicate and risky exercise.

Nevertheless, on 28 March 2003 the DRC announced its first formal investigation (albeit of a 'general' nature) into website accessibility. The purpose of the investigation was threefold: to conduct a systematic evaluation of the extent to which the current design of websites helps or hinders use by disabled people; to produce an analysis of the reasons for any recurrent barriers; and to recommend further work that might contribute to the enjoyment of full access for disabled people.[39] Website access is not, of course, the only area of service provision where the letter and spirit of the DDA are not universally observed. Unusually, however, the Web is part of the social environment that is still relatively new. Whereas access to the built environment, for instance, frequently entails tackling barriers unthinkingly created many years ago, the relative immaturity of the Web creates a unique opportunity to make an intervention in favour of disability rights at a much earlier stage.

If successful in achieving rapid and widespread change, this first DRC formal investigation[40] will help establish a course for future enforcement activity that sees the achievement of a new balance between interventions in individual cases and the use of the full range of the available strategic enforcement powers. In short, it may represent a significant step towards securing social justice, not just through the realisation of individual rights, but in the form of increased and widespread participation for all disabled people in social, economic and political life.

6 CODES OF PRACTICE AND BEYOND

In the belief that prevention is better than cure, the DRC has produced comprehensive statutory codes of practice. These relate to the extension of Part 3 DDA to physical alterations, which came into force in October 2004; and

---

[38] DRCA 1999 ss 3–5.
[39] For terms of reference, see public notices in *The Financial Times* and *The Guardian* for 28 March 2003.
[40] For a report of the findings and fifteen recommendations, see DRC, *The Web: Access and Inclusion for Disabled People* (London, TSO, 2004).

the new Part 4 provisions relating to disability discrimination in education (both pre- and post-16).[41] Other codes were published in 2004, covering new law relating to employment and other forms of occupation, and trade associations and qualifications bodies. The publication of statutory codes is not legal enforcement in the conventional sense. It is, on the other hand, an aspect of the 'mobilisation' of the law in the cause of promoting equality for disabled people. Statutory codes do not have legislative force, nor do they usurp the function of the courts and tribunals. They do, however, set the framework for future judicial interpretation of the law and for its practical implementation by those most affected.

In the absence of an express power to audit and monitor performance, statutory codes, the other materials that flow from them, and the development of good practice models, represent the DRC's most concrete instruments for embedding or 'mainstreaming' equality and translating legislative theory into social practice. Activity of this sort points towards a new regulatory regime; a school of 'enforcement' which places the emphasis upon challenging the potential 'perpetrator' of discrimination rather than assimilating, or restoring, its potential 'victim'; and which recognises that, in this context, the very notion of 'perpetrator' may be misconceived, being, in reality, a mere proxy for that elusive concentration of economic, social and cultural forces which is 'society'.

7 CONCLUSION

In May 1999 the Better Regulation Task Force produced its report on anti-discrimination legislation.[42] It suggested that, given the limited resources of the equality commissions, it may be more effective for the Government to provide support to individuals seeking redress, in the more straightforward cases, through the Community Legal Service, through the reform and extension of legal aid, and through partnership between the commissions and local advice centres.[43] As the report put it,

> [t]his would leave [the commissions] free to target their own investigative and enforcement activity on novel or test cases, and on flagrant or persistent offenders.[44]

The argument for strategic prioritisation was adopted in the Report of the Independent Review of the Enforcement of UK Anti-Discrimination Legislation (the Hepple Report), according to which:

---

[41] Code of Practice: Rights of Access to Goods, Facilities, Services and Premises (London, TSO, 2002); Code of Practice for Schools (London, TSO, 2002); Code of Practice: Post-16 (London, TSO, 2002).
[42] *Better Regulation Task Force: Anti-discrimination Legislation Review* (London, TSO, 1999).
[43] *Ibid* at p 9.
[44] *Ibid*.

The primary objective [of an equality commission] is not to represent interest groups or to give them a voice. That is the function of non-governmental organisations and organised groups such as those promoting racial equality or women's rights, or the rights of disabled persons, and those of other disadvantaged groups. The main objective of the commission is to act as an organ of government promoting change in organisations and, where appropriate helping individuals to assert their rights. The commission's essential role is to promote equality and to ensure that resources are focussed on the most important strategic issues.[45]

For Hepple, the lessons of 'modern' regulatory theory are clear enough. First, private forms of social control are often more effective than state law enforcement, so that more can be achieved by harnessing enlightened self-interest than through conventional 'command and control.' Secondly, the quality of regulation is improved by bringing into the regulatory process the experience and views of those directly affected (eg trade unions, community organisations and public interest bodies), so that 'enforcement' becomes as much a matter of educating, informing and enabling as of the direct imposition of legal sanction.[46] From these lessons emerges Hepple's seven-level 'enforcement pyramid', with persuasion at the base, supporting a structure that includes, eventually, commission investigation and the subsequent imposition of sanctions as a last resort.[47]

In the space of thirty-five years, then, the discussion has come almost full circle. While, in 1975, the Race Relations Board was lamenting the limitation of the law to acts of discrimination in 'places of public resort' and the fact that the primary mechanism of redress was conciliation, at the turn of the century, conciliation was being embraced as a distinctively 'modern' instrument of enforcement, and the emphasis of anti-discrimination legislation upon employment law and litigation was acknowledged to be an impoverishment of the law's potential to harness social change.

The DRC's enforcement activities represent an attempt to share that 'modern' strategic vision and to reach beyond the incorrigible individualism of the 'common law mind.'[48] They have been influenced by a desire to

---

[45] B Hepple, M Coussey and T Choudhury, *Equality: A New Framework (Report of the Independent Review of the Enforcement of UK Anti-Discrimination Legislation* (Oxford, Hart, 2000), pp 52–3.

[46] *Ibid* at p 57.

[47] *Ibid* at pp 58–9.

[48] On the modern 'common law mind', see D Sugarman, 'Legal theory, the common law mind and the making of the textbook tradition' in W Twining (ed), *Legal Theory and Common Law* (Oxford, Blackwell, 1986); and M Lobban, *The Common Law and English Jurisprudence 1760–1850* (Oxford, Oxford University Press, 1991). For its historical roots, see JGA Pocock, *The Ancient Constitution and the Feudal Law: A Study of English Historical Thought in the Seventeenth Century* (revised edition) (Cambridge, Cambridge University Press, 1987), especially chs 2 and 3 on the 'common law mind'.

ensure that domestic anti-discrimination legal activity extends into all areas of life, despite having initially become closely associated with employment law rather than with broader constitutional or human rights principles of the type which have frequently nurtured equality legislation elsewhere in Europe and the Commonwealth.

The common law mind, in asserting that the law is essentially case-based and that the analysis of precedent is capable of yielding a satisfactorily unified and internally coherent body of principle, conveys the important practical message that case-law and the legal profession (especially the judiciary) play the decisive role in protecting individual rights. To counter this constraining mentality there is a need, at every turn, to maximise the extra-legal impact of individual legal cases; to tackle structural inequality by promoting systemic rather than individual change; and to achieve such outcomes, not in the workplace alone, but also in other arenas of social, cultural and economic life.

The DRC has drawn, quite deliberately, upon the experience of the CRE and EOC. It has also had regard to the steady stream of constructive criticism emanating from those bodies over the years: criticism of the limitations of law; of the legal system, its process, its personnel and its priorities; and of the mixed benefits and risks of the various self-help and conciliatory alternatives to the legal process.[49] It is that wider mobilisation of the law and the legal framework that has exercised the DRC in its individual casework and that justifies the application of the epithet 'strategic' to otherwise unsystematic litigious reaction to individual cases.

In the context of race, the Race Relations (Amendment) Act 2000 imposed a positive duty on the public sector to promote race equality. Such a duty constitutes an invaluable tool in the hands of those wishing to tackle institutional discrimination. No such 'fourth generation' duty yet exists in relation to disability. The Disability Discrimination Bill (published in December 2003) seeks to remedy this omission and thus offers the prospect of transforming, beyond recognition, the 'strategic enforcement', and effective securing, of disability rights. The legislative framework for the realisation of disability equality may well then be placed beyond the reach of the potentially stifling constraints imposed by the common law mind and its over-identification of law and legal activity with the judicial decision-making process.

In conclusion, I have argued here that discrimination against disabled people cannot be tackled by simply conferring on them the right to sue those who discriminate against them. Though such rights have an important role to play, meaningful social change cannot occur unless they are supplemented by a more strategic, far-reaching approach to the problem than the lottery of individual litigation is able to provide. The existence

---

[49] CRE and EOC, Annual Reports 1977–2003. See A McColgan (above n 35) ch 5.

of an appropriately funded and empowered enforcement body is crucial to the development of such a strategic approach. The experiences of the GB DRC, in its attempts to work strategically within the constraints imposed upon it, will, it is hoped, be instructive in the creation of other such bodies elsewhere in Europe and beyond.

14

Mind the Gap! Normality, Difference and the Danger of Disablement Through Law

ANNA LAWSON*

1 INTRODUCTION

T HIS CHAPTER WILL examine some of the dilemmas which disability
has posed for non-disability-specific law in European countries. The
term 'non-disability-specific law' is used here to refer to law other
than that primarily designed to deal with disability-related issues. Anti-
discrimination legislation and welfare law therefore fall outside the scope
of this chapter. So too does human rights legislation.

My aim is to draw attention to the way in which adherence to a narrow
conception of the 'normal' can result in laws which have the effect of excluding people with impairments or of undermining their independence and
dignity. In the language of the social model of disability, such laws represent
disabling barriers to people with impairments in the same way as do exclusionary building designs and hostile attitudes. The fact that this effect may
be unintended and uncontemplated does not reduce its impact. Effort
invested in designing effective anti-discrimination legislation is at risk of
being undermined in countries where other aspects of law are allowed to
disable people in this way.[1]

It will be immediately apparent that the limits of this subject are
extremely wide. There is no space here to provide a comprehensive account
of relevant legal doctrines and principles across Europe. I will, instead,
attempt to draw attention to the importance of developing mainstream
domestic law in a manner which will facilitate the inclusion of disabled
people. I will draw on a number of examples from different countries. Most
of these examples concern issues which have arisen in the law of tort,

---

* Lecturer in Law and member of the Centre for Disability Studies and the Human Rights
Research Unit, University of Leeds.
[1] See generally, M Jones and LA Basser Marks, *Disability, Divers-ability and Legal Change*
(London, Martinus Nijhoff, 1999), p 6.

though the first concerns an aspect of property law and the second is contractual in nature. I have selected these examples not because I believe them to be the most powerful or instructive, but simply because they have arisen in areas of law with which I am most familiar; equally striking examples could, without doubt, be drawn from other fields.

In the next section, I will focus on legal issues that concern the extent to which society in general can be required to have regard to the presence within it of people with impairments. Three issues will be considered—the determination of the precise entitlements of those who own easements (or rights of way) to cross land belonging to another; the assessment of the limits of a duty of care in negligence claims; and the entitlement of holiday-makers to be untroubled by the presence of disabled people. Section 3 will examine some legal issues which have centred round the question of the extent to which disabled people (or their parents) should be compensated for their impairments despite the fact that those impairments themselves were not caused by the defendant in question. It will examine three related issues: wrongful-life claims brought by disabled people; wrongful-conception claims brought by parents of disabled children; and wrongful-conception claims brought by disabled parents.

2 ASSESSING NORMALITY: WHAT SHOULD SOCIETY EXPECT?

2.1 The Rights of Disabled Easement Owners[2]

Two Scottish cases illustrate the challenges posed to traditional property law doctrines by the fact that property owners are sometimes disabled. In both these cases the impairments were physical in nature, affecting the strength and mobility of the people concerned. In the first, *Middletweed v Murray*,[3] the issue was whether, in the absence of express declaration on the point, a right of way along a track suitable for vehicular transport should be interpreted so as to allow the owners of that right of way to use vehicles along it. In the second, *Drury v McGarvie*,[4] the issue was whether a badly constructed gate, erected across a track along which the disabled owners had a right of way, amounted to an obstruction of that right of way.

Middletweed concerned the extent of a right of way across a farm track to reach a particular bank of the river Tweed where three disabled people owned fishing rights. Due to their impairments, these people were not able to reach the relevant bank other than by vehicle. The right of way had been created impliedly and there was, therefore, no express agreement as to

---

[2] A similar discussion of this issue is contained in A Lawson, 'Land law and the creation of disability' in A Hudson (ed), *New Perspectives on Property Law: Human Rights and the Family Home* (London, Cavendish Publishing Ltd, 2004), pp 117–30.
[3] 1989 SLT 11.
[4] 1993 SLT 987.

whether it extended to vehicular transport or was confined to foot traffic. The question turned on whether vehicular access *was* necessary in order for the owners of the fishing rights to have 'full beneficial use' of those rights.[5]

The argument advanced on behalf of the disabled fishers, that vehicular access was necessary for full beneficial user, was rejected. It was held that the right of way should be no more extensive than would be required to confer full beneficial use of the fishing rights on a person 'of average strength and mobility'.[6] Because such a person would be able to walk along the track, vehicular access was denied and the disabled fishers effectively prevented from enjoying their fishing rights.

In *Drury*, the pursuers were an elderly, disabled couple who accessed their cottage by means of a track across the defender's farmland over which they had a right of way. The defender placed gates across this track, which were heavy and awkwardly designed.[7] The pursuers' physical impairments made it almost impossible for them to open the gates and, consequently, they became 'virtually house-bound'.[8] They argued that the gates constituted an obstruction which the defender should remove or alter so as to allow them access.

The pursuers' claim failed. The gates would have amounted to an obstruction, according to Lord Hope, only if it could be shown that they would have caused 'material inconvenience' to a 'person of average strength and agility or ... the ordinary, able-bodied adult.'[9] The fact that they had caused material inconvenience to the pursuers was not relevant. The pursuers, however, were entitled to rely on the right of the owner of an easement to repair a track over which they have a right of way and alter the gates at their own expense.

Thus, in *Drury*, the pursuers were held to be entitled to improve the gates so as to allow them access to and from their home. Significantly, though, this adjustment had to be at their own expense. Further, the decision raises the possibility of other cases where a right to repair may not provide an appropriate means by which to resolve the dispute. An example might be a case in which a gate had been fixed with a combination number operated padlock unusable by a disabled easement owner because of an impairment affecting sight or manual dexterity. A key-operated padlock may provide a workable alternative but could such a substitution be classified as a repair? If the dominant owner objected to it (perhaps on grounds of reduced security) how should the dispute be resolved?

In both *Drury* and *Middletweed*, the judges were keen to uphold the long-standing property law policy of minimising burdens on land subject to easements. They achieved this by adopting a narrow conception of the

---

[5] Following *Miller v Blair* (1825) 4 Shaws 214.
[6] 1989 SLT 11 at p 14 *per* Lord Davidson.
[7] 1993 SLT 987 at p 988.
[8] *Ibid.*
[9] *Ibid* at p 991.

normal easement owner—an 'ordinary able-bodied adult' with 'average strength and mobility'. Widening that conception to include people with impairments, or reformulating the law on some basis other than that of the normal person, would have imposed heavier burdens on the owners of the land affected. It would, however, have resulted in a law which placed the cost of constructing properly hinged gates on the defender in *Drury* and which allowed disabled people to fish in *Middletweed*. Unfortunately, in neither case was the policy of inclusion and participation weighed against that of minimising burdens on landowners. The decisions therefore give the impression of having been reached without full consideration having been given to their disabling results. Should similar cases arise in the future, disabled litigants would be well-advised to force an explicit consideration of such issues by pressing arguments based on the need to develop domestic law consistently with their right to a home and family and private life under Article 8 of the European Convention for the Protection of Human Rights and Freedoms 1950.[10]

2.2 A Duty of Care to Disabled People?

In order for a plaintiff to succeed in a negligence action in England and Wales, they must establish that they were owed a duty of care by the defendant. Such a duty can arise only if it was foreseeable that the defendant's actions might cause them injury. The effect of the plaintiff's impairments on this question lay at the heart of *Haley v London Electricity Board*.[11] This case was decided nearly forty years ago but nevertheless provides a good illustration of the relevant issues.

The plaintiff in *Haley* was blind. When walking alone to work, he tripped over a long hammer which had been placed across the pavement by the defendants. They had used the hammer to guard a shallow trench which they had dug in the pavement. The head of the hammer was on the ground near the kerb and the other end rested on a fence, on the other side of the pavement, at a height of some two feet. The plaintiff fell heavily and lost his hearing as a result.

It was accepted that the defendants had taken adequate steps to protect 'ordinary people with good sight'[12] from falling into their trench. It was also accepted that these steps did not provide adequate protection for blind people. The hammer would not have been easily detected by skilful long cane users such as the plaintiff. The use of something in the nature of a two foot fence, such as that commonly used by the Post Office at the time to guard

---

[10] See further the discussion of *Botta v Italy* (24 February 1998) *Reports and Decisions of the ECtHR* 1998–I, No 66 412 in O De Schutter, 'Reasonable accommodations and positive obligations in the European Convention on Human Rights' ch 4 above.
[11] [1965] AC 778.
[12] *Ibid* at p 790 *per* Lord Reid.

pedestrians from dangers, would have provided sufficient protection to blind people.

Given these facts, it was argued for the defendants that they owed a duty of care only to 'ordinary able-bodied people'[13] or to 'normal road users.'[14] The particular circumstances of blind people, who did not fall within such a category, did not have to be considered when assessing appropriate levels of protection. The case of *Pritchard v The Post Office*[15] had been decided on this basis and the argument was accepted by both the trial judge and the Court of Appeal in *Haley*. Lord Denning, in the Court of Appeal, observed that:[16]

> It would be too great a tax on the ordinary business of life if special precautions had to be taken to protect the blind.

He did qualify this remark by limiting it to places, such as the street in *Haley*, where defendants would have 'no particular reason to expect blind persons to be.'[17]

The approach of the Court of Appeal in *Haley* is based on an understanding of normality which does not embrace unaccompanied blind pedestrians. On its view, the concerns of such people are not part of 'the ordinary business of life'. If foolish enough to step outside alone, blind people should do so entirely at their own risk. The price of a duty to have regard to their safety would be too high—a view that is perhaps unsurprising given the concern that it might extend to padding lampposts![18]

The House of Lords in *Haley* took a different view. It held that it was reasonably foreseeable that an unaccompanied blind person would pass along a Greater London street and that, consequently, the defendants owed a duty of care to the plaintiff. In reaching this decision on foreseeability, their Lordships relied on the common knowledge that blind people used city streets. According to Lord Morton:

> Everyone living in Greater London must have seen blind persons walking slowly along on the pavement using a white stick in front of them so as to touch any obstruction which may be in their way.

Lord Reid indicated, however, that there were many places other than city streets where one would not expect to find an unaccompanied blind person.[19] In such unspecified places, no duty of care would arise as their presence would not be foreseeable.

---

[13] *Ibid.*

[14] *Ibid* at p 802 *per* Lord Hodson.

[15] [1950] 114 JP 370.

[16] [1964] 2 QB 121 at p 129.

[17] *Ibid.*

[18] See Lord Denning *ibid*; and *McKibbin v Glasgow Corp* [1920] SC 590 at p 598 *per* Lord Salvesen.

[19] [1965] AC 778 at p 791.

The decision of the House of Lords in *Haley* accepts the presence of blind people as an ordinary part of city life—at least as far as walking on the streets is concerned. It refused to frame the law around the narrow conception of the normal adopted by the Court of Appeal. Interestingly, however, Lord Hodson's judgment indicates continued adherence to a narrow understanding of the 'normal' but a willingness to accept that the abnormal would sometimes be foreseeable. He observed, refreshingly, that 'road users' to whom a duty of care might be owed 'include all sorts of people who cannot be described as normal'.[20]

Though a satisfactory result was reached in *Haley*, there is no guarantee that such an outcome will be arrived at in other cases turning on the same legal principle. Much will depend on the view taken by the particular judge as to whether it would be common knowledge that people with impairments of the relevant kind would ordinarily be expected to be found in the type of place where the defendant had created a danger. Common knowledge about disability-related matters, as all disabled people will know, is an unpredictable creature at the best of times.

2.3 Holiday Entitlements

In 1992 it was held by a German District Court[21] that holidaymakers were entitled to a 10 per cent reduction in the price of their holiday because of the discomfort they had experienced when sharing a hotel with a group of disabled people.[22] The plaintiffs were a married couple who, along with their two young children, had paid for full board in a hotel for 20 days. Their stay overlapped, for one week, with that of 10 disabled people. The report does not disclose the precise nature of the impairments of these people, though it does indicate that some of them were wheelchair users and that most of them could not eat 'in the normal way'. Food sometimes ran from their mouths onto bibs around their necks and some required assistance and were fed using implements similar to syringes.

The plaintiffs were unable to avoid the sight of their fellow guests eating because meal times were fixed and the dining room was small. In the words of the translated report:

> The inescapable sight of disabled persons in the small place at each mealtime caused disgust and constantly reminded [the plaintiffs] of the potentials of human suffering in a haunting way. ... [T]hese experiences do not belong in the expected course of a vacation. If it were possible, the average holidaymaker

---

[20] *Ibid* at p 805.
[21] District Court of Flensburg, 11 August 1992, case no 63 C 265/92. I am grateful to Theresia Degener for providing me with an English translation of this case.
[22] Under paras 651(d) of the German Civil Code (472 Buergerliches Gesetzbuch (BGB)). See generally BS Markesinis, *The German Law of Torts: A Comparative Treatise* (Oxford and Portland Oregon, Hart Publishing, 2002), pp 931–2.

would avoid these experiences. A holidaymaker does not necessarily have to be selfless or have high ethical standards ...

The court rejected the defendant's argument that granting a price reduction would offend good morals contrary to para 138 of the German Civil Code. This was because, in the court's view, the number of people who would regard a successful claim as disturbing or distasteful was insufficient. The defendant also argued that granting the claim would violate the human dignity of the disabled hotel guests.[23] This, too, was rejected. The court considered that no such violation would occur because:

> The disabled persons are neither directly nor indirectly affected by these proceedings. The case is not about their rights but about the question of which party has to bear the risk of the circumstances which led to the unavoidable impairment of the plaintiffs' vacation.

It is to be hoped that the court seriously underestimated the number of people who would find its decision disturbing and distasteful. When one books a place in a hotel, one assumes the risk of sharing it with people one might find unpleasant or offensive. Indeed, the disabled guests in this case might well have experienced considerable discomfort because of the attitude displayed towards them by the plaintiffs. Could they too have recovered compensation for an 'impaired vacation'? The answer would almost certainly be 'no', as the court's reasoning is grounded on a conception of the 'normal' holiday as one in which disabled people cannot be seen or heard. The disabling implications of this decision are obvious. It encourages hotel owners, and the tourism and leisure industries more generally, to refuse access to disabled people or, at best, to grant them services on a segregated basis.

3 IDENTIFYING DIFFERENCE: WHAT CAN DISABLED PEOPLE (AND THEIR PARENTS) CLAIM?

3.1 Wrongful-Life Claims by Disabled People

Wrongful-life claims have caused great concern in a number of European countries over recent years.[24] Such claims, if successful, allow disabled people to recover damages for having been born. They are based on the negligent failure of the defendant (generally a doctor or midwife) to provide the

---

[23] Contrary to Art 1 Grundgesetz—Basic Law (GG).
[24] They have also proved controversial in the US. See further M Laudor, 'In defence of wrongful life-bringing political-theory to the defence of a tort' (1994) 62 *Fordham Law Review* 1675; GE Garfinkle, 'Towards a more rational approach towards wrongful pregnancy' (1991) 36 *Villanova Law Review* 1805; and M Waldman, 'Pre-natal injuries: wrongful life, birth or conception' (1990) *American Jurisprudence* 2nd s 62A 393–518.

opportunity for their impairments to have been prevented by means of an abortion.

The decision of the French Cour de Cassation in November 2000 to allow the wrongful-life claim brought by Nicholas Perruche[25] attracted considerable publicity. Nicholas, at that time seventeen years old, had been born with brain damage. His mother had not been warned that the rubella she suffered during pregnancy posed risks to Nicholas' health. Had such a warning been given, she would have had an abortion and, consequently, Nicholas would not have been born. He was thus entitled to recover damages simply for being alive. The *Perruche* case was quickly followed by two more successful French claims, brought by children with Down's Syndrome, whose mothers (through negligence) had not been offered an amniocentesis and thus had not aborted them.[26]

The outcry caused by the development of the wrongful-life doctrine led the French Assembly to enact legislation prohibiting such actions in 2002.[27] In other countries, however, judges remain willing to allow disabled people to succeed in wrongful-life claims. In the Netherlands, for instance, nine year old Kelly Molenaar recently became the first successful claimant in such an action.[28] She was born with multiple impairments which had not been identified before her birth. Her mother, during the pregnancy, had expressed concern about giving birth to a disabled child based on the fact that a family member had a number of physical impairments. The midwife had reassured her without referring her for screening or further investigation. This case may well be appealed to the Supreme Court and has already led to calls for Dutch legislation similar to that introduced in France.[29]

Why, then, has the wrongful-life doctrine been greeted with so much hostility? It has caused alarm amongst the medical profession because it places onerous obligations upon them to provide screening for potential impairments and advice as to the risks. The possibility of mistakes and consequent lawsuits also has significant implications for the price of medical insurance policies.

More important for this paper is the hostile reaction of the disability community to wrongful-life claims. There is an argument that the actual outcome of these actions is desirable—a disabled person is awarded a sum of

[25] Ass Plén 17 November 2000. Gaz Pal 24–25 January 2001, 4–30: Bull civ no 9; D.2000.332; JCP 2000.I.279 and II.10438, (2001) *Revue trimestrielle de droit civil* 149. For a translation of the decision, see T Weir, 'The unwanted child' (2002) 6 *Edinburgh Law Review* 244, Appendix 1 p 251.

[26] See further L Eaton, 'France outlaws the right to sue for being born' (2002) 324 *British Medical Journal* 129.

[27] Based on a Bill introduced by a private member, Dr Mattéi, and enacted on 19 February 2002 as an amendment to the Code de la Santé Publique. See further T Weir, 'The unwanted child' (2002) 6 *Edinburgh Law Review* 244 (Appendix 2 of which provides a translated text of the relevant legislation—p 252); and A Dorozynski, 'Highest French court awards compensation for "being born"' (2001) 323 *British Medical Journal* 1384.

[28] Reported in Disabled People's International Electronic Update, 2 May 2003.

[29] See further T Sheldon, 'Court awards damages to disabled child for having been born' (2003) 326 *British Medical Journal* 784.

money which will help to counteract the poverty often associated with disability. On this view it would come as a surprise to learn that disabled people gathered outside the court buildings to protest against the Nicholas Perruche ruling.[30] It is important, however, that arguments like this one are not allowed to distract attention from the ideology on which the doctrine is based.

At the heart of the wrongful-life doctrine lies the assumption that it is better not to live at all than to live as a disabled person. The right it recognises is that of a child 'to be born whole or not at all, not to be born unless it can be born perfect or "normal", whatever that may mean.'[31] To confer legitimacy on such a view by enshrining it within a legal doctrine is both humiliating to disabled people and dangerous. Disabled people have long fought against the assumption, sometimes made by members of the medical profession, that their lives are not worth living. It is an assumption which not only has implications for decisions about whether disabled people should be born but also for whether they should continue to live.[31A] It is, therefore, not surprising that a doctrine which strengthens such a view has caused concern amongst the disability movement.[32]

The fact that a wrongful-life action might alleviate the poverty of a disabled individual, then, is not sufficient to justify the doctrine. The problem of poverty should be tackled in other ways—by the removal of disabling barriers to education and employment and by an appropriately constructed social security system.[33] Such an approach would draw upon a social model understanding of disability as opposed to a purely medical, individual one. As Mark Priestley has pointed out:[34]

> From this position, it is not biological differences that need to be removed from the world, but disabling barriers; it is not disabled lives that are 'wrongful' but disabling societies.

3.2 Wrongful-Conception Claims by Parents of Disabled Children

Wrongful-conception claims may be brought by parents whose child was born due to the defendant's negligent failure to prevent conception (eg by a

---

[30] A Dorozynski, 'Highest French court awards compensation for "being born"' (2001) 323 *British Medical Journal* 1384.

[31] *McKay v Essex Area Health Authority* [1982] 1 QB 1166 at p 1181 *per* Stevenson LJ— the English Court of Appeal rejected the doctrine in this case. See also s 1 of the Congenital Disabilities (Civil Liability) Act 1976.

[31A] See *R v GMC ex parte Burke* [2004] EWHC 1879.

[32] See more generally R Mullender, 'Racial harassment, sexual harassment and the expressive function of law' (1998) 61 *Modern Law Review* 236.

[33] See, however, the argument that wrongful-life actions should found damages covering the economic loss associated with being a disabled person—I Kennedy and A Grubb, *Medical Law* (London, Butterworths, 2000) pp 1547–8.

[34] *Disability: A Life Course Approach* (Oxford, Polity, 2003) p 39. See also A Asche, 'Disability, bioethics and human rights' in G Albrecht, KD Seelman and M Bury (eds), *Handbook of Disability Studies* (London, Sage, 2001), pp 297–326.

failed sterilisation operation or by inadequate advice). They have given rise to much debate in the UK over the past few years. Wrongful-birth claims (based on a negligent failure to terminate a pregnancy, eg by a failed abortion or by a failure to advise parents of risks which would have led them to have the child aborted) raise similar issues but will not be explored in depth here due to lack of space.[35]

Before *McFarlane v Tayside Health Board*,[36] the law of England and Wales[37] allowed parents in wrongful-conception claims to recover damages for the pain and discomfort associated with the pregnancy and delivery; for the economic cost of bringing up the child to adulthood; and, where the child was disabled, for the 'additional anxiety, stress and burden involved in bringing up a handicapped child.'[38] If the child was not disabled, however, no damages could be recovered for the 'tiredness and wear and tear' associated with their care as this was offset by the benefits of having such a child.[39] Recent developments have focussed on the question of whether parents should be able to claim for the costs of bringing up their initially unwanted child.

In *McFarlane* the House of Lords held that the economic cost of bringing up an unwanted child could not be recovered, at least where, as was constantly repeated in that case, the child was 'normal' and 'healthy'. All five of their Lordships delivered judgements which differ slightly in emphasis.[40] Lords Slynn, Steyn and Hope considered that it would not be 'just, fair and reasonable' to allow the claim to succeed. Lord Clyde held that to allow recovery would be to over-compensate parents for the wrong done to them. Lord Millet relied on the fact that the birth of a 'normal healthy' child was a blessing and that the advantages of parenthood could not be weighed against its costs or disadvantages. Lord Hope took the view that it could not be just, fair or reasonable to award damages as the costs would have to be set off against the benefits of having the child, which could not be calculated, a view echoed in the other judgments. Lord Steyn relied on principles of distributive justice to determine on whom burdens and losses should fall. These required him to have regard to what the ordinary person would consider morally acceptable. In his view:[41]

---

[35] This categorisation appears to have been favoured in recent UK cases. It is not universally used, however—see eg I Kennedy and A Grubb, *Medical Law* (London, Butterworths, 2000) at p 1553, and GE Garfinkle, 'Towards a more rational approach towards wrongful pregnancy' (1991) 36 *Villanova Law Review* 1805 at 1807–8, where wrongful conception and birth claims are distinguished according to whether the unwanted child was disabled.

[36] [1999] 3 WLR 1301. This was a Scottish case but recognised as representing the law in England and Wales by the Court of Appeal in *Greenfield v Irwin (A Firm)* [2001] 1 WLR 1279.

[37] As set out in *Allen v Bloomsbury Health Authority* [1993] 1 All ER 651 at p 657 *per* Brooke J.

[38] *Ibid*. See also *Emeh v Kensington and Chelsea and Westminster Area Health Authority* [1985] 1 QB 1012.

[39] *Ibid*.

[40] See further LCH Hoyano, 'Misconceptions about wrongful conception' (2002) 65 *Modern Law Review* 883 and J Thomson, 'Abandoning the law of delict? *McFarlane v Tayside Health Board* in the Lords' 2000 SLT 43.

[41] [1999] 3 WLR 1301 at p 1318.

Instinctively, the traveller on the Underground would consider that the law of tort has no business to provide legal remedies consequent upon the birth of a healthy child, which all of us regard as a valuable and good thing.

In *Rees v Darlington Memorial Hospital*,[42] a seven member House of Lords refused to overturn the *McFarlane* ruling and expressed agreement with the view that, as a matter of legal policy, it should not be possible to recover damages for the costs of bringing up a normal, healthy child.[43] Lord Nicholls[44] observed that perceptions of fairness and reasonableness underlay the different judgments in *McFarlane* while Lords Steyn[45] and Millett[46] identified two guiding principles: first, the impossibility of calculating the benefits of parenthood and, second, the view that the birth of a normal, healthy child must be regarded as a benefit to society (regardless of how it might be regarded by the particular parents). By a four to three majority, however, it was held that a conventional award of £15,000 should be made to the reluctant parent, not to meet the costs of caring for the child but because their right to choose to limit the size of their family had been infringed.

The question of how a claim should be treated if the unwanted child were disabled arose in *Parkinson v St James and Seacroft University Hospital NHS Trust*.[47] The Court of Appeal there held that *McFarlane* did not prevent the recovery of damages where the child was not a 'normal healthy baby'. Damages, however, should not cover the entire costs of the child's upbringing but be limited to the additional costs created by the child's impairments. The implications of this case for disabled people are not clear-cut. At face value it appears attractive as it provides a means of reducing the financial disadvantage often experienced by disabled people and their families.[48] However, as was argued in relation to wrongful-life claims, this result should not be purchased at the price of reasoning which devalues disabled people or threatens the principle of inclusion. What, then, was the reasoning underlying *Parkinson*?

Hale LJ relied on what she termed the 'deemed equilibrium' theory to explain *McFarlane*.[49] According to this, the benefits of having a child are

---

[42] [2004] 1 AC 309. See generally C Dixon, 'An unconventional gloss on unintended children' (2003) 153 *New Law Journal* 1732; R Barr, 'Baby blues' (2003) 147 *Solicitors Journal* 1356; and RL Denyer, 'Failed sterilisations and child costs revisited' [2004] *Family Law* 123.

[43] Cf *Cattanach v Melchior* 18 July 2003 and P Baugher, 'Fundamental protection of a fundamental right: full recovery of child-rearing damages for wrongful pregnancy' (2000) 75 *Washington Law Review* 1205.

[44] *Ibid* para 15. See also Lord Bingham at para 6, drawing attention to the unfairness of placing costs such as those involved in privately educating the unintended child on a struggling health service.

[45] *Ibid* at para 28.

[46] *Ibid* at paras 109–10.

[47] [2001] 3 WLR 376.

[48] For accounts of which see S Baldwin, *The Costs of Caring: Families with Disabled Children* (London, Routledge and Kegan Paul, 1985) and B Dobson and S Middleton, *Paying to Care: The Cost of Childhood Disability* (York, Joseph Rowntree Foundation, 1998).

[49] *Ibid* at pp 401–2, para 90.

deemed to cancel out the 'ordinary costs of the ordinary child'. Because a disabled child costs more, those extra costs should be treated as upsetting the equilibrium and therefore as being recoverable. She was at pains to stress that:[50]

> This analysis treats a disabled child as having exactly the same worth as a non-disabled child. It affords him the same dignity and status. It simply acknowledges that he costs more.

While it is encouraging (and slightly surprising) to find such an assertion in this line of cases, Hale LJ's deemed equilibrium theory is unconvincing and was roundly rejected in *Rees*.[51] Their Lordships there stressed that *McFarlane* was not grounded on the idea of some notional balance between the benefits and costs of having a child but on the sheer impossibility (and undesirability) of calculating those costs and benefits.

Brooke LJ did not rely on the deemed equilibrium theory in *Parkinson*. He took the view simply that it would be just, fair and reasonable to allow recovery of the costs associated with the child's disability. He adopted the following words of a decision of the Florida Supreme Court:[52]

> Special medical and educational expenses, beyond normal rearing costs, are often staggering and quite debilitating to a family's financial and social health ... There is no valid policy argument against parents being recompensed for these costs of extraordinary care in raising a deformed child to majority.

He also approved a recent observation of Toulson J[53] that it would be wrong for the law to deem the birth of a disabled child always to be a blessing or the care of such a child to be so enriching as to make a successful claim unjust.

The decision in *Parkinson* was considered, obiter, by the House of Lords in *Rees*. Lords Steyn,[54] Hope[55] and Hutton[56] expressed agreement with it. Lords Bingham[57] and Nicholls[58] disagreed, taking the view that the *McFarlane* principle prevented recovery even for additional costs connected with the

---

[50] *Ibid*.
[51] [2004] 1 AC 309 at para 28 *per* Lord Steyn, at para 59 *per* Lord Hope, at para 94 *per* Lord Hutton and at para 111 *per* Lord Millett. It was also criticised by the Court of Appeal in *Rees* [2002] 2 WLR 1487 at p 1494 paras 34–6 *per* Walker LJ and at p 1496 para 50 *per* Waller LJ; though cited with approval by Judge LJ in *AD v East Kent Community NHS Trust* [2002] EWCA Civ 1872.
[52] *Fassoulas v Ramey* (1984) 450 *Southern Reporter* 2d 822 at 824; considered at [2001] 3 WLR 376 at pp 390–1 paras 49–50.
[53] *Ibid* at para 47, quoting from *Lee v Taunton and Somerset NHS Trust* [2001] 1 FLR 419 at 430.
[54] [2004] 1 AC 309 at para 35.
[55] *Ibid* at paras 55–7.
[56] *Ibid* at paras 88–91.
[57] *Ibid* at para 9.
[58] *Ibid* at para 18.

child's disability. This view was shared by Lord Scott, though he did suggest that recovery may be appropriate in cases where parents had decided against having a child specifically because of the risk that that child might be disabled.[59] Lord Millett, though wishing to leave the point open, favoured the approach taken in *Parkinson*.[60] Thus, *Parkinson* was disapproved by three of their Lordships and approved by the remaining four, one of whom wished to leave the question open. Debate on the issue, therefore, is far from over.

Hale LJ was clearly keen that the law should be developed in a way which respects the dignity and equal worth of disabled people. The judgements in *McFarlane* and *Parkinson*, however, are littered with references to the 'blessings' and 'joys' associated with the birth of 'normal', 'healthy' children. Disabled or, in the terminology of Lord Millett in *McFarlane*,[61] 'defective' children, on the other hand, are portrayed as a 'sorrow' and 'burden'[62] or an 'affliction'[63] to their parents. Attention was recently drawn to the inappropriateness of such language by Kirby J in the High Court of Australia. He pointed out that:[64]

> In Australia, even the use of the description of such parents as 'afflicted with a handicapped child' would be offensive to most such parents and contrary to their attitudes about themselves, their child and others.

Interestingly, this form of negative language is far less evident in the judgements of the House of Lords in *Rees* than in the earlier UK cases. Indeed, several references are made there to the equal worth of disabled people and to the fact that they too bring incalculable benefits to their parents. Such observations, however, would not sit easily with a rule which allowed recovery of the costs relating to a disabled child's disability while preventing recovery of any of the costs of an 'ordinary' child. This tension is well illustrated by the following words of Lord Millett:[65]

> A disabled child is not 'worth' less than a healthy one. The blessings of his or her birth are no less incalculable. Society must equally 'regard the balance as

[59] *Ibid* at paras 145–6.
[60] *Ibid* at para 112.
[61] *McFarlane v Tayside* [1999] 3 WLR 1301 at p 1344.
[62] *Ibid* at p 1318 *per* Lord Steyn. See also *Allen v Bloomsbury* [1993] 1 All ER 651 at p 662 *per* Brooke J.
[63] *Ibid* at p 1316 *per* Lord Steyn, citing other cases in which this view was taken.
[64] *Cattanach v Melchior* 18 July 2003, para 163. This view is supported (at least for a very substantial proportion of parents of disabled children) by studies such as AM Bower and A Hayes, 'Mothering in families with and without a child with disability' (1998) 45 *International Journal of Disability, Development and Education* 313; P Kearney and T Griffin, 'Between sorrow and joy: being a parent of a child with developmental disability' (2001) 34 *Journal of Advanced Nursing* 582; GH Landsman, 'Reconstructing motherhood in the age of "perfect" babies: mothers of infants and toddlers with disabilities' (1998) 24 *Signs: Journal of Women in Culture and Society* 69; B Patching and B Watson, 'Living with children with an intellectual disability: parents construct their reality' (1993) 40 *International Journal of Disability Development and Education* 115.
[65] [2004] 1 AC 309.

beneficial'. But the law does not develop by strict logic; and most people would instinctively feel that there was a difference, even if they had difficulty in articulating it. Told that a friend has given birth to a normal, healthy baby, we would express relief as well as joy. Told that she had given birth to a seriously disabled child, most of us would feel (though not express) sympathy for the parents. Our joy at the birth would not be unalloyed; it would be tinged with sorrow for the child's disability. Speaking for myself, I would not find it morally offensive to reflect this difference in an award of compensation.

In *McFarlane*, however, he insisted that:[66]

> It is morally offensive to regard a normal, healthy baby as more trouble and expense than it is worth.

There is a danger that the *Parkinson* approach will give legal sanction to the assumption that it is not morally offensive to regard the birth of a disabled child in this way. One of its probable consequences is that doctors will be particularly keen to encourage parents, who have conceived due to medical negligence, to abort the child if there is any risk of even a slight impairment. The distinction drawn here between normal and disabled children is far from value-neutral and conjures the image of a society in which people with impairments are not welcome.[67] The High Court of Australia refused to draw such a distinction in *Cattanach v Melchior*,[68] a refusal, however, which one recent commentary considers likely to be dismissed by English observers as no more than 'a strange combination of Australian nationalism and political correctness.'[69]

3.3 Wrongful-Conception Claims by Disabled Parents

In the previous section I outlined the exception to the *McFarlane* ruling according to which damages covering the additional costs of an unwanted child's disability are recoverable. This section will focus on the questions raised when the unintended child is normal and healthy but the parent is disabled. This was the scenario in *Rees v Darlington Memorial Hospital*.

In *Rees*, the plaintiff chose to be sterilised because she felt that her severe visual impairment would make it impossible for her to care for a child. The operation was carried out negligently and resulted in the birth of a 'normal, healthy' son. The plaintiff brought up her child with the help of her mother and other relatives. The report does not disclose many

---

[66] [1999] 3 WLR 1301 at p 1348.
[67] See further, on the value-laden nature of judicial law-making, S Lee, *Judging Judges* (London, Faber and Faber, 1988) and JAG Griffith, *The Politics of the Judiciary* (London, Fontana Press, 1997).
[68] 18 July 2003.
[69] RL Denyer, 'Failed sterilisations and child costs revisited' [2004] *Family Law* 123 at p 123.

details of the practical arrangements, though it mentions that she did not cook as she considered this dangerous, but that she did 'try' to dress her son.[70] The following observation suggests that the court knew little more than this:[71]

> We can only imagine the sort of difficulties facing them both. We have no evidence as to how, if at all, it is more costly to look after Anthony than it would be for a mother who does not have her disability.

At first instance it was held that the plaintiff was not entitled to recover any of the costs of bringing up her child. Her loss was no different in kind from that suffered by other women who had chosen to undergo sterilisation operations. Two examples were used. First, that of a high-flying career woman who would either need to give up a career or engage expensive childcare and, second, that of a hard-pressed single mother whose life would be ruined by the extra burden of care.[72] This view was also adopted by Waller LJ, who delivered a dissenting judgment in the Court of Appeal. He elaborated on the single mother example, postulating that she had four children already, no support from her family, was poor, and was so exhausted that an extra child would push her to the edge of a breakdown. To refuse her claim and grant that of a disabled woman who might be rich and have a supportive husband and family seemed, to him, unjust—a view he thought would be shared:[73] 'I think ordinary people would feel uncomfortable about the thought that it was simply the disability which made a difference.'

The majority of the Court of Appeal, however, held that the disability did make a 'crucial difference.'[74] Hale LJ, distinguishing the position of a disabled parent from that of the single mother and that of the high-flying career woman, expressed this difference as follows:[75]

> These able-bodied parents are both of them able to look after and bring up their child. No doubt they will both benefit from a nanny or other help in doing so but they do not need it in order to be able to discharge the basic parental responsibility of looking after the child properly and safely, performing those myriad of essential, mundane tasks such as feeding, bathing, clothing, training, supervising, playing with, reading to and taking to school which every child needs. They do not need it in order to avoid the risk that the child may have to be taken away to be looked after by the local social services authority or others to the detriment of the child as well as the parent.

This passage portrays a disturbing image of the role of social services in the lives of disabled parents, completely overlooking their supportive, facilitative

[70] [2002] 2 WLR 1483 at p 1485 para 3 *per* Hale LJ.
[71] *Ibid.*
[72] See discussion *ibid* at p 1488 para 12 *per* Hale LJ.
[73] *Ibid* at p 1497 para 54.
[74] *Ibid* at p 1490 para 22 *per* Hale LJ.
[75] *Ibid.*

obligations.[76] Its approach to parenthood is one which focuses on the individual parent operating completely outside their familial, social context.[77] It is only this misleading lack of context which enables a sharp distinction to be drawn between the capabilities of parents with impairments and those without.

On appeal, Lords Steyn, Hope and Hutton adopted the reasoning of the Court of Appeal. While recognising that the distinction between disabled and non-disabled parents would create an element of arbitrariness, they were persuaded by the argument of Walker LJ that this would be consistent with more general policy developments. The law, on this view, increasingly regarded disabled people as 'requiring special consideration';[78] the Disability Discrimination Act 1995 (DDA) was a landmark development along this road. The aim of the DDA, however, is to facilitate equality and inclusion. The 'special consideration' which the Court of Appeal (and the minority of the House of Lords) sought to give disabled people in *Rees*, on the other hand, is one which would place a higher duty on doctors to carry out successful sterilisations on disabled women than non-disabled ones. Though this result was contemplated with equanimity by Hale and Walker LJJ, it is not one which speaks of equality and inclusion. It resonates, instead, with the message that disabled people are unlikely to make competent parents.[79] It is, in short, a special consideration which would be best avoided.

By a bare majority, the House of Lords allowed the appeal in *Rees*. It held that no distinction should be made between disabled and non-disabled parents for the purpose of the *McFarlane* rule. Much reliance was placed on Waller LJ's account of the anomalies which would arise from a ruling to the contrary. Reference was also made to the fact that it was the responsibility of the state to provide disabled people with benefits and support to meet the additional costs consequent on their impairments.[80] Lord Bingham[81] acknowledged that there was force in the observations of Kirby J in the Australian case of *Cattanach v Melchior*[82] about a disability-based exception to *McFarlane*. According to him:[83]

---

[76] For a review of which, see S Goodinge, *A Jigsaw of Services: An Inspection of Services to Support Disabled Adults in their Parenting Role* (London, Social Services Inspectorate/ Department of Health, 2000).

[77] For further discussion of such an approach and its role in decisions to take children away from disabled parents, see MA Priestley, *Disability: A Life Course Approach* (Oxford, Polity, 2003), pp 128–31.

[78] [2002] 2 WLR 1483 at p 1495, para 41.

[79] For discussion of the perceived incompetence of disabled parents, see M Campion, *Who's Fit to be a Parent* (London, Routledge, 1995); S Brady, 'Sterilisation of girls and women with intellectual disabilities—past and present justifications' (2001) 7 *Violence Against Women* 432–61.

[80] [2004] 1 AC 309, at para 9 *per* Lord Bingham and para 118 *per* Lord Millett.

[81] *Ibid* at para 9.

[82] 18 July 2003 (High Court of Australia).

[83] *Ibid* at para 166.

It reinforces views about disability and attitudes towards parents and children with physical or mental impairments that are contrary to contemporary Australian values reinforced by the law.

This provides a welcome contrast to the views of the minority in *Rees* as to the implications of the UK anti-discrimination legislation. The decision of the majority in *Rees* on this point is to be welcomed. There is a risk, however, that its benefits may be undermined by continued adherence to a different approach in cases where, as in *Parkinson*, it is the unintended child who is disabled.

4 CONCLUSION

The law plays a fundamental part in shaping societal attitudes and responses to disabled people. It can be a powerful tool in the breaking down of barriers to their inclusion and participation. Anti-discrimination law and human rights law are the most obvious examples of laws that are specifically designed to achieve this aim. Welfare law, too, should play an important part in facilitating inclusion by ensuring that those disability-related costs, which have recently troubled the courts in another context, do not have to be borne by particular individuals and their families. In our campaigns for new or strengthened rights in these areas, it is easy to overlook the more subtle, but nonetheless powerful, influences exerted by other areas of law over the lives of disabled people. This paper has sought to draw attention to some of these.

Section 2 focused on a number of cases in which courts were required to rule on the extent to which other members of society were required to take into account the existence of people with impairments. This question will continue to come before judges in every country and in all sorts of contexts. The answer given will determine the extent to which disabled people can be regarded as part of ordinary, mainstream society. If the resulting law is framed around a narrow conception of the normal, the effects will inevitably be disabling. This prospect brings to mind the following optimistic words:[84]

> [E]ventually the folly of this will dawn on people and we shall all joyously realise that we are all abnormal, disabled, impaired, deformed and functionally limited, because, truth be told, that is what it means to be a human being.

In section 3, consideration was given to a number of cases in which disabled people (or their parents) have claimed damages relating to their impairments even though the defendant did not cause these impairments. Success

---

[84] JE Bickenbach, *Minority Rights or Universal Participation: The Politics of Disablement* in M Jones and LA Basser Marks (above n 1), at p 114.

in these actions is grounded on the view that people with impairments are, in some way, crucially different from (or, more precisely, less than) others. The identification of such differences plays an important role in the way in which the law constructs its notion of a disabled person. This notion is one which will lie at the heart of a society's relationship with its disabled members. It is important, therefore, that it is not based on assumptions that it would be better not to live than to live with an impairment and that it does not otherwise devalue or underestimate the capabilities of appropriately supported individuals.

Normality and difference are two sides of the same coin.[85] Too often these concepts have been used to fashion legal doctrines which separate disabled people from the rest of the population. The non-disability-specific law of a truly inclusive society would be grounded on the notion that people with impairments are an integral part of ordinary society. This is not a call for sameness. Indeed, it may require others to alter their behaviour—to take into account the safety of disabled pedestrians when carrying out work on pavements, for instance, or to make reasonable adjustments to practices and buildings to facilitate their access. The law of such a society would not regard disabled people as afflictions or exceptions. It would not regard them as any more defective, burdensome, abnormal, special or extraordinary than anybody else. It would, instead, regard them simply as ordinary people trying to lead ordinary lives. Until this happens there will continue to be a danger that the law itself will operate as an exclusionary, disabling force.

---

[85] See further A Hendriks, 'The significance of equality and non-discrimination for the protection of the rights and the dignity of disabled persons' in T Degener and Y Koster-Dreese (eds), *Human Rights and Disabled Persons: Essays and Relevant Human Rights Instruments* (London, Martinus Nijhoff Publishers, 1995), pp 40–62.

Appendix I

List of statutes covered in chapter 6

1. Australia:	Disability Discrimination Act 1992	
2. Austria:	Federal Constitutional Law as amended in 1997	
3. Bolivia:	Act No 1678 about the Person With Disability (1985)	
4. Brazil:	Constitution of the Federal Republic of Brazil as amended in 1988	
5. Canada:	(a) Charter of Human Rights and Freedoms, Constitution Act 1982 (b) Canadian Human Rights Act, RSC 1985 (c) Employment Equity Act, SC 1994–95	
6. Chile:	Act No 19.284	
7. China:	Law of the People's Republic of China on the Protection of Disabled Persons (1990)	
8. Costa Rica:	(a) Law 7600 on Equal Opportunities for Persons With Disabilities (1996) (b) Decree No 19101–S–MEP–TSS	
9. Ethiopia:	Rights of Disabled Persons to Employment. Proclamation No 101/1994	
10. Finland:	(a) Constitution as amended in 1995 (2000) (b) Penal Code as amended in 1995 (39/1889) (c) Employment Contracts Act (55/2001)	
11. Fiji:	Constitution as of 1997	
12. France:	(a) Criminal Code: Law No 90–602 of 12 July 1990 (b) Labour Code as amended in 1992	
13. Gambia:	Draft of a Constitution for the Second Republic of Gambia (1996)	
14. Germany:	(a) Basic Law of the Federal Republic of Germany as amended in 1994 (b) Act on the Equalization of Persons With Disabilities (BGG) of 2002 (c) Social Law Code, Book Nine of 2001 (SGB IX) (d) Social Law Code, Book One (SGB IX) as amended in 2001	

	(e) Social Law Code, Book Ten (SGB X) as amended in 2001
15. Ghana:	(a) Constitution as of 1992
	(b) Disabled Persons Act 1993
16. Guatemala:	Act for the Protection of Persons With Disabilities, Decree No 135–96
17. Hong Kong:	Disability Discrimination Ordinance 1995
18. Hungary:	Act No XXVI of 1998 on Provision of the Rights of Persons Living with Disability and Their Equality of Opportunity 1998
19. India:	Persons With Disabilities Act (Equal Opportunities, Protection of Rights and Full Participation) Act 1995
20. Ireland:	(a) Employment Equality Act (1998)
	(b) Equal Status Bill (1999)
21. Israel:	Equal Rights for Persons With Disabilities Law 1998
22. Korea:	(a) Welfare Law For Persons With Disabilities, Law No 4179 (1989)
	(b) Act Relating to the Employment Promotion, etc of the Handicapped, Law No 4210 (1990)
	(c) Special Education Promotion Law (1994)
23. Luxembourg:	Penal Code as of 1997
24. Madagascar:	Code of Labour of 29 September 1994
25. Malawi:	Republic of Malawi (Constitution) Act 1994
26. Malta:	Equal Opportunities (Persons With Disability) Act 2000
27. Mauritius:	Training and Employment of Disabled Persons Act 1996
28. Namibia:	Labour Act 1992
29. Netherlands:	Act on Equal Treatment on Grounds of Disability and Chronic Disease of 2003
30. New Zealand:	Human Rights Act 1993
31. Nicaragua:	Act No 202 Regulations and Policies for the Disabled in Nicaragua
32. Nigeria:	Nigerians With Disability Decree 1993
33. Panama:	Code of the Family, Act No 3 (1994)
34. Philippines:	Magna Carta for Disabled Persons 1992

35. Portugal:	Labour Code of 27th August 2003 (no 99/2003)
36. South Africa:	(a) Constitution as of 1996 (b) Employment Equity Bill 1998 (c) Skills Development Bill 1998
37. Spain:	(a) Statute of Workers' Rights (Royal Legislative Decree 1/1995 of 24 March) (b) Law on the Social Integration of the Disabled (Law 13/1982, 7 April) (c) National Criminal Code (Organic Law 10/1995, 23 November)
38. Sri Lanka:	Protection of the Rights of Persons With Disabilities Act, No 28 of 1996
39. Sweden:	Act 1999:132 on the Prohibition of Employment Discrimination Against Persons With Disabilities (1999)
40. Switzerland:	(a) Constitution as of 1999 (b) Federal Act on the Elimination of Discrimination Against Persons With Disabilities of 13 December 2002
41. Uganda:	(a) Constitution as of 1995 (b) Local Government Act of 1997
42. United Kingdom:	(a) Disability Discrimination Act 1995 (b) Disability Rights Commission Act 1999
43. United States of America:	(a) Americans With Disabilities Act of 1990 (b) Rehabilitation Act of 1973
44. Zambia:	Persons With Disabilities Act 1996 (Act No 33 of 1996)
45. Zimbabwe:	Disabled Persons Act 1992

Appendix II

Directive 2000/78/EC of 27 November 2000
Establishing a General Framework for Equal Treatment in
Employment and Occupation

THE COUNCIL OF THE EUROPEAN UNION,

Having regard to the Treaty establishing the European Community, and in particular Article 13 thereof,

Having regard to the proposal from the Commission,

Having regard to the Opinion of the European Parliament,

Having regard to the Opinion of the Economic and Social Committee,

Having regard to the Opinion of the Committee of the Regions,

Whereas:

1. In accordance with Article 6 of the Treaty on European Union, the European Union is founded on the principles of liberty, democracy, respect for human rights and fundamental freedoms, and the rule of law, principles which are common to all Member States and it respects fundamental rights, as guaranteed by the European Convention for the Protection of Human Rights and Fundamental Freedoms and as they result from the constitutional traditions common to the Member States, as general principles of Community law.

2. The principle of equal treatment between women and men is well established by an important body of Community law, in particular in Council Directive 76/207/EEC of 9 February 1976 on the implementation of the principle of equal treatment for men and women as regards access to employment, vocational training and promotion, and working conditions.

3. In implementing the principle of equal treatment, the Community should, in accordance with Article 3(2) of the EC Treaty, aim to eliminate inequalities, and to promote equality between men and women, especially since women are often the victims of multiple discrimination.

4. The right of all persons to equality before the law and protection against discrimination constitutes a universal right recognised by the Universal Declaration of Human Rights, the United Nations Convention on the Elimination of All Forms of Discrimination against Women, United Nations Covenants on Civil and Political Rights and on Economic, Social and Cultural Rights and by the European Convention for the Protection of Human Rights and Fundamental Freedoms, to which all Member States are signatories. Convention No 111 of the International Labour Organisation (ILO) prohibits discrimination in the field of employment and occupation.

5.   It is important to respect such fundamental rights and freedoms. This Directive does not prejudice freedom of association, including the right to establish unions with others and to join unions to defend one's interests.

6.   The Community Charter of the Fundamental Social Rights of Workers recognises the importance of combating every form of discrimination, including the need to take appropriate action for the social and economic integration of elderly and disabled people.

7.   The EC Treaty includes among its objectives the promotion of coordination between employment policies of the Member States. To this end, a new employment chapter was incorporated in the EC Treaty as a means of developing a coordinated European strategy for employment to promote a skilled, trained and adaptable workforce.

8.   The Employment Guidelines for 2000 agreed by the European Council at Helsinki on 10 and 11 December 1999 stress the need to foster a labour market favourable to social integration by formulating a coherent set of policies aimed at combating discrimination against groups such as persons with disability. They also emphasise the need to pay particular attention to supporting older workers, in order to increase their participation in the labour force.

9.   Employment and occupation are key elements in guaranteeing equal opportunities for all and contribute strongly to the full participation of citizens in economic, cultural and social life and to realising their potential.

10.   On 29 June 2000 the Council adopted Directive 2000/43/EC implementing the principle of equal treatment between persons irrespective of racial or ethnic origin. That Directive already provides protection against such discrimination in the field of employment and occupation.

11.   Discrimination based on religion or belief, disability, age or sexual orientation may undermine the achievement of the objectives of the EC Treaty, in particular the attainment of a high level of employment and social protection, raising the standard of living and the quality of life, economic and social cohesion and solidarity, and the free movement of persons.

12.   To this end, any direct or indirect discrimination based on religion or belief, disability, age or sexual orientation as regards the areas covered by this Directive should be prohibited throughout the Community. This prohibition of discrimination should also apply to nationals of third countries but does not cover differences of treatment based on nationality and is without prejudice to provisions governing the entry and residence of third-country nationals and their access to employment and occupation.

13.   This Directive does not apply to social security and social protection schemes whose benefits are not treated as income within the meaning given to that term for the purpose of applying Article 141 of the EC Treaty, nor to any kind of payment by the State aimed at providing access to employment or maintaining employment.

14.   This Directive shall be without prejudice to national provisions laying down retirement ages.

15. The appreciation of the facts from which it may be inferred that there has been direct or indirect discrimination is a matter for national judicial or other competent bodies, in accordance with rules of national law or practice. Such rules may provide, in particular, for indirect discrimination to be established by any means including on the basis of statistical evidence.

16. The provision of measures to accommodate the needs of disabled people at the workplace plays an important role in combating discrimination on grounds of disability.

17. This Directive does not require the recruitment, promotion, maintenance in employment or training of an individual who is not competent, capable and available to perform the essential functions of the post concerned or to undergo the relevant training, without prejudice to the obligation to provide reasonable accommodation for people with disabilities.

18. This Directive does not require, in particular, the armed forces and the police, prison or emergency services to recruit or maintain in employment persons who do not have the required capacity to carry out the range of functions that they may be called upon to perform with regard to the legitimate objective of preserving the operational capacity of those services.

19. Moreover, in order that the Member States may continue to safeguard the combat effectiveness of their armed forces, they may choose not to apply the provisions of this Directive concerning disability and age to all or part of their armed forces. The Member States which make that choice must define the scope of that derogation.

20. Appropriate measures should be provided, i.e. effective and practical measures to adapt the workplace to the disability, for example adapting premises and equipment, patterns of working time, the distribution of tasks or the provision of training or integration resources.

21. To determine whether the measures in question give rise to a disproportionate burden, account should be taken in particular of the financial and other costs entailed, the scale and financial resources of the organisation or undertaking and the possibility of obtaining public funding or any other assistance.

22. This Directive is without prejudice to national laws on marital status and the benefits dependent thereon.

23. In very limited circumstances, a difference of treatment may be justified where a characteristic related to religion or belief, disability, age or sexual orientation constitutes a genuine and determining occupational requirement, when the objective is legitimate and the requirement is proportionate. Such circumstances should be included in the information provided by the Member States to the Commission.

24. The European Union in its Declaration No 11 on the status of churches and non-confessional organisations, annexed to the Final Act of the Amsterdam Treaty, has explicitly recognised that it respects and does not prejudice the status under national law of churches and religious associations or communities in the Member States and that it equally respects

the status of philosophical and non-confessional organisations. With this in view, Member States may maintain or lay down specific provisions on genuine, legitimate and justified occupational requirements which might be required for carrying out an occupational activity.

25. The prohibition of age discrimination is an essential part of meeting the aims set out in the Employment Guidelines and encouraging diversity in the workforce. However, differences in treatment in connection with age may be justified under certain circumstances and therefore require specific provisions which may vary in accordance with the situation in Member States. It is therefore essential to distinguish between differences in treatment which are justified, in particular by legitimate employment policy, labour market and vocational training objectives, and discrimination which must be prohibited.

26. The prohibition of discrimination should be without prejudice to the maintenance or adoption of measures intended to prevent or compensate for disadvantages suffered by a group of persons of a particular religion or belief, disability, age or sexual orientation, and such measures may permit organisations of persons of a particular religion or belief, disability, age or sexual orientation where their main object is the promotion of the special needs of those persons.

27. In its Recommendation 86/379/EEC of 24 July 1986 on the employment of disabled people in the Community, the Council established a guideline framework setting out examples of positive action to promote the employment and training of disabled people, and in its Resolution of 17 June 1999 on equal employment opportunities for people with disabilities, affirmed the importance of giving specific attention inter alia to recruitment, retention, training and lifelong learning with regard to disabled persons.

28. This Directive lays down minimum requirements, thus giving the Member States the option of introducing or maintaining more favourable provisions. The implementation of this Directive should not serve to justify any regression in relation to the situation which already prevails in each Member State.

29. Persons who have been subject to discrimination based on religion or belief, disability, age or sexual orientation should have adequate means of legal protection. To provide a more effective level of protection, associations or legal entities should also be empowered to engage in proceedings, as the Member States so determine, either on behalf or in support of any victim, without prejudice to national rules of procedure concerning representation and defence before the courts.

30. The effective implementation of the principle of equality requires adequate judicial protection against victimisation.

31. The rules on the burden of proof must be adapted when there is a prima facie case of discrimination and, for the principle of equal treatment to be applied effectively, the burden of proof must shift back to the respondent when evidence of such discrimination is brought. However, it is not for the respondent to prove that the plaintiff adheres to a particular religion

or belief, has a particular disability, is of a particular age or has a particular sexual orientation.

32. Member States need not apply the rules on the burden of proof to proceedings in which it is for the court or other competent body to investigate the facts of the case. The procedures thus referred to are those in which the plaintiff is not required to prove the facts, which it is for the court or competent body to investigate.

33. Member States should promote dialogue between the social partners and, within the framework of national practice, with non-governmental organisations to address different forms of discrimination at the workplace and to combat them.

34. The need to promote peace and reconciliation between the major communities in Northern Ireland necessitates the incorporation of particular provisions into this Directive.

35. Member States should provide for effective, proportionate and dissuasive sanctions in case of breaches of the obligations under this Directive.

36. Member States may entrust the social partners, at their joint request, with the implementation of this Directive, as regards the provisions concerning collective agreements, provided they take any necessary steps to ensure that they are at all times able to guarantee the results required by this Directive.

37. In accordance with the principle of subsidiarity set out in Article 5 of the EC Treaty, the objective of this Directive, namely the creation within the Community of a level playing-field as regards equality in employment and occupation, cannot be sufficiently achieved by the Member States and can therefore, by reason of the scale and impact of the action, be better achieved at Community level. In accordance with the principle of proportionality, as set out in that Article, this Directive does not go beyond what is necessary in order to achieve that objective.

HAS ADOPTED THIS DIRECTIVE:

CHAPTER I: GENERAL PROVISIONS

Article 1 Purpose

The purpose of this Directive is to lay down a general framework for combating discrimination on the grounds of religion or belief, disability, age or sexual orientation as regards employment and occupation, with a view to putting into effect in the Member States the principle of equal treatment.

Article 2 Concept of Discrimination

1. For the purposes of this Directive, the "principle of equal treatment" shall mean that there shall be no direct or indirect discrimination whatsoever on any of the grounds referred to in Article 1.

2. For the purposes of paragraph 1:

A. direct discrimination shall be taken to occur where one person is treated less favourably than another is, has been or would be treated in a comparable situation, on any of the grounds referred to in Article 1;

B. indirect discrimination shall be taken to occur where an apparently neutral provision, criterion or practice would put persons having a particular religion or belief, a particular disability, a particular age, or a particular sexual orientation at a particular disadvantage compared with other persons unless:

   i. that provision, criterion or practice is objectively justified by a legitimate aim and the means of achieving that aim are appropriate and necessary,
   or
   ii. as regards persons with a particular disability, the employer or any person or organisation to whom this Directive applies, is obliged, under national legislation, to take appropriate measures in line with the principles contained in Article 5 in order to eliminate disadvantages entailed by such provision, criterion or practice.

3. Harassment shall be deemed to be a form of discrimination within the meaning of paragraph 1, when unwanted conduct related to any of the grounds referred to in Article 1 takes place with the purpose or effect of violating the dignity of a person and of creating an intimidating, hostile, degrading, humiliating or offensive environment. In this context, the concept of harassment may be defined in accordance with the national laws and practice of the Member States.

4. An instruction to discriminate against persons on any of the grounds referred to in Article 1 shall be deemed to be discrimination within the meaning of paragraph 1.

5. This Directive shall be without prejudice to measures laid down by national law which, in a democratic society, are necessary for public security, for the maintenance of public order and the prevention of criminal offences, for the protection of health and for the protection of the rights and freedoms of others.

Article 3 Scope

1. Within the limits of the areas of competence conferred on the Community, this Directive shall apply to all persons, as regards both the public and private sectors, including public bodies, in relation to:

A. conditions for access to employment, to self-employment or to occupation, including selection criteria and recruitment conditions, whatever the branch of activity and at all levels of the professional hierarchy, including promotion;

B. access to all types and to all levels of vocational guidance, vocational training, advanced vocational training and retraining, including practical work experience;

C. employment and working conditions, including dismissals and pay;

D. membership of, and involvement in, an organisation of workers or employers, or any organisation whose members carry on a particular profession, including the benefits provided for by such organisations.

2. This Directive does not cover differences of treatment based on nationality and is without prejudice to provisions and conditions relating to the entry into and residence of third-country nationals and stateless persons in the territory of Member States, and to any treatment which arises from the legal status of the third-country nationals and stateless persons concerned.

3. This Directive does not apply to payments of any kind made by state schemes or similar, including state social security or social protection schemes.

4. Member States may provide that this Directive, in so far as it relates to discrimination on the grounds of disability and age, shall not apply to the armed forces.

Article 4 Occupational Requirements

1. Notwithstanding Article 2(1) and (2), Member States may provide that a difference of treatment which is based on a characteristic related to any of the grounds referred to in Article 1 shall not constitute discrimination where, by reason of the nature of the particular occupational activities concerned or of the context in which they are carried out, such a characteristic constitutes a genuine and determining occupational requirement, provided that the objective is legitimate and the requirement is proportionate.

2. Member States may maintain national legislation in force at the date of adoption of this Directive or provide for future legislation incorporating national practices existing at the date of adoption of this Directive pursuant to which, in the case of occupational activities within churches and other public or private organisations the ethos of which is based on religion or belief, a difference of treatment based on a person's religion or belief shall not constitute discrimination where, by reason of the nature of these activities or of the context in which they are carried out, a person's religion or belief constitute a genuine, legitimate and justified occupational

requirement, having regard to the organisation's ethos. This difference of treatment shall be implemented taking account of Member States' constitutional provisions and principles, as well as the general principles of Community law, and should not justify discrimination on another ground.

Provided that its provisions are otherwise complied with, this Directive shall thus not prejudice the right of churches and other public or private organisations, the ethos of which is based on religion or belief, acting in conformity with national constitutions and laws, to require individuals working for them to act in good faith and with loyalty to the organisation's ethos.

Article 5 Reasonable Accommodation for Disabled Persons

In order to guarantee compliance with the principle of equal treatment in relation to persons with disabilities, reasonable accommodation shall be provided.

This means that employers shall take appropriate measures, where needed in a particular case, to enable a person with a disability to have access to, participate in, or advance in employment, or to undergo training, unless such measures would impose a disproportionate burden on the employer. This burden shall not be disproportionate when it is sufficiently remedied by measures existing within the framework of the disability policy of the Member State concerned.

Article 6 Justification of Differences of Treatment on Grounds of Age

1.   Notwithstanding Article 2(2), Member States may provide that differences of treatment on grounds of age shall not constitute discrimination, if, within the context of national law, they are objectively and reasonably justified by a legitimate aim, including legitimate employment policy, labour market and vocational training objectives, and if the means of achieving that aim are appropriate and necessary. Such differences of treatment may include, among others:

A.   the setting of special conditions on access to employment and vocational training, employment and occupation, including dismissal and remuneration conditions, for young people, older workers and persons with caring responsibilities in order to promote their vocational integration or ensure their protection;

B.   the fixing of minimum conditions of age, professional experience or seniority in service for access to employment or to certain advantages linked to employment;

C.   the fixing of a maximum age for recruitment which is based on the training requirements of the post in question or the need for a reasonable period of employment before retirement.

2. Notwithstanding Article 2(2), Member States may provide that the fixing for occupational social security schemes of ages for admission or entitlement to retirement or invalidity benefits, including the fixing under those schemes of different ages for employees or groups or categories of employees, and the use, in the context of such schemes, of age criteria in actuarial calculations, does not constitute discrimination on the grounds of age, provided this does not result in discrimination on the grounds of sex.

Article 7 Positive Action

1. With a view to ensuring full equality in practice, the principle of equal treatment shall not prevent any Member State from maintaining or adopting specific measures to prevent or compensate for disadvantages linked to any of the grounds referred to in Article 1.

2. With regard to disabled persons, the principle of equal treatment shall be without prejudice to the right of Member States to maintain or adopt provisions on the protection of health and safety at work or to measures aimed at creating or maintaining provisions or facilities for safeguarding or promoting their integration into the working environment.

Article 8 Minimum Requirements

1. Member States may introduce or maintain provisions which are more favourable to the protection of the principle of equal treatment than those laid down in this Directive.

2. The implementation of this Directive shall under no circumstances constitute grounds for a reduction in the level of protection against discrimination already afforded by Member States in the fields covered by this Directive.

CHAPTER II: REMEDIES AND ENFORCEMENT

Article 9 Defence of Rights

1. Member States shall ensure that judicial and/or administrative procedures, including where they deem it appropriate conciliation procedures, for the enforcement of obligations under this Directive are available to all persons who consider themselves wronged by failure to apply the principle of equal treatment to them, even after the relationship in which the discrimination is alleged to have occurred has ended.

2. Member States shall ensure that associations, organisations or other legal entities which have, in accordance with the criteria laid down by their national law, a legitimate interest in ensuring that the provisions of this

Directive are complied with, may engage, either on behalf or in support of the complainant, with his or her approval, in any judicial and/or administrative procedure provided for the enforcement of obligations under this Directive.

3.   Paragraphs 1 and 2 are without prejudice to national rules relating to time limits for bringing actions as regards the principle of equality of treatment.

Article 10 Burden of Proof

1.   Member States shall take such measures as are necessary, in accordance with their national judicial systems, to ensure that, when persons who consider themselves wronged because the principle of equal treatment has not been applied to them establish, before a court or other competent authority, facts from which it may be presumed that there has been direct or indirect discrimination, it shall be for the respondent to prove that there has been no breach of the principle of equal treatment.

2.   Paragraph 1 shall not prevent Member States from introducing rules of evidence which are more favourable to plaintiffs.

3.   Paragraph 1 shall not apply to criminal procedures.

4.   Paragraphs 1, 2 and 3 shall also apply to any legal proceedings commenced in accordance with Article 9(2).

5.   Member States need not apply paragraph 1 to proceedings in which it is for the court or competent body to investigate the facts of the case.

Article 11 Victimisation

Member States shall introduce into their national legal systems such measures as are necessary to protect employees against dismissal or other adverse treatment by the employer as a reaction to a complaint within the undertaking or to any legal proceedings aimed at enforcing compliance with the principle of equal treatment.

Article 12 Dissemination of Information

Member States shall take care that the provisions adopted pursuant to this Directive, together with the relevant provisions already in force in this field, are brought to the attention of the persons concerned by all appropriate means, for example at the workplace, throughout their territory.

Article 13 Social Dialogue

1.   Member States shall, in accordance with their national traditions and practice, take adequate measures to promote dialogue between the social partners with a view to fostering equal treatment, including through the monitoring of workplace practices, collective agreements, codes of

conduct and through research or exchange of experiences and good practices.

2. Where consistent with their national traditions and practice, Member States shall encourage the social partners, without prejudice to their autonomy, to conclude at the appropriate level agreements laying down anti-discrimination rules in the fields referred to in Article 3 which fall within the scope of collective bargaining. These agreements shall respect the minimum requirements laid down by this Directive and by the relevant national implementing measures.

Article 14 Dialogue with Non-governmental Organisations

Member States shall encourage dialogue with appropriate non-governmental organisations which have, in accordance with their national law and practice, a legitimate interest in contributing to the fight against discrimination on any of the grounds referred to in Article 1 with a view to promoting the principle of equal treatment.

CHAPTER III: PARTICULAR PROVISIONS

Article 15 Northern Ireland

1. In order to tackle the under-representation of one of the major religious communities in the police service of Northern Ireland, differences in treatment regarding recruitment into that service, including its support staff, shall not constitute discrimination insofar as those differences in treatment are expressly authorised by national legislation.

2. In order to maintain a balance of opportunity in employment for teachers in Northern Ireland while furthering the reconciliation of historical divisions between the major religious communities there, the provisions on religion or belief in this Directive shall not apply to the recruitment of teachers in schools in Northern Ireland in so far as this is expressly authorised by national legislation.

CHAPTER IV: FINAL PROVISIONS

Article 16 Compliance

Member States shall take the necessary measures to ensure that:

A. any laws, regulations and administrative provisions contrary to the principle of equal treatment are abolished;

B. any provisions contrary to the principle of equal treatment which are included in contracts or collective agreements, internal rules of undertakings or rules governing the independent occupations and professions and workers' and employers' organisations are, or may be, declared null and void or are amended.

Article 17 Sanctions

Member States shall lay down the rules on sanctions applicable to infringements of the national provisions adopted pursuant to this Directive and shall take all measures necessary to ensure that they are applied. The sanctions, which may comprise the payment of compensation to the victim, must be effective, proportionate and dissuasive. Member States shall notify those provisions to the Commission by 2 December 2003 at the latest and shall notify it without delay of any subsequent amendment affecting them.

Article 18 Implementation

Member States shall adopt the laws, regulations and administrative provisions necessary to comply with this Directive by 2 December 2003 at the latest or may entrust the social partners, at their joint request, with the implementation of this Directive as regards provisions concerning collective agreements.

In such cases, Member States shall ensure that, no later than 2 December 2003, the social partners introduce the necessary measures by agreement, the Member States concerned being required to take any necessary measures to enable them at any time to be in a position to guarantee the results imposed by this Directive. They shall forthwith inform the Commission thereof.

In order to take account of particular conditions, Member States may, if necessary, have an additional period of 3 years from 2 December 2003, that is to say a total of 6 years, to implement the provisions of this Directive on age and disability discrimination. In that event they shall inform the Commission forthwith. Any Member State which chooses to use this additional period shall report annually to the Commission on the steps it is taking to tackle age and disability discrimination and on the progress it is making towards implementation. The Commission shall report annually to the Council.

When Member States adopt these measures, they shall contain a reference to this Directive or be accompanied by such reference on the occasion of their official publication. The methods of making such reference shall be laid down by Member States.

Article 19 Report

1. Member States shall communicate to the Commission, by 2 December 2005 at the latest and every five years thereafter, all the information necessary for the Commission to draw up a report to the European Parliament and the Council on the application of this Directive.

2. The Commission's report shall take into account, as appropriate, the viewpoints of the social partners and relevant non-governmental organisations. In accordance with the principle of gender mainstreaming, this report shall, inter alia, provide an assessment of the impact of the measures taken on women and men. In the light of the information received, this report shall include, if necessary, proposals to revise and update this Directive.

Article 20 Entry into Force

This Directive shall enter into force on the day of its publication in the Official Journal of the European Communities.

Article 21 Addressees

This Directive is addressed to the Member States.

Appendix III

European Disability Forum Proposal for a Directive Implementing the
Principle of Equal Treatment for Persons with Disabilities

THE COUNCIL OF THE EUROPEAN UNION,

Having regard to the Treaty establishing the European Community, and
in particular Article 13 thereof,

Having regard to the proposal from the Commission,

Having regard to the Opinion of the European Parliament,

Having regard to the Opinion of the Economic and Social Committee,

Having regard to the Opinion of the Committee of the Regions,

Whereas:

1.   In accordance with Article 6 of the Treaty on European Union, the
European Union is founded on the principles of liberty, democracy, respect
for human rights and fundamental freedoms, and the rule of law, principles which are common to all Member States and it respects fundamental
rights, as guaranteed by the European Convention for the Protection of
Human Rights and Fundamental Freedoms and as they result from the constitutional traditions common to the Member States, as general principles
of Community law.

2.   The right to equality before the law and protection against discrim-
ination for all persons constitutes a universal right recognised by the
Universal Declaration of Human Rights, the United Nations Standard
Rules on the Equalisation of Opportunities for Persons With Disabilities,
the United Nations Covenants on Civil and Political Rights and on
Economic, Social and Cultural Rights, the United Nations Convention on
the Elimination of all Forms of Discrimination Against Women and the
United Nations Convention on the Elimination of all Forms of Racial
Discrimination and by the European Convention for the Protection of
Human Rights and Fundamental Freedoms, to which all Member States
are signatories.

3.   The Charter of Fundamental Rights of the European Union, which
was solemnly proclaimed by the European Parliament, the Council and the
Commission in Nice on 7 December 2000 affirms, in Article 21, that any
discrimination on the ground of disability shall be prohibited and, in Article 26, recognises and respects the right of persons with disabilities to
benefit from measures designed to ensure their independence, social and
occupational integration and participation in the life of the community.

4.   The principle of equality of opportunity for all, including people
with disabilities, represents a core value shared by all Member States.

5.   The overall purpose of the United Nations Standard Rules on the Equalisation of Opportunities for Persons with Disabilities, adopted by the General Assembly on 20 December 1993 is to ensure that all people with disabilities may exercise the same rights as others and have the same opportunities. These Rules call for action at all levels both within States as well as through international cooperation to promote the principle of equality of opportunity for people with disabilities.

6.   People with disabilities contribute to and enrich the social, cultural and economic life of the European Community.

7.   At least 10 percent of the population of the European Union, or some 37 million people, have a disability and many more are affected by a disability of a family member or close acquaintance.

8.   Disability arises out of an interaction between the environment and a person with a physical, sensory, intellectual, psychological, communication or developmental impairment or multiple impairments or chronic illness.

9.   Given the heterogeneous nature of disability, persons with disabilities form a diverse group and may experience different forms of discrimination which should be combated in different ways.

10. The Council has adopted a Resolution on Equality of Opportunity for People with Disabilities.

11. The Commission has issued a Communication entitled 'Equality of opportunity for people with disabilities—a new European Community disability strategy'.

12. The Commission has issued a Communication entitled 'Towards a Barrier Free Europe for People with Disabilities'.

13. The European Parliament has adopted a Resolution on 'Towards a Barrier Free Europe for People with Disabilities'.

14. The European Parliament has adopted Resolutions on Sign Language in 1988 and 1998.

15. The European Congress on Disability held in Madrid on 20–23 March 2002 adopted the Madrid Declaration on 'Non discrimination plus positive action result in social inclusion'.

16. On 27 November 2000 the Council adopted Directive 2000/78/EC establishing a general framework for equal treatment in employment and occupation on the grounds of religion or belief, disability, age and sexual orientation. That Directive already provides protection against disability discrimination in the field of employment and occupation.

17. On 29 June 2000 the Council adopted Directive 2000/43/EC implementing the principle of equal treatment between persons irrespective of racial or ethnic origin.

18. To ensure the full participation of all persons with disabilities, and bearing in mind their heterogeneity, specific action needs to be taken to address areas such as education, social protection including social security, healthcare, social advantages and access to and supply of services, facilities and goods, including culture, leisure and sports, insurance, transportation,

the communications environment, the built environment, housing and man-ufactured and designed products.

19. To this end, any direct or indirect discrimination or discrimination in the form of failure to make a reasonable accommodation on the grounds of disability falling within the scope of this Directive shall be prohibited.

20. All persons with disabilities should have full and equal access to all types of education at all levels, including higher education and adult educa-tion, and to lifelong learning according to their abilities and needs. Partici-pation in mainstream education will be considered as the general rule, while special education shall only be considered as an option, if so preferred by the disabled person or his parents, guardians or designated advocates, when the disabled person is a child or adult unable to represent himself.

21. Large institutions which permanently or for a long period of time provide housing and living facilities and services exclusively to persons with disabilities and which do not further the goal of self-determination and equal participation in the life of the community of persons with disabilities, should be dismantled and replaced, when required, by community based services that further the above mentioned goals.

22. In implementing the principle of equal treatment for persons with a disability, the Community should, in accordance with Article 3(2) of the EC Treaty, aim to eliminate inequalities, and to promote equality between men and women, in particular as women with disabilities are often the victims of multiple discrimination.

23. Women with disabilities and women who are associated with a per-son with a disability through a family or other relationship are particularly vulnerable to disability based gender discrimination and Member States should pay specific attention to combating such discrimination.

24. Persons with intellectual disabilities, persons with psychological dis-abilities, persons with multiple disabilities, and older persons with disabi-lities and children with disabilities are particularly vulnerable to disability based discrimination and Member States should pay specific attention to combating such discrimination.

25. People adversely affected by discrimination based on disability are frequently also adversely affected by discrimination on other grounds, such as race or ethnic origin, age, religion or belief or sexual orientation, and Member States should ensure that adequate attention is paid to combating multiple discrimination.

26. The appreciation of the facts from which it may be inferred that there has been discrimination is a matter for national judicial or other com-petent bodies, in accordance with national law or practice. Such rules may provide, in particular, for indirect discrimination to be established by any means including on the basis of statistical evidence. However, given the difficulties associated with obtaining reliable statistical evidence in this area, sole reliance on statistical evidence to demonstrate indirect discrimi-nation is not appropriate for the purposes of this directive.

27. Appropriate measures should be provided, ie effective and practical measures to ensure the full access and participation of persons with a disability, for example amending policies and practices, adapting premises, equipment, services, goods and the means by which information is conveyed through the making of a reasonable accommodation. Such a reasonable accommodation should include, where appropriate, the provision of personal assistance to a person with a disability.

28. The duty to make a reasonable accommodation as provided for under this directive shall be based on an anticipation of the needs of disabled people. However, when the needs of an individual with a disability have not been foreseen, the obligation to provide a reasonable accommodation remains to ensure compliance with the principle of equal treatment.

29. To determine whether the measures in question give rise to a disproportionate burden, account should be taken in particular of the financial and other costs entailed, the scale and financial resources of the organisation or undertaking, the possibility of obtaining public funding or any other assistance, as well as the increase in the income of the organisation or undertaking, resulting from the making of their goods or services accessible to a wider public.

30. Persons with disabilities frequently face discrimination in the form of inaccessible public transportation, an inaccessible built environment, including housing, as well as an inaccessible communications or information environment.

The requirement to provide for accessibility for persons with disabilities in these areas is essential to put into effect the principle of equal treatment for people with disabilities.

The provision of accessibility does not exclude the need for a reasonable accommodation in individual cases to ensure compliance with the principle of equal treatment.

31. Insulting portrayals of disability and the failure to respect the dignity of persons with disabilities in political and public life, in advertising and the media reinforce negative stereotypes of persons with disabilities and undermine the principle of equal treatment.

32. The prohibition of discrimination should be without prejudice to the maintenance or adoption of measures intended to prevent or compensate for disadvantages experienced by persons with a particular impairment.

33. To ensure the full participation of people with disabilities, positive action is necessary to overcome discriminating and stereotyping perceptions of disability and to promote positive attitudes. Public education programmes can help to increase the understanding of the needs and rights of people with disability.

34. This Directive lays down minimum requirements, thus giving the Member States the option of introducing or maintaining more favourable provisions. The implementation of this Directive shall not serve to justify any regression in relation to the situation which already prevails in each Member State.

35. Persons who have been subject to disability discrimination should have adequate means of legal protection. To provide a more effective level of protection, associations or legal entities should also be empowered to engage in proceedings, as the Member States so determine, either on behalf of or in support of any victim or have an independent right of action, without prejudice to national rules of procedure concerning representation and defence before the courts.

36. For many persons, particularly persons on a low income, the provision of free legal aid and representation are essential prerequisites to start a judicial and/or administrative procedure to enforce obligations under this Directive.

37. The effective implementation of the principle of equal treatment requires adequate judicial protection against victimisation for complainants and witnesses.

38. The rules on the burden of proof must be adapted where there is a prima facie case of discrimination and, for the principle of equal treatment to be applied effectively, the burden of proof must shift back to the respondent when a presumption of such discrimination is established.

39. Member States need not apply the rules on the burden of proof to proceedings in which it is for the court or other competent body to investigate the facts of the case.

The procedures thus referred to are those in which the plaintiff is not required to prove the facts, which it is for a court or competent body to investigate.

40. Close cooperation with representative non-governmental organisations of persons with disabilities and of parents, guardians or designated advocates of persons with disabilities unable to represent themselves is a prerequisite for combating disability discrimination effectively and for implementing the principle of equal treatment.

41. Member States should promote dialogue with representative non-governmental organisations of persons with disabilities and of parents, guardians or designated advocates of persons with disabilities unable to represent themselves, to address different forms of discrimination covered by this Directive.

42. Protection against discrimination based on disability would itself be strengthened by the existence of a body or bodies, such as an ombudsman or an equal opportunities commission, in each Member State, with competence to analyse the problems involved, to study possible solutions and to provide concrete assistance for the victims, including receiving and pursuing complaints from persons of discrimination on grounds of disability. Member States may opt to establish a body or bodies dealing exclusively with disability discrimination or to establish a body or bodies dealing with a variety of grounds of discrimination.

43. Member States should provide for effective, proportionate and persuasive sanctions in case of breaches of the obligations under this Directive.

44. Compliance with the obligations under this Directive would be strengthened if Member States excluded public or private entities with a record of non-compliance with the national provisions adopted pursuant to this Directive from publicly funded or administered grants.

45. In accordance with the principles of subsidiarity and proportionality as set out in Article 5 of the EC Treaty, the objectives of this Directive, namely ensuring a common high level of protection against disability discrimination in all the Member States, cannot be sufficiently achieved by the Member States and can therefore, by reason of the scale and the impact of the proposed action, be better achieved by the Community. This Directive does not go beyond what is necessary in order to achieve those objectives.

CHAPTER I: GENERAL PROVISIONS

Article 1 Purpose

The purpose of this Directive is to lay down a framework for combating discrimination on the ground of disability, with a view to putting into effect in the Member States the principle of equal treatment.

Article 2 Concept of Discrimination

1.   For the purposes of this Directive, the principle of equal treatment shall mean that there shall be no direct or indirect discrimination whatsoever on the grounds of disability and no discrimination in the form of a failure to make a reasonable accommodation.

2.   For the purposes of paragraph 1:

   a.   direct discrimination shall be taken to occur where one person is treated less favourably than another is, has been or would be treated in a comparable situation on grounds of disability;

   b.   indirect discrimination shall be taken to occur where an apparently neutral provision, criterion or practice would put a person having a particular disability at a particular disadvantage compared with other persons unless that provision, criterion or practice is objectively justified by a legitimate aim and the means of achieving that aim are appropriate and necessary;

   c.   the failure to make a reasonable accommodation where this cannot be objectively justified shall be regarded as a form of discrimination.

This means that the persons, including public bodies, referred to in Article 3 shall take appropriate measures, whenever possible in an anticipatory way, to enable a person or persons with disabilities to have equal access to the activities in the areas referred to in the Article 3, unless such measures would impose a disproportionate burden on the provider or supplier.

3. Harassment shall be deemed to be a form of discrimination within the meaning of paragraph 1, when an unwanted conduct related to disability takes place with the purpose or effect of violating the dignity of a person or of creating an intimidating, hostile, degrading, humiliating or offensive environment, in particular if a person's rejection of, or submission to, such conduct is used as a basis for a decision which affects that person. In this context, the concept of harassment may be defined in accordance with national laws and practice of the Member States.

4. A failure to comply with the requirements referred to in Articles 4, 5 and 6 shall be deemed to be a form of discrimination within the meaning of paragraph 1.

5. An instruction to discriminate against persons on grounds of disability shall be deemed to be discriminatory within the meaning of paragraph 1.

6. For the purposes of this Directive, the provision of services, including those provided by institutions, in particular but not only residency, education, culture, health care, transportation and housing, which impede independence, social and occupational integration and participation in the life of the community of a person with a disability shall be regarded as a form of discrimination unless objectively justified by a legitimate aim and the means of achieving that aim are appropriate and necessary.

7. For the purposes of this Directive, a person shall be regarded as having a disability if they currently have a disability, they have had a disability in the past, they may have a disability in the future, they are associated with a person with a disability through a family or other relationship, or they are assumed to fall into one of these categories.

Article 3 Scope

1. Within the limits of the powers conferred upon the Community, this Directive shall apply to all persons, as regards both the public and private sectors, including public bodies, in relation to:

   a. social protection, including social security;

   b. healthcare, including access to all forms of medical treatment, while fully respecting the responsibilities of the Member States for the organisation and delivery of health service and medical care;

   c. social advantages;

   d. education;

   e. access to, including conditions regulating access, and supply of services, facilities and goods which are available to the public, including culture, leisure and sports, insurance, transportation, the communications environment, the built environment, housing and manufactured and designed products.

2. Member States shall introduce such measures as are necessary to enable them to promote the objective of equal treatment for persons with disabilities by its incorporation, in particular, into all laws, regulations, administrative provision, policies and activities in the areas referred to in paragraph 1 of this Article.

3. In all measures implementing this Directive, the Member States shall consider the interests and needs of the different groups of persons with disabilities according to their sex, age, race or ethnic origin, religion or belief, sexual orientation or any other grounds for discrimination, and place particular importance on combating multiple discrimination.

4. Member States shall actively take into account the objective of equality of all persons irrespective of disability when formulating and implementing laws, regulations, administrative provisions, policies and activities in the areas referred to in paragraph 1.

Article 4 Access to Information and Procedures

The public and private sectors, including public bodies, shall take account of a disabled person's preferred means of communication when seeking to provide accessible information and procedures in the areas referred to in Article 3 of this Directive and in the areas referred to in Article 3(1) of Directive 2000/78/EC. In particular information shall be provided in writing, braille, large print, electronic formats, through sign language, recordings, subtitling and easy to understand text which is accessible to people with intellectual disabilities. This information and these procedures shall be made available without undue delay and without extra cost to the recipient.

Article 5 Access to Buildings, Telecommunication, Transport Modes and Other Public Spaces and Facilities

1. For the purposes of this Directive, the provision of accessibility involves the removal of barriers and prevention of new barriers that hamper the equal access of persons with disabilities to the areas referred to in Article 3 of this Directive and in the areas referred to in Article 3(1) of Directive 2000/78/EC, irrespective of the nature of the barrier or disability. This removal should be done in an anticipatory way, without prejudice to the requirement to provide reasonable accommodation to a person with disabilities, whose needs have not been foreseen.

2. Insofar as the following areas fall within the scope of this Directive and Directive 2000/78/EC, Member States shall introduce such measures as are necessary to ensure that:

a. all forms of public transport and all buildings and structures providing access to public transport, whether provided by the public or private sector, are accessible to persons with disabilities.

Member States shall require that all new and, wherever possible, re-fitted transportation vehicles and buildings are accessible and shall set appropriate deadlines for providers of public transport with regard to achieving accessibility for existing vehicles, buildings and structures, subject to the following maximum deadlines:

— [5 years after the publication of this Directive in the Official Journal] for taxis and hackney cabs

— [10 years after the publication of this Directive in the Official Journal] for road and rail transport

— [10 years after the publication of this Directive in the Official Journal] for air and sea carriers

— [10 years after the publication of this Directive in the Official Journal] for buildings and structures providing access to public transport.

b. all new buildings open to the public, whether in the public or private sectors, are accessible, and that existing buildings that are open to the public are made accessible within [10 years after the publication of the Directive in the Official Journal].

c. all new public spaces, whether in the public or private sectors, such as parks, playgrounds, pavements and squares, car parks, sports facilities and information facilities, are accessible and that existing public spaces are made accessible [within 15 years after the publication of the Directive in the Official Journal.]

d. all new housing developments consisting of three or more residencies are capable of being adapted to provide accessible housing and the areas and facilities open to all residents are accessible.

e. all new telecommunications, and existing and new services provided by Internet service providers, and electronic services provided by public authorities, are accessible, and that existing telecommunications are made accessible within [5 years after the publication of the Directive in the Official Journal].

f. all new buildings which are places of employment or vocational training are accessible, and that existing places of employment or vocational training are made accessible within [10 years after the publication of the Directive in the Official Journal].

3. Member States may exclude the vehicles, buildings and sites of historical or cultural importance referred to in paragraphs 2a and 2b of this

Article, from the accessibility requirement where the exclusion is objectively justified and the exclusion is appropriate and necessary and the vehicles or buildings cannot be made accessible without fundamentally changing their historical or aesthetical character. In such cases, the accessibility requirement will be ensured through provisional structures or equipment.

4.   Member States shall ensure the access of guide and service dogs where needed in order to provide equal access of people with disabilities.

5.   Member States shall ensure that representative non-governmental organisations of persons with disabilities and parents, guardians or designated advocates of persons with disabilities unable to represent themselves, are involved in the setting of appropriate accessibility standards.

6.   Member States shall provide for an independent body to monitor compliance with the requirements established in this Article.

Article 6 Access to Education

In addition to the measures already foreseen under articles 4 and 5, in order to ensure equal access to education, Member States shall ensure that all disabled children and adults in mainstream education and in special education benefit from reasonable accommodations covering their individual needs, including, among others, tuition in Braille, special equipment, special educational material and assistive educational devices. Member States shall ensure that persons who are deaf and who are sign language users are given the opportunity to receive tuition through the medium of sign language.

While considering participation in mainstream education as a general rule, Member States shall ensure that in determining which form of education or training is appropriate, the views of the person with a disability will be considered as a significant factor. Where the person is a child or adult who is unable to represent himself, the views of their parents, guardians or designated advocates will also be considered as a significant factor.

Article 7 Images of Persons with Disabilities in the Media

Member States shall ensure that broadcasts, advertisements and the media do not contain insulting portrayals of disability or contain any incitement to hatred on the grounds of disability and shall ensure respect for the dignity of persons with disabilities in political and public life.

Article 8 Positive Action

1.   With a view to ensuring full equality in practice, the principle of equal treatment shall not prevent any Member State from maintaining or adopting specific measures to prevent or compensate for disadvantages linked to disability.

2.   The principle of equal treatment shall be without prejudice to the right of Member States to maintain or adopt provisions on the protection of health and safety of persons with disabilities or to measures aimed at creating or maintaining provisions or facilities for safeguarding or promoting the integration of persons with disabilities, and in particular women with disabilities, people with severe and multiple disabilities and their families and people facing multiple discrimination.

Those laws, regulations and administrative provisions contrary to the principle of equal treatment where the concern for protection that originally inspired them is no longer well founded shall be revised.

Article 9 Minimum Requirements

1.   Member States may introduce or maintain provisions which are more favourable to the protection of the principle of equal treatment than those laid down in this Directive.

2.   The implementation of this Directive shall under no circumstances constitute grounds for a reduction in the level of protection against discrimination already afforded by Member States in the fields covered by this Directive.

CHAPTER II: REMEDIES AND ENFORCEMENT

Article 10 Defence of Rights

1.   Member States shall ensure that judicial and/or administrative procedures, including where they deem it appropriate conciliation procedures, for the enforcement of obligations under this Directive are available to all persons who consider themselves wronged by failure to apply the principle of equal treatment to them, even after the relationship in which that discrimination is alleged to have occurred has ended.

In order to ensure equal and effective rights of access and participation in judicial and/or administrative procedures, such procedures shall be organised and conducted in a manner which is accessible to all persons with disabilities.

2.   Member States shall introduce into their national legal systems such measures as are necessary to ensure real and effective compensation or reparation as the Member States so determine for the loss and damage sustained by a person injured as a result of discrimination contrary to Article 2, in a way which is dissuasive and proportionate to the damage suffered; such compensation or reparation may not be restricted by the fixing of a prior upper limit.

3.   Member States shall ensure that associations, organisations or other legal entities, which have, in accordance with the criteria laid down by their

national law, a legitimate interest in ensuring that the provisions of this Directive are complied with, may engage, either on behalf or in support of the complainant, with his or her approval, in any judicial and/or administrative procedure provided for the enforcement of obligations under this Directive.

Member States shall also ensure that such associations, organisations or other legal entities may engage in judicial and/or administrative procedures have an independent right of action in order to enforce the obligations provided for under this Directive in those cases where an individual complainant is not required. An individual complainant will not be required in any judicial and/or administrative procedure where it is alleged that the act in question discriminates against, or is likely to discriminate against, more than a nominal number of persons with disabilities.

4.   Paragraphs 1 and 3 are without prejudice to national rules relating to time limits for bringing actions as regards the principle of equal treatment.

Article 11 Burden of Proof

1.   Member States shall take such measures as are necessary, in accordance with their national judicial systems, to ensure that, when persons who consider themselves wronged because the principle of equal treatment has not been applied to them establish, before a court or other competent authority, facts from which it may be presumed that there has been discrimination within the meaning of Article 2 and it shall be for the respondent to prove that there has been no breach of the principle of equal treatment.

2.   Paragraph 1 shall not prevent Member States from introducing rules of evidence which are more favourable to complainants.

3.   Paragraph 1 shall not apply to criminal procedures.

4.   Paragraphs 1, 2 and 3 shall also apply to any proceedings brought in accordance with Article 10(3).

5.   Member States need not apply paragraph 1 to proceedings in which it is for the court or competent body to investigate the facts of the case.

Article 12 Victimisation

Member States shall introduce into their national legal systems such measures as are necessary to protect individuals and associations, organisations or other legal entities, from any adverse treatment or adverse consequence as a reaction to a complaint or to proceedings aimed at enforcing compliance with the principle of equal treatment.

Article 13 Dissemination of Information

Member States shall take care that the provisions adopted pursuant to this Directive, together with the relevant provisions already in force, are, in an appropriate and accessible way, brought to the attention of the persons concerned by all appropriate means throughout their territory.

Member States shall encourage the involvement of representative non-governmental organisations of persons with disabilities and parents or designated advocates of persons with disabilities unable to represent themselves, in the dissemination of information about national measures adopted pursuant to this Directive.

Article 14 Dialogue with Non-governmental Organisations

1.   Member States shall encourage and maintain dialogue with representative non-governmental organisations of persons with disabilities and parents, guardians or designated advocates of persons with disabilities unable to represent themselves, which have, in accordance with their national law and practice, a legitimate interest in contributing to the fight against discrimination on grounds of disability with a view to promoting the principle of equal treatment.

2.   Member States shall take account of the diverse nature of disability when entering into dialogue with the representative non-governmental organisations referred to in Article 14(1).

CHAPTER III: BODIES FOR THE PROMOTION OF EQUAL TREATMENT

Article 15

1.   Member States shall provide for an independent body, such as an ombudsman or an equal opportunities commission, for the promotion of the principle of equal treatment of all persons without discrimination on the grounds of disability. This body may form part of one or more independent, pre-existing agencies charged at national level with the defence of human rights or the safeguarding of individuals' rights and shall cover the areas referred to in Article 3 of this Directive and the areas referred to in Article 3 of Directive 2000/78/EC.

2.   Member States shall ensure that the functions of the independent body referred to in paragraph 1 include:

— without prejudice to the alleged victims of discrimination and of associations, organisations or other legal entities referred to in Article 9(2), receiving and pursuing complaints from individuals of discrimination on grounds of disability,

— starting and conducting investigations or surveys concerning discrimination on grounds of disability,

— publishing independent reports and making recommendations on any issue relating to such discrimination,

— monitoring compliance with this Directive and related national laws and practices.

3.   Member States may charge the independent body with the creation of conciliation procedures as referred to in Article 10(1).

4.   Member States shall ensure that where the independent body referred to in paragraph 1 consists of members, persons with disabilities and parents, guardians or designated advocates of people with disabilities unable to represent themselves shall be included in the membership. Where the independent body is only concerned with the promotion of the principle of equal treatment on the grounds of disability, the Member State shall ensure that the membership is broadly representative of the national disability community, and that a majority of the membership of the body is made up of persons with disabilities and parents, guardians or designated advocates of people with disabilities unable to represent themselves.

CHAPTER IV: FINAL PROVISIONS

Article 16 Compliance

Member States shall take the necessary measures to ensure that:
a.   any laws, regulations and administrative provisions contrary to the principle of equal treatment are abolished;
b.   any provisions contrary to the principle of equal treatment which are included in individual or collective contracts or agreements, internal rules of undertakings and rules governing profit-making or non-profit-making associations are or may be declared null and void or are amended.

Article 17 Sanctions

Member States shall lay down the rules on sanctions applicable to infringements of the national provisions adopted pursuant to this Directive and shall take all measures necessary to ensure that they are applied. The sanctions, which may comprise the payment of compensation to the victim, must be effective, proportionate and persuasive. The Member States shall notify those provisions to the Commission by [date two years after publication in Official Journal] at the latest and shall notify it without delay of any subsequent amendment affecting them.

Candidates for public contract award procedures relating to works, services and supplies, and private and public entities wishing to enter into contractual relations with State, regional or local administrations or other bodies governed by public law shall be required to present to the contracting authorities proof of compliance with the national provisions adopted pursuant to this Directive and, with regard to disability, pursuant to Directive 2000/78/EC, prior to submitting a tender.

Public or private entities found in breach of the national provisions adopted pursuant to this Directive or, with regard to disability, pursuant to

Directive 2000/78/EC by a court of law or administrative procedure, shall be deemed ineligible for grants awarded by Member States in the framework of the European Structural Funds for a period of ten years following the final judgment or final administrative decision.

Article 18 Implementation

Member States shall adopt the laws, regulations and administrative provisions necessary to comply with this Directive by [date two years after publication in Official Journal]. They shall forthwith inform the Commission thereof.

When Member States adopt these measures, they shall contain a reference to this Directive or be accompanied by such a reference on the occasion of their official publication. The methods of making such a reference shall be laid down by the Member States.

Article 19 Report

1.   Member States, in consultation with the representative non-governmental organisations of persons with disabilities and parents, guardians and designated advocates of persons unable to represent themselves, shall communicate to the Commission by [date three years after publication in Official Journal], and every three years thereafter, all the information necessary for the Commission to draw up a report to the European Parliament and the Council on the application of this Directive.

2.   The Commission's report shall include a comparative assessment of the measures adopted by the Member States and shall take into account, as appropriate, the viewpoints of the representative non-governmental organisations of persons with disabilities and parents, guardians or designated advocates of persons with disabilities unable to represent themselves. In accordance with the principle of gender mainstreaming, this report shall, inter alia, provide an assessment of the impact of the measures taken on women and men. In light of the information received, this report shall include, if necessary, proposals to revise and update this Directive.

Article 20 Entry into Force

This Directive shall enter into force on the day of its publication in the Official Journal of the European Communities.

Article 21 Addressees

This Directive is addressed to the Member States.

Appendix IV

Council of Europe European Social Charter (Revised)

Article 15—The right of persons with disabilities to independence, social integration and participation in the life of the community.

With a view to ensuring to persons with disabilities, irrespective of age and the nature and origin of their disabilities, the effective exercise of the right to independence, social integration and participation in the life of the community, the Parties undertake, in particular:

1. to take the necessary measures to provide persons with disabilities with guidance, education and vocational training in the framework of general schemes wherever possible or, where this is not possible, through specialised bodies, public or private;

2. to promote their access to employment through all measures tending to encourage employers to hire and keep in employment persons with disabilities in the ordinary working environment and to adjust the working conditions to the needs of the disabled or, where this is not possible by reason of the disability, by arranging for or creating sheltered employment according to the level of disability. In certain cases, such measures may require recourse to specialised placement and support services;

3. to promote their full social integration and participation in the life of the community in particular through measures, including technical aids, aiming to overcome barriers to communication and mobility and enabling access to transport, housing, cultural activities and leisure.

Index